SATIRE AND SENTIMENT 1660–1830

SATIRE
AND SENTIMENT
1660–1830
STRESS POINTS IN THE
ENGLISH AUGUSTAN TRADITION

CLAUDE RAWSON

YALE UNIVERSITY PRESS
NEW HAVEN AND LONDON

First published in 1994 by Cambridge University Press
This edition first published in paperback in 2000 by Yale University Press

Printed in Great Britain by St Edmundsbury Press, Ltd

Library of Congress Card Number 99–68561
ISBN 0–300–07916–8 (pbk.)

A catalogue record for this book is available from the British Library.

2 4 6 8 10 9 7 5 3 1

For Florence and Maynard Mack

Contents

Preface

The studies collected in this book are concerned with the energies of a patrician culture in decline. In a sense, that culture was perhaps always in decline, or under stress, although the literary expressions or reflections of this were themselves extraordinarily vital. They were mostly the work of non-patrician authors. Rochester, at the beginning of my period, and Byron and Shelley at the end, are among the exceptions (as is Fielding, about whom I have written elsewhere): but most of the authors treated extensively in these pages, Oldham, Dryden, Swift, Pope, Johnson, Reynolds, Burke, Austen, are non-patrician writers whose characteristic idiom, and whose loyalties and aspirations, are rooted in the classicising and patrician subculture we sometimes call 'Augustan' (it is in this restricted sense that the term is used in this book, and not as a description of the period as a whole or any chronological subdivision of it).

Certain incongruities or contradictions were inherent in the situation: the age-old love-hate relationship of the English with their aristocracy, the feeling that lords did not live up to lordly standards (proclaimed in lordly accents by unlordly censors like Swift or Pope), the filtering down to Grub Street of a rhetoric of uppish contempt. Inevitably, the lordly ethos underwent various forms of *embourgeoisement* (the mutation by Steele, Richardson, and others of old chivalric codes into the phenomenon Swift derided as 'fair-sexing', and the resublimation of this in Burke's political writings lamenting the ill-treatment of noble ladies in India and France, are examples; as is Jane Austen's domestication of ironies she derived, to an extent still underestimated, from Fielding). The literary idiom was permeated by what Chesterfieldian censors were quick to put down as linguistic or social solecism, and by a linguistic self-consciousness which is as vividly evident in Swift, Addison, and Steele as in Richardson,

Johnson, and Austen. Forms of verbal egotism and self-display which would have earned the contempt of Chesterfield received proleptic parody in Swift, who thought he was mimicking Dryden (a writer whose affectations of lordly rakishness were cruelly put down by Rochester) but came much closer to the Shandean or Boswellian manifestations of a later time. (Such parody *avant la lettre*, and subsequent acts of unparodying or resublimation of mock-forms, are phenomena which have not had the attention they deserve).

Some of these tensions appear in an exacerbated form in authors in whom the Augustan element or survival may be thought to exist in a modified or attenuated state, who were committed to a popularising or levelling down of polite letters, like Addison and Steele, or to a style of self-exploration which, even in private diaries, closely mirrored their restless and hardly 'polite' self-promotion in the drawing-rooms of the great, like Boswell or Thomas Moore (who appears in this book as a minor Boswellian avatar, rather than in his better-known guise as an unreadable poet). The same might be said of Richardson, the only radically anti-Augustan writer considered here in his own right, in so far as he is himself caught up in mannerisms and attitudes he rejects. (Other great writers of this period who belong to alternative traditions, Defoe, Blake, Wordsworth, Coleridge, do not in general fall within the scope of this book except for specific illustrative purposes, sometimes in adversarial roles).

The period 1660–1830 is especially interesting in the history of English satire. Its earlier phase, to about 1750, is the only time when satire was a dominant mode of literary expression, practised by some of the best writers at the height of their powers, and the only time when mock-heroic in particular emerged as an important genre in its own right, a mode of cultural commentary transcending its bookish origins and its jokey parodic dimension. Pope's two best-known poems, one of them, the *Dunciad*, arguably his most ambitious imaginative undertaking, belong to this genre. Its official tendency, as everyone knows, was to deride not the heroic itself, but a lowered modern reality deemed to have fallen short of heroic standards and aspirations.

But official tendencies, particularly when their expression takes the form of ironic mimicry, are vulnerable to subversion even in innocent contexts. The mock-heroic masterpieces of this period had no such context. They flourished in an atmosphere inhospitable to heroic celebration, when the heroic ethos was hardly felt to be tenable by anyone, and when the value of the great epics of classical antiquity was increasingly contested. Declared admirers, who continued to assert that a heroic poem, truly such, was undoubtedly the greatest work which the soul of man was capable to perform, were not, in fact, conspicuously undoubting. The form, in all its embattled loyalism to epic originals, is fraught with subtextual anxieties over the morality of war, the ethos of a warrior caste, the uppish aloofness and pride of rank of an aristocratic culture no longer sure of itself, whose most eloquent defence was being carried out by ambivalent outsiders. In an earlier book, *Order from Confusion Sprung* (1985, 1992), I drew attention to the fact that, even as Dryden, Pope, and others went on proclaiming the official view of the epic's primacy over other genres, no good poet finished an epic after Milton, though Dryden and Pope both tried, and those poets who did (Blackmore, who wrote six, is the paradigm case) were likely to be of an adversarial persuasion, Modern rather than Ancient and in other ways aligned against, and much scorned by, Dryden, Swift and Pope. Dryden and Pope wrote their epics by proxy, translating the ancient masters, or else through a parodic filter, distanced by irony.

This irony was self-protective, but also, as I argue in chapters 3 and 4, protective of epic: a striking feature of all Augustan mock-heroics which are still read today is the lengths to which they go to minimise or obliterate reminders of war in a genre whose principal subject-matter was war. A complementary tendency in non-epic writings was to minimise or obliterate reminders of epic when the atrocities of war were being related. By the time of Byron and Shelley, the protective-ness disappears. There is no feeling that heroic poetry deserves to be shielded from military disrepute, an index of changes within a patrician literary tradition brought about by a number of pressures: of anti-war feeling, of conflicting attitudes to violence, of unresolved elements in the Ancient–Modern controversy, of ideological and social change associated with the French Revolution (the run-up to it, and its aftermath, as much as the event itself), of a progressive *embourgeoisement* of the intellectual life.

My intention has been to capture and analyse stress points, rather than to provide a progressive narrative. This seems to me more naturally adapted to the density and the complex, volatile, and nuanced character of the issues and texts I discuss, than a treatment which offered the satisfaction of a simplifying coherence of outline. This is as true of the extended chapters which in a sense form the core of the book (chapters 3 to 5) as it is of the volume as a whole. Chapter 3 and most of chapter 5 (approximately half the book) are published here for the first time. They are given a more intensive documentation than other parts, because the unfamiliarity, complexity or controversial nature of the material seemed to me particularly to call for this. The shorter chapters, more circumscribed in subject-matter, invited a different treatment. I have also thought it best to preserve the format and atmosphere of their first publication, and in particular to leave in their natural unannotated state pieces which first appeared in such papers as the *TLS* or *London Review of Books*. I have, however, revised, corrected or expanded the substance of many of the chapters, while leaving the format unchanged.

Several chapters began as papers read to learned institutions and conferences: the English Institute, the David Nichol Smith Memorial Seminar, the DeBartolo Conference on Eighteenth-Century Studies, the British Society for Eighteenth-Century Studies, the Fédération Internationale des Langues et Littératures Modernes (FILLM), the American Society for Eighteenth-Century Studies, the International Association of University Professors of English, and the Colloques on the eighteenth-century sponsored in December each year by the Université de Paris III. To the organisers, and in particular to the late Robert C. Elliott and to Jocelyn Harris, Pat Rogers, Barry Nisbet, Thomas Lockwood, Marshall Brown, Maynard Mack, Paul-Gabriel Boucé and Suzy Halimi, I owe debts not only for the original stimulus, but also for many acts of personal, as well as professional, kindness. I have profited from discussion with audiences in many universities in Britain, the United States, and elsewhere. These are too numerous to name individually, but I feel a special gratitude to Donald Mell and his colleagues at the University of Delaware, who have provided me with an almost annual forum for the discussion of many of the topics which are explored in this book.

To the editors past and present of the *Times Literary Supplement* and the *London Review of Books*, and especially to Jeremy Treglown, Karl Miller, and Mary-Kay Wilmers, who invited me to write some of the pieces which became chapters of this book, I owe special thanks for encouragement, editorial wisdom, and personal kindness.

The Huntington Library, the National Endowment for the Humanities, and the John Simon Guggenheim Memorial Foundation awarded fellowships which gave me time to write parts of this book. To Yale University I am indebted for periods of leave, and for a

Senior Faculty Fellowship. Most of the research for this book was done in the various libraries of the Yale University Library system and in the Huntington Library, but I have also frequently used the British Library, the Bodleian Library, and the University of Warwick Library. I am grateful to the librarians and staff for their helpfulness and hospitality.

The following friends and colleagues have helped by offering information, answering questions, correcting errors or reading parts of the manuscript: Christine Battersby, Victor Bers, David Bromwich, Marie Devine, Howard Erskine-Hill, Michel Fuchs, Knud Haakonssen, Ian Higgins, George Hunter, Claudine Kahan, George Kennedy, Ilona Kinzer, Diana Kleiner, Peter Larkin, F. P. Lock, Maynard Mack, Lawrence Manley, Richard Martin, David Marshall, Louis L. Martz, Jenny Mezciems, John Mulryan, Susan Naulty, Marjorie Perloff, John Valdimir Price, Martin Price, Judy Rawson, Bruce Redford, Marie-Cécile Révauger, Pat Rogers, Vasily Rudich, Florian Stuber, Joan Sussler, Gordon Turnbull.

Kevin Taylor of the Cambridge University Press has been a model editor, encouraging, helpful, and patient beyond all normal standards of tolerance; the same praise is due to Gillian Maude as copy-editor.

Last, but certainly not least, I am deeply grateful to Liza Cluggish and Phyllis Gibson for heroic labours in typing the manuscript.

PREFACE TO THE PAPERBACK EDITION

I have taken the opportunity of this edition to correct some typographical and other errors and to add one or two references which were unavailable to me at the time of original publication. I owe thanks to Linda Bree, Jenny Davidson and Leo Lemay for supplying information and pointing out corrigenda.

Claude Rawson
March 1999

Acknowledgements

Several chapters have appeared, sometimes under different titles, in the following publications, and are reprinted (with revisions) by permission of the editors and publishers:

Chapter 1   'Rochester', *The Times Literary Supplement*, 29 March 1985, pp. 335–6;

Chapter 2   'Oldham', *London Review of Books*, 5 January 1989, pp. 19–21;

Chapter 4   'Mock-heroic and war, II: Byron, Shelley and heroic discredit', *Byron: Augustan and Romantic*, ed. Andrew Rutherford, Macmillan and The British Council, 1990, pp. 82–116;

Chapter 6   'The *Tatler* and *Spectator*', *The Times Literary Supplement*, 2–8 December 1988, pp. 1336–7;

Chapter 7   'Richardson, alas', *London Review of Books*, 12 November 1987, pp. 15–16;

Chapter 8   'Boswell's Life and Journals', 1. *New York Times Book Review*, 13 January 1985, p. 37; 2. *London Review of Books*, 7 May 1987, pp. 18–21;

Chapter 9   'Boswell's *Life of Johnson*', Introduction to *Life of Johnson*, Everyman Library, 1992;

Chapter 10   'Dining Out in Paris and London: Thomas Moore's Journal', *The Times Literary Supplement*, 6 September 1985, pp. 963–4;

Texts and editions used

Dryden
Quotations are from *The Poems of John Dryden*, ed. James Kinsley, Oxford, Clarendon Press, 1958, 4 volumes, and *Of Dramatic Poesy and other Critical Essays*, ed. George Watson, London and New York, Everyman's Library, 1962, 2 volumes (abbreviated as Watson).

Swift
Prose Works, ed. Herbert Davis and others, Oxford, Blackwell, 1939–74, 16 volumes (abbreviated as *Works*); Harold Williams (ed.), *Poems*, 2nd edn., Oxford, Clarendon Press, 1958, 3 volumes, and *Correspondence*, Oxford, Clarendon Press, 1963–5, 5 volumes.

Pope
Twickenham Edition of the Poems of Alexander Pope, ed. John Butt, Maynard Mack, and others, London, Methuen, 1939–69, 11 volumes in 12 (abbreviated as TE).

Fielding
Unless otherwise noted, qutations are from W. B. Coley, Martin C. Battestin and others (eds.), *The Wesleyan Edition of the Works of Henry Fielding*, Oxford, Clarendon Press, 1967 – (in progress); *Jonathan Wild*, World's Classics edition, London, Oxford University Press, 1961 reprint.

Greek and Latin writers, and translations from them, are generally cited from the Loeb Classical Library; translations from Homer, unless otherwise noted, are by Richmond Lattimore.

Satire

Lordly accents
Two Restoration satirists

· I ·

Rochester

According to John Aubrey, Marvell, 'who was a good judge of witt', said Rochester 'was the best English satyrist and had the right veine'. We don't think of him as a satirist *comme les autres*, writing formal verse satires and epistles and Horatian imitations, though his 'Allusion to Horace' is said to have taught the genre to better-known practitioners, and the remarkable epistle 'From Artemiza to Chloe' is now enjoying a vogue, partly fuelled by feminist preoccupations. Our view of satire is still largely Pope-centred, and, although Rochester had a substantial influence on both Swift and Pope, their feelings about him seem to have been lukewarm. And he is really very unlike. He was of 'the Mob of Gentlemen who wrote with Ease', a Popeian put-down meaning 'holiday writers'. The 'Ease' was not quite the quality which Pope meant when he praised Petronius for uniting 'the *Scholar's Learning*, with the *Courtier's Ease*', and which he mythologised into that witty urbanity, neither Roman nor strictly courtly, which is sometimes, to the dismay of latter-day pedagogues, called 'Augustan'.

That Rochester was both a lord and a courtier, as Pope was not, is one of the paradoxes which surround the English Augustan style and its curious patrician pretensions. He came closer perhaps than Pope's description did to the Petronius who is remembered as the raffishly elegant sophisticate of Nero's court portrayed by Tacitus, and as the author of the exuberantly obscene *Satyricon* (if they were indeed the same person). Rochester's 'ease' was of a sort which, in wit as in other things, spilled over into excess. It thus differed from the Popeian version, which suggests containment and measure, but its way of being excessive included a sense of command. The dramatist Lee called him 'Lord of Wit' in a sycophantic dedication, but he also gave, after Rochester's death, one of the best accounts of what this might seriously mean: 'his Genius was so luxuriant, that he was forc'd to

tame it with a Hesitation in his Speech to keep it in view'. If this
sounds a bit like a calculated stammer raised to the level of art, the fact
is appropriate: Rochester's poetry, like Pope's in its different way, is
never far removed from the social ploy. But what is more importantly
implied, I think, is a unique form of *sprezzatura* which readily expresses
itself in passionate or high-spirited accents. It may accommodate
coarseness and even obscenity, as Fielding's manner sometimes could
but Pope's could not (or not without loss of 'ease', which is perhaps
one test of the lordly):

> You Ladyes all of Merry England
> Who have been to kisse the Dutchess's hand,
> Pray did you lately observe in the Show
> A Noble Italian call'd Signior Dildo?

It is a low-pitched example, from a poem which has been praised
for having 'the characteristic uncertainty of accent of the street
ballad'. There's justice in this. A command of low styles, and a taste
for them, have often been paraded as badges of patrician freedom, a
specialised expression, perhaps, of the cultural antinomy mythologised, with a fervid gravity Rochester might have scorned, in Yeats'
'Dream of the noble and the beggarman', both poets excluding the
intermediate figure of the cit or merchant at his greasy till. But
'uncertainty' hardly describes the masterly hint of metrical disloca-
tion, the colloquial stumble which is part of the poem's thrusting
plasticity, and which seems a prosodic manifestation of the 'hesitation' Lee was talking about. The hard finish of the lines comes over
with none of the bland orderliness of Waller or Denham, and is
equally unlike the strong coupleteering summations of Dryden or
Pope. Demotic vitality is mimicked with a buoyancy which is really
quite *un*hesitant, just as elsewhere some gnarled muscularities in the
'strong lines' idiom are transfigured by a species of headlong grace.
The stanzas of 'Signior Dildo', the driving phantasmagoric couplets
of 'A Ramble in Saint James's Parke', the bravura quatrains of 'The
Disabled Debauchee', bring home, as much as any stylistic evidence
can, how unlikely Rochester is to have composed the yokel couplets of
Sodom, capable though he was of every obscenity in that feeble play.
Pope thought Rochester's versification 'bad', a remark approximately on a par with his reported statement to Voltaire that Milton
had not written in rhyme 'because he could not'.

'One Man reads *Milton*, forty *Rochester*', wrote Defoe. This had little to do with the prosody of either: 'One wrote *the Lewd*, and t'other *the Sublime*.' As Fielding's Squire Booby made clear when he found Shamela in the act of reading, '*Rochester's* Poems' was more or less synonymous with 'dirty book'. Rochester is not 'pornographic'. He is obscene but not, like *Fanny Hill*, arousing: he would, I think, have shared Fielding's distaste for those 'whose Devotion to the Fair Sex . . . wants to be raised by the Help of Pictures'. This was not a matter of prudery, but of patrician cool. Fielding's jibe included Richardson's love-scenes along with *Venus in the Cloister*, a book also owned by Shamela. Rochester uses every bad word in the language, and reports more deeds than will be familiar to most readers of this book, but never enticingly, or intimately, or graphically. It's partly a matter of distance, of the unruly knowingly kept at arm's length, and not unconnected with 'excess'. Those much-quoted mandrakes 'Whose lewd Topps Fuckt the very Skies', or the Duchess who 'Has Swallow'd more Pricks, then the Ocean has sand', are phantasmagoric enormities, as of a Rabelaisian gigantism worked over by a Gothick imagination. It's overheated if you like, but as a brilliant virtuosity of fantastication, like some of the wilder flights of Swift's *Tale of a Tub*, not as any sort of sensuous daydream. There could hardly be much in it for the auto-erotist.

Hyperbolic fantastication, like any other form of excessive utterance, is usually more preoccupied with itself than with its ostensible subject. It flourishes on a built-in assumption that the reader will discount a good deal, providing its own ironic guard. The limitation in turn acts as an enabling or releasing force, since the self-unrealising that attends the more colossal sexual imaginings offers a dispensation from reticences which are normally activated when we mean to be taken 'seriously'. Obscenity grows gigantic as arousal is neutralised, as well as vice versa. Something similar may happen with invective, whose great masters (Rabelais, Swift, Céline) are fantasists of an enormity which signals that the calls to hatred or to massacre don't really mean what they say, but don't not mean it either. Invective often borrows the rhetoric of sexual obscenity, in Rochester as in Rabelais, with both forms of incitement held in check by the play of aggressive utterance:

> Bawdy in thoughts, precise in Words,
>   Ill natur'd though a Whore,
> Her Belly is a Bagg of Turds,
>   And her Cunt a Common shore.

The style of these lines more particularly suggests a late-Swiftian exuberance of imprecation, in the drumming manner of *Traulus* or the *Legion Club*. There's also a grandiloquent triumphalism that is almost celebrative, cheekier and more light-hearted, as well as more reject-ing, than Yeats' 'foul rag-and-bone shop of the heart', but with something of the same excitability bordering on eloquence. In a related poem,

> By all *Loves* soft, yet mighty *Pow'rs*,
>   It is a thing unfit,
> That *Men* shou'd Fuck in time of *Flow'rs*,
>   Or when the *Smock's* beshit,

the squalors of the female pudenda are projected with a festive insolence which is in itself unSwiftian, but which, when coupled with Swiftian 'intensities', may produce a Yeatsian mix. The lines again express an opposite feeling to that of Yeats' 'Love has pitched his mansion in / The place of excrement', but they are closer to a Yeatsian mood than those more traditional patristic or Swiftian reminders that procreation takes place *inter urinas et faeces* which Yeats is resublimating.

Rochester's lines have a scabrous splendour, enhanced no doubt by the linguistic accident that 'flowers' meant menstrual discharge, as in French *fleurs*, from which the English term derives. (The etymology suggests 'flow' or 'flux', from Old French *flueurs*, Latin *fluor*, but colloquial usage assimilates the term to its more familiar homonym, of which it is sometimes understood as a metaphorical extension). It would be characteristic of Rochester to exploit the pun again, adding a festive insolence, so that the painful and the spectacular unite, as in those blood-stained sunsets and sunrises of Baudelaire, Laforgue or Apollinaire. Like those French poets, Rochester was a good mocker, though his style of mockery differed from theirs. His repudiations have a gaiety, a 'sudden glory' in jeering which gives the Hobbesian phrase an unexpected surplus aptness: 'I'le write upon a double Clowt/ And dipp my Pen in Flowers'. There are no Baudelairian luxuries, whether of grandeur or repudiation. The poet of 'To the Post Boy', who wrote that 'the Readyest way to Hell' was 'by Rochester', who 'for five years together ... was continually Drunk', who exper-ienced some extreme states of both debauchery and devotion, and died at 33, obviously had much in common with the *poètes maudits* of a later time. He would have rejected the phrase as too solemn, just as in

his lordly way he would have rejected the lordly guilt-ridden grandeurs of Byron's Lara or Cain (though he hoped on his death-bed that
God would not drive him 'like Cain from before His presence').

Nor would he have had much truck with the alternative solem-
nities, 'carefree' or debonair, of the later bohemian variety. Though
often broke and 'faine to borrow mony', he would have despised the
insolvent garreteers of the 1670s and the 1890s alike: in this, as in
much else, he was 'Augustan' to the core. His jokeyness on painful
subjects, and his harping on impotence, might seem to align him with
a Laforguian–Prufrockian sub-species of Romantic Agonist. But he is
self-mocking without being 'self-ironic' in the Laforguian way, and
his stanza on impotence addressed to a lady in flowers has a genial
insolence which sounds more like Macheath than like Prufrock:

> If thou wou'dst have me true, be wise,
> And take to cleanly sinning;
> None but fresh *Lovers Pricks* can rise,
> At *Phillis* in foul linnen.

The fact that we don't associate Macheath with the copulatory
indignity or with such brutal language makes the resemblance
especially arresting. Impotence is an insistent theme of Rochester's,
cheekily flaunted in what amounts to a machismo of sexual debility.
These lines are a specialised specimen, indicating that he's a jaded
(rather than a 'fresh') lover, not absolutely 'disabled'. Displays of
sexual weariness are easily presented as admissions or even boasts of
sexual excess, a recurrent feature of the Rochesterian, though not of
the Laforguian, mode. The Disabled Debauchee speaks 'of *Honourable
Scars,/* Which my too forward *Valour* did procure'. Rochester said in
'To the Post Boy' that he had 'swived more whores more ways than
Sodoms walls/ Ere knew', an exhaustiveness of possible postures
complemented in 'The Disabled Debauchee' and elsewhere by a
penchant for permutating not only the positions but the sex of his
paramours:

> And the best Kiss, was the deciding *Lot*,
> Whether the *Boy* fuck'd you, or I the *Boy*.

The Freudians sometimes go on about homosexuality as a latent
force in compulsive Don Juanism. Since everything in this domain
can be said to be latent when it isn't patent, we might feel that the ride
we're being taken on is something of a circular tour. Rochester's 'case'
is in fact one of the patent ones, and his bisexuality is declared without

fuss. What one senses about the main examples, however, is not the experience in itself, but the concern to register a kind of exhaustiveness of sexual pursuit, a *jusqu'auboutisme* of erotic transaction. This pedantry of the senses finds its mental complement in the refinements of guilt and a strong urge towards spiritual system-making. (The inordinate devotion of some learned students of erotica to their bibliographical, editorial, and biographical labours also suggests a predisposition to the perfectionisms of pedantry in a more literal sense). Like other amateurs of systematic debauchery, Rochester was drawn not only to states of introspection, but to large-scale theorising. When abetted by Burnet, Rochester's theorising turned to the theological. That of Sade, another libertine aristocrat, was antitheological and probably not so very different in its native impulse. If such intellectual system-making seems surprising in confirmed sensualists, we should perhaps remember that 'sensualism' is itself an ism. No isms are more doctrinaire or persistent than isms of excess, which readily pursue metaphysical exhaustiveness as much as physical exhaustion.

As often as not, 'impotence' is presented in Rochester as an imagined state, on a par with other erotic possibilities. In 'The Disabled Debauchee' the speaker is frankly imagining future incapacities, not describing present ones. The pleasures of memory he anticipates take the form of a comprehensive survey of the modes of modern sinning, so that the poem's present offers some of the mental satisfactions of a catalogue, to which can be added some voyeuristic joys and some refinements of pandarism, plus a future replay of past sensualities on a non-sensual plane. The impotence is thus conceived not as a cessation of erotic energy, but as an energy in its own right, a vigour not so much diminished as gone into reverse. As if to reflect this the verse has an extraordinary thrust of jeering incandescence. 'The Disabled Debauchee' must be unique among poems on this particular theme in achieving an authentically mock-heroic note. The heroic stanza which it borrows from *Gondibert* and *Annus Mirabilis* not only appropriates the grandeurs of the original it traduces as Pope's *Dunciad* appropriates Milton's, but outdoes these originals in the energy of its witty eloquence. The theme is an old one, deriving from Ovid and Petronius, with some French and English intermediaries. 'The Imperfect Enjoyment' (like Aphra Behn's 'The Disappointment', attributed to Rochester in 1680) is about premature ejaculation, a recognised variant, and afflicts the speaker with a loved

8

woman but not with whores, a matter on which Rochester is again more amusing than Freudian commentators. There's a Malamudian pathos over the languid member, 'Sapless, like a wither'd *Flow'r*'. Flowers clearly have a more versatile existence in love poetry than literary historians recognise, and Rochester's line is prettily outdone in Behn's poem, where Cloris' hand discovers the object of her ministrations 'Disarm'd ... And Cold as Flow'rs bath'd in the Morning Dew'.

The woman's helping hand is common in such poems, beginning with Ovid (*Amores* III.vii. 73ff.), and an attractive tenderness often gets into the act, displacing or softening the derision. It's especially evident in Rochester's 'Song of a Young Lady. To her Ancient Lover', which belongs to yet another sub-genre (poems about old men and young girls), especially popular in the seventeenth century:

> Thy Nobler part ...
> By Ages frozen grasp possesst,
> From his Ice shall be releast:
> And, sooth'd by my reviving hand,
> In former Warmth and Vigor stand.
> All a Lover's wish can reach,
> For thy Joy my Love shall teach:
> And for thy Pleasure shall improve,
> All that Art can add to Love.
> Yet still I love thee without Art,
> *Antient Person of my Heart.*

The woman's affectionate devotion comes over as enhanced rather than diminished by her application of technical expertise, and indeed by the sense that the man's flagging powers are part of what turns her on. There's an unforced tenderness, in Rochester's writings, for sexual configurations which others might feel impelled to scorn as bizarre or depraved: a queer geniality, which critics often miss, which erupts with an extraordinary off-beat charm in 'Fair *Cloris* in a Piggsty lay', and which even suffuses the bitter little song on 'Grecian Kindness' (a miniature *Troilus and Cressida* in the sense of being perhaps the shortest anti-heroic exposure of the Trojan War) with an afterglow of lazy good-nature: 'While each brave *Greek* embrac'd his Punk,/ Lull'd her asleep, and then grew drunk.' It is consistent with this that one of the '*Maxims* of his *Morality*', as he told Burnet, was 'that he should do nothing to the hurt of any other' in gratifying his 'natural Appetites'. In this he differed from Sade.

These flauntings of the theme of impotence were part of the sub-culture of rakish coteries to which Rochester belonged: Etherege also wrote an 'Imperfect Enjoyment'. There was no doubt some coded self-projection, which only a gull would take for autobiographical disclosure. It is hard to recapture the exact blendings of inverse machismo or playful fabulation. Rochester was more than usually given to role-playing, in both life and letters, so the now slightly faded stand-by of the critic, the persona, doubtless needs to be wheeled in. In the poem about the Ancient Lover, it is the woman who speaks, but the man who is the focus of attention. To the extent that 'persona' suggests authorial mask, it is the man who, however passively, usurps the role, his situation which is the 'interesting' one. There are poems by Laforgue and by Eliot in which a woman speaks, but in which it is similarly the man's predicament (usually of erotic incapacity of some kind) which mainly comes through. It is also curious that Rochester, Laforgue, and Eliot, all wrote, while still in their twenties, portraits of men suffering or affecting an elderly sexual debility, though the refined timidities and wilting sadness of a Prufrock differ greatly from the thrusting ostentation of the Disabled Debauchee. The latter is only elderly by future projection, but even the Ancient Person of the girl's song, though wholly passive, is energised by proxy in her imagined efforts to revive his powers. He lacks identity and consciousness, and is thus spared the Prufrockian forms of *taedium vitae*, but his body is simultaneously inanimate and responsive to stimulation, like an erotic Aeolian harp.

Rochester often imagines the penis as an autonomous being, comically separate from the body's other functions and unpredictable. This is equally true whether he is writing about impotence or about irrepressible lechery. The classic example is Signior Dildo himself, who combines passivity with an inexhaustible (because mechanical) virility. In one sense, he resembles the lifeless member of the Ancient Person: ladies pick him up, manipulate and embrace him. But he's also so 'Lusty a Swinger' (glossed by one commentator as 'a very powerful person') that 'passive' is hardly the right word, any more than it is for the voracious sexuality of those, both women and men, who court his penetrations, like the aforementioned Duchess, who 'Has Swallow'd more Pricks, then the Ocean has Sand', and who clearly rates as a very powerful person too. Henry Savile wrote to Rochester in 1671 that his presence was extreamly wanting heere to make friends at ye custome house where has been lately unfortunately seized a box of those leather instruments y^r L^p carried downe one of, but these barbarian Farmers Prompted by ye villainous instigation of theire wives voted them prohibited goods soe that they were burnt without mercy ... Y^r L^p is chosen Generall in this warr betwixt the Ballers & ye farmers.

The letter reveals that Rochester had a dildo, and was thought of as a leader of those who used them. It also records a Restoration comedy situation, the rakes pitted against the boors at the custom-house and their starchy, and doubtless seducible, wives, but transposed to that alternative utopia of gallantry, the 'real' world. As Keith Walker points out in his edition of Rochester, the poem echoes the incident, or one like it:

> Were this Signior but known to the Citizen Fopps
> He'd keep their fine Wives from the Foremen of Shops,
> But the Rascalls deserve their Horns shou'd Still grow
> For Burning the Pope, and his Nephew Dildo.

A few lines later is an episode in which the mechanical allegory replays another familiar scenario of Restoration literature and life:

> A Rabble of Pricks, who were welcome before,
> Now finding the Porter deny'd 'em the Door,
> Maliciously waited his coming below,
> And inhumanely fell on Signior Dildo.

'Signior Dildo' is a delightful foolery, the product of a social Cloud-cuckoo-land that really existed in the alleys and the drawing-rooms of late seventeenth-century London. The mechanical phallus who almost turns organic as he merges in the seething mass of metropolitan lechery may look forward to some of those machines of the modernist imagination, rhapsodically celebrated as extensions of the sensuous life. Rochester lacks both the brutal sentimentality and the preening abstraction. In the humanoid comedy of Dildo and the Pricks, we witness the altogether more genial modernism of a Disney cartoon, as the Stranger flees 'along the Pallmall', and 'the Ballocks came wobbling after' pursuing him in 'full Cry'. Both Dildo and Pricks are *re*- rather than *de*-personalised, in no mere lifeless paradox. There is an amusing fitness in the fact that after Rochester's poem, dildoes came to be known as Signiors, as though the poem had conferred person-hood on the real thing.

Oldham

'Farewell, too little and too lately known', Dryden wrote in a pompous, self-serving poem prefixed to John Oldham's *Remains in Verse and Prose* (1684). Oldham had died of smallpox the previous December, at the age of 30, at the house of the Earl of Kingston, a young nobleman who had recently become his patron. He left behind a surprisingly large body of work, now available in full (or almost in full, for a few omissions of scurrilous material have been reported in an important unpublished paper by James Turner) for the first time in a magisterial edition by Harold Brooks, begun over 50 years ago, and concluded with the assistance of the late Raman Selden. This includes the fierce 'Juvenalian' satires for which he is mainly remembered, but also much else: imitations (sometimes brilliant) of Horace, Ovid, and other Latin poets, as well as of several Greek poets, and Boileau and Voiture; 'Pindarique' odes of elaborate stanzaic architecture; and poems of Rochesterian obscenity or of libertine ideology.

Oldham is (with Dryden and Rochester) one of the three considerable satirists of the Restoration period, one of the earliest masters of 'poetical imitation' in its great English Augustan phase, and in this and other ways a model for Dryden, Swift, Pope, and Johnson. He is remembered in the textbooks, but he has always seemed too problematic for canonical assimilation. As a satirist, he was the last great practitioner of the 'rough' vitriolic style deemed to derive from 'satyrs', and Pope thought him 'undelicate ... too much like Billingsgate'. As a satellite rather than a full member of the Rochester circle, he never commanded a full share even of scandalised attention, though some of his libertine exercises (not always easily accessible before the Brooks-Selden edition) display great baroque inventiveness and some strongly powered jeering. But the full range of his writing remains, in Dryden's words, 'too little and too lately known':

an underrated poet, probably chiefly remembered, when all is said, through Dryden's overrated poem about him.

Oldham was the son of a country clergyman of puritan sympathies, who was ejected from his Wiltshire parish in 1662 and ran a school. He studied at St Edmund Hall, Oxford, and went on to earn his living as a schoolmaster and tutor while seeking for patronage and literary recognition. At the time of his death, his career looked promising enough for Dryden, who does not seem on any evidence now available to have been closely associated with him, to confer a prefatory poem on his posthumous works, mythologising him as a fellow-genius struck down in his prime.

Dryden's elegy is unctuously self-exalting. Its Virgilian gesturings (Dryden and Oldham presented as Nisus and Euryalus; Oldham as the 'young . . . *Marcellus* of our Tongue') call to mind more surely than Dryden's strong translation of Virgil the derision Swift lavished on him as a Virgilian pretender, with his 'Helmet . . . nine times too large for the Head . . . like the Lady in a Lobster, or like a Mouse under a Canopy of State'. His trumpeting of Oldham's greatness,

> For sure our Souls were near ally'd; and thine
> Cast in the same Poetick mould with mine

is self-promoting. Perhaps it also teeters on the edge of self-derision, echoing Dryden's recent description of the restless devious Achitophel: 'Great Wits are sure to Madness near ally'd;/ And thin Partitions do their Bounds divide.' The elegiac quickly turns pontifical and patronising, as Dryden suggests that the young poet couldn't scan:

> What could advancing Age have added more?
> It might (what Nature never gives the young)
> Have taught the numbers of thy native Tongue.
> But Satyr needs not those, and Wit will shine
> Through the harsh cadence of a rugged line.

As usual, Dryden was repeating what others had said in Oldham's lifetime, including Sir William Soame, a poetical gentleman now chiefly remembered, perhaps, for having translated Boileau's *Art Poétique* with Dryden's help. Oldham was sensitive on the point, answered Soame in the 'Advertisement' to *Some New Pieces* (1681) and set about refuting him with examples of what he could do in more urbane and mellifluous styles when his subject-matter didn't call for satiric harshness. By the time Dryden wrote these lines, the larger part of Oldham's work could not fairly be described in those terms. But the outdated stereotype clung to Oldham's reputation, and reappears in Pope and others.

The *Satyrs upon the Jesuits* (1681), Oldham's earliest major publication, were the notorious example of this harshness. These poems were important to Dryden. They appeared in complete form some months before Dryden's own quasi-heroic treatment of Popish Plot material, *Absalom and Achitophel*, and it has been suggested that Oldham's winning the race is what lies behind the allusion to Nisus and Euryalus in the elegy. If this is so, Dryden would be taking the credit in some way, since in Virgil's story the older Nisus helped his younger protégé by tripping an opponent. Moreover, Nisus had been winning himself, until he fell accidentally, thus implying that Dryden was not only a devoted friend, responsible for the other's success, but the more talented of the two anyway. Or Dryden may be saying, in the words of one of his editors, that he learned from the *Satyrs* 'something of [Oldham's] technique of raising satire to heroic proportions and focusing it on a national issue'.

There may be something in this, though some of the influence may have been the other way round. If the idea of raising a derided enemy to heroic proportions was derived by one poet from the other, Dryden's *Mac Flecknoe* has some claim to priority. It was not published until 1682, but was written much earlier, and Oldham transcribed much of it in 1678. Heroic aggrandisement (though not in the same sense 'on a national issue') is more prominent in this poem than in *Absalom and Achitophel*, whose satiric brilliance is built on life-size character portrayals rather than on the phantasmagoric enlargements of caricature. Oldham's grandeurs, like Juvenal's, come over as projections of the satirist's anger, rather than from a poetically realised sense of the enemy's enormity. The vitriolic invective of *Satyrs upon the Jesuits* is in this sense almost as remote from the defiled grandeurs of *Mac Flecknoe* as from the hard-edged discriminations of *Absalom and Achitophel*.

Nevertheless, the *Satyrs* do to some extent anticipate *Absalom and Achitophel* in representing the Popish Plot in a Miltonising idiom of infernal elevation, and may thus give countenance to Dryden's possible feeling of having, like Nisus, lost the race. Oldham's third 'Satyr' opens in a hothouse of Satanic scheming. This is somewhat apart, however, from the main stream of English mock-heroic. Loyola's Miltonic properties look back to Sin and Death and infernal grotesquerie, and are not the ones which mainly lead to Dryden or to Pope:

> Like *Delphick* Hag of old by Fiend possest,
> He swells, wild Frenzy heaves his panting Brest,
> His bristling Hairs stick up, his Eye-Balls glow,
> And from his Mouth long flakes of Drivel flow.

The demonic gigantifications of English mock-heroic tradition tend characteristically towards monumentality, as though bent on preserving heroic dignity even in defilement: compare *Mac Flecknoe*'s 'Thoughtless as Monarch Oakes, that shade the plain' or the *Dunciad*'s 'Slow rose a form, in majesty of Mud.' Oldham's is an alternative manner. Its nearest Augustan analogue is in Swift, who declined the 'lofty Stile' and the elevations of mock-heroic, and whose aggrandisements, like Oldham's, tended to unruly forms: Rabelaisian enumerations, hyperbolic extermination fantasies, and grotesqueries of irrepressible putrescent animation, as in his portrait of the 'bloated *M[iniste]r*' Walpole ('Of loud un-meaning Sounds, a rapid Flood/ Rolls from his Mouth in plenteous Streams of Mud').

The governing condition of such grotesqueries for Swift was that their self-defiling vitality could be relied on to neutralise all heroic suggestion. Oldham seems to have had no such inhibition, but his ideas of both the heroic and the mock-heroic were pretty crude. Sir William Soame's verses 'To the Author of Sardanapalus upon that, & his other Writeings' spoke of his mistaking 'furious Fustian for Sublime'. His poems have none of the ironic finesse of good mock-heroic. They take their grandiloquence more readily from Restoration tragedies than from classical epic, and he fulminates against the Jesuits in the same inflated accents in which he purported to mimic their imprecations.

This is partly a matter of the 'roughness' for which he was attacked early. Soame spoke of his showing 'a Monster for a Man', presumably mainly referring to the freakish sexuality of Sardanapalus but also perhaps to the grotesque villains (Garnet, Loyola) of the anti-Jesuit 'rude Satyrs'. But Soame's main complaint, like Dryden's later, was the metrical one, that he didn't 'know how to scan'. On this issue, Oldham had no difficulty in appealing to the roughness which some still deemed traditional to satire. He was less concerned to 'mind the Cadence' than to be 'keen and tuant'. But Soame's verses identified Oldham's faults as schoolmasterly gaucheries, and he was stung, in his second collection, *Some New Pieces*, into demonstrating that he could practise both the Horatian 'easie and familiar way' and the smooth fluencies of Ovid and Tibullus. From that point, relatively early in his career, the charge of 'roughness', which has dogged his reputation ever since, became obsolete.

Soame advised the 'School-master' to study Horace and Boileau, and Oldham's rendering of the *Ars Poetica*, which opens his new volume, seems to be a response to Soame's taunt. Oldham said that in attempting the Horatian style he had been 'careful to avoid stiffness', an index of how ready writers were to bow to the demands of 'urbanity' and to regard Horace as a shortcut to this. Horace became a godfather to styles which not only didn't much resemble his own, but forfeited 'ease' by straining to display it. Oldham's imitation of the *Art of Poetry* is a mildly self-conscious case of this, and of a related and equally counter-productive predisposition to heavy-handed hauteurs. His lines about scribblers of quality who behave like shopkeepers belong to a tradition of lordly put-downs of lords, usually by commoners, which became a nervous tic among English Augustan writers, resurfacing in powerfully fervid forms in Pope and Fielding. Pope's famous line, 'Scriblers or Peers, alike are *Mob* to me', occurs in a direct imitation of a famous Horatian satire, but it is not in the original, and its absence is conspicuous in the parallel text on the facing page.

The shift from Juvenalian to Horatian models nevertheless opened up an important new manner for Oldham, which shows strongly in the opening of his imitation of Horace's satire about the impertinent bore (i. ix):

> As I was walking in the *Mall* of late,
> Alone, and musing on I know not what;
> Comes a familiar Fop, whom hardly I
> Knew by his name, and rudely seizes me.

It is a powerfully assured and innovative voice within what Ronald Bottrall once described as the 'colloquial tradition' in English poetry. It has a thrusting flatness, equally free of gnarled Skeltonic overkill and of Rochesterian overheating (that charged conversational incandescence which Oldham sometimes imitated without flair in some of his rakish poems). Nor does it resemble the supple and disciplined sweep of Pope's or Byron's conversational verse. It is both animated and plain, a putting down in the sense of efficient notation as well as of satirical flattening, deceptively simple but uncommon: there is nothing quite like it in the other translations and imitations of Horace's poem examined by Paul Hammond in his useful *John Oldham and the Renewal of Classical Culture*. You find it again, perhaps, in the opening of Swift's *Legion Club* and in Auden. Its studied half-rhymes are also unusual in the period, in that they are neither merely slapdash nor a gesture of prescribed satiric 'roughness', and they do not belong to that alternative style of prosodic horseplay and cheeky rhyming which we associate with Butler, Swift, and Byron. They perhaps look forward to the sophisticated exploitation of half-rhymes by some twentieth-century poets. If, as in Butler and Swift, they subvert the firm definitional closures of the high Augustan couplet, it is not in a spirit of playfully loyalist parody, but more subtly to evoke incomplete finalities, closure or containment continuously and unspectacularly undermined by pressures of fact or perception, a sense of satirical certainties straining against order and themselves undercut by a disorderly reality. There is a fluidity of movement in its way unrivalled in Swift or in Pope, and when the poem moves into dialogue it achieves some of the most natural and vital reporting of speech in English poetry.

Oldham's Pindarique odes are by contrast inflated and metrically inert, despite the plasticity notionally encouraged by the form's metrical variety. This is true of the Horatian odes which Oldham laboriously refashioned into Pindarique stanzas, and which incongruously follow the brilliant satire on the bore. It applies equally to his own 'original' compositions, whether celebrative ('In Praise of Homer'), or elegiac ('To the Memory of Mr. Charles Morwent'), or even comic in a bibulous-libertine vein: 'A Dithyrambique on Drinking', purportedly spoken by Rochester, shows up very poorly beside Dryden's masterful ode on drunkenness, *Alexander's Feast*.

There are some odd exceptions, mainly among the 'obscene' poems. In the starchy ambience of the 'Satyr Against Vertue', with its pindaricised pedantries of libertine doctrine, a humour of baroque–Disneyan visualisation (perhaps learned from Rochester) is sometimes allowed to take off, as when Ixion's failure to win Juno turns into a ballooning fantasy of desire vainly expended on a cloud:

> When he a Goddes thought he had in chase,
> He found a gawdy Vapor in the place,
>   And with thin Air beguil'd his starv'd Embrace,
>   Idly he spent his Vigor, spent his Bloud,
> And tir'd himself t'oblige an unperforming Cloud.

An analogue from Waller cited in Brooks' commentary: 'She with her own resemblance, graced/ A shining cloud, which he embraced', serves only to highlight the inventiveness and animation of Oldham's portrayal. Perhaps he discovered in the ponderous elaboration of the Pindarique a natural medium for the comic ungainliness of erotic discomfiture and for heavy displays of sexuality in general.

'Sardanapalus', the poem which triggered Soame's monitory verses, is an interesting example:

> Far as wide Nature spreads her Thighs,
> Thy Tarse's vast Dominion lyes:
> All Womankind acknowledge its great Sway,
> And all to its large Treasury their Tribute pay.

The poem is a fantasy of unlimited potency, like Rochester's 'Signior Dildo', more laboured than Rochester's thrusting street-ballad couplets ('That Pattern of Virtue, her Grace of Cleaveland,/ Has Swallow'd more Pricks, then the Ocean has Sand') even where the Pindarique stanza itself moves into couplets:

> Ten Thousand Maids lye prostrate at thy Feet,
> Ready thy Pintle's high Commands to meet.

These come over with a power of their own: not Rochester's supple force, but a strutting starchiness amusingly incongruous in the prevailing atmosphere of phallic enormity. 'Pintle' adds to the incongruity, since the form of the word suggests a diminutive (which according to the *OED* it may etymologically have been). The comedy of bigness and littleness explodes into the baroque extravaganza of the final tableau, with the monarch's immolation on a blazing pyre of compulsive and polymorphous copulation:

> Here, glowing C—t, with flaming Beard,
> Like blazing Meteor appear'd;
> There, Pintle, squirting fiery Streams,
> Like lighted Flambeau, spending Flames.

The Disneyan fantasia of priapic rocketry is played out against a decor of heavy baroque ornamentation, for which the wedding-cake stanzas of the Pindarique are a perfect prosodic as well as visual expression. Like Signior Dildo, also Disneyan in his way and similarly unlimited in his powers, Pintle acquires a humanoid autonomy, but by a reverse process, the live phallus becoming a mechanical firework where Rochester's mechanical instrument takes on personhood. The whole joke is gathered up into a massive concluding spectacle, surreal in a John Martin way:

> Thus Lechery's great Martyr, Revelling in Fire,
>   At every Pore dripping out Scalding Lust,
>   With all thy Strength collected in one Thrust
>   At gaping C—t, thou didst give up thy mighty Ghost,
>   And 'midst a Glorious heap of burning C—ts expire.

The transitions seem unfocused or unco-ordinated, but in what adds up to an oddly ambitious orchestration. 'Orchestration' in such a context may in itself suggest a kind of overkill. As a highly crafted way of labouring a joke, it may be part of what Soame perceived as a schoolmasterly stiffness, but it is also a calculated and comic excess. The Pindarique ode is an awkward medium for jokes, and resistant to modulated transitions: an unwieldy and accumulative form, it readily gives an impression of discrete composition blocks, each enriched and ornamented (again like a wedding-cake) to maximum capacity. In a class-structure of poetic forms, it is perhaps aptly described as *nouveau riche*. Oldham seems at home with that, and the fact may reflect (stylistically rather than biographically speaking) his own odd relations with the court wits.

Sardanapalus, traditionally a figure of luxurious effeminacy, is transformed by Oldham into a paragon of baroque machismo, a mixture which replicates some contradictory features of Rochester, as viewed by contemporaries and perhaps by himself. In Oldham's two elegies from the Greek bucolic poets, 'Bion' and 'The Lamentation for Adonis', Rochester is viewed successively in the image of several mythological youths celebrated for both prettiness and erotic immolation: Hyacinth, Orpheus, Narcissus, Acis, and the fair Adonis from whose 'wide wound fast flows the streaming gore,/ And stains that skin which was all snow before.' 'There he lies, like a pale and wither'd Flower': the elegiac evocation of the dead youth recalls (in an instinctive intertextuality that is characteristic of Oldham's poetic obsession with Rochester) Rochester's own account of his spent phallus in 'The Imperfect Enjoyment', 'Shrunk up, and Sapless, like a wither'd *Flow'r*'.

It should not surprise us to see Rochester portrayed as a Hyacinth or Adonis, whose delicate and mutilated beauty assimilate them to cults of ambiguous, passive or enfeebled sexuality, in spite of the traditional image of his aggressive maleness. It was one of his gestures to blur the distinction between the two stereotypes, or rather to transform the one into a species of the other, so that, as I suggested in the previous chapter, his poems of sexual failure express a kind of machismo of impotence, and his bisexuality is paraded as a polymorphous vigour. This bravura redefinition is one of the things which distinguishes him from later *poètes maudits*, with whom he nevertheless has some features in common. Hyacinth is named in the opening lines of Oldham's 'Bion', which he says were 'begun by another Hand', adding: 'I have been told that they were done by the Earl of *Rochester*'. Oldham claimed, truthfully or otherwise, that he didn't believe the attribution. But the suggestion, right or wrong, is securely planted in Oldham's prefatory statement, and enters willy-nilly into our reading, as it was inevitably part of Oldham's. The mythologised identification of Rochester with the entire roll-call of beautiful dead youths is teasingly enhanced by the possibility that Rochester himself may have been a party to it.

Oldham said he resisted the attribution on the grounds that Rochester 'seldom meddled with such Subjects, and more especially by reason of an uncorrect line or two to be found amongst them, at their first coming to my hands, which never us'd to flow from his excellent Pen'. Nevertheless it was this fragment that gave him the idea of dedicating an imitation of the entire elegy 'to the memory of that incomparable Person'. By a queer coded fortuity, a passage about Hyacinth triggered a poem about Rochester. But Oldham's words about metrical incorrectness also seem coded in another more deliberate sense. They occur in the same 'Advertisement' in which he protested against the imputation that his own writing was 'rough', pleading that harsh Juvenalian satires should not be expected to 'flow so smoothly as *Ovid*, or *Tibullus*, when they are describing Amours and Gallantries, and have nothing to disturb and ruffle the evenness of their Stile'.

One would not think of Rochester in such terms. He was indeed a consummate metrist, as Oldham suggests, but hardly a 'smooth' one, whether in the manner ascribed to Ovid and Tibullus or, more pertinently, in the impeccably mellifluous style in which Oldham went on to complete the poem about him, or which he ascribed to him in that poem:

> Not harsh like the rude *Cyclops* were thy lays,
> Whose grating sounds did her soft ears displease:
> Such was the force of thy enchanting tongue,
> That she for ever could have heard thy Song.

Some of Rochester's finest effects, by contrast, come precisely from a mastery of metres which were indeed 'uncorrect' by the conventional standards of the heroic couplet, and Oldham's defence of him shows how much he internalised Rochester into the image he wished to project of himself.

The rankling accusation that he couldn't write smoothly thus led Oldham not only to undertake the 'easy' urbanity of Horatian epistles or the unruffled flow of Ovidian or pastoral elegies, but to mythologise his dead friend against all the evidence into a soft poet of love: 'And his soft lays did *Venus* ever please'. This revisionist reading, which never once suggests that Rochester's erotic poetry contained the slightest hint of obscenity, is almost as unfounded as (and not unconnected with) Oldham's apparent intimation that his own work resembles Rochester's:

> If I am reckon'd not unblest in Song,
> 'Tis what I ow to thy all-teaching tongue.

Brooks comments reasonably: 'I have never found the lessons easy to trace . . . no poem of Oldham's is like a poem of Rochester's.' 'Owing' is not the same as being like, of course, but few readers would deny the pervasiveness of Rochester as a presence in Oldham's poems, as a perpetual focus of self-definition, and as a model in the choice of subject-matter or the affectation of certain stylistic routines. But the point of interest about the description of Rochester in the elegies as well as in the prose 'Advertisement' is that it bears little real resemblance to the work of either poet.

Oldham, as Brooks says, was always 'ambivalent' about 'Rochester and his circle'. This shows not only in the gestures of retractation, in the 'Apology' for the 'Satyr Against Vertue' or in the 'Counterpart' to the 'Satyr', where, 'In Person of the Author', he denounces the principles enunciated in the original poem, 'Suppos'd to be spoken by a Court-Hector at Breaking of the Dial in Privy-Garden'. The subtitle, which refers to an exploit of Rochester's in the royal gardens, indicates an element of derision even before the later disavowals, and the fact that the original poem, including the derision, seems to have pleased Rochester and to have led him to seek Oldham out, confirms that 'ambivalence' existed in Rochester himself. Mockery or self-mockery on the subject of hectoring or of libertine exploits is often a form of celebration. But disclaimers and denunciations, fits of moralistic self-righteousness and even of repentant self-abasement, are themselves part of the natural idiom of libertine sub-cultures (especially perhaps among aristocrats of the more self-publicising sort, like Sade or even Byron): as gestures of inverse boastfulness, as more or less contemptuous sops to opinion, as expressions of a connoisseurship in sensations purportedly large enough to include the pleasures of antithetical or oppositional states of mind, as enhancements of transgression, or whatever. Periodic, or even terminal, accesses of self-castigation (like Rochester's own death-bed repentance) may be a natural part, or counterpart, of the pathology of states of excess, where extreme sensualism borders on an exacerbated spirituality. Acts of contrition may be as conscious of their own excess as any transgression, and this may or may not be part of Oldham's meaning when he asks us in the 'Apology' to 'excuse Th'Extravagance of a repenting Muse'.

But it is apparent in Oldham's case that even as he mimicked the postures of the Rochesterian rakes, he displayed a class-conscious awareness of not being to the manner born. This is not surprising, considering how quick Rochester and his circle were to spot clumsiness in unlordly pretenders to the 'mannerly obscene': Dryden's dry bawdy bobs are the best-known casualty of their put-downs. Oldham's references to the libertine poets keep harping on their lordly rank ('damn'd Placket-Rhimes, Such as our Nobles write', 'our witty bawdy Peer'), sometimes with a note of hoity-toity *tu quoque* conveying that the peers are no better than an 'Illiterate Cit' or 'Prentices and Carmen'. The 'Scriblers of Quality' would see this as a case of underlings aping their betters. But lordly accents, directed against lordly victims, were part of the rhetorical armoury of unlordly poets: as I suggested, this assumed arrogance did not sit easily on Oldham, though he tried, nor even on Dryden, whereas Swift, Pope, and Fielding played it freely and with blistering point.

As to the 'Mannerly Obscene', Dryden at least could do it quite as well as the noble rakes, though Rochester wanted it known that he was loud and gauche in such things, and would cry 'Cunt' to seem a 'tearing Blade'. Dryden may for a time have tried to be something of a sexual Hector in his social behaviour, which may have been part of what Rochester meant. But in 'obscene' poems both he and occasionally Oldham could claim to be more 'mannerly' than their betters, if 'mannerly' implies a less emphatic touch than crying cunt: at all events 'cunt', freely in evidence in Rochester's poems, doesn't appear in the Dryden concordance, whereas Dryden's song 'Whilst Alexis lay prest' (from a play dedicated to Rochester), perhaps the wittiest erotic poem of the time, uses no bad words. Oldham cries cunt a good deal in 'Sardanapalus', but he is guying Rochester in that poem: even so, it was 'To the Author of Sardanapalus' that Soame addressed his 'School-master' rebuke.

What Rochester himself conceived as well-bred obscenity was not the delicate touch he affected to praise in his friends, but a more thrustingly outrageous thing, a *sprezzatura* paradoxically sustained in the teeth of a foul-mouthed strenuousness. What he ascribed to Dryden, on no great surviving evidence, was presumably an oafish version of the same thing, which failed the patrician litmus test. The imputation that Dryden's efforts were poetic and sexual non-events, 'dry Bawdy bobs', derives piquancy from Rochester's poetic interest in impotence or sexual burn-out, whether flaunted confessionally or in mythologised self-projection.

It was to this particular vanity, indulged by Rochester with boastful brio, that Oldham addressed himself, in real or pretended condemnation or both, in the imprecations of 'Upon the Author of the Play call'd *Sodom*':

> Thou covet'st to be lewd, but want'st the Might
> And art all over Devil, but in Wit.
> Weak feeble strainer at meer Ribaldry,
> Whose Muse is impotent to that degree,
> 'T had need, like Age, be whipt to Lechery.
>
> Vile Sot! who clapt with Poetry art sick,
> And voidst Corruption like a Shanker'd Prick,
> Like Ulcers, thy Imposthum'd addle Brains
> Drop out in Matter, which thy Paper stains:
> Whence nauseous Rhymes by filthy Births proceed,
> As Maggots in some Turd ingendring breed,
> Thy Muse has got the Flowers, and they ascend
> As in some greensick Girl, at upper End.
> Sure Nature made, or meant at least 't have done 't,
> Thy Tongue a Clitoris, thy Mouth a Cunt.
> How well a Dildoe would that place become,
> To gag it up, and make 't for ever dumb!

Whether or not Rochester wrote *Sodom*, these driving sexual curses are a good imitation of several of his canonical poems, not only in the general idiom, at once overheated and arrogantly insouciant, but in the specific vocabulary of flowers (menstruation), dildoes, frigging and the rest: the flowers ascending 'at upper End' anticipate Swift's analysis of genital forces rising to the brain. The poem concludes with Rochester's book being sent, in the common satirical formula, to the public jakes for bum-paper. There, however, it will 'bugger wiping Porters when they shite,/ And so thy Book itself turn Sodomite', exceeding the formula and becoming, instead of the inert cloacal matter sanctioned by tradition, a sexually active humanoid, like Signior Dildo himself.

It's a very Rochesterian effect. The customary metaphors, venereal or scatological, for literary shortcomings are realised anthropo-morphically, beyond traditional analogies between muse and mistress or conceits about the 'lust of Poetry', which Oldham uses freely. This is of a piece with Rochester's rendering of sexual functions, even in failure, as self-powered humanoids: as when phalluses, intermittently and unpredictably impotent, become paradoxically like the omnipotent Dildo, autonomous beings independent of their owner. As I argued in chapter 1, this is part of what gives impotence in Rochester's poems the boastful vitality of an active function rather than a passive or merely helpless state.

Oldham was quite willing to apply to himself and his own art images of aged incapacity ('More tedious than old Doaters, when they woo') and outright impotence that 'Upon the Author of *Sodom*' applied to Rochester and indeed borrowed from him. The analogies between bad writing and sexual failure have in both poets a forceful-ness and immediacy quite different from their better-known counter-parts in Pope's *Essay on Criticism*. Oldham's 'Letter from the Country' is not only an extended orchestration of such analogies, but acquires a quickened energy of formulation at precisely the point where impotence is contemplated:

> As a dry Lecher pump'd of all my store,
> I loath the thing, 'cause I can do't no more.

Typically this comes over with almost more animation than the ensuing account of recovery, in which the poet finds again 'Recruits of matter in my pregnant Brain'. It's evident that Rochester's set-pieces on impotence made an enduring impression on Oldham's verse, haunting his rhythms even when the subject-matter did not especially connect. The passage from the third *Satyr upon the Jesuits*, for example, where the dying Loyola addresses his followers:

> Yet, as a wounded General, e're he dies,
> To his sad Troops, sighs out his last Advice ...
> So I to you my last Instructions give ...

24

undoubtedly derives from 'The Disabled Debauchee' ('As some brave *Admiral*, in former *War*,/ Depriv'd of force, but prest with courage still ...'), though Brooks' commentary does not record it.

'Upon the Author of *Sodom*' may read like devastating invective, but the poem was designed for circulation within the group, and Rochester would be likely to have relished its virtuosities as a kind of compliment. They belong to the type of aggressive hyperbole that disarms itself in the sport. The badnesses it purports to decry are ones which the group would normally boast, and the taunts of impotence were no more than Rochester directed at himself in defiant self-jeering. Brooks is surely right to relate Oldham's 'vein of comic exaggeration' to the 'joshing' freely practised within Rochester's circle, but he also sees the speaker as ill-bred in a way that separates him from 'the elite fellowship of true antinomian gallants'. His harangue mimics Rochester more than Dryden's poems ever did, and his way of crying 'cunt' is not the show-off way imputed to Dryden, whose poems don't do it anyway, but very close to the ranting derision with which Rochester 'cried' the word himself: if anything, the poem is more sparing in this matter than the master usually was, though (if numerical counts mean anything) 'Sardanapalus' amply compensates for any shortfall.

Oldham's aspiration to membership of the Rochester coterie seems to have differed from Dryden's, though both felt themselves, and were doubtless made to feel, outsiders by virtue of inferior rank. At least it expressed itself differently. He had the instinctive street-wisdom not to be self-abasing, as Dryden was self-abasing when cultivating the rakish Earl. The forms of obscene mimicry and the mock-imprecations he practised instead were not only a less solemn idiom and closer to that of the group, but also in its very nature protected, as overt compliment was not, from a too obvious appearance of sycophancy. Oldham more than once declared his dislike of flattering dedications: when he did praise Rochester fulsomely, it was in the posthumous context of 'Bion', when the flattery would no longer seem self-serving. He was less pompous or self-important than Dryden, and as an unestablished figure doubtless had less to lose. He could more easily adopt coterie postures of outrageous scurrility or frivolous insolence, thus avoiding Drydenian unctuousness.

Even so, there's no evidence that Oldham was admitted to intimate membership of the group. He does not appear in the index of Rochester's correspondence, and the degree of friendship or even of active patronage on Rochester's part is unclear. Tradition has it that

it was the 'Satyr Against Vertue' which led Rochester and his friends
to seek Oldham out at the school in Croydon where he taught. If true
it confirms that they were happy enough to be the objects of a parody
of libertine hectoring and even to be described as court hectors. But
the poem must have appeared especially clumsy in its impersonation
of lordly speech: mimicry of the order of 'haughty scornful I', 'dull
unbred Fools ... Who act their Wickedness with an ill Grace',
convicts itself of the 'ill Grace'. It is arguable that the satirical point is
precisely to indicate that the 'breeding' the speaker pretends to is itself
oafish, which might or might not indicate that the wits were even
more tolerant of derision, and on a broader front, than one might have
assumed. But it is unlikely that the poem would have suggested to
them that the author had an easy familiarity with their normal modes
of speech. I find it hard to imagine that they would overtly declare
themselves to be the 'grandees' of sin any more than Rochester would
refer to himself as 'haughty scornful I', or that they would expound
their libertine code with the laboured explicitness (not to mention the
arthritic cadences) of the speaker:

> In Us [Sin's] a Perfection, who profess
> A studied and elab'rate Wickednes:
> We're the great *Roya'l Society* of Vice,
> Whose Talents are to make Discoveries,
> And advance Sin like other Arts and Sciences:
>   'Tis I, the bold Columbus, only I,
>   Who must new Worlds in Vice descry,
> And fix the Pillars of unpassable Iniquity.

Oldham picks up some traditional items of ideology: the notion of
libertines as self-styled explorers, analogous to scientists or discoverers
of new worlds, living at the frontiers of known experience, dedicated
to the pursuit of all possibilities of transgression or pleasure, learned to
a perfectionism or exhaustiveness of pedantry, and 'studied' too in the
sense of the fastidious and the *recherché*. Hero-worshipping gestures to
Satan, Cain, and Nero, are also guyed, with the same humourless
spelling-out. Pretensions of daring and refinement, *éxalté* pompous-
ness parading a dandy cool, are captured with real insight. Oldham
can diagnose the codes of aristocratic immoralism, and the blend
of romance and doggedness, or glamour and pedantry, that peren-
ially attach to such subcultures. But his laboured mimicry resembles
nothing in Rochester's manner, and reads as much like the soliloquies
of a stage Machiavel as any speech from the *Satyrs upon the Jesuits*.

Lurid principles are projected into that indeterminate fictional zone between private unspoken reflection and the need to spell things out to an audience, in which both matter and manner tend to lose all conviction. This is another example of the legacy in Oldham's work of the manner and rhetoric of Restoration heroic plays. A fascinating appendix to Brooks' edition shows that the working drafts for *Satyrs upon the Jesuits* are full of passages from plays by Lee, Dryden, Settle, and Otway. The Rochesterian speaker's aspiration to have 'done some great and unexampled Deed' comes from the same generic source. Rochester may have liked the poem, but could never have spoken in the way it represented him. Oldham's borrowings from theatrical speeches, however ironic their subtext, show a nervous sense of the needs of an audience, of explanations due to the uninitiated, which is exceptionally incongruous in what purports to be a coterie document. What is most actively in evidence is that essential feature of Oldham's character and formation, his schoolmasterliness, as Sir William Soame, responding to a rather more flamboyantly successful of his libertine impersonations, perceived exactly.

· 3 ·
Mock-heroic and war
I: Swift, Pope and others

THE GREAT DIVERSION OF ALL THE SPECTATORS

In the fourth book of *Gulliver's Travels*, Gulliver discourses to the Master Houyhnhnm about war:

being no Stranger to the Art of War, I gave him a Description of Cannons, Culverins, Muskets, Carabines, Pistols, Bullets, Powder, Swords, Bayonets, Sieges, Retreats, Attacks, Undermines, Countermines, Bombardments, Seafights; Ships sunk with a Thousand Men; twenty Thousand killed on each Side; dying Groans, Limbs flying in the Air: Smoak, Noise, Confusion, trampling to Death under Horses Feet: Flight, Pursuit, Victory; Fields strewed with Carcases left for Food to Dogs, and Wolves, and Birds of Prey; Plundering, Stripping, Ravishing, Burning and Destroying. And, to set forth the Valour of my own dear Countrymen, I assured him, that I had seen them blow up a Hundred Enemies at once in a Siege, and as many in a Ship; and beheld the dead Bodies drop down in Pieces from the Clouds, to the great Diversion of all the Spectators. (IV.V.247)

The passage belongs to an old tradition of descriptions of battle, both in its general accumulation of horrors and in the specific details listed. There is a general awareness that such things belong to a family type, whose earliest-known versions go back to Homer, where they are already likely to have been assembled from traditional materials, used in some degree as prefabricated building blocks: 'dictional formulae, formulaic lines, typical details, typical groupings of details, recurrent situations'.[1] Homeric accounts of carnage have left their mark on many set pieces of battle-description by poets and historians, both ancient and modern.

---

[1] References to *Gulliver's Travels* in the text give book, chapter & page in *Works*, XI. See Bernard Fenik, *Typical Battle Scenes in the Iliad* (*Hermes: Zeitschrift für Klassische Philologie*, 21), Wiesbaden, 1968, pp. 229, *et passim*; also J. C. Bramble, 'Lucan', in *Cambridge History of Classical Literature. II: Latin Literature*, ed. E. J. Kenney and W. V. Clausen, Cambridge, 1982, pp. 545–7.

Later war-descriptions have increasingly had to accommodate details belonging to more advanced technologies in siege-warfare, and in other land and sea combat. The tradition came eventually to include gunpowder war, in some celebrated enumerations of Erasmus or Rabelais, as well as of Swift, without radically modifying the sense of the generic or habitual that seems naturally to attach to such passages, or to individual components. A glimpse in a text by Norman Mailer of 'a dismembered arm ... flying across the sky after an explosion' looks back not only to Swift's 'Limbs flying in the Air', but also to the exuberant routines of non-explosive mutilation in Ariosto or Lucan or Homer.[2] Aerial bombardment and 'smart weapons' also produce most of the effects Swift catalogued, and they doubtless tend to elicit similar portrayals.

New technologies in this sphere almost always have the function of increasing the scale of devastation, though the changes they introduce are not only of scale, or even of technology. They penetrate modes of perception, the style of moral thought, the entire cultural fabric, and the impact of gunpowder, or aviation, or nuclear bombs, is one whose range of cultural consequences extends beyond the limits of this study of mock-heroic and war. I shall, however, be concerned with an important moment in the history of the European conscience on which the war-descriptions of Swift and of some other writers seem to me to throw light.

That there were continuities as well as discontinuities is my starting point. The 'typical details, typical groupings of details', which derive from Homeric portrayals and permeate innumerable later exercises in the genre, remained sufficiently 'typical' in Swift's day to be comprehensively anthologised in the *Battle of the Books* (1704). The war-description of *Gulliver's Travels*, IV.v, is a technologically updated version (though the earlier work also takes in gunpowder), and one which carries a highly individual ironic charge. But its generic character is unmistakable. It is an enlarged, as well as intensified, version of the kind of thing Dryden described as 'common notions' in poetical battle-descriptions: 'the thundering of guns, the smoke, the disorder, and the slaughter'.[3] Educated contemporaries of Swift would be likely to sense an almost allusive kinship with descriptions of

---

[2] Norman Mailer, *The Fight* (1975), II.13, London, 1976, p. 158; Ariosto, *Orlando Furioso*, XV.lxxxii, trs. Barbara Reynolds, Harmondsworth, 1975, 1.467; Lucan, *De Bello Civili*, II.181 *et passim* (for a special effect, discussed below, of dismembered limbs dropped by birds of prey from the sky, see VII.838–40); *Iliad*, XI.145–7 (cited Fenik, p. 19, who says this is infrequent in Homer; but cf. V.81–2 and XVI.323–4).   [3] Watson, 1.96

carnage in epic poems (violent epics like Lucan's even more, perhaps, than Homer's or Virgil's), and especially in the writings of some historians, notably of the Carthaginian wars (Polybius, Livy, Appian) in whom Swift was particularly well read.[4]

There is a small body of critical writing which hints at models for such descriptions: earliest (and furthest from Swift, because focused more on family catastrophes than on the portrayal of physical devastation), a passage in the *Rhetorica ad Herennium* on how to describe a besieged town; Quintilian on the same subject, and somewhat closer to another of Gulliver's war-descriptions, to the King of Brobdingnag (ii.vii.134); and Erasmus' *De Copia*, which cites the passage from Quintilian and goes on to instance Lucan's third book (siege and naval battle of Massilia or Marseille) for the proper description of 'seditions, armies, battles, slaughter, destruction, sackings, single combat, naval battles', a rhetorician's enumeration of enumerations.[5] Both Quintilian and Erasmus present warfare less as a topic in its own right than as one among several subjects providing illustrative examples of the art of description. But one senses, in Erasmus especially, the resonances of a substantive critique of war of the kind he provides in the discussion of the adage *Dulce bellum inexpertis* (*c.* 1513), with its generalised list of devastations, which resembles Gulliver's and may have been one of the models for it:

Imagine now that you see before you the barbarous cohorts whose very faces and shouts strike terror to the heart: the iron-clad troops drawn up in battle array, the terrifying clash and flash of arms, the hateful noise and bustle of a

---

[4] Swift left copies of Polybius and Livy annotated by himself, Nos. 367 and 384 of the Sale Catalogue of his books (Harold Williams, *Dean Swift's Library*, Cambridge, 1932; Williams, p. 45 and n., says he owned three copies of Livy and two of Appian's *Roman History*). These histories are frequently cited in his works, and he was well read in them by the time the *Battle of the Books*, a work of epic parody whose battle descriptions are discussed in this chapter, appeared in 1704. He used Polybius extensively as an authority on constitutional history, and cited Livy and Appian, in his *Discourse of the Contests and Dissensions in Athens and Rome*, 1701 (ed. Frank H. Ellis, Oxford, 1967, *passim*); Livy appears briefly as a character in the *Battle* (*Works*, i.152), and is cited a number of times in his works.

[5] *Rhetorica ad Herennium*, iv.xxxix.51, a passage which has its own Homeric prototype (*Iliad*, ix.591ff.), cited by Harry Caplan in the excellent Loeb edition of this work once attributed to Cicero. Caplan also cites analogues in other rhetorical and historical texts (pp. 358–9n.); see also Quintilian, *Institutio Oratoria*, viii.iii.67–8; Erasmus, *De Copia*, translated by Betty I. Knott, ii, Method 5, i, 'Description of Things', *Collected Works*, xxiv (Toronto, Buffalo and London, 1978), 577, 580; the example cited by Erasmus is Lucan, *De Bello Civili*, iii.453–762. For some useful remarks about Quintilian's siege scenario, its relation to treatments by poets and historians (and adaptations and reversals by Lucan of traditional elements), see J. C. Bramble, 'Lucan', pp. 545ff.; on 'epic ... formulae for treating the pitched battle', and Lucan's variations, see pp. 548–57.

great multitude, the threatening looks, harsh bugles, startling peal of trumpets, thunder of the bombards (no less frightening than real thunder, but more harmful); a mad uproar, the furious shock of battle, and then wholesale butchery, the cruel fate of the killers and the killed, the slaughtered lying in heaps, the fields running with gore, the rivers dyed with human blood.[6]

Gulliver's account, even more than Erasmus', is a curious cross between the highly specific account of a particular event which might be found in an epic poet or a historian, and the rhetorician's 'typical' or exemplifying list. The headlong enumeration of weapons seems to derive immediately from some enumerations of artillery in Rabelais (i.xxvi; iv.lxi), Swift's 'dynamic productivity' betokening death and sterility, in a peculiarly advanced form of that 'copiousness' which presupposes the opposite of healthy expansive abundance.[7]

The number 20,000 occurs in another of Gulliver's war-descriptions (iv.xii.293), in Swift's *Fragment of the History of England*, and in the *Conduct of the Allies (Works*, v.19; vi.33). Swift's collaborator, Thomas Sheridan, said in late November 1728 in *Intelligencer*, 18, that the Drapier had 'prevented that by his PEN, which perhaps *Twenty thousand* Swords, could not have done'. It appears to have settled into a rhetorical formula, either denoting large military forces or as a figure for great slaughter. It occurs in the Old and New Testaments and in classical writers, including (with special frequency) Polybius, Livy, Plutarch, and Appian, and also in Shakespeare; it later figures in Sade (who was well-versed in numerations of slaughter, including Swiftian ones) and in Flaubert (who studied Polybius and other ancient sources for *Salammbô*).[8] In Graeco-Roman letters it seems to be a

---

[6] Erasmus, *Adages*, iv.i.1, in Margaret Mann Phillips, *The 'Adages' of Erasmus: A Study with Translations*, Cambridge, 1964, p. 313. For a parallel enumeration see p. 313n.1; also pp. 296–353 for Erasmus' general attitude to war.

[7] The phrase 'dynamic productivity' is borrowed from Terence Cave, *The Cornucopian Text*, Oxford, 1979, p. 183; Cave's discussion, throughout the book, of the negative properties of cornucopia is of special interest.

[8] Jonathan Swift and Thomas Sheridan, *The Intelligencer*, ed. James Woolley, Oxford, 1992, p. 199. In *A Modest Proposal*, it is suggested that 'Twenty thousand [children] may be reserved for Breed' – a perhaps unusual non-martial example (*Works*, xii.111). For biblical examples, see 2 Samuel, 8.4, 10.6, 18.7; 1 Chronicles, 18.4; Psalms, 68.17; Luke, 14.31. For ancient historians, see for example Polybius, *Histories*, i.lxvii.13; iii.lxxii.8; v.lxv.9; Livy, viii.xxx.7; ix.xxxi.16; ix.xliv.7; xxii.lx.20; Plutarch, *Sulla*, xxiv.1; *Camillus*, xxvi.1; *Pompey*, xii.3; xxviii.2; *Antony*, vii.2; l.1; lxiv.1; Appian, *Civil Wars*, i.vi.48, 50; i.x.92; ii.i.7, etc. (The above are extracted from a much larger list of examples in the corpus of Greek and Latin literatures, retrieved from two databases; Thesaurus Linguae Graecae, CD ROM c, University of California, Irvine; and, for the Latin examples, Packard Humanities Institute, CD ROM 5.3; both databases were searched by means of *Ibycus*, Search Programme Version 91.08.10. The

historian's figure rather than an epic one. It does not appear even in an 'historical' epic of mass-carnage like Lucan's *De Bello Civili*, though Robert Graves, one of Lucan's translators, slips 'twenty thousand corpses' into a footnote on the Pharsalian battlefield, a figure remarkable because it is neither in Lucan nor in standard accounts by Caesar, Plutarch, and Appian, all of whom give different numbers for Pompey's dead.[9]

If Graves invented or mechanically slipped into this particular number, he presumably did so much in the way Gulliver did, and the fact offers additional confirmation of its peculiar hypnotic attraction in such contexts. Despite its frequency among historians, however, the number does not seem to occur in any of the major Graeco-Roman epics, presumably because of their tendency to focus on individual warriors rather than on details of mass-confrontation. This tendency is perhaps less evident in Lucan, who was sometimes disparagingly described as more a historian than a poet, and whose poem gives an unusually marked sense of large-scale troop-movements and of tactical deployment, as well as showing a concern with the horrors of war and the cruel waste of civil strife which is often more prominent than any attention to individual prowess. One critic has spoken of Lucan's reversal of conventional epic patterns and expectations, and of the fact that his poem has only one *aristeia*, and that an 'inverted' one (the episode of Scaeva, in VI.140ff.).[10] Even so, he does not offer Graves' statistic, any more than other epic poets do. There is an odd Homeric exception, at *Iliad*, IX.383–4, a reference to 'Thebes of the hundred gates, where through each of the gates two hundred/ fighting men come forth to war with horses and chariots'. The arithmetic happens

New Testament is included in the Greek database and the Vulgate in the Latin). It should be said that this is usually a figure among many in extended historical narratives, but a frequent one, whose subsequent use in subsequent literary texts suggests that it acquired a quasi-formulaic status as a rhetorical round number, whether or not based on specific statistical information. It occurs repeatedly in Shakespeare and other authors, as well as Swift. For Shakespeare, *Richard II*, III.ii.76, 85, IV.i.59; *3 Henry VI*, I.ii.51; *Coriolanus*, III.iii.69; *Hamlet*, IV.iv.60. Sade, *Aline et Valcour*, lettre LXCI, Paris, 10/18, 1971, II.432. Flaubert, *Salammbô*, chs. 4, 6, 14 in *Oeuvres Complètes*, ed. Bernard Masson, Paris, 1964, 1.710,721,785, and letters about *Salammbô*, of 2 January 1862 to Jules Duplan and Edmond and Jules de Goncourt, in *Correspondance*, ed. Jean Bruneau, III (Paris, 1991), 193, 195.

9 See Lucan, *Pharsalia*, trs. Robert Graves, Harmondsworth, 1956, p. 171n; Caesar, *Civil War*, III.99, gives 15,000; Plutarch, *Caesar*, XLVI.2–3, and *Pompey*, LXXII.3, gives 6,000, from the historian Asinius Pollio; Appian, *Civil Wars*, II.xi.82, cites 25,000 from 'exaggerating writers' and 6,000 from Asinius Pollio. For a general account of the numbers at Pharsalus, see *De Bello Civili*, VII, ed. J. P. Postgate, rev. O. A. W. Dilke, Introduction, pp. 12–30.

10 Bramble, 'Lucan', pp. 538, 543. For Lucan as a 'historian' rather than poet, see pp. 39–40 and n.23 below.

to come to 20,000, but the reader would need to make the calculation, and what comes over is the sense of ceremony and symmetry rather than large undifferentiated numbers. Swift's readiness to use this figure repeatedly may reflect a subtextual predisposition to evoke the historians rather than epic poets.

Other things in Gulliver's list are, however, strongly reminiscent of heroic poetry, though not confined to it. 'Fields strewed with Carcases left for Food to Dogs, and Wolves, and Birds of Prey' is a familiar epic commonplace (the *Iliad* actually begins with it),[11] and so are many other items, the sense of mass carnage and plunder, the murderous crowdedness of a siege or a sea-battle, 'trampling to Death under Horses Feet'.[12]

A number of things in the passage are more 'modern', notably 'the great Diversion of all the Spectators'. The shocking pay-off erupts as a kind of rhetorical afterthought, a turn purportedly so outrageous and unexpected that it has to be assumed to be new-fangled, in the way we call appalling things 'unheard of'. This 'modernism', like all modernisms Swift deals in, has always existed. In *A Tale of a Tub*, Swift's completest anatomy of the topic, it embraces a complex of depravities, moral and intellectual, which go back, like the '*TRUE CRITICK*, whose Original is the most Antient of all', to the earliest manifestations of the unregulated intellect. (The issue is given a mock-epic orchestration at this point in the *Tale*: 'Every *True Critick* is a Hero born, descending in a direct Line from a Celestial Stem.')[13] The present-day manifestations are bad because new, but in a way that shows humanity as atavistically disposed to the 'new' – to the transgressions against norms of virtue or sense that are from the earliest time endemic to the radical character of the human animal. Readers are caught up in an unresolved contradiction, projecting an either-way-you-lose atmosphere which is part of what is nowadays, in

---

[11] *Iliad*, 1.4–5; see also *Gulliver's Travels*, IV.iv.241, where Gulliver tells the Houyhnhnms that this is what happens to dead horses in the human world.

[12] For examples of this commonplace in the Graeco-Roman epic tradition, including comic derivatives in Ariosto and Rabelais, see *Iliad*, v.588, xi.531ff., xx.498ff.; *Aeneid*, xii.324–40, 532–4; Lucan, vii.528ff.; *Orlando Furioso*, iii.lv, trs. Reynolds, i.171; Rabelais, i.xxxvi. The detail is anthologised in the *Battle of the Books* (see below). On the Homeric passages, see also Edouard Delebecque, *Le Cheval dans l'Iliade*, Paris, 1951, pp. 97ff., 115, who argues that Homer falsifies, because horses do not tread on bodies. If so, Homer is followed by other writers, and by pictorial examples, ancient and modern.

The passage at *Iliad*, v.580–9, is discussed in Pope's 'Essay on Homer's Battels', which is inserted after Book iv in his translation of the *Iliad*, TE, vii.253.

Classical historians also include this detail, for example Appian, viii.xix.129 (part of an extended set-piece).   [13] *A Tale of a Tub*, iii, *Works*, 1.57.

Swift studies, called 'entrapment'. Modern is old and new at the same time, in a way that defies conventional expectations of orderly discourse, leaving no sense of a definite proposition to resist, let alone assent to, only an awareness of aggression diffusely and comprehensively targeted.

Cruel laughter was no new thing, and gratuitous unmotivated pleasure in suffering had been a matter of note in imperial Rome as in Renaissance Europe, often in relation to spectacles in Roman amphitheatres or to the perverse cruelties of emperors (some examples are considered below). The 'modernity' of such things was itself of classical origin or a matter of ancient report, though the charged exploitation of contradictory signals is Swift's own. An especially interesting case may be found in Montaigne's essay on cruelty ('De la cruauté', II.xi). A passage in the first edition (1580) records one of Montaigne's most painful obsessions, the extreme cruelties perpetrated in the French religious wars, not exceeded by anything in ancient writings ('ne voit on rien aux histoires anciennes de plus extreme que ce nous en essayons tous les jours'). The harping on the modernity of these phenomena should be seen against the background of a deep distrust of innovation, which derived from ancient sources, chiefly Plato, and which Montaigne shared with Swift. Both saw civil war and religious strife as destabilisations proceeding from a refusal to accept established order and the state religion, with the Huguenots in Montaigne playing a role similar to that of the Dissenters in Swift. For the cruelties perpetrated in such unnatural convulsions to be presented as 'new' was a further twist of the knife. A rhetoric of the appallingly 'unheard of' reinforces the logic of a belief that innovations bring atrocities, by suggesting that the atrocities are themselves innovative as atrocities go.

At all events, Montaigne says of the awful 'unprecedented' doings of the religious wars that he can't get used to them, and could hardly persuade himself, without personally witnessing the fact, that people could undertake such cruelties out of sheer pleasure in killing ('pour le seul plaisir du meurtre'), committing mutilations, sharpening their wits in the invention of unusual tortures and new styles of killing, without hostility or profit ('sans inimitié, sans profit'), merely to enjoy the pleasant spectacle:

A peine me pouvoy-je persuader, avant que je l'eusse veu, qu'il se fut trouvé des ames si monstrueuses, qui, pour le seul plaisir du meurtre, le voulussent commettre: hacher et détrencher les membres d'autruy; esguiser leur esprit à inventer des tourmens inusitez et des morts nouvelles, sans inimitié, sans profit, et pour cette seule fin de jouïr du plaisant spectacle des gestes et mouvemens pitoyables, des gemissemens et voix lamentables d'un homme mourant en angoisse. Car voylà l'extreme point où la cruauté puisse atteindre.

The harping on new, unusual or unheard of atrocities may derive from las Casas, writing about the cruelty of Spanish invaders towards their Amerindian victims. But the wording which most clearly emphasises pure motivelessness, *sans inimitié, sans profit, et pour ... jouïr du plaisant spectacle*, is a close variation on a passage in Seneca's letters, about killing without anger or fear, *non iratus, non timens, tantum spectaturus*, not included in the first edition or A-text (1580), which stressed the modernity of the phenomenon, but added in manuscript as a c-passage subsequent also to the expanded edition (B) of 1588. As it happens, a B-addition a page or so later concerns the killing of animals and men in Roman shows, and the final disposition of the essay combines (with some appearance of reluctance, but also with Montaigne's serendipitous hospitality to afterthoughts, complicating peculiarities, and even contradiction) ideas of a perverse modernity with a simultaneous recognition of its atavistic character. That recognition, more or less subtextual, was itself in some ways an extension of the understanding that if the argument against 'innovation' was an ancient one, then 'innovation' was ancient too. It exists in a quizzical relation with that abhorrence of novelty which led Montaigne, in 'De la coustume' (I.xxiii) and elsewhere, to suggest that the established customs or barbarities of outlandish peoples ought not lightly to be reversed, though they sometimes resembled what he would think of as atrocities in Europe.[14]

---

[14] Montaigne, *Essais*, ed. Pierre Villey, rev. V.-L. Saulnier, Paris, 1988, II.432–3. For an explanation of A, B, and c notations, see 'Note de l'éditeur', I.xv. For speculative identifications of the kind of 'plaisant spectacle' Montaigne may have meant, see III.1276n.

For Bartolomé de las Casas' insistence on the outrageous novelty of Spanish atrocities, for example in his *Brevísima relación de la destrucción de las Indias* (1552), see *Très brève relation de la destruction des Indes*, trs. (into French) Fanchita Gonzalez Batlle, Paris, 1991, pp. 50, 61, 63, 81, 83, 123. See Montaigne's account in 'Des Coches' (III.vi) of the 'horrible et inouy' treatment of the Indians in Peru and Mexico, including burnings alive (III.912–13 and 1320–1nn.). The adjective 'inouy' is similarly used of the extent of the devastation caused by Spanish conquest, and of the cruelties of popular wars in *Essais*, II.xviii, xxvii (II.667, 693). The Senecan quotation is from *Epistulae Morales*, xc.45. A related passage in III.vi ('Des coches'), which, like Book III as a whole, first appeared in B (1588), describes the progression in Roman spectacles from atrocities with wild beasts to those involving gladiators (III.905).

For some perceptive comments on Montaigne's views on custom and innovation, see the commentary on I.xxiii by Jacob Zeitlin, in his translation of the *Essays*, New York, 1934, 1.333ff.

The passage from *Gulliver's Travels*, and others like it in Swift's writings, embody a similar coexistence of apparent contradiction, but with a somewhat less relaxed targeting on the contradiction as culpable in itself. The war-description blends a suggestion of habitual turpitudes, deriving from the entranced automatism of Gulliver's enumeration, with the 'unexpected' sting of the 'great Diversion'. Its modernity comes over as a 'refinement' (a favourite Scriblerian term of abuse) of viciousness, but the outrageousness is that of the perverse, rather than the temporally new, as the notion of a 'novelty' or an 'original' sometimes refers to the eccentric or abnormal, rather than the unprecedented. Part of the trap is that abnormal acts like laughing at calamities are all too normal, so that, in another imprisoning turn, a relatively late, literally modern, technology like gunpowder merges with the perennial perversity of rejoicing in carnage and cruelty.

That perversity had become something of a *topos*, amply confirmed by real life. In the famous account of the Sack of Rome in *A Dialogue Concerning Heresies* (1529), More described the sadistic triumphalism of Lutheran mercenaries at the dismemberment of victims of their atrocities: 'Now than was all theyr cruell sporte and laughter eyther to se ye sely naked men in shrynkyng from the pykys to tere of theyr membres or for payn of yt pullynge to runne theyr naked bodyes in depe uppon the pykes.' In the discourse of Amerindian conquest, it might manifest itself in the behaviour of a Spanish captain, reported in las Casas's *Brevísima relación*, who killed Indians while singing of Nero and the burning of Rome; or in the behaviour of Indians, when a cannibal *canaille* is said by Jean de Léry to have displayed with peals of laughter the chopped parts of a captured prisoner. Las Casas' sense of new and unheard of atrocities, like Montaigne's, blends with an evocation of ancient continuities. The gaiety of Nero as Rome burned, and the pleasures of gladiatorial shows, were frequently invoked as gruesome parallels in Agrippa d'Aubigné's epic of the French religious wars, *Les Tragiques* (1616). Even without classical reminders, the phenomenon is one which naturally provokes surprised recognition, a rhetoric which blends ideas of predictability as well as unnaturalness, and which may be seen as prefiguring Swift's perception of an atavistic modernism. Fielding's account, in the *Voyage to Lisbon* (1755), of the unfeeling ribaldry of the sailors and watermen who jeered at his crippled state as he was embarking, is a later example (discussed from another perspective in the fifth chapter of this book).[15] These instances have the reek of the real, warm and immediate beyond joke or sarcasm. They have no need of pay-off lines, and do not come over as ironic fictions or as pointed literary play.

But they reflect something which has also been appropriated from an early date into some of the more stylised forms of the literature of cruelty. The garish violence of Roman epics of the Silver Age (Lucan, Statius, Silius Italicus) has been seen as an instance of it, to which mock-heroic discourse paid early attention. A classical analogue to the 'great Diversion' occurs in the little epic on the *bellum civile*, recited by Eumolpus in Petronius' *Satyricon* (sometimes thought to contain a parody of Lucan's poem on the same subject, along with other excessively rhetorical poetry), in a purportedly typical scene in which a captured 'tiger is wheeled in a gilded palace to drink the blood of men while the crowd applauds' (*ut bibat humanum populo plaudente cruorem*).[16] Swift knew his Petronius and wrote an imitation of one of his poems.[17] If he was the author of *A Letter of Advice to a Young Poet* (1721), he cited from Eumolpus' speech on poetry (which is the preamble to the mock-poem) the comment that a poet's mind ought to be 'steeped in the vast flood of literature' (*mens ... ingenti flumine litterarum inundata*), adding that the words are 'no better than an invidious and unhandsome Reflection on all the *Gentlemen-Poets* of these Times'. If he did not write it, whoever passed it off as his knew how to catch something of his sarcasm, and evidently assumed that an allusion to Petronius' treatment of poets would sound like him.[18]

---

[15] Thomas More, *Dialogue Concerning Heresies* (1529), VI.7, in *Complete Works of St. Thomas More*, VI, ed. Thomas M. C. Lawler and others, New Haven and London, 1981, Part i, p. 371. For discussion, see Appendix C, Part ii, pp. 773–7, and Robert P. Adams, *The Better Part of Valor: More, Erasmus, Colet, and Vives, on Humanism, War, and Peace, 1496–1535*, Seattle, 1962, pp. 266–7; las Casas, *Très brève relation*, p. 81; Jean de Léry, *Histoire d'un voyage fait en la terre du Brésil*, 2nd edn., 1580, ed. Jean-Claude Morisot, Geneva, 1975, pp. 226–7; d'Aubigné, *Les Tragiques*, I.813–14, 1105ff., v.963ff., in *Oeuvres*, ed. Henri Weber and others, Paris, 1969, pp. 40, 47, 173; Henry Fielding, *Journal of a Voyage to Lisbon*, ed. Harold E. Pagliaro, New York, 1963, pp. 44–5.

[16] Petronius, *Satyricon*, CXIX.17–18. For the vexed question of the relation to Lucan, see the 'Additional Note' in the revised Loeb edition (Cambridge, MA, and London, 1975), pp. 380–4; William Arrowsmith's introduction and commentary to his translation of the *Satyricon*, Ann Arbor, 1959, pp. xx–xxi, 208–10 (Arrowsmith omits the line about crowds applauding the drinking of blood, speaking only of 'fangs in demand', i.e. for use in amphitheatres, pp. 138, 210); J. P. Sullivan, *The Satyricon of Petronius*, London, 1968, pp. 165–86; Bramble, 'Lucan', p. 538 (cf. F. R. D. Goodyear, 'Prose Satire', in the same volume of the *Cambridge History of Classical Literature*, p. 637).

[17] 'On Dreams. An Imitation of Petronius' (1724?); *Poems*, II.363–64; for the original, *Somnia quae mentes ludunt*, see the Loeb edition, p. 429.

[18] *Letter to a Young Poet* (1721), in Swift, *Works*, IX.332–3, citing *Satyricon*, CXVIII (there is another

Whether or not Swift thought of Petronius' applauding crowd as aimed at Lucan (the notion of Lucan as Petronius' target was certainly in circulation in his time),[19] its parody of epic extravagance in a late decadent phase, and its glimpse of Roman mores under Nero, would not have escaped him. His view of Lucan himself was cool. In the *Battle of the Books* Lucan appears 'upon a fiery Horse, of admirable Shape, but head-strong', making a 'mighty Slaughter' among the Modern cavalry. He is impressive, as Ancients have to be in any battle with Moderns, but a bit over the top. In an exchange of gifts, paralleling the close of Hector's encounter with Ajax in *Iliad*, VII.201–312, Lucan's modern adversary, Blackmore, gives him a bridle.[20]

Lucan's reputation was mixed. His supercharged, extravagantly rhetorical style was already a matter of comment in Petronius and Quintilian, and is frequently noted by Dryden.[21] Boileau spoke of his heaped corpses and his inflated style and asked if there was anyone who didn't prefer Virgil (it is said that Corneille didn't but was ashamed of it).[22] Lucan is refused a place next to Homer and Virgil at the Table of Fame in Addison's *Tatler*, No. 81, and told by Virgil that he should sit with the historians (not taken as a compliment by Lucan, a sign of the inferior standing not only of himself, but of history, a view

---

ironic appeal to Petronius at p. 329); see the introduction to *Works*, IX.xxivff. for the contemporaneous attribution to Swift, whose name appeared on the title-page of the London reprint of the first Dublin edition, which had appeared anonymously over the signature E. F. (p. 345). Oddly, Petronius was also invoked in another work doubtfully attributed to Swift, the *Second Letter from a Friend to the Right Honourable* --- (i.e. to Chief Justice Whitshed) by 'N. N.', in 1725, which quotes from the opening of the *Satyricon*; see *Works*, X.170, and introduction p. xxv. For a canonical reference to Petronius, see *Works*, VIII. 134–5.

For Swift's copy of Petronius, see Sale Catalogue, No. 47: 'Petronii Arbitri Satyricon cum notis Variorum Plant. L. Bat. 1696'.   [19] See Watson, I.160, II.158.

[20] *Works*, I.158. Arbuthnot remembered this passage in a letter to Swift of 11 December 1718, in a scornful reference to Rowe's recently published translation of Lucan (*Correspondence*, II.303–4). Swift owned copies both of Rowe's translation and of the Latin text; he seems to have given away another copy of the original, and a third copy is lost, according to Harold Williams, who also states that the copy of Rowe's translation must have been Stella's (*Dean Swift's Library*, pp. 23–5, 43, Sale Catalogue, Nos. 50, 420).

[21] *Satyricon*, CXVIII; Quintilian, x.i.90; for Dryden, see Watson, I.201, II.82, 118–19, 158, 204. Dryden adds that Lucan's errors were exceeded by Petronius in *his* civil war poem (1.158).

[22] Boileau, *Art Poétique*, 1.98–100, IV.83–84 (lines 98–100, 939–40 in the Soame–Dryden translation); see *Epîtres*, VIII.53 (Boileau is partly attacking Lucan's French translator G. De Breboeuf). See *Epîtres, Art Poétique, Lutrin*, ed. Charles-H. Boudhors, Paris, 1952, pp. 268–9, 302, for comments by Rapin on Lucan as a bad influence on youthful taste, and for the suggestion about Corneille, which Boudhors questions; but see *Le Lutrin, L'Art Poétique*, ed. René d'Hermies, Paris (Classiques Larousse), n.d., p. 104n.1, which cites Huet on 'le grand Corneille' and his embarrassed preference, assumed by some editors to be aimed at by Boileau in IV.83–84. Corneille praised Lucan strongly in *Pompée* (1641), 'Au lecteur'.

which may go back to Petronius, and is shared by Davenant, Dryden and others;[23] the inferior status of history is germane to my argument, and discussed in later parts of this chapter and the next). The poor taste of people who preferred Lucan to Virgil was itself a critical commonplace, inevitably reaffirmed by Dryden more than once.[24] And Bolingbroke, in a letter to Swift of 1721, spoke of Cato 'so Sung by Lucan in every page, & so much better sung by Virgil in half a line'.[25]

The passage in Petronius is an analogue rather than a source. Swift undoubtedly knew it, but was unlikely to be thinking of it when writing *Gulliver's Travels*. We may assume that he was broadly sympathetic to Petronius' criticism of the excesses of Silver Epic, but that he would not have been if the targets had been Homer or Virgil. Homer, in fact, provides an example of spectators laughing at suffering, in which the foul-mouthed Thersites is beaten by Odysseus for his scurrilous attacks on the whole heroic business. 'A bloody welt stood up between his shoulders', and he wept in pain and fright, while the Greek soldiers 'laughed over him happily'. In this case, unlike that of Petronius' spectators, Swift's sympathy as well as Homer's would be with the spectators and not the victim. He rewrote the episode in the *Battle of the Books*, where Bentley takes the place of Thersites and Scaliger that of Odysseus.[26] What is interesting is that Swift omits any hint of the beating or the laughter of the soldiers, as well as of Thersites' substantive anti-heroic sentiments (Bentley merely utters general insults, calling the generals 'a Pack of *Rogues*, and *Fools*, and *Sons of Whores*'), three instances of a protective *pudeur* over the status of epic to which should be added a fourth, applicable to the *Battle* as a whole. By transferring the animus to Bentley, Swift further sidesteps the issue of heroic morality: since, throughout the *Battle*, books are fighting and not men, revulsion at any wounding or killing is

[23] Addison, *Tatler*, No. 81, 15 October 1709, ed. Donald F. Bond, Oxford, 1987, II.18–19; for Petronius, see *Satyricon*, CXVIII; for Dryden and Davenant, see Watson, I.95 and n., 160 and n.
[24] Watson, II.22, 243, 279. Of two useful studies of Lucan's reputation, O. A. W. Dilke, 'Lucan and English Literature', in *Neronians and Flavians*, ed. D. R. Dudley, London and Boston, 1972, pp. 83–112, and Charles Martindale, 'The Epic of Ideas: Lucan's *De bello civili* and *Paradise Lost*', *Comparative Criticism*, 3 (1981), 133ff., the first offers little evidence from Swift's lifetime, while Martindale's view that his reputation was very high in this period requires adjustment. Some of Martindale's discussion is reprinted in his *John Milton and the Transformation of Ancient Epic*, London and Sydney, 1986, pp. 197–227, a volume which in general contains valuable accounts of Renaissance views of Homer, Virgil, and Ovid, as well as Lucan.   [25] Bolingbroke to Swift, 28 July 1721, *Correspondence*, II.397.
[26] *Iliad*, II.211–77, esp. 267, 270; Swift *Works*, I.160–1.

neutralised. No such neutralising takes place in *Gulliver's Travels*, where, however, the epic reminders are of limited force.

The episode is different from Petronius' in that the spectators' laughter is at the punishment of a character deemed to deserve it, and in that it is supported by Homeric authority. Even so, Swift won't allow any response that might suggest a punitive gloating on Homer's part, just as he eliminates those parts of Thersites' speech which might make a reader side with him rather than with the official Homeric point of view. The passage is quite far removed from the congratulatory glee with which Gulliver imagines European faces being battered into mummy by the hooves of 20,000 Houyhnhnms (IV.xii.293), in what is, but might not readily be noticed as, a gigantic multiplication of the epic topos of 'trampling to Death under Horses Feet', and by that multiplication stripped of any essentially epic character; or from the reflection in the *Sentiments of a Church-of-England Man* that 'the Bigots of both Parties are *equally* entituled' to the extermination they wish upon each other;[27] or any of Swift's other expressions of a desire to shoot, hang or root out off the face of the earth various classes of people, including politicians, bankers, beggars, and Irishwomen who didn't buy Irish manufactures.

The readiness to entertain or to register complicity with punitive imaginings, or to be made both 'merry' and murderously punitive by a contemplation of the depravities which aroused them, is part of an old rhetoric, whose most explicit formulation in Swift is in the *Epistle to a Lady*: 'All their Madness makes me merry . . . I would hang them if I cou'd.'[28] The prototype Swift invokes is 'the ever-laughing Sage', Democritus. Juvenal's *ridet et odit*, in Satire xv, the reaction of a god contemplating human turpitude, is an even closer analogue.[29] When the Houyhnhnm General Assembly debates 'Whether the *Yahoos* should be exterminated from the Face of the Earth' (IV.ix.271), they are repeating what God said in Genesis 6.7: 'I will destroy man whom I have created from the face of the earth.' The implication is not that God, or the Houyhnhnms, are genocidal tyrants, but that man deserves the punishment. If laughter, generally a scarce commodity in Houyhnhnmland, is not immediately evident in either Houyhnhnms or God, a form of black humour or cruel joke is undoubtedly at work on Swift's part. The whole flat-voiced reversal, in which it is beasts who contemplate the extermination of human or humanoid pests,

[27] *Works*, II.13.   [28] *To a Lady*, lines 164–70, *Poems*, II.635.   [29] Juvenal, xv.71.

and consider alternatives like castration (what humans usually do to horses, as Gulliver explains), 'which, besides rendering them tractable and fitter for Use, would in an Age put an End to the whole Species without destroying Life' (273), cannot be read without recognition of a humorous grotesquerie, cheekily colluding with the whole put-down of human self-esteem. It is a dry version of a familiar pattern in which satirists of widely differing character (Rabelais, Flaubert, Jarry or Céline) exuberantly entertain extermination fantasies or participate in a righteous counterpart of the murderous velleities of enemies or malefactors.

Nevertheless, when Bentley gets his comeuppance, he is spared even the limited beating which he received in the Homeric original, even though the point of the episode is to humiliate him. A marginal gloss, referring conspicuously to Homer's Thersites, ensures that readers won't miss the connection, and one supposes that the reminder is calculated further to compound the insult. That being so, one has to ask whether Swift was instinctively and subtextually sanitising his Homer in the very act of putting him on display, as Pope was to do more overtly in his translation.

The Homeric episode is localised, and the soldiers' laughter is motivated by battle-hardened partisanship and a just sense of Thersites' shortcomings, while 'the great Diversion of all the Spectators' suggests a large, quasi-universal body of people (a bit like Flaubert's *bourgeois, c'est-à-dire tout le monde*),[30] with no motive but pleasure in the contemplation of carnage: the mirror antithesis of the satirist's posture I have been describing. The characteristic oscillation between contrary states which this suggests occurs within *Gulliver's Travels* itself, as well as between it and some of Swift's other writings. Gulliver's war-list differs from the scenario of the Houyhnhnm rout of European armies in that, instead of Gulliver's righteous delight at the slaughter of defeated invaders, implying deserved punishment, it offers an entranced evocation of the copious murderousness of modern war, which nobody deserves – or perhaps everybody. This comes over simultaneously from Gulliver as an admiring enthusiasm for the belligerents on all sides, and from Swift as a virtuosity of indictment.

Petronius' crowd applauding man-eating tigers, is likewise small-scale beside Swift's spectators, though unlike the Homeric episode it reports a motiveless pleasure in atrocities which aligns it with the war-

[30] Flaubert to Ernest Feydeau, 17 August 1861, *Correspondance*, III.170.

list. The tigers whose gory performances were staged in the amphitheatres are presented by Petronius as the fruits of imperial conquest,
and the spectators' applause exposes the decadence of Roman mores
under Nero, an emperor whose reign and personal character have
always been associated with a hedonism of gratuitous cruelty. The
fascination which he and a number of other Roman emperors held not
only for Sade and Flaubert, but also for Artaud, Camus, and other
exponents of 'cruelty' and the absurd has to do with a mythologised
perception of imperial omnipotence as the enabling condition for
'gratuitous acts' and the gratification of every impulse, unchecked by
morality and free of motive.

Both Petronius and Lucan, the author and a presumed target of
Eumolpus' recitation on the civil war, were personal victims of the
emperor: both 'died through the enmity of Nero, and both by the
same cause [i.e. suicide] and in effect at the same time'.[31] As courtiers
and critics of Nero, they were privileged real-life witnesses of those
'great tragical Farces in which one Half of Mankind was with much
Humour put to Death and Tortures, for the Diversion of the other
Half,'[32] as Fielding described the antics of Nero and other emperors
and tyrants. The passage luridly echoes Swift's remark about 'life
being Farce ... in every sense but the most important one, for it is a
ridiculous tragedy, which is the worst kind of composition'.[33] Like
Petronius' poem, Fielding's remarks encompassed cruel popular
entertainments and the behaviour of tyrants, and he insisted on a
connection between 'little jocose Mischiefs' (practical jokes), imperial
pleasures like Domitian's 'Fly-spitting', and such performances of
'exquisite Humour' as Alexander's 'burning the City of Persepolis'.[34]

These were enacted on the stage of history rather than in the
revered epic masterpieces. A traditional linkage existed between
tyrants and epic heroes, which Swift and some contemporaries
showed a need to uncouple or repress. There was a well-known story
that Alexander carried the *Iliad* with him as his 'viaticum of the
military art' and was an ostentatious devotee of Achilles.[35] Suetonius

---

[31] 'Additional Note' in Loeb *Satyricon*, p. 380.
[32] Henry Fielding, *Covent-Garden Journal*, No. 19, 7 March 1752, ed. Bertrand A. Goldgar,
   Oxford, 1988, pp. 132–3; Swift to Pope, 20 April 1731, *Correspondence*, III.456; see also Claude
   Rawson, *Henry Fielding and the Augustan Ideal under Stress*, new edn., New Jersey and London,
   1991, pp. 191ff., for fuller discussion of several examples discussed here.
[33] Swift to Pope, 20 April 1731, *Correspondence*, III.456.
[34] *Covent-Garden Journal*, Nos. 19 and 24, 7 and 24 March 1752, pp. 132, 156.
[35] Plutarch, *Alexander*, VIII.2, XV.7–9, XXVI.1–2.

reports that Nero owned 'two favourite drinking cups, which he called "Homeric", because they were carved with scenes from Homer's poems'; and Suetonius' version of a better-known story is that having whimsically set fire to Rome, Nero observed 'the conflagration from the tower of Maecenas and exulting, as he said, in "the beauty of the flames", he sang the whole of the "Sack of Ilium", in his regular stage-costume.'[36] Tacitus wasn't sure whether Nero started the fire, and merely reports as a rumour Nero's singing his *Troica*.[37] (Tacitus' account of the conflagration bears a broad family resemblance to the disaster scenarios of the rhetoricians cited earlier.)[38] Ironically, both Lucan and Petronius also wrote poems on the Fall of Troy. Lucan's is lost, but Petronius', a parody, is included in the *Satyricon*. Lucan is said also to have written a prose work on the fire, accusing Nero of starting it.[39]

Some of the tragical farces in which 'one Half of Mankind' was slaughtered 'for the Diversion of the other Half', as I have argued in an earlier discussion of Fielding, were perceived as charged with epic associations, and Nero's burning of Rome as literally executed to the tune of the Iliadic story.[40] Swift's contempt for Nero's murderous lusts and 'Thousand Caprices of Cruelty' was similar to Fielding's, and he had a similar understanding of Alexander the Great.[41] Like Fielding, Swift was well-read in Suetonius and Tacitus on Roman emperors, as well as Plutarch and others on Alexander, and equally aware of traditional associations between such tyrants and conquerors, and epic heroes in their more nefarious aspect.[42] The discomfort of the epic association was commonly side-stepped or repressed by a number of familiar manoeuvres. One was to insist, more or less overtly, on distinctions between historical villains and epic protagonists (who

[36] Suetonius, *Nero*, XLVII.1, XXXVIII.1–2.

[37] Tacitus, *Annals*, XV.xxxviii–xxxix. On the fire, and on Nero's poem on the Trojan War, see Miriam T. Griffin, *Nero: The End of a Dynasty*, New Haven and London, 1985, pp. 128–32, 147–52, 164, 268–76nn.

[38] *Annals*, XV.xxxviii; see the passages from the *Rhetorica ad Herennium* and from Quintilian cited n.5 above (the stress on conflagration, civilian disruption, wailing women and children is shared by all three, in a somewhat different emphasis from Swift's).

[39] On Lucan's *Iliacon*, see Griffin, *Nero*, pp. 153, 276n.71; on his work about the Fire, pp. 158–9, 269n.54, 278nn.96,103, and Sullivan, *The Satyricon of Petronius*, p. 189; on Petronius' *Troiae Halosis* (*Satyricon*, LXXXIX), see Sullivan, pp. 186–9.

[40] *Henry Fielding and the Augustan Ideal under Stress*, p. 193.

[41] *Works*, II.22; also I.198, 222; II.100; V.85. On Alexander, *Works*, I.107, 205, 247; also in Glubbdubdrib (*Gulliver's Travels*, III.vii.195); for an admiring glimpse of Alexander, V.83.

[42] The Sale Catalogue shows Swift to have owned 4 editions of Tacitus, 3 Latin and 1 English, 2 of the Latin editions annotated in his hand (Nos. 46, 289, 393, 638), as well as a Suetonius and a Dio Cassius (Nos. 285, 95). On Alexander, he owned copies of Plutarch, Arrian and Quintus Curtius (Nos. 243, 362, 150).

could at least be thought of as fictional). Another was to suppress analogies that might create embarrassing recognitions, or to omit or soften portrayals of disreputable or sanguinary behaviour in contexts likely to evoke the epic tradition. Another was to emphasise the difference between the deeds and character of epic heroes like Achilles and the greatness of the poems in which they appeared: as Addison said, Achilles was 'Morally Vicious, and only Poetically Good'.[43] Such uncouplings were especially important to writers of conservative and classicising allegiance like Swift and Pope, at a time when the old view that 'A heroic poem, truly such, is undoubtedly the greatest work which the soul of man is capable to perform'[44] was becoming increasingly difficult to square with anxieties about the morality of 'Warrs, hitherto the onely Argument/ Heroic deemd.'[45]

The urge to effect such uncouplings may be seen in discursive form in Pope's Preface and notes to the *Iliad*. Its poetic applications include his Homeric renderings and the remarkable avoidance of sanguinary war in all the important mock-heroic poems from Boileau's *Lutrin* to the *Dunciad*. The tenacity of the impulse in Swift is the expression of an anxious attachment to the putatively menaced values of *ancienneté*, in conflict with an equally powerful commitment to the Humanist critique of war, now no longer the marginal or minority position that it was at the time of Erasmus and More.[46]

Writers not in the same way attached to classicising canons of taste,

[43] *Spectator*, No. 548, 28 November 1712, ed. Donald F. Bond, Oxford, 1987, IV.464; see Bond's note for some analogous usages, including one by Dryden about Achilles.

[44] Dryden, Dedication of *Aeneis* (1697), in Watson, II.223 (for other examples, see *Discourse Concerning Satire*, 1693, Watson II.96; and references in *Order from Confusion Sprung*, pp. 201, 218nn.1–2). [45] Milton, *Paradise Lost*, IX.28–29.

[46] On the Humanist critique of war, see Adams, *Better Part of Valor, passim*. For the rarity of anti-war sentiment in the sixteenth and seventeenth centuries, see J. R. Hale, *War and Society in Renaissance Europe, 1450–1620*, Leicester, 1985, pp. 35ff. Hale argues in particular that the quasi-pacifism of More, Erasmus, Budé, Vives, and Castiglione lasted for a generation and 'soon died away' (pp. 40–1), and had a restricted effect anyway (pp. 35–45); also several essays in Hale, *Renaissance War Studies*, London, 1983, in particular, 'Sixteenth-Century Explanations of War and Violence', 'War and Public Opinion in Renaissance Italy', and 'Incitement to Violence? English Divines on the Theme of War, 1578–1631' (pp. 335–58, 359–87, 487–517), which suggest that influential and principled objections to war were uncommon, while celebrations, both secular and clerical, of war and the martial arts were plentiful, notably 'in the age's only mass medium', the pulpit (p. 511). James A. Freeman, *Milton and the Martial Muse*, Princeton, 1980, pp. 4, 16ff., 117ff.; another study, Robert T. Fallon, *Captain or Colonel: The Soldier in Milton's Life and Art*, Columbia, Missouri, 1984, pp. 128ff. also minimises pacifist sentiment in the seventeenth century, disagreeing with Freeman's portrayal of Milton's hostility to war. For the period 1618–1789, see Matthew Anderson, *War and Society in Europe of the Old Régime*, Leicester, 1988, which concurs with Hale's analysis, extending it to and beyond the seventeenth century as a whole, and indicating a growing hostility to war 'in educated and opinion-forming circles' in the 1740s to the 1770s (p. 185).

notably Defoe and Richardson, felt no corresponding obligation to protect the status of Homeric epic, and no inhibition about implicating it in their condemnation of war, as Ian Watt showed long ago.[47] Both novelists display a broad cultural antipathy towards classical epic, in which objections to a warlike morality combined with issues of class-antagonism (the identification of epic with an aristocratic warrior-class and its modern avatars, and the association of classical interests with a conservative and patrician caste). Richardson wrote of 'the fierce, fighting Iliad' that 'this poem . . . and its copy the Eneid' have created a 'savage spirit' that has 'ravaged the earth, and made it a field of blood'.[48] He also urged Aaron Hill to publish his epic *Gideon* without calling 'it epic in the title-page; since hundreds who see the title, will not, at the time, have seen your admirable definition of the word', a far cry from calling epic the noblest achievement of the human mind.[49]

Watt thinks Richardson was referring to an 'unpopularity' which 'must have been connected with the fact' that the epic excluded the novelistic 'expectations of everyday contemporary life'. Hill did in fact publish the poem as *Gideon . . . an Epic Poem*, but his apologetic gestures to a public not normally 'dispos'd . . . for *giving Fame to Epic Poetry*' are concerned with other issues, protesting, in a protracted access of political correctness, that his poem in its present form extolled sound principles of limited monarchy, and exposed the 'political defect' of a '*Military Care disjoin'd from the Imperial*'. He stressed in his notes an unusually bald conception of the view, not in itself unusual, of epic as a 'noble Lesson in Morality': 'A Man, who undertakes an *Epic Poem*, is not to write a *History*; but to propagate a *Moral*'. Hill retained a view of the importance and virtue of the military factor in ways Richardson may or may not have liked, as included among 'the chief Virtues of a People: *Intrepidity* in foreign *War* – and Spirit of domestic *Liberty*'.[50]

Swift might have found some of Hill's political ideals acceptable, though he is likely to have found his poem (whose first three books

---

[47] Ian Watt, 'Defoe and Richardson on Homer: A Study of the Relation of Novel and Epic in the Early Eighteenth Century', *Review of English Studies*, NS III (1952), 325–40, and *The Rise of the Novel*, London, 1957, pp. 240–59.

[48] Richardson to Lady Bradshaigh, 1749, in *Correspondence*, ed. A. L. Barbauld, 1804, IV.287; see also *Sir Charles Grandison*, ed. Jocelyn Harris, Oxford, 1986, III.197; cited *Rise of the Novel*, pp. 243–44.

[49] Richardson to Hill, 27 October 1748, *Correspondence*, I.122, cited *Rise of the Novel*, p. 246.

[50] Hill, *Gideon*, 1749, pp. 7–8, 39.

appeared in 1749, four years after Swift's death) as feeble as he or Pope or Dryden had thought Blackmore's epics were. And the Richardsonian interest in the reporting of sub-epic quotidian existence would have seemed 'modern' in Swift's special sense as well as the one now in use: a predisposing factor, for example, for the emergence of the novel (domestic, realistic, non-heroic), and especially of that confessional and digressive mode which we associate with Richardson and Sterne and which Swift derided *avant la lettre* in *A Tale of a Tub*. The baldest statement of its anti-military component is probably Blake's frequently cited exclamation in 'On Homer's Poetry' (*c.* 1820) that it is 'the Classics! & not Goths nor Monks, that Desolate Europe with Wars'. For many early eighteenth-century writers, this was precisely the connection which had to be minimised. The tenacity of Swift and Pope in this regard is observable in varying degrees in other writers, and may be seen to falter in Fielding, from *Jonathan Wild* onwards. By the time of Byron and Shelley, which is also the time of Blake's 'On Homer's Poetry', the urge to uncouple epic poems from the realities of military carnage has broken down, even in writers who, unlike Blake, might be thought to have a patrician-classicising formation (though Blake's own feelings about Homer were ambivalent).[51] In the epic traffickings of Byron and Shelley, modern war and the things Homer wrote about are seen as much the same thing.

Gulliver's diverted spectators create an effect of alienated recoil, unlike the laughing soldiery of the Homeric episode, with its opposite intimations of secret (or not so secret) sharing, which Swift eliminated in his rewriting of Homer. The stinging parable contained in Gulliver's pay-off line looks forward to a group of later fictions: for example to the audience's laughter at a newsreel showing the capture and rough treatment of a young militia man in Genet's *Pompes funèbres* (1947); the film in Bellow's *Humboldt's Gift* (1975) at which 'thousands of people were laughing' as a plane crashed into the sea or as 'pictures of man-eating comedy unrolled on the screen' (in this example, the disasters are actually played for laughs, Humboldt having, before his death, insisted on this, predicting to an unbelieving Charlie Citrine 'that it would be extremely funny'); and closest of all, and perhaps consciously half-echoing Swift, the war-film reported by Winston Smith in *Nineteen Eighty-Four* (1949), with its 'wonderful shot of a

---

[51] See the admirably succinct entries on Homer and Virgil in S. Foster Damon, *A Blake Dictionary*, rev. ed., Hanover, NH, and London, 1988, pp. 187–9, 435–6.

child's arm going up up up right up into the air' as a ship is blown up, while the audience are 'shouting with laughter'.[52]

It is curious that in all three passages the spectators' diversion is at cruelties witnessed through the mediation of the cinema, a technological interposition which distances and sanitises the event, and provides the laughter with a species of grotesque unfeeling freedom: 'it was pleasing hundreds of thousands, millions of spectators ... the whole theatre rocked with delight, shouting with laughter.'[53] An interesting variation occurs in Elmore Leonard's *LaBrava*, whose hero takes a shot on his telephoto lens of a man thrown off an overpass: 'they're holding the guy up in the air and he got the one of the guy falling, arms and legs out like he's flying, the one that was in *Newsweek* and all the papers ... Cleared about twelve grand so far, the one shot!'[54] The wording oddly resembles Orwell's passage, and the note of sanitised aloofness from the horror comes over even more strongly than in the examples reporting laughter. There is a sense in which the cinematic medium mirrors, in a way Swift could not have predicted, the effects of that other modern technology which *was* very much on his mind, and which was said to have introduced a 'vulgar impersonality' into warfare, distancing its deadliness from those who inflict it: gunpowder.[55]

GUNPOWDER

Gunpowder is what, in Gulliver's description, sends 'Limbs flying in the Air'. The flying is a detail Orwell includes, and quite commonplace in modern imaginations, but might seem less likely to be

---

[52] Jean Genet, *Pompes Funèbres*, in *Oeuvres Complètes*, Paris, 1976, III.40ff., and see Jean-Paul Sartre, *Saint Genet: Comédien et Martyr*, Paris, 1969, p. 194; Saul Bellow, *Humboldt's Gift*, Harmondsworth, 1977, pp. 449–51; George Orwell, *Nineteen Eighty-Four*, I.i, Harmondsworth, 1954, pp. 10–11 (the latter episode is discussed in Claude Rawson, *Gulliver and the Gentle Reader*, new edn., New Jersey and London, 1991, where Gulliver's two war-descriptions are considered in relation to modern analogues, from a somewhat different perspective: pp. 15–16, 50–1, 104, 156 n.45). For Orwell's intense interest in Swift, and especially in *Gulliver's Travels*, see his essay 'Politics vs. Literature: An Examination of *Gulliver's Travels*' (1946), in *Collected Essays, Journalism and Letters of George Orwell*, ed. Sonia Orwell and Ian Angus, Harmondsworth, 1970, IV.241–61, and the many references to Swift in the indexes to all four volumes. For other twentieth-century examples of this motif of laughter at cruel things, see R. D. Laing, 'The Bird of Paradise', in *The Politics of Experience and The Bird of Paradise*, Harmondsworth, 1967, p. 141; Ted Hughes, 'In Laughter', *Crow*, London, 1974, p. 48–49.   [53] *Humboldt's Gift*, p. 450.

[54] Quoted by John Sutherland, 'No. 1 Writer', *London Review of Books*, 5 September 1985, p. 16.

[55] The phrase 'vulgar impersonality' is from James A. Freeman, *Milton and the Martial Muse*, p. 214.

featured in the ancient texts, epic or historical, which contemporaneous readers of Gulliver's account would feel called upon to remember. This point should be taken with caution, in view of the remarkable continuity in the tradition of war-descriptions I have noted. There had, moreover, been an early belief, 'mentioned by Petrarch, that gunpowder had been known to the ancients and invented by Archimedes', which made it possible, as J. R. Hale says, 'for those humanists who believed that the ancients had anticipated everything ... to read accounts of ancient sieges, especially those employing some form of Greek fire, in terms of guns'. Thus Pius II (pope from 1458 to 1464) is cited as saying that 'in Homer and Virgil could be found descriptions of every kind of weapon which our age used'.[56]

As this suggests, there are in ancient texts, both epic and historical, instances which later imaginations tend to assimilate to gunpowder war. Crumbling walls and battlements, brought down by missiles or fire, are common from Homer onwards,[57] becoming increasingly frequent and spectacular in later writers. Severed limbs or heads are also common, and occur with increasing frequency and in increasingly large-scale or collective manifestations, until the extremely violent epics of the Latin Silver Age, where even individual acts of carnage occur in industrial quantities. Typically, one or more warriors will inflict these (often multiple) mutilations, or one or more projectiles (spears, arrows, slings, firebrands (*faces*) and flame-carrying missiles like the *falarica*) will hit several bodies 'at once'. They may even 'fly' in some restricted sense: and there are set-pieces in which mutilated parts, or whole bodies, alive or dead, are hurled from walls or battlements or burning houses or ships, or in which, as in Lucan's description of the Battle of Pharsalus, the flesh and limbs of dead warriors are dropped by birds of prey from the sky.[58] In Lucan's account of the siege of Massilia (III.459ff.), missiles are powerfully in evidence: boulders are catapulted, breaking all things in their course, flaming torches cause buildings to crumble, other missiles fly over

---

[56] See J. R. Hale, 'Gunpowder and the Renaissance: An Essay in the History of Ideas', in *Renaissance War Studies*, p. 392; see also 'War and Public Opinion', pp. 368–69. Hale also writes of a different development, in which artillery began to be pictured in fifteenth-century illuminated manuscripts portraying the armies of Alexander or of the Crusades, and canons and handguns in the earliest illustrated printed editions of Livy (p. 407).

[57] For Homer, see for example *Iliad*, XII, 154ff., 257ff.

[58] Lucan, III.464ff.; Silius Italicus, *Punica*, I.347ff.; Appian, *Roman History*, VIII.xviii.118, xix.128,129; Lucan, VII.838–40.

heads, or stray into the sea, killing survivors from wrecked ships; so powerful are the projectiles that in one case the resulting rush of blood expels both javelins from a man hit front and back (III.585–91), while in another it causes both eyes to jump out of the head of a warrior hit by a Balearic slinger's 'bullet' (Latin *glans*, acorn or ball discharged by sling, and *plumbum*, lead, III.709–14).

It is such scenes which give readers of the gunpowder age a misleading impression of ancient battle-descriptions. The word 'bullet', not used in English before the sixteenth century even in non-gunpowder contexts, occurs in the eighteenth-century translation of Lucan by Nicholas Rowe, as well as in the Loeb rendering, a small example of the way in which modern usage appropriates to such material wordings evocative of gunpowder war.[59] The most recent translator of the *Iliad* uses phrases like 'explosive blasts of flame' and 'explode in a burst of fire', for example, and the Loeb translator's rendering of an intensive missile engagement in Silius Italicus' *Punica* speaks of combatants killed 'by the cross-fire.'[60] It is interesting to set Lucan's 'bullet', which drove the victim's eyes out of his sockets, beside a superficially similar passage from Flaubert's *Salammbô*, which is set in the Punic Mercenary War, in which balls of lead ('boules de plomb', cf. Lucan's *plumbum*) and pellets of clay ('amandes d'argile') fly whistling through the air, causing blades to jump from hands, and brains from skulls: 'passant dans l'air, sifflaient, faisaient sauter les glaives des mains, la cervelle des crânes.'[61] This is the work of a novelist scrupulously concerned with exactitude of detail and atmosphere, who researched his material in sources in which we know Swift to have been steeped (these include Homer and Lucan as well as Polybius), and who was alive to traditions of battle-description in classical poets and historians.[62]

---

[59] *Lucan's Pharsalia. Translated into English Verse, by Nicholas Rowe*, 1718, pp. 123, 288 (III.1060 and VII.746, corresponding to Lucan, III.711 and VII.513; the Loeb translator adds a 'bullet' at I.228–9).

[60] Homer, *The Iliad*, trs. Robert Fagles, New York and London, 1990, pp. 521, 531 (XXI.16, 380, from Homer XXI.12–14, 333); Silius Italicus, *Punica*, IX.311ff. (Loeb, II.25).

[61] *Salammbô*, ch. 8, *Oeuvres Complètes*, I.744.

[62] The 'Notice' at the end of the Conard edition of *Salammbô*, Paris, 1910, pp. 415ff., is still a serviceable guide to Flaubert's sources, though somewhat out of date. The fullest information on Flaubert's sources is to be found in the Appendices to the Club de l'Honnête Homme edition of the *Oeuvres Complètes*, of which *Salammbô* is the second volume, Paris, 1971, pp. 277–512. This reprints his manuscript plans and notes (pp. 279ff.), a file of notes specifically concerned with sources (pp. 489ff.), and some reviews and replies by Flaubert,

All too alive, he might have said. Gautier described Flaubert as the supreme battle-painter, who mixed together Homer, Polybius, and Vegetius, author of the *De Re Militari*; and Flaubert's manuscripts and letters confirm that these were indeed among the authors he studied. In particular, he complained of the difficulty of describing ancient battles because of the sameness with which *l'éternelle bataille épique* had been treated by all great writers (*tous les écrivains nobles*) on Homer's model. Flaubert worried persistently about this problem of sameness, and his friend Louis Bouilhet wrote to him that the *Iliad* was nothing but a series of more or less identical battles.[63] These comments were excessive. They may lie behind some of Flaubert's minor variations, especially those which tend to intensify the carnage. A competitive *diablerie*, determined to outdo his predecessors in the production of horrors, would be consistent with the tone and spirit of his correspondence at the time *Salammbô* was being written.

Flaubert's difference from Lucan is that the effect of the missiles is collective, and simultaneous, on a large scale. This would not be likely in the absence of explosive weaponry, and is not found, even in Lucan, in this generalised form. A related glimpse in *Salammbô* of severed hands flying out, 'des mains s'envolaient coupées',[64] comes over, like the passage about blades and brains, with a collective force never quite matched in Lucan's slaughter-saturated poem, yet equally distinct from Mailer's exploding arm flying across the sky. This should guard us from easy imputations of anachronism, unlikely anyway in a

some of which deal with sources (pp. 371ff.). The transcriptions from Flaubert's manuscripts are often grossly inaccurate, however (see Alison Fairlie and Anne Green in *French Studies*, 27 (1973), 287–315, and Isabelle Strong in *Modern Language Review*, 72 (1977), 538–54). The introduction to this edition contains some discussion of the relation of Flaubert's novel to ancient epic (pp. 20ff.). Flaubert said in a manuscript note that his models for siege-warfare were the sieges of Saguntum, Syracuse and Jerusalem (p. 497), and in a letter to Ernest Feydeau of 29 November 1859 he described the novel as a *Thebaid* which he was pushed into by his disgust with modern life (*Correspondance*, ed. Jean Bruneau, Pléiade, III (Paris, 1991), 59). There is some relevant information in Anne Green, *Flaubert and the Historical Novel: Salammbô Reassessed*, Cambridge, 1982, which reprints some additional manuscript material (pp. 118ff.) and gives a valuable bibliography, including earlier studies of Flaubert's sources (pp. 167ff.).

   The commentary to Edouard Maynial's edition of *Salammbô*, Paris (Garnier), 1961, has useful information on sources of particular passages, including notes on war-machines (pp. 423–24,nn.76off., and 426–27n.822).

[63] For Flaubert's worries about the sameness of epic battles, see the 'Notice' at the end of the Conard edition, pp. 472–3, including the remarks of Bouilhet. See also the Pléiade edition of *Oeuvres*, ed. A Thibaudet and R. Dumesnil, Paris, 1951, 1.692. Gautier's comment is from a review of *Salammbô* in *Le Moniteur*, 22 December 1862, in the Club de l'Honnête Homme edition, p. 453.   [64] *Salammbô*, ch. 8, *Oeuvres Complètes*, 1.775.

writer of Flaubert's fastidious habits. What his passage shares with Gulliver's 'Limbs flying in the Air' is not gunpowder but the sickening shock of the habitual. It is one of the properties of Flaubert's use of the imperfect tense (brilliantly observed by Proust),[65] whose satiric applications are observed in their purest state in *Bouvard et Pécuchet*, but are likely to erupt anywhere in his fiction, evoking prolonged states and dogged recurrence. It is an extraordinary adaptation of 'free indirect discourse', offering quizzical entry into some murky consciousnesses, and at the same time suggestive of a narrator's ironic contemplation of human turpitudes as possessed of a quotidian normality. His kinship with Swift has more to it than the fact that both were good haters of humankind.[66]

Nevertheless it is doubtful whether the terms of Flaubert's descriptions of mass carnage would have been quite the same if the effects of explosive weaponry had been unavailable to his imagination. In that sense, his writing is the product of a post-gunpowder imagination operating in a pre-gunpowder setting. His 'flying hands' will more or less pass, in naturalistic terms, but their effective force is moral rather than naturalistic. In this too he may resemble Swift, except that Swift was overtly addressing, in moral terms, the issue of gunpowder itself, rather than principally concerned with the vividness of his fiction. The more advanced pieces of ancient weaponry, slings and catapults and ballistas, were capable of sending limbs flying, but this would not be one of their most notable effects, and no such weapon would be able to 'blow up a Hundred Enemies at once'. In Swift, gunpowder is explicitly at work, and Swift is at pains to stress the fact. By the time of Orwell, it is taken for granted.

Gunpowder was not, of course, new. It was an old 'modern' bugbear. References to it in Europe go back to the fourteenth century

[65] Marcel Proust, 'A Propos du "style" de Flaubert' (1920), in *Contre Sainte-Beuve* (and other works), ed. Pierre Clarac and Yves Sandre, Paris, 1971, pp. 586–600, esp. 587–91; see also the earlier fragment 'A ajouter à Flaubert' (*c.* 1910), and Proust's early pastiche 'L'affaire Lemoine par Gustave Flaubert' (1908), in *Contre Sainte-Beuve*, pp. 300, 12–15. See also some observations on Flaubert's imperfect in Mario Vargas Llosa, *The Perpetual Orgy*, London, 1987, especially the sections 'Circular Time or Repetition' and 'The "Style Indirect Libre"', pp. 172–7, 206–9. These stand out from the many run-of-the-mill accounts of free indirect style in containing the perceptions of working novelists into the expressive functioning of grammatical technicalities and especially verb tenses.

[66] For two perspectives on this, see John Lawlor, 'Radical Satire and the Realistic Novel', *Essays and Studies*, N.S. 8 (1955), 58–75, and my 'Cannibalism and Fiction: Reflections on Narrative Form and "Extreme" Situations. Part I: Satire and the Novel (Swift, Flaubert and Others)', *Genre*, 10 (1977), 667–711.

or earlier, and there was a belief, evidently correct, that it was invented in China earlier still.[67] Montaigne, rebuking Western vanity, said the Chinese had invented both gunpowder (not, he thought, very useful or effective) and printing a thousand years earlier. Swift offered an alternative deflation: 'The greatest Inventions were produced in the Times of Ignorance; as the Use of the *Compass, Gunpowder,* and *Printing*; and by the dullest Nation, as the *Germans.*'[68] Although there was controversy about the date of its invention, including some attributions of it to the ancients, it was invoked in the Ancient–Modern debate as a major example of Modern progress (the cannon, Hale says, was one of the foremost status symbols for Renaissance princes, evidently somewhat like long airport runways at the present time). Francis Bacon recommended the study of gunpowder manufacture. On the second frontispiece in large-paper copies of Sprat's *History of the Royal Society* (1667), 'Bacon, "Artium Instaurator", is portrayed pointing to a gun', and Sprat's book shows that guns and gunpowder were prominent among the Society's interests.[69] It naturally has a place on the Modern side in the *Battle of the Books.* Sixteenth-century Humanists, notably Erasmus and Rabelais, denounced it as the invention of the Devil; so did *Don*

[67] On the early origins in Europe, and the belief in Chinese invention, see Hale, 'Gunpowder', pp. 391–93. For recent information on Chinese origins, going back to the ninth century, see Joseph Needham, 'The Guns of Khaifêng-fu', *Times Literary Supplement*, 11 January 1980, pp. 39–42, and subsequent correspondence by James Chambers and Anthony Davey, 1 and 22 February and 7 March 1980, pp. 117, 208, 267. Needham reports Arabic references in the thirteenth century (p. 39), and dates the first transmission to the Western world in the second half of that century (p. 41). For fourteenth-century uses, see H. C. B. Rogers, *A History of Artillery*, Secaucus, NJ, 1975, pp. 11ff.

[68] For Montaigne, see note 72, below. Swift, 'Thoughts on Various Subjects', *Works*. 1.242. The compass, printing, and gunpowder were given as three of the four causes (together with the revival of learning) of the decline of the balanced Gothic government, according to the neo-Harringtonian Andrew Fletcher in *A Discourse of Government with Relation to Militias* (1698): see J. G. A. Pocock, 'Machiavelli, Harrington, and English Political Ideologies in the Eighteenth Century', in his *Politics, Language and Time*, London, 1972, pp. 138–9 (I owe this information to Ian Higgins). For German origins, see Hale, 'Gunpowder', pp. 391–3.

[69] Hale, 'Gunpowder', pp. 404–6: Hale inaccurately says the portrayal of Bacon occurs on the title-page. It can also be seen as a frontispiece to the edition of Sprat's *History* by Jackson I. Cope and Harold Whitmore Jones, St Louis and London, 1959, rptd. 1966. Sprat's *History* includes papers read to the Royal Society by various scientists on 'Experiments of the Recoiling of Guns', 'The History of the Making of Salt-Peter' ('of which Gunpowder is made'), and 'The History of Making Gunpowder' (*History*, 1667, pp. 233–83). For the rest of this chapter I shall use Ancients and Moderns, with capitals, to indicate allegiances, and in lower case in the chronological sense. Thus Swift is an Ancient and Homer an ancient. Lucan is an ancient who is also, in the *Battle of the Books*, an Ancient, fighting the Modern Blackmore.

Quixote; Ben Jonson spoke of the friar 'who from the Devil's Arse did guns beget'; the point survives strongly, as is well known, in Milton.[70] More's Utopians have missiles (arrows) and war machines pointedly not said to have to do with gunpowder.[71] Rabelais satirised elaborate artillery inventions, along with Homerican war-gastronomy and the Virgilian wooden horse, as well as a specific application to fourteenth-century warfare, in the Great Sow of iv.xl, and has some energetic satire on gunpowder (some of it directly anticipating *Gulliver's Travels*) in iv.lxi–lxii.

GUNPOWDER AND CHIVALRY

Its power as an improved agency of destruction and an increased source of suffering was widely (though not universally) recognised.[72] Men of the Renaissance, including notably Ariosto and Don Quixote,

[70] For some references to the diabolical origins of gunpowder and artillery, see Hale, 'Gunpowder', pp. 394–6, 401; Erasmus, *The Complaint of Peace* (1517), trs. Betty Radice, *Collected Works*, xxvii (Toronto, Buffalo and London, 1986), 306–7; Ariosto, *Orlando Furioso*, ix.xci, xi.xxiii, trs. Reynolds, 1.310, 350 (Ariosto's patron, Alfonso, Duke of Ferrara, had a cannon called *Il Diavolo*: see Reynolds, Introduction, 1.22, and note to *Orlando Furioso*, xxv.xiv, ii.61, 681); Spenser, *Faerie Queene*, i.vii.13; Cervantes, *Don Quixote*, i.xxxviii, trs. J. M. Cohen, Harmondsworth, 1954, p. 344; Ben Jonson, 'An Execration upon Vulcan', line 202, *Poems*, ed. Ian Donaldson, Oxford, 1975, p. 201; *Paradise Lost*, vi.470ff. (the literature on Milton and gunpowder is very extensive; for a convenient discussion of the Satanic dimension, from Milton's early gunpowder poems to *Paradise Lost*, see Stella Purce Revard, *The War in Heaven: Paradise Lost and the Tradition of Satan's Rebellion*, Ithaca and London, 1980, esp. pp. 86–107). See also, Boileau, *Satires*, viii.153–4, and John Oldham, *The Eighth Satyr of Monsieur Boileau, Imitated*, lines 205–6 (the lines are an 'imitation' of Juvenal, xv.165–71, about man's inhumanity to man, replacing Juvenal's references to cannibalism by the example of gunpowder, among others). Erasmus had preceded Boileau in saying that gunpowder warfare was worse than cannibalism (*Dulce bellum inexpertis*, in Phillips, *Adages of Erasmus*, p. 316).

[71] The possession of arrows among Utopians is consistent with their preference for cunning over force and bloodshed in warfare. They also have secret war machines, not specified as related to gunpowder, perhaps, as the Yale editors suggest, because More shared Erasmus' view of the 'hellish inventions' of artillery: see *Utopia*, in *Complete Works of St Thomas More*, iv, ed. Edward Surtz, S. J., and J. H. Hexter, New Haven and London, 1965, pp. 212–15, and 511–12nn.

[72] See Hale, 'Gunpowder', pp. 393f., for claims that gun warfare reduced casualties. Montaigne thought guns of little effect, except through deafening loudness (*l'estonnement des oreilles*), nowadays so familiar that no one fears it. He hoped we would soon give it up (*Essais*, i.xlviii, 'Des Destriers' ('Of Steeds')). In iii.vi, 'Des Coches' ('Of Vehicles'), he spoke of the surprise effect of European artillery in conquering the defenceless Amerindians. This essay also derides the wonder of Europeans at the invention of artillery, saying the Chinese enjoyed it a thousand years earlier (*Essais*, i.290, iii.909, 908). The more elementary guns, which took a long time to reload, were less efficient than archery, and one sixteenth-century estimate had it that 'an archer would shoot fifteen arrows while a matchlockman was loading once': see Noel Perrin, *Giving up the Gun: Japan's Reversion to the Sword, 1543–1879*, Boston, 1979, pp. 15, 97n.35, a short book of exceptional interest.

hated it also as anti-chivalric, a subverter of nobility, ignoble or anti-noble: its use created a situation in which battle was no longer won by the noblest warrior in close combat, and in which, as Don Quixote complained, 'a base and cowardly hand [could] take the life of a brave knight' at a distance, anonymously. In *1 Henry IV*, Hotspur mocked 'a certain lord ... a popinjay' who affected outrage at the 'villainous saltpetre .../ Which many a good tall fellow had destroy'd/ So cowardly', using it as an excuse for not becoming a soldier himself.[73] This particular Renaissance revulsion did not greatly trouble such Humanist thinkers as Erasmus, More, and Rabelais, who disliked gunpowder, but who also held chivalric codes in contempt.[74] But it is an extension of very ancient codes of battle, much earlier than the invention of gunpowder, according to which prowess in hand-to-hand combat was thought of as the heroic norm. Homer established a standard prototype for describing close combat, 'shield against shield ... man against man', which was imitated by Virgil, 'haeret pede pes, densusque viro vir', and by later Latin and Renaissance authors.[75] This was deemed superior to anything that might be achieved by the more impersonal agencies of arrow or sling, both of which have in common with gunpowder the fact that (unlike spears) they rely on a 'technological' rather than merely personal force. The low status of archery is a commonplace in Homer, as well as in plays of Aeschylus and Euripides, and in later Latin epics. It is more often than not practised by ethnically and ethically, as well as socially, inferior groups: foreigners, mercenaries, common troops rather than chieftains, or chiefs (like Paris) of low or ambiguous reputation.[76]

[73] *Don Quixote*, i.xxxviii, trs. Cohen, p. 344; for Ariosto's complaints about gunpowder and its anti-chivalric character, see Reynolds, Introduction, 1.21–4, and *Orlando Furioso*, ix.xxviii–xxxi (Olimpia's father killed by a 'traitor's' gun), lxxxviii–xci; xi.xxi–xxviii (Reynolds, 1.295, 310, 350–2, and commentary, 1.749). Earlier than both, in 1499, the Italian Humanist Polydore Vergil denounced gunpowder as having destroyed chivalry (Adams, *Better Part of Valor*, pp. 59, 317n10); Shakespeare, *1 Henry IV*, 1.iii.32–63. On the survival of chivalric outlooks, see Hale, *War and Society*, pp. 37ff.

[74] For the Humanist contempt for chivalry, see Adams, *The Better Part of Valor*, pp. 77–8 (and see p. 182), 152ff., 158ff., 184, 223ff., 227–8, 231–2, 285. For More's *Utopia* as expressing anti-chivalric conceptions of warfare, see Adams, 152ff., 227–8.

[75] *Iliad*, xiii.130–31, xvi.215–17; *Aeneid*, x.361; Quintus Curtius, *History of Alexander*, iii.ii.13; Statius, *Thebaid*, viii.398–99; Thomas Kyd, *Spanish Tragedie*, 1.ii.55–6.

[76] For succinct accounts, see *Oxford Classical Dictionary*, 2nd edn., Oxford, 1984, s.v. 'Archers'; also *A Companion to Homer*, ed. Alan J. B. Wace and Frank H. Stubbings, London, 1962, pp. 518–20; Hale, 'Gunpowder', p. 396; Edith Hall, *Inventing the Barbarian: Greek Self-Definition through Tragedy*, Oxford, 1989, pp. 42, 84–6, 138–9. Hall's discussions in particular draw attention to the fact that 'since in classical times archery was despised and considered suitable only for Cretans and Scythians, this has been taken to imply the cowardice and

This pattern seems universal. Firearms were regarded as cowardly not only by Montaigne, but by a nineteenth-century Sudanese people.[77] The Slav hero Marko Kraljevic, discovering the powers of the musket, said 'Henceforth valour is of no avail, for now the meanest wretch may slay the bravest knight.'[78] While the Chinese, like More's Utopians, preferred to fight at a distance,[79] the Japanese, after being ahead of Europe in gun-technology in the sixteenth century, virtually abolished firearms for 250 years, a deliberate reversal of the technological clock in favour of the *samurai* sword.[80] All the familiar arguments are replayed in this Japanese context: guns 'tend to overshadow the men who use them', and to transfer skill 'from the soldier to the manufacturer ... and ... from the soldier to his commander' in the familiar transition from *aristeia* to strategy; 'a farmer with a gun could kill the toughest samurai', and, as a seventeenth-century nobleman noted, 'there is no difference between soldiers and peasants, because firearms are used'.[81] Even a relatively specialised observation (found, as we shall see, in Pope) that gunpowder tended to eliminate heroic speeches before battle, is replayed, or anticipated, in slow motion, the epic *Heike Monogatari* featuring a speech before shooting, and history recording that warriors 'learned to skip the introductions, and just shoot'.[82]

Similar feelings about 'modern' warfare and 'the old-fashioned notion of chivalric war' may be found in the mythologies, past and present, of the American Civil War. In Robert Penn Warren's version, for example, gallant Southern generals led their troops personally into battle, an aristocracy fighting hand to hand, while

inferiority of the Trojans', but that the Homeric presentation is not fully consistent with this. Thus Diomedes insults Paris, calling him an archer (XI.385), but 'the poem does not support Diomedes' opinion' of Paris or the low status of archery, and 'two of the most conspicuous archers in the poem, Teucer and Meriones, are Greeks' (p. 42; see also Fenik, *Typical Battle Scenes*, pp. 20–1, 95–6): Hall's view suggests the presence in the *Iliad* of 'two different and historically discrete views' on this question.

[77] See Alan Moorehead, *The Blue Nile*, new edn., London, 1974, p. 160; Montaigne, III.vi. loc. cit.

[78] See *The Ballads of Marko Kraljevic*, trs. D. H. Low, New York, 1968, p. 183; see also 'The Death of Marko', in Clarence A. Manning and Roman Smal-Stocki, *History of Modern Bulgarian Literature*, Westport, CT, 1974, p. 169.

[79] Needham, 'Guns of Khaifêng-fu', p. 39. On Utopian warfare, and the absence of any chivalric exaltation of close-fighting, see *Utopia*, ed. Surtz and Hexter, pp. 198–217.

[80] Perrin, *Giving up the Gun, passim*, esp. pp. 8ff., 25ff., 76–7. For the exceptional importance of the sword as a badge of caste, see p. 36.

[81] Perrin, pp. 24, 25, 73. See also p. 28, on Japanese gunners defeating Korean archers, while samurai fought with swords and spears against Korean knights: 'Upper-class soldiers could be, and were, heroes; lower-class soldiers easily triumphed through technological superiority.'   [82] Perrin, pp. 16, 17. Cf. Pope, below n. 85.

Sherman favoured the new kind of 'total war', anticipating mass-bombings from Coventry and Dresden to Hiroshima. So did 'Grant the butcher', smoker of fat cigars, who knew 'the balance sheet of blood', but 'flinched from the sight of blood and could eat only overdone meat'. Not all Southern officers, of course, were to the manner born. Some achieved it, or had it thrust upon them. Take General Forrest, for instance: 'not a perfect example, for he rose from private to general, but, *main à main*, he slew twenty-nine adversaries in his lifetime and had thirty horses shot from under him – three at Fort Pillow alone'. In any case, 'the modern men won'.[83]

The script, doubtless rewritten in every generation, is of the victory of the new men over gentlemen, of money over class and of the machine over nature. In Ted Hughes' early poem, 'The Ancient Heroes and the Bomber Pilot', the pilot who can destroy whole cities 'at a turn of my wrist' is humbled by the thought of ancient heroes, who are much like anglicised Homeric Myrmidons, 'tearing boar-flesh and swilling ale' and thinning down 'their fat fulsome blood in war': humbled not because his bombs are more destructive, but because they are lacking in the old immediacies of bloodshed. The new technology, in this exceptionally crude version of an old scenario, is not scorned for its greater deadliness, but because it is experienced as less deadly, at an impersonal or cowardly distance from the killer.[84]

At all events, there was a perception in the lifetime of Swift and Pope that, for better or worse, the introduction of artillery was a direct threat to the codes of honour which traditionally animate epic poetry. As Pope said in his 'Essay on Homer's Battels', 'before the Use of *Fire-Arms* there was infinitely more Scope for personal Valor than in the modern Battels'. He added, in a revised form, the complaint of Don Quixote that 'a Soldier of far inferior Strength may manage a Rapier or Fire-Arms so expertly as to be an Overmatch to his Adversary' (the connotations of strength are evidently intended to shade into valour and thence into nobility). This was said to support the view that the refusal of single combat by men of lesser strength is not to be thought dishonourable in Homer. It also explains 'those Harangues his Heroes make to each other in the Time of Combate', since before gunpowder

[83] Robert Penn Warren, *Jefferson Davis Gets his Citizenship Back*, Lexington, Kentucky, 1980, pp. 63–69. In this and the next example, I draw on two discussions of mine in the *London Review of Books*: 'Southern Comfort', 16 April-6 May 1981, pp. 17–19, and 'War and Pax', 2–15 July 1981, pp. 15–16.

[84] Ted Hughes, *The Hawk in the Rain*, London, 1957, p. 57; and see previous note.

there was 'more *Leisure*' for making speeches in mid-battle.[85] Pope's special pleading seems desperate, but there is no mistaking his perception of an inverse connection between firearms and epic codes of honour, and there seems to have been a general sense that artillery and ballistics had abolished the epic hero along with single combat.[86]

The hostility to gunpowder in the Renaissance and after was not unanimous. But it was widespread. On the other hand, it should not be mistaken for a hostility to war: 'in an age almost innocent of pacifism', according to Hale, 'war was thought to be necessary to the state and good for the individual, even when it included cannon'.[87] This view of war seems to have been the prevailing one in the seventeenth and into the eighteenth centuries. It is not until the Enlightenment years 'from the 1740s to the 1770s' that M. S. Anderson, in his *War and Society in Europe of the Old Regime, 1618–1789*, finds strong signs, 'in educated and opinion-forming circles in western Europe', of a 'growing hostility to war'.[88] Swift was no pacifist, but his attack on most forms of warfare in *Gulliver's Travels* was perhaps something of a minority position, as was that of Erasmus and More (also no pacifist). Like them, and unlike many of the contemporaries of all three, he merged his dislike of gunpowder war into a larger principled hostility to war.

Although his thinking partly looked back to these Humanist models, and especially to More, times had changed, and influential voices denouncing war were perhaps more evident than Anderson's bald scenario suggests. More specifically, hostile identifications of military carnage and brutality with the ethos of Homeric and Virgilian poetry were being heard not only from new spokesmen of a sceptical Enlightenment, but from middle-class moralists like Defoe and Richardson, in the former case substantially before the period 1740–80. These could be put down, and were, as Moderns, and of low caste, but they reached a substantial public, and put under pressure of serious moral questioning a number of cultural monuments of considerable symbolic importance to those who saw themselves as guardians of an *ancienneté* under threat.

This critique in any case touched a nerve that had been raw for some time. The implications of Cowley's statement of 1656 that 'a

---

[85] TE, vii.260.
[86] See Dustin Griffin, *Regaining Paradise: Milton and the Eighteenth Century*, Cambridge, 1986, p. 50. See below, chapter 4, n. 26.   [87] Hale, 'Gunpowder', p. 393.
[88] See note 46 above; Anderson, *War and Society*, p. 185.

warlike, various, and tragical age is best to *write of*, but worst to *write in*' reverberates in Thomas Blackwell's hope in 1735 '*That we may never be a proper subject of an* Heroic Poem'.[89] A current of anxiety about what, in his Preface to the *Iliad*, Pope called 'those Ages, when a Spirit of Revenge and Cruelty, join'd with the practice of Rapine and Robbery, reigned thro' the World',[90] and about their reflection in admired poems, was part of the so-called *querelle d'Homère* and thus of the larger Ancient–Modern controversy of which it was an episode. One sees in Pope's formulation, as I have suggested, the impulse to uncouple the poem from the age it is set in or belongs to, as well as from the deeds it describes.

It seems that the issue of embarrassing analogies between the fictions of poetry and the realities of war was especially sensitive in the lifetime of Swift and Pope, and indeed in their own work. It is only in writers of an alternative allegiance, like Defoe, that they are confronted without fuss or protective anxiety. In the later generation of Byron and Shelley, the protectiveness has disappeared, even in writers of an Augustanising cast, as though the epic muse had been demystified beyond anyone's power or wish to sanitise it. In the *earlier* time of Erasmus and More and Rabelais, on the other hand, there appears also to be an unfussy readiness to contemplate awkward analogies, not only between epics and the realities they portray, but between epics and the debased chivalric derivatives of the heroic ethos. Erasmus writes in the *Education of a Christian Prince* (1516):

But first, indeed, comes the selection of authors, for it matters a great deal what books a boy reads and absorbs first. Bad conversation defiles the mind, and bad reading does so no less. For those silent letters are transformed into conduct and feelings, especially if they have taken hold of the mind which is prone to some defect; for example, it will take very little to incite a naturally wild and violent boy to tyranny if, without being equipped with an antidote, he reads about Achilles or Alexander the Great or Xerxes or Julius Caesar.

But today we see a great many people enjoying the stories of Arthur and Lancelot and other legends of that sort, which are not only tyrannical but also utterly illiterate, foolish, and on the level of old wives' tales, so that it would be more advisable to put one's reading time into the comedies or the myths of the poets rather than into that sort of drivel,[91]

[89] Abraham Cowley, *Poems*, ed. A. R. Waller, Cambridge, 1905, p. 7; Thomas Blackwell, *Enquiry into the Life and Writings of Homer*, 1735, p. 28. See Claude Rawson, *Order from Confusion Sprung*, new edn., New Jersey and London, 1992. p. 215.

[90] Pope, Preface to *Iliad*, TE, VII.14.

[91] Erasmus, *The Education of a Christian Prince*, ch. 2, trs. Neil M. Cheshire and Michael J. Heath, *Collected Works*, XXVII.250.

a statement which, as Robert P. Adams says, acquires extra resonance in the context of 'the immense Renaissance fascination ... with the idea that war was itself ... potentially a work of art'.[92]

The remarkable thing about this statement is that Erasmus can make both of his damaging comparisons, and in addition issue his educational warning, without the slightest surrender of the genuine admiration he demonstrably had for the poem of which Achilles was the hero, who is, in this very work, frequently cited for his wisdom as a guide to princely behaviour.[93] In this as in other things, Erasmus is echoed in the *Governour* (1531) of Sir Thomas Elyot, an author who praised Homer for containing 'incomparable wisedomes, and instructions for politike governaunce', but was, in the same sentence, more hospitable to the idea of Homer as an educator in the 'documentes marciall and discipline of armes', adding to Homer's honour the story of Alexander keeping Homer's works 'under his pillowe'. Elyot actually praised the *Education of a Christian Prince* for offering instruction comparable to that which Alexander found in Homer. Elyot also praised archery as 'the moste excellente artillerie for warres', better, so to speak, than artillery: better exercise and deadlier in war.[94] The point I wish to stress is that the issue of Homeric carnage can not only be absorbed without strain by a moderately militarist admirer of Erasmus, but can coexist with a secure and unselfconscious admiration of Homer in the anti-militarist Erasmus himself. Indeed, there is no more anxiety in the *Education of a Christian Prince* that Homer will suffer from the anti-militarist juxtaposition of Achilles with Alexander, than there is in the *Lusiads* (1572), a nationalist epic more representative of sixteenth-century attitudes to war, and more dedicated than most to overt celebrations of martial conquest, when Camoens recalls that 'Alexander read Homer so assiduously that he seems to have made of him his bedside book.'[95] The passage is one in which the poet seems engaged in a comparison between poems and wars, to the disadvantage of the latter, which is superficially similar to

---

[92] Adams, *Better Part of Valour*, p. 116.

[93] *Education of a Christian Prince*, pp. 203, 229, 239, 242, 279. For Erasmus' warnings about bad examples in Homer and other authors, see the adage *Aut fatuum aut regem nasci oportere* (i.iii.1; Phillips, *Adages of Erasmus*, pp. 214–16).

[94] Sir Thomas Elyot, *The Boke Named the Governour* (1531), i.x (on Homer's political wisdom, Alexander, etc.); i.xi and iii.xi (on Erasmus and the *Education of a Christian Prince*), i.xxvii (on archery etc.); ed. H. H. S. Croft, rpt. New York, 1967, 1.58–9, 95; ii.280–1; 1.290–306.

[95] Camoens, *The Lusiads*, v.xcvi; trs. William C. Atkinson, Harmondsworth, 1952, p. 139. For an anti-militarist collocation by Erasmus, see *Education of a Christian Prince*, p. 250.

the project which can be observed in some contemporaries of Swift and Fielding.

Thus Camoens asserts that Alexander valued Achilles' prowess less 'than the harmonious verse in which Homer sang of them', adding that good warriors ought to be men of learning, as Caesar was, who fought 'with lance in one hand and pen in the other'. There is a grievance about philistinism in high places, which explains why 'we have neither Virgils nor Homers; and soon ... shall have no pious Aeneases or fierce Achilles either'[96] – a train of thought asking to be set beside the 'Renaissance fascination' with war as 'a work of art' as much as any of Erasmus'. It leads in an opposite direction, of course, and the aggrieved bard opens his poem with praises of Portuguese heroes, men used to 'war and ... dangers', who spread 'havoc among the infidels of Africa and Asia', exceeding the travels of Ulysses and Aeneas and the victories of Alexander and Trajan.[97] Collocations of epic and history which were to generate much subtextual pointmaking in Fielding's *Jonathan Wild* come fast and free to Camoens. If Erasmus seems largely untroubled admiring Homer, while acknowledging that heroism and hated war were not far apart, Camoens was totally unabashed in his paeans to martial glory.

If Camoens exhibited any ambivalence, it was not over war as such, but over gunpowder. Ambivalence may be too honorific a term for the mixture of have-it-both-ways enthusiasm and brassy muddle. But certainly his writing on this question has neither the outright hostility of Erasmus, Rabelais or Swift, nor the celebration of the power, efficacy, and modernity which made gunpowder attractive to rulers like Ariosto's patron, Alfonso of Ferrara.[98] In Canto I, Vasco da Gama is asked by the Governor of Mozambique to show his weapons, and orders his men to

show their armament: coats of armour, gleaming breastplates both solid and laminated, fine mail, shields of divers designs, cannon-shot, muskets of pure steel, longbows with their quivers full of arrows, sharp halberds, trusty pikes. Then they brought out the fire-bombs, sulphur-pots, and mortars ...[99]

This panoply of armour combines the trappings of knightly chivalry, and the sort of array of modern artillery which might, with a minimal addition of irony, easily shade into one of Swift's war-lists: a merging

[96] *Lusiads*, v.xciii–xcviii; pp. 138–9.   [97] *Lusiads*, I.i–iii; p. 39.
[98] Hale, 'Gunpowder', pp. 401ff.; Ariosto, trs. Reynolds, Introduction, I.21.
[99] *Lusiads*, I.lxvii–lxviii; p. 49.

of two opposite enthusiasms almost equally discreditable in Humanist eyes.

The sequence 'fire-bombs, sulphur-pots, and mortars' is set in relief, opening a new stanza:

> As bombas vêm de fogo e juntamente
> As panelas sulfúreas, tão danosas;
> Porém aos de Vulcano não consente
> Que dêm fogo às bombardas temerosas.

The second half of the stanza, however, backs away from the enumeration to pay a 'chivalric' obeisance to the idea that gun-powder may be ungentlemanly. At least, 'it is no part of breeding or valour to make a display of might before a few timorous strangers'. Eventually, however, the timid Moslems turn treacherous, so gunfire is used, causing panic and flight. 'The Portuguese followed up the victory with more killing and destruction', and those Moslems who could 'crowded into canoes, on which the Portuguese rained shot, smashing many to pieces'. *Arrombam as miúdas bombardadas* has some-thing of Gulliver's entranced surrender, in his war-lists, to the rolling wonder of the thing, and there is a familiar set-piece of punitive devastation:

the settlement had no walls or other defenses, and under bombardment its dwellings collapsed and burst into flames ... The old and the helpless, the mother with the child at her breast, might be heard cursing all war.[100]

It is a standard portrayal, clearly derived from rhetorical instruc-tion, and closest perhaps to the model in Quintilian, viii.iii.68, on how to describe a besieged town: burning houses, falling roofs, the old, the mothers and their children in lamentation. Since towns have walls and defences (not as it happens specified in Quintilian, but routine in siege-pieces in poems), Camoens mentions them as non-existent in the Moslem settlement, on the familiar rhetorical principle that mention-ing what you mention that you're not mentioning is mentioning it. And if the old, the mother, and child, are cursing war, it is clear the poet is not. Before the end of Canto i, the 'breeding' that withholds gunfire has turned to a triumphal cannonade, and the poem crackles with the sound of guns, as the poet relates gun-salutes to a frightened

---

[100] *Lusiads*, i.xc–xcii; p. 53.

Moslem monarch, or extols the idea of shelling 'the walls of Byzan-
tium and Turkey'.[101]

Camoens' poem is full of chivalric paraphernalia, and brings within
a single text the amalgam of epic, chivalry, and quasi-historical
militarism which Erasmus admonishingly brought under one head in
the passage from the *Education of a Christian Prince*, with gunpowder
thrown in for good measure. It was perhaps an early indication of a
truth that writers of Ancient persuasion in Boileau's or in Swift's time
sensed about the French writers of Biblical epics or the poems of
Blackmore, that a genuine Homeric epic was no longer possible for
good writers, and that the only writers likely to make the attempt were
Moderns like Blackmore, who wrote six. The irony or paradox is that
it takes a Modern to think they can do it.

Blackmore's poems included much sub-Homeric bloodshed, as did
none of the epic imitations of the leading Ancient contemporaries,
Boileau, Garth, Swift or Pope. Garth's *Dispensary* is the only one (with
the special exception of Swift's *Battle of the Books*) briefly to feature epic
gore ('*Blood, Brains, and Limbs the highest Walls distain*') and this turns
out to be part of a string of ranting quotations from the epics of
Blackmore, who is a character in Garth's poem, as in Swift's *Battle* and
later in Pope's *Dunciad*.[102] Blackmore took for two of his poems the
chivalric subject that both Milton and Dryden had considered for
epic treatment and dropped: King Arthur. In the *Battle*, he is pitted
against Lucan, in an episode in which both are treated quite genially.

Of all conservative writers of his time, Swift was the least likely to be
easily impressed by heroic pretensions. His loyalty to Ancient canons
of taste was strong and even rigid, but there was a subversive potential
for negation in which scepticism of grand gestures went hand in hand
with an intensified protectiveness of hallowed institutions. His feelings
about chivalry may be inferred from his admiration for *Don Quixote*.
One would not suppose him to be more attached to chivalric
flummery than the sixteenth-century Humanists with whom he
shared some of his most important feelings about war and about
society in general (including his opposition to standing armies). He
was also, of all writers, the least likely to be impressed by the more
irrational or inflated codes of martial correctness associated with

---

[101] *Lusiads*, II.cvi–cvii, VII.xii; pp. 75, 163.
[102] See *Order from Confusion Sprung*, pp. 205, 219n.17; Garth, the *Dispensary*, 2nd edn., 1699,
IV.190, 178ff. in *Poems on Affairs of State ... volume 6: 1697–1704*, ed. Frank H. Ellis, New
Haven, 1970, p. 101.

chivalry in its quixotic guise. But although More, along with Socrates and four other revered ancients, was a member (the only modern one) of that '*Sextumvirate* to which all the Ages of the World cannot add a Seventh' which is celebrated by Gulliver in Glubbdubdrib (III.vii.196), and although *Utopia* is a major influence on *Gulliver's Travels*, Swift seems to have made sure that his Houyhnhnms, unlike the Utopians, were 'perfect Strangers' to war and to 'missive Weapons', though well able to defend themselves (IV.xii.293).

Missiles play a minor part in his mock-epic allegory, the *Battle of the Books*, as does gunpowder. Swift did not mix these with chivalry, and if his views on chivalry were those not of Don Quixote but of his satirical author, something of Quixote's chivalric feelings on gunpowder entered into his own attitude. The indecorum of a base and cowardly hand killing a brave knight at a distance is one that has a special application of its own in the *Battle*. And something of the sense of underhandness, of fighting that is furtive and dishonourable, gets into the generally minor attention that missiles are given in the *Battle*.

Although the army of the Ancients in the *Battle of the Books* contains some bowmen, whose leaders are Plato and Aristotle, it is the Modern troops who are portrayed as flingers of missiles, especially noxious and sneaky:

Paracelsus brought a *Squadron* of *Stink-Pot-Flingers* from the snowy Mountains of *Rhoetia*. There, came a vast Body of *Dragoons*, of different Nations, under the leading of *Harvey*, their great *Aga*: Part armed with *Scythes*, the Weapons of Death; Part with *Launces* and long *Knives*, all steept in *Poison*: Part shot *Bullets* of a most malignant Nature, and used *white Powder* which infallibly killed without *Report*.[103]

White powder has never been confidently identified. One of the connotations may be of arsenic or rat's poison.[104] Medical quackery might be consistent with the presence of Harvey and Paracelsus, whose stink-pots may suggest pharmaceutical jars as well as missiles (in the *Dispensary*, jars had been used *as* missiles).[105] Since the powder is deadly, an allegory suggesting the death-dealing powers of medical men would be an apposite example of the moral standing of modern

---

[103] *Works*, I.152.
[104] See *The Battle of the Books*, ed. Hermann J. Real, Berlin and New York, 1978, p. 56n.
[105] Guthketch and Nichol Smith point out that Swift's patron Temple had cast doubt on Harvey's discovery of the circulation of blood (*Tale of a Tub*, Oxford, 1973, p. 236n.); Garth, *Dispensary*, V.177ff., pp. 113–14.

science, and is consistent also with a pattern in the *Battle* in which epic parody is frequently side-tracked to competing parodic discourses.

The principal suggestion, however, has to do with gunpowder, clearly reinforced by juxtaposition with malignant bullets. (Similarly the dominant sense of 'stink-pots', like that of the 'sulphur-pots' in the *Lusiads*, is that of missiles, though the *OED* offers a single citation from 1665 in the sense of 'pot containing a disinfectant.'). Bacon thought the idea of a silent gunpowder improbable, but 'a dangerous experiment, if it should be true'. Browne's *Pseudodoxia Epidemica* says that 'of white powder and such as is discharged without report, there is no small noise in the world', and has an extended discussion of possibilities, noting that 'Alphonsus Duke of Ferrara' (Ariosto's patron) was said to have 'invented such a Powder'.[106] Hale lists, among means of destruction so wicked that their inventors concealed the secret, a noiseless powder by Niccolò Tartaglia, a sixteenth-century mathematician and author of the *Nova scientia* (1537), said to be the first printed book on artillery.[107] We now have silencers, but to Swift it doubtless had a touch of contradiction, of alchemical absurdity, like squaring the circle, or converting air into a dry tangible substance. Arbuthnot spoke of 'exploded Chimeras' like 'the *perpetuum Mobile*, the circular Shot, Philosopher's Stone, and silent Gunpowder'.[108] Gunpowder was itself alchemical, implying quackery as well as viciousness.[109] White powder would have the real nastiness of any gunpowder, plus the furtiveness of what Bacon called 'secret murders'.[110] If it exists it is doubly evil. If not, the quest for it speaks tellingly of the modern mind.

Swift's list of modern warriors and their weapons highlights the more dishonourable or 'unchivalrous' aspects of war. Poisoned lances and arrows, 'treacherous, ungentlemanly', were, according to Gilbert Murray, removed from the *Iliad*, where there are surviving traces of their presence from earlier states of the poem.[111] Silius Italicus' epic, *Punica*, lists among the 'foul weapons' of the barbarian Nabis 'a bow and quiver and javelins steeped in the venom of asps; for he used

[106] Francis Bacon, *Sylva Sylvarum*, 120, in *Works*, ed. James Spedding and others, New York, 1968, II.392–3; Sir Thomas Browne, *Pseudodoxia Epidemica*, II.v.5, ed. Robin Robbins, Oxford, 1981, I.129–34, II.756–60. See also John Cleveland, 'To P. Rupert' (*c.* 1642), lines 39–40, in *Poems*, ed. Brian Morris and Eleanor Withington, Oxford, 1967, p. 34.
[107] Hale, 'Gunpowder', pp. 412, 454.
[108] John Arbuthnot, *The History of John Bull* (1712), II.iii, ed. Alan W. Bower and Robert A. Erickson, Oxford, 1976, p. 53.
[109] Hale, 'Gunpowder', pp. 391–3, for the reputed alchemical origins.
[110] Bacon, *Works*, II.392.
[111] Gilbert Murray, *The Rise of the Greek Epic*, New York, 1960, p. 130.

poison for his weapon of war' (xv.672–91). It is, one might say, the pre-industrial version of gunpowder, a secret link between epic and barbarism; 'poisoned darts' are mentioned in the same breath as the 'hellish inventions' of artillery in Erasmus' *Dulce bellum inexpertis*.[112] For poisoned arrows speak of barbarian tribes, not usually in the epic front line, except in the vicious late epics of the Silver Age, and then presumably not in organised troop formations. When Gulliver, leaving Houyhnhnmland, lands in a savage country and is wounded by a native, he 'apprehended the Arrow might be poisoned' (IV.xi.284). Readers would be reminded of travel narratives rather than epics, and the inclusion of poisoned weapons in the *Battle* flickers with unresolved suggestions. One is that the mock-epic is signalling derision of something else, whether travel-narratives or a foul apothecary's brew (poison goes with stink-pots and deadly powders); another is that any modern epic, especially one featuring Modern warriors, is going to be so unlike the real thing that it will derealise the closest kind of formal imitation; and it is modern states of mind, their ingenuities of furtive malice, that are the focus of interest, more than the formal ingenuities of the epic correspondences (which are, throughout the *Battle*, teasingly close).

THE ABSTRACTIONS OF TECHNOLOGY

White powder belongs with these suggestions. It is a peculiarly Swiftian variation on the idea that gunpowder is unchivalric. But his substantive complaint about gunpowder, of course, is that, in a way which would not be so vividly evident to Ariosto or Cervantes, and which is sometimes glimpsed in the wholesale gigantifications of Rabelais, it raises cruelty to a new, and technological, scale of power. It is on these grounds that Gulliver seeks to interest the king of Brobdingnag:

In hopes to ingratiate myself farther into his Majesty's Favour, I told him of an Invention discovered between three and four hundred Years ago, to make a certain Powder; into an heap of which the smallest Spark of Fire falling, would kindle the whole in a Moment, although it were as big as a Mountain; and make it all fly up in the Air together, with a Noise and Agitation greater than Thunder. That, a proper Quantity of this Powder rammed into an hollow Tube of Brass or Iron, according to its Bigness, would drive a Ball of Iron or Lead with such Violence and Speed, as nothing was able to sustain its

[112] Phillips, *Adages of Erasmus*, p. 316.

Force. That, the largest Balls thus discharged, would not only Destroy whole Ranks of an Army at once; but batter the strongest Walls to the Ground; sink down Ships with a thousand Men in each, to the Bottom of the Sea; and when linked together by a Chain, would cut through Masts and Rigging; divide Hundreds of Bodies in the Middle, and lay all waste before them. That we often put this Powder into large hollow Balls of Iron, and discharged them by an Engine into some City we were besieging; which would rip up the Pavement, tear the Houses to Pieces, burst and throw Splinters on every Side, dashing out the Brains of all who came near. That I knew the Ingredients very well, which were Cheap, and common; I understood the Manner of compounding them, and could direct his Workmen how to make those Tubes of a Size proportionable to all other Things in his Majesty's Kingdom; and the largest need not be above two hundred Foot long; twenty or thirty of which Tubes, charged with the proper Quantity of Powder and Balls, would batter down the Walls of the strongest Town in his Dominions in a few Hours; or destroy the whole Metropolis, if ever it should pretend to dispute his absolute Commands (II. vii. 134).

It differs from Rabelais' gigantifications, because in Rabelais everything is gigantified, and one comes away with impressions of extravagant imagination rather than of grinding precisions of war damage. Foreign to Rabelais also is the sober-sided practicality of the idiom, its emphasis on cheapness, on compactness of effort in relation to magnitude of effect, and on the satisfactions of technical know-how.

Like Gulliver's other war-list, it has a self-intoxicated exuberance, doubtless resembling Rabelais', but a Rabelais, as Coleridge said, *habitans in sicco,* its arithmetic intimating operational practicalities rather than the energies of a free-wheeling and self-delighting *copia*.[113] Its enormities belong to the drawing-board, and its scenarios of absolute tyranny or mass-killing are a foretaste of the mock-science of the Flying Island and the mock-economics of *A Modest Proposal*. It is closer to 'the balance sheet of blood' which Robert Penn Warren identified with Ulysses S. Grant, than to the vast slaughters of Célinian daydreaming, the true modern heir of a Rabelaisian style turned mass-destructive.[114] The scene of a destroyed city, with its pavements ripped up and houses torn to pieces is the product of technology: epics contain such scenes, but as massive attritions, caused by fire or a piecemeal accumulation of missiles, not as huge single bursts. And on either side of this scene are two types of personal annihilation, one more or less familiar in epic, the other deriving from

---

[113] Coleridge, *Table Talk*, 15 June 1830; for sources of the phrase in Rabelais, see *Gulliver and the Gentle Reader*, p. 174n.19.   [114] Warren, *Jefferson Davis Gets his Citizenship Back*, p. 67.

an epic commonplace. The first is the dividing of 'Hundreds of Bodies in the Middle', which is a gigantic multiplication of the kind of thing that happens *individually* in the grimmer scenes of mass-carnage in Silver Epic. There are two examples within twenty lines in Lucan's account of the siege of Marseille, and there are parallels in a historian like Appian, but the nearest thing to collective mutilation on this Gulliverian scale can only be a rhetorical fantasy, like Caligula's wish, reported by Suetonius, that the Roman people had a single neck so that he could behead it at a stroke.[115]

The atmosphere of Gulliverian war has something of the density of the military engagements in Lucan or Silius Italicus, so that the essential difference is telling, since these authors of extremely violent epics are masters of scenes of mass-carnage. In them, as in Homer, and unlike modern novelists like Flaubert recounting ancient wars, battles are related to some extent as a cumulation of *individual* combats, even where the focus has ceased to be on the *aristeia* of a named protagonist, so that they are without the bizarre Swiftian sense, already discussed in relation to Gulliver's other war-description, of the single identical wound affecting hundreds indiscriminately at once. Any reader conscious of epic parallels would sense the difference as an additional allusive illustration of the revolutionary mass-murderousness of gunpowder. Swift himself cannot have been unaware of making epic parallels in the matter: the body cut in two is an item specifically parodied in that systematic 'compleat collection' of epic styles, the *Battle of the Books*. But such a reader, also likely to be familiar with a more recent poetry of gunpowder wars, with Waller's 'the angry Bullets fly,/ And of one Wound hundreds together die', for example, would sense in Gulliver's sweeping allusion to hundreds of bodies a quality of *disembodied* abstraction, quite unlike Waller's hundreds dying, although they do so in an equally collective and simultaneous way.[116]

[115] Lucan, III.637ff.; Appian, *Roman History*, VIII.xix.129; Suetonius, IV.xxx.2. Caligula's wish became an object of interest to English poets: see Milton, *Eikonoklastes, Complete Prose Works*, III, ed. M. Y. Hughes (New Haven, 1962), 579; Cleveland, 'Smectymnuus, or the Club-Divines', lines 65–67, *Poems*, p. 25; Oldham, *Satyrs upon the Jesuits*, I. 321–25. For bodies cut in two in tank warfare in World War II, see John Keegan, *Times Literary Supplement*, 17 May 1991, p. 11, citing Robin Neillands, *The Desert Rats: 7th Armoured Division, 1940–1945*.

[116] Edmund Waller, 'Of a War with Spain, and Fight at Sea, by General Montague. In the Year 1656', *Poems ... Written upon Several Occasions*, 1711, p. 195. Gulliver's account here deals with chain-shot rather than a barrage of bullets, as Robert C. Gordon points out, 'Jonathan Swift and the Modern Art of War', *Bulletin of Research in the Humanities*, LXXXVIII (1980), 198n.

My second example, which shows the bursting houses hitting and 'dashing out the Brains of all who came near', is even more pointed in its effects, simultaneously evoking epic and neutralising or derealising the evocation, because the dashing or spilling of brains, the despatching of a warrior in a mess of brains and blood, is so frequent in Homer, and even in the more restrained Virgil, as to be virtually formulaic, and it recurs in Silver Epic, sometimes with special increments of grotesquerie.[117] In the *Battle of the Books* Homer takes two Moderns, 'with the same Blow dashing out both their Brains'.[118] The modern imagination is responsive to such things, not only in Ubuesque routines of *décervelage* and similar repositories of *humour noir*, but in realistic depictions of killing in such special-effects movies as *Soldier Blue* and *Catch-22*, and even in TV newsreels of war-scenes. It is also the sort of detail which, however formulaic in Homer and however common in later literature and life, tends to be conceived, in its very nature, as an individual rather than a mass event. A more 'general' example in epic, when Athena tells Odysseus 'I look for endless/ ground to be spattered by the blood and brains of the suitors', seems to be a special case, involving castigation of a homogeneous group of malefactors concentrated in one place, and in an issue of domestic rather than military concern.[119] Normally the concentration is on the individual warrior killed. This is true even in the reportorial artefacts of a fully technologised age of mass-violence like the present. My most vivid memory of such an emphasis is of a single trickle from the head of a recently killed old woman, in some news-footage from Vietnam showing a mass of fleeing refugees. Comparable effects from the streets of Sarajevo can be seen on TV now, a pavement covered with corpses, but the shock coming mainly from individual mutilations. The imagination and the TV camera seem to find their natural focus in these.

W. J. T. Mitchell has interestingly described a contrast between television coverages of the Vietnam and the Gulf Wars, the former typified by 'the innumerable flag-draped caskets, the massacres, atrocities and mass-burials seen on television, as well as singular images like the naked Vietnamese girl, her flesh aflame with napalm,

---

[117] *Iliad* xi, 97–8, xii. 186; *Aeneid*, ix.750ff., x.416, xi.699–700; Lucan, vi.177–8; for added special effects, Silius Italicus, *Punica*, ix.395–400.   [118] *Works*, i.157.
[119] *Odyssey*, xiii.394–5.

and the dismembered American soldiers returning home.'[120] His point has to do with the role played by television in the public's revulsion against the Vietnam war, and the care taken by the authorities and the media to ensure that exposure of Desert Storm was sanitised against this. 'The famous image-sequences transmitted from the noses of the smart bombs descending on their targets' in Iraq also took 'a dazzled American public directly into the heart of mass destruction', but in the 'abstract, like a display in a video game'.

Mitchell's argument is that 'the media managers of Desert Storm realised that physical alienation and detached spectacle would best serve the purposes of anaesthetising the American public from the consequences of a high-tech massacre', emphasising in particular that exposure of bodies was to be minimised. But there is a sense in which large numbers, even of *bodies*, achieve abstraction almost as effectively as the substitution of images of smart weapons for mutilated casualties. Gulliver is similarly concerned to laud the prowess of technology, but it is through the blanket plurality of the casualties, as much as in the listing of weapons, that Gulliver's enumerations are able to dream themselves away from a full realisation of epic carnage (and by the same token enable Swift, as distinct from Gulliver, to neutralise or at least subdue the epic reminders generated by his descriptive vocabulary: a sensitiveness protective not so much of a war-mongering government, as of the warrior ethos of a hallowed poetic institution, of cultural allegiances felt to have become tarnished, however subtextually or unwittingly the feeling is manifested).

Plurality is anonymous, and by the time it reaches Ted Hughes' Bomber Pilot alone with his lever it can be expressed with an abstraction more total and laconic than Gulliver is able to achieve: 'The enemy capital will jump to a fume/ At a turn of my wrist.' But it is this as well as the technology which gives it distance that separates the Pilot from the Ancient Heroes who kill man to man.[121] That the poem's solidarity is with the latter ('The grandeur of their wars humbles my thought'), not because they kill fewer victims, but because their killing is more viscerally immediate, shows something of

---

[120] W. J. T. Mitchell, 'Culture Wars', *London Review of Books*, 23 April 1992, pp. 7–10. A related perception about the anaesthetising effect of stylish weaponry of large-scale destruction, in the third movie of the *Lethal Weapon* series, was registered by Anthony Lane in the *Independent on Sunday*, 10 August 1992, p. 19: 'Destruction on the grand scale is easy to take; only down among the small fry does real pain bare its teeth, which is more than this film dares to contemplate.'   [121] Hughes, *The Hawk in the Rain*, p. 57.

the nature of the 'epic' sympathy Swift was signalling some unac-knowledged disengagement from. I think an important distinction is blurred when Mitchell speaks indiscriminately of 'coverage of body counts, the innumerable flag-draped caskets ... as well as singular images like the naked Vietnamese girl aflame with napalm'. The flag-draped caskets, though sometimes numerous, were seldom anony-mous. They were usually accorded individual ceremonial attention, even, I suspect, in 'mass-burials', and tended to translate themselves into 'one of our boys' or 'the boy next door'.

The dashed out 'Brains of all who came near' enforce Gulliver's argument that gunpowder kills masses and not just individuals, and it evokes epic discourse in a spectacularly self-neutralising way. Its shockingness is at an opposite pole, for example, from that of an early seventeenth-century account of the siege of Ostend, describing how 'the Lord of Chatillon ... met with an unhappy mischance ... he had his head struck off, above the teeth, with a cannon shot; and his brains dashed upon the Colonel's left cheek'.[122] The difference is striking, not least because this account is in its own way 'Swiftian', with its mixture of colloquial understatement ('met with an unhappy mischance') and brutal brevity, quite close to the stylistic strategy of 'Last Week I saw a Woman *flay'd*, and you will hardly believe, how much it altered her Person for the worse.'[123] Swift's strongest glimpses of brutalised bodies tend to turn up in brief shocking eruptions, and almost always (as I shall be suggesting) outside contexts of epic reminder. As a graphic apprehension of mutilation, the collective dashed brains of Gulliver's list do not compete with even the most routinely formulaic examples in Homer.

The example of Flaubert, a writer whose vision of the horror and the vacuity of human doings is sometimes compared to Swift's, and the only other major writer known to me who, in an episode discussed earlier, portrayed the spilling of brains as a mass-phenomenon rather than as an accumulation of particular cases, suggests that the distinction between an individual victim and a generalised sense of collective casualties does not wholly account for the unusual quality of Gulliver's account. Although both share the same diffused reach, and a broadly comparable ironic perception of the habitual, Flaubert's bullets causing brains to fly from heads have more in common, as an actualised apprehension of atrocities, with the highly particular case

[122] Cited in Freeman, *Milton and the Martial Muse*, p. 36.
[123] *Tale of a Tub*, IX, *Works*, I.109.

of the Lord of Chatillon than with their panoramically focused Swiftian counterpart.

This is doubtless partly because Flaubert, unlike Gulliver, is describing a particular battle, so that the tendency of particular accounts to be stronger is at work in a variant form. In both Gulliver's set-pieces, however, the characteristic energy comes not from 'generality' as such, but from the peculiar effect of making Gulliver speak in elaborately specific detail about what is not, in fact, a specific battle, but a kind of common denominator of war, so that a sense of grotesquely or grimly comic disconnection is registered. The vitality of Swift's descriptions comes from a sense of headlong lists of madness and badness (lists of weapons, or of types of destruction), not from a realised portrayal of combat, and their animation is an abstract animation, reflecting crazy and vicious energies of the human mind, not the actualities of war that Flaubert, or for that matter Homer, take for their subject.

This maximises the satiric definition of belligerent depravity while anaesthetising the display of carnage, and in that process, among other effects, preventing the satire from cutting, so to speak, too close to the epic bone. In this sense, 'the great Diversion of all the Spectators' is a decisive focus of energy in the parallel war-description to the Houyhnhnm. Its eruptive effect is to shift the force of the passage from the battle details to the fundamental human nastiness, which is in the mind. The battle has become a spectator sport, and the turn of the satiric screw lies in the fact that, however wicked the doings of the belligerents, they pursue purposes, or are forced to pursue the purposes of others, as well as endure appalling consequences, whereas the 'spectators' express a gratuitous delight in meaningless carnage.

This spectatorial twist only comes at the end. But Gulliver's delight, in both descriptions, in his own rapturous enumeration of modes of slaughter, makes it clear that the whole thing has for him been a spectator sport throughout. He is no less 'diverted' than the spectators he reports, who have no particular name or place, as the wars he describes have no identifiable combatants, locations, or causes. If we can detect in Gulliver's dithyrambic celebration of 'Cannons, Culverins ... Sieges, Retreats ... Bombardments, Seafights', something of the purposes of the media managers who concentrated on smart weapons, and preferred wherever possible to give statistics of carnage rather than displays of the casualties, then there is another analogy to be drawn. To the extent that their purpose, as Mitchell

argues, was to avoid alienating public opinion, they largely succeeded. The public was not alienated, but its entranced following of
the television coverage shows that it was 'greatly diverted', and the
media managers must also have sensed, as Genet, and Orwell, and
Bellow evidently sensed in the episodes I discussed earlier, that the
public are particularly responsive to such pleasures when they are
mediated through a TV or movie screen.

It seems likely that Swift understood a pre-electronic version of this
truth, and included the spectators in his indictment rather than
catering to their pleasures, as well as distancing the carnage through
strategies of ironic presentation which the modern media make
possible by other means. Swift's denunciation would have included
these other means too, if they had been available. He did not shrink
from alienating his spectators, and he differs from the managers of
Mitchell's scenario in not being concerned to sanitise war, or to shrink
from exposing cruelty. It is Homer that he shrank from exposing. He
had his own version of an instinct he shared with Pope and others, to
ensure that revered ancients who dealt with such realities were
distanced from the kind of inculpation to which Defoe, Richardson,
Blake or Byron, showed or were to show them to be vulnerable. In
Gulliver's Travels he achieved this not, in the manner of Pope's
translation, by softening Homer, but by neutralising potential
reminders of him in incriminating contexts.

Indeed, the sanitising is remarkable, and characteristically Swiftian, in that it softens nothing. Derealising the epic connection and
viewing war through the eyes of 'spectators' like Gulliver, enabled
Swift to bring a particularly damning and extensive verdict on the
human taste for massacre. The King of Brobdingnag's famous
declaration to Gulliver, 'I cannot but conclude the Bulk of your
Natives, to be the most pernicious Race of little odious Vermin that
Nature ever suffered to crawl upon the Surface of the Earth'
(II.vi.132), comes just before Gulliver's praise of gunpowder technology and his offer to make it available. But it says it all, and the war-
description is absorbed into the king's comment, one of the judicial
climaxes of this book of indictments.

A large part of Gulliver's advocacy of gunpowder, moreover, is
controlled by a celebration, to which bloody deeds are secondary, of
totalitarian control. His portrayal of war yields, in less than a page, to
the king's scornful rejection and to ironies about the European
method of reducing '*Politicks* into a *Science*', as well as about converting

73

scientific discoveries into political excesses. In the Flying Island, where tyranny raises the spectre of annihilation from the air (including, for latter-day readers, thoughts of nuclear stalemate, since the king will never use the ultimate deterrent for fear of self-destruction), political violence is allegorised rather than described or enacted (III.iii.167–72). The Flying Island's oppression is in effect metaphorical, and its atrocities are never actualised on the 'realistic' plane. Physical horror of the kind briefly evoked by the war-descriptions is actually kept at bay by means of allegorical displacement. The destruction of cities comes up in the School of Political Projectors, where one researcher studied political forces by examining the excrement of 'suspected Persons' and discovered that,

when he used merely as a Trial to consider which was the best Way of murdering the King, his Ordure would have a Tincture of Green; but quite different when he thought only of raising an Insurrection, or burning the Metropolis. (III.vi.190)

The squalor of the researcher's mind, like that of the quest for white powder, is clear, but actual burning of the metropolis, touched on in both war-descriptions, is kept at several removes.

Swift was in many ways a violent writer. His most memorable scenes of violence tend to be individual, specific, and brief, like the image of the flayed woman, not general, diffused, or extended, and they usually occur off the battlefield. A characteristic Swiftian counterpart to the Homeric dashing of brains is the scheme, in the School of Political Projectors, for reconciling party differences by taking a hundred leaders of each party, sawing off 'the *Occiput* of each Couple at the same Time' and redistributing their brains (III.vi.189) – a piecemeal intramural counterpart to the war-list's idea of dividing a hundred bodies in the middle, but transposed to a mode of mock-scientific discourse, and thus wholly free of epic reminder.

THE 'BATTLE OF THE BOOKS'

Swift was not innocent of epic analogy, however. The *Battle of the Books* suggests that he was likely to have, in almost every case, a detailed and specific consciousness of epic reverberation, item by item. It is his only sustained mock-heroic work (and an interesting question arises as to why this most parodically minded of eighteenth-century writers should have attempted the mock-heroic so seldom, at the only time in English literary history when the genre absorbed the most creative energies of some of the best writers). It actually isolates every epic commonplace that was later to find its way into *Gulliver's Travels*, almost in the manner of a sottisier or 'tritical essay', even the relatively uncommon one of the hero cut in two.

In a passage particularly full of echoes from Virgilian and Homeric poems, Pindar despatches Cowley:

he raised his Sword, and with a mighty Stroak, cleft the wretched *Modern* in twain, the Sword pursuing the Blow; and one half lay panting on the Ground, to be trod in pieces by the Horses Feet, the other half was born by the frighted Steed thro' the Field.[124]

What in *Gulliver's Travels* was to be generalised into hundreds here remains the specific fate of an individual, as in an epic poem, undisarmed by Gulliver's generalising fantasy. The body cut in two is a more excessive detail than one normally finds, except in the sensationally violent world of Silver Epic. Lucan offers two analogues and is presumably in Swift's mind, since he figures by name in the preceding paragraph of the *Battle*.[125] (Homer and Virgil, as well as the later authors, also give severed parts of bodies in posthumous animation, like Cowley's panting half: heads that go on talking or hands that clutch swords or ships after being severed).[126]

The example is self-neutralising, however, since the gory scene is not literal. The battle is a learned foolery, allegorising an intellectual debate; and, even if we attend literally to the narrative, the battle is not between men but, in the words of the title, *Between the Antient and the Modern Books in St. James's Library*. If the tenor of the allegory is sometimes forgotten because the reader is too caught up in the epic vehicle, Swift frequently issues reminders. The next sentence shows us Venus attending one of the halves of Cowley's remains: 'This *Venus* took, and wash'd it seven times in *Ambrosia*, then struck it thrice with a Sprig of *Amarant*; upon which, the Leather grew round and soft, the Leaves turned into Feathers, and being gilded before, continued gilded still.' This reminder that Cowley is a book is followed by a

---

[124] *Works*, I.159. Quotations from the *Battle* will for the rest of this chapter be identified by page-numbers in the text.

[125] Lucan, III.637ff., see above, n. 115. The two analogues cited by Real from *Aeneid*, IX.749–51, and *Paradise Lost*, VI.630–1, are inexact (*Battle*, ed. Real, p. 90).

[126] Severed heads continuing to speak: *Iliad*, X.457; *Odyssey*, XXII.329; Silius Italicus, XV.470; body still running after decapitation: Silius Italicus, XIII.246–8; severed hands seeking their owner, clutching at sword or side of ship, or otherwise in motion: *Aeneid*, X.395–6; Lucan, III.609–13, 661–9; Silius Italicus, XIV.489–91, 537–8; Ariosto, *Orlando Furioso*, XXXIX.lxxxiv; Tasso, *Gerusalemme Liberata*, IX.lxix.

mock-editorial note reminding us that the allegory is an allegory ('*I do not approve the Author's Judgment in this, for I think* Cowley's *Pindaricks are much preferable to his* Mistress'). Any residue of horror is dissolved by the relative geniality to Cowley, one half of whom is complimented in Swift's text and the other half in Swift's note, reflecting a special loyalty Swift clearly still felt towards his early poetic model, as one of the less degraded Moderns (Swift is normally more given to double-barrelled insults than double-barrelled compliments, but here introduces a mildly stinging either-way-you-win irony, instead of the either-way-you-lose sort which is more usual with him).[127]

Thus, despite its violent epic language, the telling of Cowley's mutilation is given an unusually benign orchestration. It looks forward to a type of mock-heroic with which we do not normally associate Swift, although its author was to learn much from Swift, that of the *Rape of the Lock* and its ultimate refinement of the act of cutting a hero in two:

> Fate urg'd the Sheers, and cut the *Sylph* in twain,
> (But Airy Substance soon unites again).[128]

There are Homeric and Miltonic sources for this passage, but they have to do with the healing aspect, not with cutting in twain, and a comic analogue in Ariosto.[129]

Into such genial fantasy, Swift will not enter too far. The language is sustainedly that of battlefield atrocities, which, although not taken at face value, have an unsettling power: 'he ... cleft the wretched *Modern* in twain ... and one half lay panting on the Ground, to be trod in pieces by the Horses Feet, the other half was born by the frighted Steed thro' the Field'. This narrative sequence is itself a mini-anthology of epic *topoi*, like the *Battle* as a whole, and like Gulliver's war-lists, with which it shares many details. The anthologising predisposition is one which Swift shared (though in a highly indivi-

---

[127] A similar geniality is accorded to Denham, 'a stout *Modern*, who from his Father's side, derived his Lineage from *Apollo*, but his Mother was of Mortal Race' (p. 157), another earlier English writer (slain by no less than Homer) with a special claim on Augustan affections, who likewise gets a footnote to himself explaining that his '*Poems are very Unequal, extremely Good, and very Indifferent*'. In addition, Blackmore is saved from Lucan's lance by Aesculapius because of his medical skills, and given a pair of spurs by Lucan, because his poems are dull and move slowly (p. 158: Lucan, as I said earlier, gets a bridle in return). Both examples occur close to the passage about Cowley and mark a benign phase in the *Battle*.

[128] *Rape of the Lock*, III.151–2, TE, III.179.

[129] *Iliad*, v.339ff., 416ff.; *Paradise Lost*, vi.330ff.; 433–6.*Orlando Furioso*, xv.lxxxiiff., trs. Reynolds, I.467ff. and Introduction I.43–4.

dual form) with many of his contemporaries, and with the Flaubert of *Salammbô* (in a sense an anthology of real atrocities, as the *Battle* is of mock-atrocities, drawn from the same ancient sources), as well as of *Bouvard et Pécuchet* and the dictionary of 'received ideas' – a topic raised in later chapters of this book. The highly localised narrative of the *Battle*, and the zanily generalised enumerations of Gulliver, are miniaturised 'compleat collections' of the 'typical details, typical groupings of details' which are the prefabricated building blocks of Western heroic poetry.

Anthologising is in Swift's hands as in Flaubert's a virtual declaration of ironic perspectives, anything but a neutral selection. Flaubert's principles of narrative were dedicated to concealing this, but the nature of *Salammbô* as a sottisier of carnage, its resemblance in some ways to the manner of *Bouvard et Pécuchet*, its transformation of the grossly specific into instances of habitual turpitude, are never far below the surface, and a reading of his letters during the composition of the book brings out the vast stores of derision whose overt display was, in a formal sense, suppressed in the narrative itself. The atrocities of *Salammbô* have a quality of uncompromising excess that is simultaneously true to its sources and teetering on the edge of a grotesque self-deflation, abetted by the subtle and gruelling monotony (a masterful monotony that is a great narrative power) of Flaubert's telling.

The enumerative telescoping of the same things in Swift wears its derision on its sleeve. The anthologising is, almost generically, an announcement of satiric disengagements, but it leaves unresolved its exact relation to its subject matter and the exact targeting of the mockery. In the episode of Pindar and Cowley, the note is in some ways so genial that it is difficult to see who is meant to be hurt. Yet the fiction of martial brutality is so specific that it is difficult to accept that nobody is. Irresolutions of this sort are characteristic of Swift, and are instruments of satiric aggression in themselves. In the Gulliver lists, warfare is targeted and the epic reminders are accompanied by suggestions that it is not epics that are under attack, only the things which are their subject, and specifically when the things are enacted rather than sung. But the language evokes the songs, and also half-suppresses the evocation. The ambivalence is real, more protective of epic than aggressive towards it. But the two impulses are in tension, and the tension is not given the kind of open discursive articulation which Pope offered in the editorial matter of his Homer translation.

77

Pope, close to Swift in friendship and cultural allegiance, is very different in satiric temper, and Swift's adumbration of the *Rape of the Lock* in the episode of the cleaving and partial restoration of Cowley is highly unexpected. The *Rape of the Lock* is surely the least Swiftian of all Pope's poems, and the *Dunciad* (Pope's darkest satiric work, indebted to the *Tale*, abetted by Swift, and dedicated to him) the most closely related, in subject-matter, technique, and intellectual sympathy, to the *Battle of the Books*. But it happens more than once that the *Battle* shows surprising prefigurations of the *Rape*, while it never comes near the peculiar degraded massiveness of the *Dunciad*. An example is the system 'of light, nimble Gods, menial Servants to *Jupiter*: . . . his ministring Instruments in all Affairs below', who 'are call'd by mortal Men, *Accidents*, or *Events*; but the Gods call them, *Second Causes*' (p. 153). The passage derives, as is well-known, from Homer, and the *topos* of different names occurs in virtually every epic and mock-epic work ever since.[130] But the closest resemblance is to the airy spirits of the *Rape of the Lock*, that 'light *Militia* of the lower Sky' who intercede in all affairs below, and who are known under one name by the gods, and another by men: ''Tis but their *Sylph*, the wise Celestials know,/ Tho' *Honour* is the Word with Men below.'[131] (Swift had not read the *Rape*, and the *influence* is of course the other way, although the *Battle* is virtually unmentioned in the Twickenham commentary. The system was derived by Pope from the Rosicrucian fiction by Montfaucon de Villars, the *Comte de Gabalis*, a work Swift is known to have read in 1697 while at work on the *Battle* and the *Tale*, and which is pertinent to his anti-Rosicrucian satire in the *Tale*.)[132]

A Dunciadic version of the double naming comes over with a weightier and gloomier cadence, which might in principle be thought more appropriate to Swift's vision. The poetic fact is not Swiftian at all, however. The antiquarian counterfeiter Annius appeals to Dulness to propitiate his frauds by an appropriate supply of cloud:

> Grant, gracious Goddess! grant me still to cheat,
> O may thy cloud still cover the deceit!
> Thy choicer mists on this assembly shed,
> But pour them thickest on the noble head.
> So shall each youth, assisted by our eyes,

[130] *Iliad*, 1.403–4, II.813–14, XIV.291, XX.74 and see Pope's notes to his translation of *Iliad*, 1.523 and XIV.328–30 (TE, VII.113, VIII.178–9); Rabelais, IV, Prologue; Dryden, *The Hind and the Panther*, III.823–4; Thomas Parnell, *Homer's Battle of the Frogs and Mice*, III.189–90, 'Allegory on Man', lines 2–4, in *Collected Poems*, ed. Claude Rawson and F. P. Lock, Newark, DE and London, 1989, pp. 96, 164, 474, 524.   [131] *Rape of the Lock*, 1.42, 77–8; TE III.149, 151.
[132] TE, III.378–83; *Tale of a Tub*, ed. Guthkelch and Smith, pp. lvi, lviii, 186, 353–60.

See other Caesars, other Homers rise;
Thro' twilight eyes hunt th'Athenian fowl,
Which Chalcis Gods, and mortals call an Owl ...

The last line, as Pope tells us in a note, is lifted from Hobbes'
translation of *Iliad*, xiv.291, in a passage where Sleep, instructed by
the scheming Hera to lull Zeus into slumber, assumes the form of a
bird whom, in Lattimore's version, 'the immortal gods call chalkis,
but men call him kymindis'. Pope's translation of the *Iliad* had given
the Homeric passage a majestic montage:

Dark in embow'ring Shade, conceal'd from Sight,
Safe *Sleep*, in Likeness of the Bird of Night,
(*Chalcis* his Name with those of heav'nly Birth,
But call'd *Cymindis* by the Race of Earth.)

Pope added a note describing the bird, as 'about the Size of a Hawk,
entirely black', and complaining that Hobbes' version, identifying it
as an owl, had lowered the dignity of the original, and in particular of
its suggestion that the poet is 'no Stranger to the Language of the
Gods.'[133]

Pope's translation is itself not without mild and unsubversive
intimations of mock-ponderous inflation, but by the same token the
Dunciad's version is remarkable for its contrary resistance to some of
the expected *de*flationary tendencies of the mock-form – a double
index of the ease with which Pope could maintain in delicately poised
coexistence varying proportions of majesty and mockery, without
allowing either to cancel or overwhelm the other. The bathetic drop
suggests disparagement or degradation, but no diminution of substance or mass, a characteristic feature of the *Dunciad*, whose polluted
grandeurs extend in rich and unexpected ways the reach of Dryden's
perception of mock-heroic in Boileau's *Lutrin* as 'finely mixing' the
venom of satire with 'the majesty of the heroic'.[134] The couplet which
closes with Hobbes' line, brilliantly naturalised into an authentically
Popeian idiom, retains a stubborn sense of brassy stupor and impen-
etrable brooding vacancy which has analogues in Dryden's *Mac
Flecknoe* and Fielding's *Jonathan Wild*, but is seldom found in Swift.
The speech is suffused with enveloping mists of such density and mass
that they almost acquire suggestions of statuary, like the 'Monument
of vanisht minds' in *Mac Flecknoe*'s Barbican fantasia (the line is lifted

[133] Pope, *Dunciad*, iv.355ff., and Pope-Warburton note to iv.361, and translation of *Iliad*,
xiv.327–30 and note, TE, v.377–8, viii.178–9.
[134] Dryden, 'Discourse Concerning Satire' (1693), in Watson, ii.149.

from Davenant's *Gondibert*, where it referred to a library containing books by great authors now dead and not to modern mindlessness); and with something too of the *Dunciad*'s own 'Monumental Brass', itself a good example of original majesties (from Horace's *Exegi monumentum aere perennius*) preserved in a powerful degraded form.[135]

Brass is an explicit presence in Annius' speech. The Pope–Warburton note explains that 'th'Athenian fowl' refers to 'The Owl stamp'd on the reverse of the ancient money of Athens', a transformation of both Homer and Hobbes. In the poem itself, Annius goes on to pray that those who hunt it through the 'twilight ages', the dupes of his forgeries, may 'Be rich in ancient brass, tho' not in gold.'[136] The associations of brass are also subtextually furthered by the fact that the word χαλκις (*chalkis*), for the bird Hobbes miscalled an owl (which remains unidentified under either of its Homeric names), is very close to the Greek word for brass or copper, χαλκός (*chalkos*): the city of Chalkis in Euboea is sometimes said to take its name from neighbouring copper-mines. The atmosphere of fraudulent brazenness and mindless gullibility has its subheroic dimensions too, and Pope's lines evoke a deadpan unsmiling owlishness which might be associated with one of the Swiftian guises Pope apostrophised in addressing the *Dunciad* to his friend: that of the straight-faced joker, choosing 'Cervantes' serious air'.[137] It coexists in Pope with the gigantifications of a perverse heroic survival, a vivid example of his success in mimicking primary majesties and offering up his parody as a genuine tribute to them.

This is precisely what Swift would not allow himself to do. He shied from mock-heroic partly because of an instinctive guardedness lest any primary residue of 'lofty Stile' should rub off on the parody in a manner which Dryden had claimed as a peculiar strength of mock-heroic, 'the most beautiful and most noble kind of satire', and 'undoubtedly a species' of heroic poetry itself. Dryden's praise would be enough to make Swift draw back, but he had inhibitions of his own that made him feel that he would 'make a Figure scurvy' in any high style, even a derisive one.[138] This complements the fear lest the other

[135] Dryden, *Mac Flecknoe*, line 82; Sir William Davenant, *Gondibert* (1651), II.v.36; *Dunciad*, II.313, TE, v.311; Horace, *Odes*, III.xxx.1.

[136] *Dunciad*, IV.361 and Pope-Warburton note 365, TE, v.378.

[137] *Dunciad*, I.21, TE, v.270.

[138] Dryden, 'Discourse Concerning Satire', Watson, II.149; Swift, *Epistle to a Lady*, lines 218–20, in *Poems*, II.637; on Swift's rejection of the lofty style, see Rawson, '"I the Lofty Stile decline": Self-apology and the "Heroick Strain" in some of Swift's Poems', in *The English Hero, 1660–1800*, ed. Robert Folkenflik, Newark, DE and London, 1982, pp. 79–115, esp. 85–7.

half of the mock-heroic package, the *mockery*, should, against his official intentions, contaminate the status of epic itself. Pope had neither fear: secure as Swift never was in his allegiances, he was able in his mock-heroic both to welcome its grandeurs and to control the modulations of his mockery.

Such control was never easy for Swift. He knew only too well that his irony was not of the decorously manageable sort, though he desired decorum, and management, in all things; and that this irony risked damaging all it touched, including what he himself regarded as his most cherished positives. The fortunes of *A Tale of a Tub*, accused to his dismay of undermining the Church of England itself, were later to bring this home to him more painfully, but it would be surprising if he was not already aware of it in the writing (witness the evasion of any extended treatment of Martin, and the undercutting of him on the one occasion when he is allowed to speak, and most sensibly too, from something like Swift's own point of view).[139]

If the church was vulnerable to the unofficial energies of his style, so *a fortiori* was any other object of his loyalty. It is not therefore surprising to see Swift, in his one mock-heroic work, taking uncharacteristic pains to reduce the corrosive potential of his irony, particularly when frequent and damaging features of epic are involved. Hence perhaps the softening of epic horrors by an uncharacteristic geniality in the *Battle*, and the element of fantasticated generality in those obviously far from genial mock-descriptions in *Gulliver's Travels*, in places where they risk recalling epic treatments of similar material. It is even possible that, just as he delayed and reduced to a minimum Martin's important speech in the *Tale*, Swift began by holding back from descriptions of combat altogether: more than two-thirds of the *Battle* elapse before there is any actual battling, and the first onset of battle is nipped in the bud by the insertion of three large gaps or *hiatuses* in the manuscript (one of them huge, 'Ingens'), where much carnage would otherwise have been. The third of these *hiatuses* follows a passage where Descartes is hit in the eye by Aristotle's arrow, and we are spared details of that frequent epic event, the gouging out of eyes:[140] 'The Steel Point quickly found a *Defect* in his *Head-piece*; it pierced the Leather and the Past-board, and went in at his Right Eye.

[139] *Tale of a Tub*, VI, *Works*, 1.87.
[140] e.g. *Iliad*, XIV.493ff.; *Odyssey*, IX.387ff.; Lucan, II.184ff., III.709–14, VI.218–19, 541–3; Statius, *Thebaid*, IX.751–2. In Swift's *Battle*, Wotton has his eyeballs squeezed out on the previous page (p. 155).

The Torture of the Pain, whirled the valiant *Bow-man* round, till Death ... drew him into his own *Vortex.*' Four lines of asterisks follow, indicating *Ingens hiatus hic in MS*, and so drawing attention to the fact that the *Battle* is among other things a learned edition of itself (p. 156).

LATERAL DISPLACEMENTS: THERSITES

The traffic between the mock-heroic and the mock-learned parodies, signalled by this editorial mimicry and inherent in the very conception of the *Battle of the Books*, is part of a sustained displacement of 'heroic' material away from epic or epic parody to an altogether non-epic discourse, which runs across the expected vertical drop from heroic to unheroic or anti-heroic. It may be described as a lateral movement which intercepts the downward fall at some point and removes it sideways to an area of feeling not preoccupied with the heroic either way. The setting up of the chief Modern protagonist Bentley into a ludicrous heroic guise departs from the predictable vertical process when he is given a physical description and a character-portrayal in which he is neither hero nor a hero's mock-heroic opposite. Crooked-legged, hump-shouldered, and railing, he evokes that rather special and separate Homeric personage, Thersites, as Swift indicates explicitly in a marginal gloss, adding in a footnote: '*The Person here spoken of, is famous for letting fly at every Body without Distinction, and using mean and foul Scurrilities*' (p. 160).

This lateral departure is a special case, because it has its own Homeric source, which was sometimes singled out as 'burlesque' and beneath heroic dignity in Homer himself.[141] Scaliger addresses Bentley as Odysseus had addressed Thersites:

Miscreant Prater, said he, *Eloquent only in thine own Eyes, Thou railest without Wit, or Truth, or Discretion. The Malignity of thy Temper perverteth Nature; Thy* Learning *makes thee more* Barbarous, *thy Study of* Humanity, *more* Inhuman; *Thy* Converse *amongst Poets more* groveling, miry, *and* dull. *All Arts of* civilizing

---

[141] René Rapin, *Comparaison d'Homère et de Virgile*, ch. 8, where it is not Homer who is to blame but his impolite times; on the other hand, in his *Réflexions sur la Poétique*, I.x, Rapin said Thersites was introduced in order to arouse contempt (*Oeuvres*, 1725, 1.126–7, II.117); see Addison, *Spectator*, No. 279, 19 January 1712, ed. Bond, II.589, to the effect that the portrayal of Thersites had a 'Burlesque Character' which took away 'from that serious Air which seems essential to the Magnificence of an Epic Poem'. For another Swiftian use of Thersites in an attack on a contemporary see 'Mad Mullinix and Timothy' (1728), lines 51–6, *Poems*, III.775. For Thersites in the English vernacular tradition, perceived through Latin rhetoric books rather than directly from Homer, as the type of the railing detractor, see Robert Kimbrough, *Shakespeare's Troilus and Cressida and its Setting*, Cambridge, MA, 1964, pp. 37–9.

others, render thee rude *and* untractable; Courts *have taught thee* ill Manners, *and* polite Conversation *has finish'd thee a* Pedant. *Besides, a greater Coward burdeneth not the Army* ... (p. 161)

The speech begins and ends Homerically. Odysseus had denounced Thersites as a railer and as the worst man in all the Greek armies. But the true burden of Scaliger's speech is in the middle, and has no correspondence with Homer, whether as parallel or as sub-heroic opposite. Scaliger's comment that 'Courts *have taught thee* ill Manners, *and* polite Conversation *has finish'd thee* a Pedant' calls to mind the low courtiers ('from the gentleman-usher ... downward to the gentle-man-porter') of Swift's essay 'On Good-Manners and Good-Breeding': 'With these kind of pedants, the court ... was always plentifully stocked'; they lacked 'the smallest tincture of good-manners'; as masters of the trifles of courtly knowledge, they and their like, Swift says, were 'greater pedants, than LIPSIUS, or the elder SCALIGER', a coincidence whose piquancy seems only slightly diminished by the probability that in the *Battle* Swift was alluding to the younger, rather than the elder, Scaliger.[142]

Scaliger's speech against Bentley treats him as an offender not primarily against the heroic virtues, but against good-manners, against the classical scholarship, the humanity, and humane letters of which he professed himself a champion, and against the civilised good breeding which is a presumed product of devotion to the classics. There is no pedantry in Homer and no concern, either way, with *humanitas*. Not only does the 'politeness' against which Bentley offends have nothing Homeric about it, but Homer himself might indeed be thought (and often was thought) to offend against it, every bit as much as Bentley, though doubtless in different ways.

Turning Bentley into a ragged sub-courtier, reminiscent of the motley crew of dancing-masters and gentleman-ushers of the essay on good-manners, is an example of the displacement from the heroic mode which I am discussing. It is accompanied by interesting departures from Homer not only in the speech of Scaliger and the characterisation of Bentley, but in the amount of characterisation supplied, indeed in the fact of characterisation itself (not normally bestowed by Homer on lower personages), and in the action which accompanies it. Odysseus speaks as lengthily as Scaliger, or more, in

---

[142] Swift, 'On Good-Manners and Good-Breeding' (posthumously published in 1754), in *Works*, IV.215–16; for opinions as to which of the two Scaligers is intended, see *A Tale of a Tub*, ed. Guthkelch and Smith, p. 252n., and *Battle of the Books*, ed. Real, p. 93.

his speech to Thersites, but, beyond noting his railing and his military uselessness, offers no other information about his character. He goes on instead to threaten to send Thersites naked and howling back to the ships if he ever catches him 'playing the fool' again. Then, in the passage I discussed earlier, Odysseus wounds him with his sceptre and makes him weep, while the dispirited Greek soldiers 'laughed over him happily'. This is a Homeric 'humanity', which has nothing to do with the *humanitas* Swift was talking about, but which is capable of taking in the pathos as well as the despicability of the beaten Thersites, and the pathos as well as the malicious triumphalism of the laughing soldiery, and his own partisanship with it and against the victim. Virtually all these elements, including the threat, the beating, the soldiers' cruel laughter and their own sad state, belong to a Homeric amplitude which Augustan 'politeness' would have found more or less difficult to accommodate, and their omission speaks almost as eloquently as Scaliger's displacing *additions*.

The difference does not lie in the fact that Bentley received a lordly putdown, establishing him as socially and morally low, rather than unworthy of heroic dignity. The treatment *de haut en bas* has a good deal of Homeric sanction. Thersites is the only named low-class character in the *Iliad* (and also, as we are told in Kirk's *Commentary*, the only named character in the poem who is not given either a patronymic or a place of origin).[143] Thersites is the main carrier in Homer of an anti-heroic perspective, and the poet's treatment of him is adversarial and loftily contemptuous. This does not seem to imply whosesale dismissal. The home-truths Thersites delivers about Agamemnon, for example, are similar to those which Achilles delivers in Book I, so that the discredit attaching to them may have less to do with their substance (with much of which Swift, as well as Achilles, might be sympathetic), or at least with any radical untenability, than with the character of the speaker and the subversive implications of allowing low persons to express such views. As Pope put it, Homer 'rebuk'd the Seditious in the Person of *Thersites*', and the treatment of Thersites by Odysseus follows precisely the scenario, spelt out a few lines earlier, for dealing with low-born as distinct from lordly cowards, of the type Lattimore renders as 'man of the people', and Pope as 'clam'rous vile Plebeian'.[144]

The sympathies which align Swift with Homer against the victim of

[143] G. S. Kirk, *The Iliad: A Commentary. Volume I: Books 1–4*, Cambridge, 1985, pp. 138–9.
[144] Pope's note to his *Iliad*, II.348; *Iliad* translation, II.235, TE, VII.144, 138.

Odysseus' punishment are obvious. He would be unlikely to position himself against the Homeric prototype, especially in a work allegorising the contest between Ancients and Moderns, even though some of the views of the original Thersites were not far removed from what Swift himself might have said about heroic thuggery and the exaltation of war. By translating Thersites into Bentley he made it easy for himself not to enter into the Homeric character's actual opinions. The change released him into freedoms of non-Homeric castigation which raised no awkward issues about heroic morality, and which he articulates through the additional matter in Scaliger's speech.

Scaliger's additions assert values which Swift nearly always showed in a beleaguered state, and they are invoked in a classic counter-attack in the name of an English Augustan conception of polite learning: '*The Malignity of thy Temper perverteth Nature; Thy* Learning *makes thee more* Barbarous, *thy Study of* Humanity, *more* Inhuman ... *All Arts of* civilizing *others, render thee* rude *and* untractable; Courts *have taught thee* ill Manners, *and* polite Conversation *has finish'd thee* a Pedant.' The speech, and the satire as a whole, are sustained by a huge tacit irony, that the Modern Bentley, librarian of the Royal Library in St James' Palace (where the *Battle* takes place) and keeper since 1694 of all the king's libraries, was a classical scholar of great distinction, more learned in the classics than anyone on the Ancient side, and nowadays recognised as one of the foremost figures in the history of classical scholarship. The paradox by which the most learned authorities on classical antiquity, in their commitment to a scholarly professionalism at odds with the relatively insubstantial connoisseurship of their lordly betters, came to be of the Modern allegiance, has been magisterially explored in Joseph M. Levine's recent book.[145]

Swift had little conception of the distinction, or indeed the nature, of Bentley's scholarship, but he was in his cultural loyalties, if not in his own social rank, aligned on the lordly side. The *hauteurs* uttered by Scaliger are Swift's by proxy, and in them Bentley's central failings as a Modern are tested against standards of decency and civilisation which have to be admitted to be post-classical. If one calls them Horatian, it is largely in terms of a specialised Renaissance or post-Renaissance conception of Horace, and this certainly has little to do with the Homeric world, or any features of the Homeric original in reference to which the particular passage is orchestrated. Indeed, one

[145] Joseph M. Levine, *The Battle of the Books: History and Literature in the Augustan Age*, Ithaca and London, 1991.

implication of such displacements of simple (vertical) mock-heroic is that merely showing Bentley as unheroic or subheroic, unHomeric or sub-Virgilian, is not felt to be enough. To fail the standards of heroic grandeur has come to seem, in itself, less than culpable, not because we can't all be heroes, but because being a hero could no longer be assumed, unquestioningly and unambiguously, to be a reputable thing, either in social behaviour or in common morality. To drama-tise an enemy's full iniquity, a different set of shortcomings is called for, and in the *Battle of the Books* the failures of the Moderns are partly set against a code of gentlemanly virtue which, as formulated, is not very much more ancient than themselves.

The satirical weapon which displaces or transforms an often meticulously worked-out epic parallel is an appeal to the uppish gestures of high rank. Near the end, Wotton hurls a lance at Swift's patron, Sir William Temple, 'General of the *Allies* to the *Antients*', in a passage which crackles with echoes of epic commonplaces, goddesses intervening to guide or deflect a throw, warriors saved by the providentially arranged protection of belt or buckle: 'Away the Launce went hizzing, and reach'd even to the Belt of the averted *Antient*, upon which, lightly grazing, it fell to the Ground. *Temple* neither felt the Weapon touch him, nor heard it fall' (pp. 162–3). This is an amusing transcendence or overcoming of the chivalric concern, expressed by Don Quixote and others in relation to gunpowder, that missile warfare makes it possible for base persons to kill knights from afar. Sir William proves not to be vulnerable, in ways which activate the kind of lateral displacement I have been describing. A Homeric precedent for a projectile deflected by a goddess and hitting a belt, and for a hero consequently unconcerned by the impact, occurs at *Iliad*, IV.127ff., where Menelaus is struck on the belt, and makes light of the wound: it is one of the passages which Gilbert Murray identifies as a survival from an earlier version, in which the arrow was poisoned.[146] Temple's ignoring of Wotton's lance can be seen as a mock-version of this heroic unconcern, except that the lack of acknowledgement is so absolute that the ignoring is a literal ignorance.

At this moment, the passage ceases to be a mere heroic lowering, and becomes a social ploy, something like a literalisation of the

---

[146] *Rise of the Greek Epic*, p. 130: see above, n.111. For another example of a spear stopped by a belt, see *Iliad*, XI.234–7; for a goddess strengthening the hero's arm or deflecting a spear, see *Iliad*, XVII.569–70, *Aeneid*, IX, 743ff.

colloquial phrase (satirised by Fielding in *Joseph Andrews* in an anthologised enumeration of snobbish usages) 'people one does not know': a letter in which Temple described himself in 1698 as 'having no mind to Enter the List, with such a Mean, Dull, Unmannerly PEDANT' shows that he was in real life given to ponderous versions of the kind of lofty putdown which Swift applaudingly and more amusingly allegorised in the *Battle*.[147] Perhaps such things are always more heavy-handed in reality than in fiction. In any event, it is the kind of hauteur by proxy which Swift practised with expert care. A Gulliverian analogue occurs in the afterworld of Glubbdubdrib, where Homer and Aristotle are seen surrounded by 'all their Commentators', but evidently 'perfect Strangers' to every one of them (III.viii.197). This is how gentlemen treat pedants, and Ancients treat Moderns, whatever the date, and belongs to the discourse of 'polite' social exclusion rather than that of heroic pretension.

It may seem proper, for all their witty aptness, to question the value of such gestures. If an ultimately irrelevant comparison between the heroic and the sub-heroic is displaced by frosty gestures of gentlemanly uppishness, the improvement might not seem self-evident. No doubt it is better to show uppish contempt to one's inferiors than to be a butcher (the term is in this context without class overtones) like Achilles, but not very impressive as an example of values to be set against the absurdities or depravities of bad Moderns, whatever they may be. The point, I take it, is that the gestures of superiority which Swift has invented for Temple, or Homer and Aristotle, however much they literalise the metaphors of social contempt, are themselves a metaphorical shorthand for superiorities not of rank, but of morals, manners, and culture.

The metaphorical shorthand derives its force from a climate in which the validity of distinctions of rank was assumed, or presupposed in a manner hard for present-day readers to enter into. Swift had a known distaste for arrogance of rank based merely on rank, and made no pretence to high rank for himself. Like Pope and Fielding, he poured some of his most uppish scorn on noblemen who failed by his standards of virtue, politeness, and literacy. An ideal, not actual, congruence is postulated between rank on the one hand and moral and cultural soundness on the other, and the paradox of using a kind of metaphorical snobbery to make the point was no harder for Swift or

---

[147] *Joseph Andrews*, II.xiii; Temple, letter of 30 March 1698, first published 1699 and cited in *Tale of a Tub*, ed. Guthkelch and Smith, p. xlviii.

his readers to swallow than that whereby a small tradesman like the Drapier could scorn a big financier like William Wood by calling him a mean insignificant hardwareman.[148] It does not normally occur to readers to note either the curious incongruity of the Drapier's posture, in class terms, or its unpleasantness as a crude valuation on mere grounds of rank: we recognise in it a rhetoric in which the lowness of Wood resides in its identification with the worst forms of profiteering, with the moneyed vices, with bribery, and with political oppression. (Pope's protestation that in showing the poverty of the dunces he was not attacking poverty helps us to understand the nature of this rhetoric, but also perhaps its inherent embarrassments).[149] The uppishness which Swift projects by proxy on to Temple, Homer, and Aristotle is as obviously rooted in something other and worthier than simple superiorities of rank as those he projects through the Drapier, in that both occur in contexts primarily and overtly concerned with the probing of literary and cultural values and with their bearing on morals and manners. Scaliger's denunciation of Bentley's malignity and 'inhumanity' seem designed to call us back to the ideal equivalences in which 'noble' means 'high' in a good human sense, and 'ignoble' is 'low' in an equal and opposite way.

We have seen, in some of these examples, a displacement of epic material into an essentially non-epic realm of activity, and that one of the possible implications of this is that the set of positive values which the epic was assumed to enshrine, however indirectly and at whatever distance, was sensed as no longer sufficient. There is also a related and opposite process, in which epic material is offered, not in the form of thoroughly elaborated mock-epic sequences like the throwing and deflection of Wotton's lance, but with some of its epic appurtenances missing. Instead of a transformation of mock-epic material by the addition of a new and non-epic perspective or the insertion of non-epic discourses or narrative details, we are given images or episodes or speeches in which parts of the original model are eliminated. Just as non-epic discredit is added in one case, so, in the other, material which would discredit the epic from within is removed. In the example of Thersites and Bentley both processes may be detected: Scaliger's speech adds the wholly unHomeric piece about humanity and

---

[148] See Rawson, 'The Injured Lady and the Drapier: A Reading of Swift's Irish Tracts', *Prose Studies*, 3 (1980), 32.

[149] Pope, 'A Letter to the Publisher', prefixed to the *Dunciad*, TE, v.14–16. On Pope's probable authorship of this letter, which is signed 'William Cleland', see the Introduction, TE, v.xxv.

pedantry, but the episode loses the Homeric detail in which Thersites is beaten, hurt, and mocked.

LATERAL DISPLACEMENTS: MAJESTIES OF MUD

Swiftian parody frequently operates in a mode of generic displacement or side-tracking. *Gulliver's Travels* is not principally concerned to deride the travel-books whose form it mimics, and the same might be said of *A Modest Proposal*'s relation to economic tracts, though in both cases a secondary derision of the parodied text is sometimes present. The *Battle of the Books* is a little different from both, in the sense that the parodic genre to which it belongs was most characteristically practised in his time as a positive tribute to the genre it mimics. The textbook principle is that a lowered modern reality can, through mock-heroic exposure, be shown to be unworthy by appeal to an older and loftier standard. In practice, mockery does not necessarily settle where an author thinks it should, and the risk of subversion from within is one against which Swift had special reasons to be on his guard.

Swift's usual avoidance of mock-heroic was, in addition, consciously powered by an opposite risk, as though in recoil from the residue of primary majesties from which *Mac Flecknoe* and the *Dunciad* derive their most characteristic strength, and which is a species of second-remove 'loftiness' included in Swift's feeling that he would 'make a Figure scurvy' in any 'lofty Stile'.[150] Another motive probably was his sense of his own inability to leave 'loftiness', whether primary or second-remove, unsubverted. The *Battle of the Books* is his only sustained mock-heroic, a detailed and systematic parody of Homeric and Virgilian doings, but flattened by the prose-medium and by an interposed dimension of mock-journalese ('A Full and True Account of the Battel Fought Last Friday'). This exists as a shield between Swift and the twin risks of allowing heroic parody to turn either into a species of the heroic, as Dryden defined it, or into an attack on the heroic. The interposition is insistently kept alive. The ministrations of Fame (p.152) are a replay of well-remembered Homeric and Virgilian prototypes, [151] but in the context of a public demand for scandal sheets and the gossip-columnist: 'Now, because the Talk of this Battel is so fresh in every body's Mouth, and the Expectation of the Town so great to be informed in the Particulars; I,

---

[150] See above, n.138.   [151] *Odyssey*, xxiv.413ff.; *Aeneid*, iv.174ff.

being possessed of all Qualifications requisite in an *Historian*, and retained by neither Party; have resolved to comply with the urgent *Importunity of my Friends*, by writing down a full impartial Account thereof' (p. 145).

The 'historian' is no more a historian than the journalistic hacks whom Fielding was to grace by the same name, in an ironic usage that remained common as late as Byron. He is a party hack protesting independence of party, a Grub Street scribbler whose writings no one wants protesting that he only writes because friends pressed him to, the standard low scribbler of Augustan satire. Much of the mockery that might otherwise have subverted the heroic norm is transferred to him, though further complexities attach to the usage and will be addressed in the next chapter.

This, it might be objected, is after all what happens in the *Dunciad*, with its Scriblerian prefaces and annotations. But is it? The Scriblerian material in the *Dunciad* is notable precisely for the fact that it is largely relegated to prefaces and annotations. The poem in its first conception existed without them, and Pope's ability to run a 'lofty' parody without inhibition or undercutting easily survives these semi-extraneous additions. Indeed they satisfy the need of the subject for a low-level exposure without harming the integrity of the grander vision.

The peculiar chemistry of Pope's mock-heroic grandeurs may be studied in the famous line in which Smedley emerges from the waters of Fleet-ditch, having been thought to have sunk without trace during the diving competition in Book II: 'Slow rose a form, in majesty of Mud.' The line has a long epic ancestry. Like other passages in Book II it evokes some ostensibly subheroic indignities in the heroic games in *Iliad*, XXIII and *Aeneid*, V, including the scatological mishaps of Ajax and Nisus, who both slip during a race and rise with their faces and mouths covered in dung. In a parallel race earlier in the *Dunciad*, Curll also slips, and then, 'Renew'd by ordure's sympathetic force ... Vig'rous he rises':

> from the'effluvia strong
> Imbibes new life, and scours and stinks along;
> Re-passes Lintot, vindicates the race,
> Nor heeds the brown dishonours of his face.[152]

[152] *Dunciad*, II.326, 103–8, TE, V.313, 300; *Iliad*, XXIII. 773–92; *Aeneid*, V.327–61.

Pope cites the Virgilian passage about Nisus in a note. But neither the Homeric nor the Virgilian episodes offer anything resembling his effect of polluted pomp. They report the sporting misadventures without apologies for lowness or any attempt to transform it into the grand monochrome mass of Pope's 'majesty of Mud' or 'the brown dishonours of his face'. The latter phrase, interestingly, has its immediate sources not in the epic originals, but in other comic or mock-heroic works by Pope's Scriblerian associates, in Gay's *Trivia* (1716), where a beau falls in the wet streets:

> Black Floods of Mire th'embroider'd Coat disgrace,
> And Mud enwraps the Honours of his Face,

and in Parnell's *Homer's Battle of the Frogs and Mice* (1717):

> This saw *Pelobates*, and from the Flood
> Lifts with both Hands a monst'rous Mass of Mud,
> The Cloud obscene o'er all the Warrior flies,
> Dishonours his brown Face, and blots his eyes.[153]

Pope's version surpasses these in sureness and economy, but it is from them and not from primary heroic sources that he took the materials for, and the main effect of, majestic transfiguration. It is in the framework of modern travesty, not in the heroic originals, that low things are raised to an imposing stature. This is not because ancient epics lacked low details, but because they saw no need to portray them as anything else. Dryden's treatment of Nisus' fall and Pope's treatment of Ajax's, in their respective translations of Virgil and Homer, show a comparable determination to assimilate these accounts to an idiom of heroic inflation which differs from their original counterparts, in the paradoxical sense that they are less differentiated from the primary heroic idiom. They are not the most successful things in either translation.[154]

Both translators, as is well known, sanitised their originals. In the episode from the games Dryden especially took care to attenuate or remove the scatological element. Virgil's 'foul dung and sacred blood', *immundoque fimo sacroque cruore*, becomes 'Filth, and Holy Gore', and Virgil's 'he displayed his face and limbs, filthy with wet excre-

---

[153] Gay, *Trivia*, II.533–4, in *Poetry and Prose*, ed. Vinton A. Dearing and Charles E. Beckwith, Oxford, 1974, I.158; Parnell, *Homer's Battle*, III.83–6, in *Collected Poems*, ed. Rawson and Lock, p. 94, and commentary, p. 473.

[154] Pope, *Iliad*, XXIII.912–13; Dryden, *Aeneid*, V.433, 468–9.

ment', *faciem ostendabat et udo/turpia membra fimo*, becomes 'he pointed to his Face, and show'd/His Hands and all his Habit smear'd with Blood'. The latter removes dung altogether (which Pope did not do, in lines otherwise partly influenced by Dryden, with the corresponding passage from the *Iliad*, XXIII, though he did so in a more momentous passage in the next book, as we shall see). Virgil tells us immediately after that 'good father Aeneas laughed', *Risit pater optimus*, which Dryden renders 'Th'indulgent Father of the People smil'd', introducing a note of sedate dignity of a kind Pope would also sometimes add to his Homeric original. The substitution of an indulgent smile for Aeneas' laughter may also be compared with Swift's removal of the soldiers' laughter in the episode of Bentley–Thersites.[155]

To return to Pope's Smedley, rising slow in majesty of mud: his lineaments are those of an Old Man River, and he resembles the account of the brown dishonours of Curll's face in having no obvious heroic prototype. If he has any 'serious' heroic analogue it is, perhaps, in some grotesqueries of Renaissance epic: in the humourless inflations of Camoens' *Lusiads*, with its riverine or maritime apparitions, Ganges and Indus, Adamastor and Triton.[156] Such figures would be likely to strike Pope as belonging to a decadence of the epic tradition, on a par with the heroic pretensions of a Blackmore. They were self-parodic in the same way as Blackmore's epics seemed self-parodic to Garth, so that they could be cited *verbatim* in the *Dispensary*,[157] or as heroic tragedies seemed to the authors of the *Rehearsal* or the Fielding of the *Tragedy of Tragedies*. During the war of the Ancients and Moderns which Swift allegorised in the *Battle*, it was the Moderns who, in a paradox which was only apparent, were more readily given to writing epic poems without irony, a phenomenon which was taken to imply a misplaced confidence in their ability to rival the ancient masters, and which offered Pope and others a monitory example of what to avoid. As is well known, Dryden and Pope contemplated, or began, epics of their own, but never finished them, and both diverted

155 Virgil, *Aeneid*, v.333, 357–8 (my translation); Dryden, v.433, 468–70; Pope, *Iliad*, XXIII.905ff., TE, VIII.525. Wakefield pointed out that Pope's 'Besmear'd with Filth' (XXIII.911) is taken from Dryden (v.433), *The Iliad of Homer, Translated by Alexander Pope*, ed. Gilbert Wakefield, 1796, VI.151n.
156 Camoens, *Lusiads*, IV.lxxii–lxxiv, v.xxxix ff., VI.xvi–xviii, trs. Atkinson, pp. 115–16, 128ff., 143–4.
157 Camoens is mentioned twice in the Scriblerian paraphernalia to the *Dunciad*, once in an unflattering or ambiguous context (TE, v.205, 340n.). On Garth's *Dispensary*, see above n. 102.

their epic aspirations into translations or ironic rewritings, a matter to which I shall refer again in the next chapter.

But, by another paradox which is also only apparent, such a line as 'Slow rose a form, in majesty of Mud' offers an instructive example of how, in an episode of comic indignity, Pope was more interested in effecting a majestic transfiguration than in stressing the comic bathos which his satire is ostensibly programmed to expose. In the poem's first versions the line read 'Lo E– rose, tremendous all in Mud!' (1728), and later 'Lo Smedley rose, in majesty of Mud!' (1729), a transition that not only indicates a change of target from John Dennis to Smedley, but also shows an early determination to disencumber the passage from any conspicuous suggestions of buffoonery. When he replaced 'tremendous' by 'majesty' in the *Dunciad Variorum*, he added a note drawing attention to a speech by Mammon in *Paradise Lost*, describing the 'majesty of darkness' with which God sometimes surrounded himself, an additional sign that brooding grandeur was what he wished to highlight, even before his own line achieved its final and most memorable form. When he came to execute the latter. he seems to have remembered a line from his own translation of the *Iliad*, 'Slow from his Seat arose the *Pylian* Sage'. The sedate stateliness of this description of Nestor was itself something Pope had felt it necessary to inject into his Homeric original in the first place: Homer mentions no slow rising, though Gilbert Wakefield perhaps went too far in asserting that Pope should have written '*Quick* from his seat *starts up* the Pylian sage'.[158]

It is not the only example of Pope's effort to raise the tone of the Homeric poems. The process is observable in his mock-heroic travesties as well as in the translations. And the final version of 'Slow rose a form, in majesty of Mud' has a defiled grandeur, or a grandeur in defilement, which Pope could achieve more easily in mock-heroic than in Homeric translation. The wonderful Homeric passage in *Iliad* XXIV.163–5, where (in Lattimore's version) Priam is grieving for the death of Hector:

> Dung lay thick
> on the head and neck of the aged man, for he had been rolling
> in it, he had gathered and smeared it on with his hands,

[158] *Dunciad*, A II.302 and Pope's note, and textual note at TE, v. 139; *Paradise Lost*, II.266; Pope's *Iliad*, I.330 (Homer, I.247–8), TE, VII.103; *The Iliad of Homer, Translated by Alexander Pope*, ed. Wakefield, I.50. Dryden translates Homer's line without fuss as 'But from his Seat the *Pylian* Prince arose', *First Book of Homer's Ilias*, line 362.

becomes in Pope's translation:

> With frantick Hands he spread
> A Show'r of Ashes o'er his Neck and Head.

Homer's word was *kopros*. Pope perhaps imported the ashes from a different passage, *Iliad*, xviii.23–5, where Achilles covers his head with dust, and ashes are scattered over his clothes.[159]

It is interesting, by the way, that Plato objected to such passages in Homer *not* because they mention 'dung', but because it is bad for youths to read about great persons in postures of weakness or grief, and he objected equally to ashes and to dung.[160] Pope's inhibitions about epic sprang from what he and most of his contemporaries perceived as its own potential indecencies. He would not allow Homer to defile himself, and it is perhaps in part this dangerous range of Homeric sympathies and of epic possibilities that prevented Pope from writing an epic of his own. But in mock-heroic, protected by irony, Pope could make majesty flower, for Pope's irony protects his loyalties rather than threatening to subvert them in the way that Swift's did.

When Swift described men covered in dung, the result was, and could only be, figures whom it was unthinkable to place in any epic or mock-epic context, the briefly glimpsed inmate of the Academy of Modern Bedlam:

raking in his own Dung, and dabling in his Urine. The best Part of his Diet, is the Reversion of his own Ordure, which exspiring into Steams, whirls perpetually about, and at last reinfunds. His Complexion is of a dirty Yellow, with a thin scattered Beard, exactly agreeable to that of his Dyet upon its first Declination,

or his colleague from the Academy of Lagado:

His Face and Beard were of a pale Yellow; his Hands and Clothes dawbed over with Filth ... His Employment from his first coming into the Academy, was an Operation to reduce human Excrement to its original Food, by separating the several Parts, removing the Tincture which it receives from the Gall, making the Odour exhale, and scumming off the Saliva. He had a

---

[159] *Iliad*, trs. Pope, xxiv.201–2, TE, viii.545. Similarly, when Homer described on the Shield of Achilles 'cattle ... wrought of gold and of tin', who 'thronged in speed and with lowing/out of the dung of the farmyard to a pasturing place', Pope omitted the dung as well as the tin: 'Here, Herds of Oxen march, erect and bold,/Rear high their Horns, and seem to lowe in Gold,/And speed to Meadows ...' (*Iliad*, xviii.572–5, Pope, xviii.665–7). *Kopros* can mean either dung or dung-yard, farmyard, as at *Odyssey*, x.411, and Pope, x.485–7, erases either suggestion in both places.   [160] Plato, *Republic*, iii.ii (387b–388c).

weekly Allowance from the Society, of a Vessel filled with human Ordure, about the Bigness of a *Bristol* Barrel.[161]

The appalling power of such passages, the energy of cloacal fantasy set off by the deadpan conciseness of the notation, would never have been possible for Swift in a framework of epic allusion. It is not that there are no epic analogues. Homer's Ajax, his mouth and nose filled with cow-dung, which comes out of his mouth as he speaks, is perhaps a prototype. It anticipates some grotesqueries in political invective by Oldham or Swift, who portrays Walpole in 'To Mr. Gay' with 'a rapid Flood' that 'Rolls from his Mouth in plenteous Streams of Mud', but neither this line nor the accounts of the two academicians occur in contexts of substantial epic association, and actual or suspected epic allusions or comparisons on isolated details tend to remain inactive.[162]

Camoens also offers some slight prefigurations. His Adamastor has an unkempt beard, yellow teeth, and hair matted with clay, and his Triton has hair and beard matted with slime and dripping water. The examples verge on mock-heroic, as I suggested, and Triton's head-dress, 'a huge lobster-shell' (*Uma mui grande casca de lagosta*), by a bizarre and delightful coincidence, anticipates Swift's passage about Dryden in the *Battle*, his 'Helmet . . . nine times too large for the Head, which appeared Situate far in the hinder Part, even like the Lady in a Lobster' (p. 157).[163] But the epic reverberations of the academicians in the *Tale* and in *Gulliver's Travels* are either too remote to be noticed or else largely displaced by an attack on science whose idiom (unlike, for example, the satire on physicians in Garth's *Dispensary*) has little to do with the heroic, whether as a respected norm or an object of parody. The mock-scientific reportage is not only a travesty of scientific reports, but evokes some older set-pieces about madcap cloacal projects, often mock-scientific or mock-alchemical, which had acquired a subgeneric status in their own right. The passage from Lagado derives from Rabelais, v.xxi, where a prototype of the Swiftian projectors in the land of the Quintessence spends his time fermenting urine in a tub full of the dung of horses and Christians. He says he supplies this to kings and princes, which may or may not be a ghostly irreverent echo of the Homeric Priam, but what is certain in

---

[161] *Tale of a Tub*, IX. *Works*, I.112–13; *Gulliver's Travels*, III.v.179–80.
[162] On Oldham, see chapter 2, above; Swift 'To Mr. Gay', lines 39–40, *Poems*, I.532.
[163] *Lusiads*, v.xxxix, vi.xvii, trs. Atkinson, pp. 128, 144.

the fabric of Rabelais' work as a whole is that no cultural reticence inhibits the evocation of Homeric enormities by Rabelaisian ones.

It is also clear that Swift was no more inhibited than Rabelais from cloacal subjects as such; and equally that, when the *anima Rabelaisii* came to inhabit a dry place, a prophylactic concern to keep such subjects away from '*ancient* Altars' became almost totally binding. If Pope needed to remove dung from Homer himself, he could freely play with it in the epic parody of the *Dunciad* in a way impossible for Swift. Pope could only write epic by proxy, translating and 'softening' Homer, or better still, through a transforming filter of irony. Swift could not safely attempt it at all, knowing his irony to be no filter but a caustic remover of filters.

The cherished genre of the epic, purporting to embody the highest values in the Augustan cultural code, was also the repository of that culture's deepest nightmares, of carnage, cruelty, and barbarism, not only reported, but celebrated by the most admired authors. A genre which 'polite learning' placed at the summit of its hierarchy of cultural properties was simultaneously perceived as inimical to the very 'politeness' which gave it its pre-eminent place. It was also a genre which could not be practised, except by Moderns presumed to lack all taste and understanding for it.

As for the Ancients of the great age of mock-heroic, Boileau, Dryden, Swift, or Pope, who would not write epic straight or leave it alone, filters were a necessity: as much to protect loyalties or forestall dismaying recognitions as to guard the practitioner from emulative failure. If irony was not of itself sufficient to provide the filter, or if it carried risks of its own, then the interposition of buffer genres, siphoning off some of the more subversive energies of allusion, was a common resource. Journalism, allegory, and Aesopic fable, continuously or intermittently, provide this function in the *Battle of the Books*, whether by organisational design or the instinctive opportunisms of a deep stylistic defensiveness. In the battle-scenes of *Gulliver's Travels* the things which risk epic reminder are similarly filtered through competing allusive associations: of historical fact and of history books, of travel books and travesties of travel books, and also of other satirists, who had already mimicked epic and created out of that a primary satiric idiom, like Lucian and Ariosto, and especially Rabelais. Rabelais' scenes of carnage are often 'Homerican'. But they are above all Rabelaisian, and the humanist attack on war to which they belong creates for Swift a focus for allusion which interposes itself between, and diverts attention from, inconvenient reminders of Homer. Even so, Rabelais subjects Homer to freedoms from which Swift would shrink. Rabelais' rewriting of an epic spilling of entrails typically includes soup and lentils as well as the gut which contained them, festive and exuberant as their few grim epic analogues could never be. In Swift such eviscerations are altogether removed from epic contexts to a world of crazed scientists, political projectors, and political surgeons.

The somewhat disreputable epics of the Silver Age, of Lucan, Silius Italicus, and Statius, their violence and their visceral horrors sometimes so extravagant as to be almost self-parodic, had in this context a parallel usefulness to that of the straightforwardly parodic or quasi-parodic models, Lucian, Ariosto, and Rabelais. Both groups served as enabling examples, absorbing material whose ready association with Homer and Virgil might be felt to be 'sensitive'. The network of multiple allusion, to individual works as well as to whole genres, usually and properly seen as a richly layered tribute to the classical tradition, also had a sceptical or subversive side, as well as a self-subversive anxiety to hold this in check. It may be that the most irreverent of eighteenth-century satirists, who at the same time proclaimed his ancient loyalties with an equal and opposite earnestness, used this hallowed form of tribute to negotiate an inherent disrespect.

· 4 ·
Mock-heroic and war
II: Byron, Shelley, and heroic discredit[1]

Byron's Augustanism is a large subject. There are certain aspects of it which I shall take for granted, mainly (1) that it is more authentically evident in the great *ottava rima* poems, which have no formal models in the English Augustan writers, than in such formally Popeian compositions as *English Bards and Scotch Reviewers* or *Hints from Horace* (the relative poverty of these couplet poems may itself imply a certain weakness in the post-Augustan transmission); and (2) that for all his celebrated championship of Pope, it is from an alternative Augustanism of Butler, Prior, and Swift that Byron derived his most successful styles[2] – a fact that he was himself predicting as early as *Hints from Horace* in the Popeian couplets he was gradually to disengage himself from:

> Peace to Swift's faults, his Wit hath made them pass,
> Unmatched by all save matchless Hudibras,
> Whose Author is perhaps the first we meet
> Who from our couplet lopped two final feet,

whose 'measure moves a favourite of the Nine ... And varied skilfully [as by Scott], surpasses far/Heroic rhyme' even in 'a theme of weight' (lines 397ff). (3) Perhaps more controversially, but not unconnectedly, that Byron's famous letters on Pope, with the exception of a handful of eloquent or amusing utterances (that Pope was 'the moral

---

[1] Quotations from Byron's poems are from the *Complete Poetical Works*, ed. Jerome J. McGann, Oxford, 1980–. Shelley's poems are cited from his *Poetry and Prose*, ed. Donald H. Reiman and Sharon B. Powers, New York, 1977. This edition has been chosen because it provides the only complete text of *Peter Bell the Third* to have been based on the Bodleian press-copy manuscript (see *The Bodleian Shelley Manuscripts*, 1, ed. Donald H. Reiman, New York, 1986, p.13). In referring to particular passages in the poem, however, I have departed from Reiman's and Powers' continuous line numbering, in favour of the more traditional stanzaic numeration.

[2] The fullest discussion of this matter is in A. B. England, *Byron's Don Juan and Eighteenth-Century Literature*, Lewisburg, 1975, esp. pp.68, 80ff.

poet of all Civilization – and as such . . . [may] one day be the National poet of Mankind'; or that it was 'of no very great consequence whether Martha Blount was or was not Pope's Mistress, though I could have wished him a better'), are not very interesting or distinguished documents, more preoccupied with a tedious and self-important wrangle with Bowles than with a genuine understanding of Pope;[3] and (4) that the self-conscious or Shandean dimension, though derived like *Tristram Shandy* itself from old traditions of 'learned wit' and the parodic fooleries of Swift's *Tale of a Tub*, is either a corrupted or debased Augustanism or something else altogether.

I shall talk principally of *Don Juan* and the *Vision of Judgment*, and also of Shelley's *Peter Bell the Third*, from a perspective, and in the context of a tradition, which seem to me crucial to any understanding of the Augustan complex in Byron: namely the tradition of epic and mock-heroic. It is the tradition which Byron invoked when he wrote in *Don Juan:*

> Thou shalt believe in Milton, Dryden, Pope;
> Thou shalt not set up Wordsworth, Coleridge, Southey;
>
> (i.ccv)

identifying in the first list the last great author of classical epic in Europe and the two greatest English practitioners of mock-heroic; and in the second list a group of poets notable in his eyes for their possession of undeserved official honours, chiefly Southey's Laureateship, or for the epic pretensions in their work, or both. Even Coleridge, the least official and least epic of the three, is conceived as 'the Laureat of the long-ear'd kind' (*English Bards*, line 264), braying like a poor man's version of sonorous Blackmore's strain. In this sense, these poets occupied the place which Shadwell, Blackmore, or Cibber had in the work of Dryden and Pope. I shall argue that there is a pervasive fixation on epic or mock-heroic in *Don Juan* especially; that the preoccupation runs very deep, as a catalyst for important acts of poetic, social, and political self-definition; but that this is paradoxically manifested through a sustained, insolently brilliant feat of trivialisation, through the formal underminings of inspired persiflage, through deflation, and ultimately through a ringing denial of the epic's moral worth.

In the Augustan cultural code, with its anguished broodings on the relation of past and present, no issue was so centrally problematic as

---

[3] Byron, *Complete Miscellaneous Prose*, ed. Andrew Nicholson, Oxford, 1991, pp.150–1, 166.

that of the 'epic', still potently celebrated in the words of Dryden, Pope and many others, as 'the greatest work which the soul of man is capable to perform',[4] yet clearly no longer writable by good poets: its military morality unacceptable, its social ethos unreal, its language out of line with a lowered sense of reality. Of all the ancient altars that still stood green, it was the most tarnished, official denials merely confirming the fact. By one of the many contradictions of the Ancient–Modern tug of war, it was the ancient faction that proclaimed the virtues of epic while failing to deliver epics of its own (except by proxy, in translations of Homer or Virgil, or in ironic guise in mock-heroic); while the moderns, Blackmore or the French biblical poets who had dismayed Boileau, went on writing to the ancient prototype without inhibition. This is how Byron often viewed Southey, supplier of 'an epic ... every spring' (*Don Juan* III.xcvii), though as Marilyn Butler has recently suggested he may have taken more from Southey than he would have wished to admit.[5]

It was frequently in mock-heroic idiom, or in the context of heroic pretension, that the forms of Augustan scorn, the gestures of patrician loftiness, the putdowns of cits by wits, expressed themselves. And the epic gestures of *Don Juan*, the *Vision of Judgment* and *Peter Bell the Third*, with their obsession with the laureate and proto-laureate figures of Southey and Wordsworth, and their identification of the Laureate-ship and the poetic establishment with a debased form of the epic muse (laurels were traditionally the rewards of martial as well as poetic prowess, and appear in both roles in *Don Juan*, sometimes with a specific epic allusion: see, for example, I.ccix, VII.lxviii), derive closely from Augustan models.

This may have harked back to an obsolete idiom. But in so far as it expressed patrician superiority, the ironic fact is that Shelley and Byron actually possessed a patrician status that Dryden, Swift, and Pope all lacked. The lordly accents of the latter were partly mimicked from the mob of gentlemen who wrote with ease, sometimes at the expense of Dryden or of Pope themselves. Byron's put-downs of Lake or Cockney poets and related riff-raff, the would-be wits and can't-be gentlemen, thus partly derive from authors who were sometimes

[4] John Dryden, *Of Dramatic Poesy and other Critical Essays*, ed. George Watson, London, 1962, II.223.
[5] Marilyn Butler, 'Revising the Canon', *Times Literary Supplement*, 4–10 December 1987, p.1360.

themselves the victims of such put-downs. When Byron said of
Southey in *Don Juan*:

> because you soar too high, Bob,
> And fall, for lack of moisture, quite adry, Bob!
>
> (Dedication, iii)

he was evoking the Drydenian nickname of Drybob, found not only in
the low Shadwell, whom Dryden scorned, but in the lordly Rochester,
who scorned Dryden, and who spoke famously, in his 'Allusion to
Horace' (whose very title seems to prefigure Byron's 'Hints') of
Dryden's 'dry bawdy bobs'. The idea was that Southey, like Dryden
in Rochester's portrayal, was a non-event, socially, sexually, and
poetically, in interchangeable and interconnected order.[6]

When Pope and his contemporaries wrote mock-epics, then,
straight epic no longer seemed possible to good poets. And the high
standing of epic which Dryden and Pope proclaimed was in practice
manifested only (as I argued) in the great mock-heroics, in which epic
grandeurs are filtered through irony, and survive not as primary
expressions of contemporary aspirations, but as a standard from
which the modern world can be shown to have lapsed. Hence the
mushrooming majesties of Pope's *Dunciad*, and even the delicate
ballooning of the *Rape of the Lock*. You sense in them the surviving
importance of the lost model, just as you sense it in a lower key in the
coarse couplets of seventeenth-century travesties of Virgil where the
high is treated in low language instead of the other way round, as in
the opening of Charles Cotton's *Scarronides* (1664): 'I *Sing the Man*
(read it who list,/ A *Trojan* true, as ever pist,) ...'[7] Coarse and
demotic, admittedly, but unthinkable even in, or especially in,
popular culture, unless a live awareness of the significance of epic
originals is taken for granted even among those who didn't or couldn't
read them. Scarron, Butler, Cotton are not demotic authors in a
simple sense. They represent a peculiar symbiosis of doggerel and
courtliness, a *rapprochement* of high and low, noble and beggarman,
which typically eschews the more constrained gentilities of the middle
ranks. Their verse is a witty and knowing exploitation of an idiom
which would not be out of place in popular farces and drolls and
puppet shows at Bartholomew and Southwark fairs. In the eighteenth

---

[6] Thomas Shadwell, *The Humorists* (1671); Rochester, 'An Allusion to Horace', line 75. See
above, chapter 2, pp. 22–3.
[7] Charles Cotton, *The Genuine Poetical Works*, 3rd edn., 1734, p.1.

century such shows sometimes dealt specifically with ancient heroic themes, including the siege of Troy.[8]

Now compare Byron 150 years or so later announcing in *Don Juan*

> My poem's epic, and is meant to be
>   Divided in twelve books; each book containing,
> With love, and war, a heavy gale at sea,
>   A list of ships, and captains, and kings reigning,
> New characters; the episodes are three:
>   A panorama view of hell's in training,
> After the style of Virgil and of Homer,
> So that my name of Epic's no misnomer,   (I.cc)

This is not demotic. It's as witty and allusive and exclusive as Pope. But I shall argue that as far as any real relationship to epic might be concerned, it is no more than a debonair flourish.[9] Epic has ceased to be more than a topic for intertextual jokerie, though there's a lot of this in *Don Juan*. But I shall first talk about Shelley.

Shelley and Byron are the two major Romantic poets who are closest to the Augustan 'aristocratic' sensibility, and both of them treat the epic with a frivolity and a lightness that would be unthinkable in Pope. *Peter Bell the Third*, a poem roughly contemporaneous with *Don Juan*, can be thought of in some ways as a low-key *Dunciad*. It mocks Wordsworth's *Peter Bell*, which Shelley may not have read at the time, a poem dedicated to Southey in 1819 and also guyed in *Don Juan*.[10] It thus has, like *Don Juan* and the *Vision of Judgment*, an honorary connection with the Laureateship, though not so direct as

---

[8] See Sybil Rosenfeld, *The Theatre of the London Fairs in the 18th Century*, Cambridge, 1960, and a brief discussion in my *Henry Fielding and the Augustan Ideal under Stress*, pp.213–14, 226. On Elkanah Settle's *Siege of Troy* (1707), and its importance in Pope's *Dunciad*, see Pat Rogers, 'Pope, Settle, and The Fall of Troy', *Studies in English Literature*, 15 (1975), 447–58.

[9] Byron's frequently quoted protestations to Thomas Medwin about the epic nature of *Don Juan* seem to me to be in the same spirit of jokey bravado (*Medwin's Conversations of Lord Byron*, ed. Ernest J. Lovell, Jr., Princeton, 1966, pp. 164–5).

[10] Shelley probably wrote his parody on the basis of reviews of Wordsworth's poem. An earlier parody, John Hamilton Reynolds's *Peter Bell. A Lyrical Ballad*, actually appeared before Wordworth's *Peter Bell* (see Reiman's discussion in *The Bodleian Shelley Manuscripts*, I.6–16.) Shelley's poem, which was not published until 1839, is sometimes seen as being in a similar spirit to Byron's *ottava rima* satires, and Mary Shelley felt impelled to deny an early reviewer's supposition that Byron had had a hand in it (*ibid*, pp. 12, 16n.28). Byron himself derided *Peter Bell*, partly in Dunciadic language, in *Don Juan*, III.c, and in an 'Epilogue' written on the first page of the prologue to Wordsworth's poem (*Complete Poetical Works*, IV.285–6, 517–18; A. E. H. Swaen, 'Peter Bell', *Anglia*, XLVII (1923), 146ff.; Leslie A. Marchand, *Byron: A Biography*, London, 1957, II.873 and notes p.95). In a letter of 31 August 1820, Byron jeered at 'Mr. Turdsworth's Peter Bell' (*Letters and Journals*, ed. Leslie A. Marchand, VII.167).

the *Dunciad*'s (but the *Dunciad* itself only came to the Laureateship second time round). In this poem, in which Peter, alias Wordsworth, goes to hell, one of the Devil's guises is said to be that of 'a bard bartering rhymes/For sack' (II.ii). There is jeering at Wordsworth's increasing alignment with the respectable (that is tyrannical and warmongering) establishment, which culminates in 'odes to the Devil' (VI.xxxvi). His consequent 'promotion' to a genteel sinecure (VII.i–viii) refers to the distributorship of stamps for Westmorland which Wordsworth obtained in 1813 (cf. *Don Juan*, Dedication, vi) but seems almost to hint, with prophetic accuracy, at a 'poetic justice' which was to make Wordsworth a suitable Laureate in the future.

As in the *Dunciad* the elevation is intimately bound up with Dulness:

> Peter was dull – he was at first
> Dull – Oh, so dull – so very dull!
> Whether he talked, wrote, or rehearsed –
> Still with this dulness was he cursed –
> Dull – beyond all conception – dull.   (VII.xi)

What has disappeared is the vast misshapen majesty of the Popeian Mighty Mother. Dulness is no longer an engulfing force of Miltonic dimensions, Daughter of Chaos and eternal Night, but reduced to chatty drawing-room proportions: 'Dull – Oh, so dull – so very dull!' If an Augustan analogue were to be sought, it would be in the low-key idiom of Swift's conversational travesties, and the cheeky rhyming of 'rehearsed/he cursed' is both Swiftian and Byronic. Byron took it from Swift (Swift, Byron said, 'beats us all hollow, his rhymes are wonderful').[11] Other Swiftian strains (not necessarily direct influences) in the poem include the portrayal of Peter as a canting dissenter, with 'eyes turned up' and 'a nasal twang' (I.ii):

> Turned to a formal Puritan,
> A solemn and unsexual man, –
> He half believed *White Obi*.   (VI.xix)

Swift didn't think puritans unsexual, though he exposed their pretences that way; and '*White Obi*' (or what Leigh Hunt spoke of as the 'methodistical nightmare' of Wordsworth's hero)[12] evokes that traditional satire of sectarian enthusiasts which Swift brought to its

---

[11] *His Very Self and Voice: Collected Conversations of Lord Byron*, ed. Ernest J. Lovell, Jr., New York, 1954, p.268.
[12] Swaen, 'Peter Bell', p.161. Hunt's review of Wordsworth's poem (*Examiner*, 3 May 1819) is reprinted in Swaen, pp.159–62.

wittiest culmination in the *Mechanical Operation of the Spirit*. Swift is
mentioned in the stanza after the one about Peter's Dulness, when
Peter is compared to a Struldbrug:

> No one could read his books – no mortal,
>   But a few natural friends, would hear him: –
> The parson came not near his portal; –
> His state was like that of the immortal
>   Described by Swift – no man could bear him. (VII.xii)

The mystifying pseudonymous 'Dedication' by Miching Mallecho,
with its Grub-Street-garret-joking, recalls *A Tale of a Tub* and its later
avatars: 'Pray excuse the date of place; so soon as the profits of this
publication come in, I mean to hire lodgings in a more respectable
street'. The words come, moreover, in a mock-nervous postscript in a
genre familiar from the *Tale*'s 'Apology' or the ending of the
Mechanical Operation, and there's some mock-learned footnoting in the
style broadly associated with Tubbaean or Dunciadic exercises.

Such generically Scriblerian routines don't call for particular
source seeking. As with Eliot's *Waste Land*, which had its origins in an
attempt to write mock-heroic couplets in the style of the *Rape of the
Lock*, and whose whole portrayal of cultural chaos has a Dunciadic
scope, there is behind Shelley's ostensibly Popeian structure a whole
system of local effects that are in a lower key and more specifically
traceable to Swift.[13] In Eliot it's a matter of satiric tone and of
scabrous detail, the 'drying combinations ... Stockings, slippers,
camisoles, and stays' (lines 225–7), which come more from 'The
Lady's Dressing Room' (lines 11ff) than from *The Rape of the Lock* (the
common source, in its way, of both Swift *and* Eliot). In Shelley, the
scope is also Dunciadic (the section 'Hell is a city much like London',
III.i, is followed as in the *Dunciad* by a satirical array of dunces from the
political and literary world), and the ostensible pretensions are epic:
'a *very heroic* poem' was how Shelley described it to Leigh Hunt in a
letter, and Shelley supplies the 'panorama view of hell' which Byron
promised in *Don Juan* and didn't get round to, offering instead the
London cantos of *Don Juan*. But Shelley pursued, as much in this
poem as in *Julian and Maddalo* (a poem about his relations with
Byron), a 'familiar style' or '*sermo pedestris* way' altogether foreign to

---

13 For further evidence on this point, see Rawson, 'The Nightmares of Strephon: Nymphs of the
City in the Poems of Swift, Baudelaire, Eliot', in *Order from Confusion Sprung*, pp.154ff., esp.
187–8n.23.

Dunciadic grandiloquence.[14] His more local evocations are often of
Swift, and it is consistent with Shelley's as well as Byron's low-key
conception of epic resonance that the Swift who rejected the 'lofty
style' should act as a catalyst in the use by both poets of a mock-heroic
idiom whose conceptual and to some extent formal character is more
readily associated with Pope.

Shelley is hardly a poet whom one would compare closely with
Eliot, who disliked him. But both poets in their mock-heroic enterprises belong to stages in cultural history when mock-heroic could no
longer act, as in Pope, in majestic and respectful homage to the heroic
original. Shelley's way is to trivialise the epic connection: not
nervously, like Cowper singing the sofa with eulogium due, but with a
confidence which (like Byron's) suffers from few or no residual epic
longings. If Pope is confident in his loyalty to epic, Shelley (and
Byron) seem confident the opposite way, where poor Cowper remains
stuck in between, coyly protesting both his seriousness and his
unseriousness, not with a bang but a whimper. When Shelley speaks
in the Dedication of the 'scene of my epic', though concerned with
'Hell and the Devil', as being 'in "this world which is"', deriding
Wordsworth's claims to have avoided 'supernatural machinery'; or
when he refers to his poem about Peter, the third treatment (after
Wordsworth and John Hamilton Reynolds) of this hero and as being
'like the *Iliad*' part of a 'series of cyclic poems'; or when he speaks of
'the full stop which closes the poem ... [as] being, like the full stops at
the end of the *Iliad* and *Odyssey*, a full stop of a very qualified import',
we are in a world of epic joking which is totally relaxed in its signalling
that no part of the mock-heroic idiom is anything but an act of
persiflage (the last example belongs with the Tubbaean or Shandean
project of letting the pen run on although there is nothing left to say,
and also with the inverse Shandeism of *Beppo*, which ends because the
'pen is at the bottom of the page'). When Garth or Pope ridiculed
Blackmore writing epics, the joke was at the idea of a puny modern
age pretending to grandeurs no longer available. But when Shelley, in
Hell the 'city much like London', reports on 'suppers of epic poets', it
is a passing glimpse of frivolous nonsense closer to *Beppo*'s Venice than
to the *Dunciad*'s bloated metropolis:

> And all these meet at levees; –
> Dinners convivial and political; –

[14] *Letters of Percy Bysshe Shelley*, ed. Frederick L. Jones, Oxford, 1964, II.134, 108, 196 (to Leigh
Hunt, 2 November and 15 August 1819, and to Charles Ollier, 14 May 1820).

Suppers of epic poets; – teas,
Where small talk dies in agonies; –
  Breakfasts professional and critical;

Lunches and snacks so aldermanic
  That one would furnish forth ten dinners . . .
                                                    (III.xii–xiii)

Even that last item, with its Dunciadic vision of aldermanic binges, lacks, as the references to aldermanic feasts and their Homeric prototypes in *Don Juan* lack, the enormity of Pope's gluttonous Lethe of city-dignitaries, and the cosmic torpor which they spread over the culture:

Now May'rs and Shrieves all hush'd and satiate lay,
  Yet eat, in dreams, the custard of the day. (*Dunciad* I.91–2)

Even the protracted account of a widespread onset of sleep at the end of Shelley's poem comes over merely as a 'drear ennui' (VII.xiii), with none of the massiveness of this single couplet, let alone Pope's larger orchestrations of the great yawn of gods and men (*Dunciad*, VI. 605–6).

Nevertheless, Shelley's hellscape should not be underestimated because of the surface frivolity, the mock-lyrical-ballad flatness of its stanza, or whatever. The theme of the great city as Hell receives at times an eloquent and laconic astringency which makes Pope's couplet seem almost genial by comparison:

Hell is a city much like London –
  A populous and a smoky city;
There are all sorts of people undone,
And there is little or no fun done;
  Small justice shewn, and still less pity.   (III.i).

The passage takes its place not only among the classic satirical accounts of the city, Juvenal's third and Boileau's sixth satires, Swift's 'Description' poems, Johnson's *London*, but specifically with those visions of a metropolitan inferno which we identify with Milton and Pope and Baudelaire and Eliot, in whose unreal city,

Under the brown fog of a winter dawn,
A crowd flowed over London Bridge, so many,
I had not thought death had undone so many.
                              (*Waste Land* lines 60ff)

Eliot, like Pope, used images of hell to bring out the urban nightmare, Pope mainly from Milton, Eliot mainly from Dante.

'Undone' reverberates, fortuitously or otherwise, from Shelley's poem, but Eliot's passage as a whole derives from Dante's *città dolente* in *Inferno* III.55–7:

> sì lunga tratta
> di gente, ch'io non averei creduto
> che morte tanta n'avesse disfatta.

Pope's Dunciadic London similarly gains its infernal resonances and its monstrous shapes from Milton's Hell and Milton's Chaos.

But if Pope and Eliot drew on Hell to portray the city, Milton and Shelley proceed the other way: the city is instead used to portray Hell. In *Paradise Lost* the comparison is both memorable and oddly brief. Satan, after prolonged exile in Hell, visits Eden:

> As one who long in populous City pent,
> Where Houses thick and Sewers annoy the Air,
> Forth issuing on a Summers Morn to breathe
> Among the pleasant Villages and Farms
> Adjoind, from each thing met conceives delight,
> The smell of Grain, or tedded Grass or Kine
> Or Dairie, each rural sight, each rural sound. (IX.445ff.)

It's a traditional country–city opposition, remarkable here mainly because the image of the city presented itself as an immediately available analogy for what Satan had been experiencing in Hell. It is so taken-for-granted as to be almost perfunctory. Milton doesn't offer much detail as to how a city might be like Hell, beyond noting populousness, confinement ('pent'), and bad atmospheric conditions: 'Where Houses thick and Sewers annoy the Air'. Shelley's 'populous and smoky city', though its phrasing echoes Milton's, is much more particularised. It's evident that Shelley is more concerned with cities than with Hell, while Milton, unlike Pope, or Shelley, or Eliot, isn't much concerned with cities at all.

A feature of Milton's passage has perhaps been unremarked, however. If you want to describe the horrors of the city, Hell may offer some useful support. If you want to describe Hell, cities might be a bit of a let-down, unless you raise the power of the city to the super-charged levels of apprehension which we variously encounter in the *Dunciad* or in Baudelaire or in Eliot, in whom the whole analogy is viewed from the other end of the telescope anyway. Milton could, like Shelley, have given more detail. He could in principle have gone the way of Pope; the argument that this would have been anachronistic in

Milton's story must be set against the fact that Milton allowed himself all the prophetic incursions into the future he chose. The germ of city-horror which helped him momentarily to actualise a sense of infernal unpleasantness wasn't developed, perhaps because that wasn't what seemed to Milton the most telling example of horror, but it was a beginning.

If there is any sense in Milton's glimpse of the city that the horrors of Hell invited a secularised representation, this might be consistent both with Milton's more generally awkward treatment of ineffable and superhuman phenomena in temporal and humanised terms, and with the persistent feeling we get in *Paradise Lost* that Milton was engaged in a critique of the heroic at the same time as writing the last distinguished European poem in the older epic mode. *Paradise Lost* is full of secularising elements, and full of uncertainty too as to whether Hell is to be conceived as a geographical place or a mental state (an issue Shelley addressed with Miltonic reminders, but with a radically trivialised reduction of scope). It is also a poem which many readers have seen as tantalisingly poised between transcendent sublimity and some brilliantly contained comic effects, often embodied in combination in the character of Satan, titanic villain–hero and comic butt. It is the only full-scale epic that includes mock-heroic resonances which prefigure the *Dunciad* not only in reverse, as we should expect, but also directly, as when:

> So eagerly the Fiend
> O'er bog or steep, through strait, rough, dense, or rare,
> With head, hands, wings or feet pursues his way,
> And swims or sinks, or wades, or creeps, or flies,   (ii.947ff.)

which Pope imitated and cited at *Dunciad* ii.63ff., describing Lintot who like 'a dab-chick waddles thro' the copse/On feet and wings, and flies, and wades, and hops' (ii.63–4).

Such ambivalences were a major issue for Milton, in whom mock-heroic was a minor strand, and they were a major issue for Pope, in whom mock-heroic was the *major* element. But when we compare Shelley's comparison of Hell to a city, we sense this ambivalence in a heightened or exacerbated form. Where Milton's comparison is 'perfunctory' in the sense that it gives little city detail, Shelley's is perfunctory in spite of a great deal of detail. In Shelley, as against Milton, the reversal of expectation (saying Hell is like London) comes over as a way of saying London is like Hell, just as in Pope (or in Eliot).

But, unlike Pope, Shelley shows no obvious interest in actualising the analogy, no real concern with an active play of infernal resonance, only a focus on the city in its specific secular unpleasantness, so that his reverse comparison functions as an extended rhetorical turn rather than as a fully realised epic fiction.

Shelley won't lightly let the Miltonic echoes and connections disappear, however. London evidently brought the anxiety of influence to the surface of his mind (though perhaps only the surface). In another poem which contains some of his pithiest literary-satirical formulations, the Horatian epistle known as the 'Letter to Maria Gisborne' (1820), Shelley wrote, a year later:

> You are now
> In London, that great sea whose ebb and flow
> At once is deaf and loud, and on the shore
> Vomits its wrecks, and still howls on for more.
> Yet in its depth what treasures! You will see
> That which was Godwin, – greater none than he
> Though fallen – and fallen on evil times – to stand
> Among the spirits of our age and land
> Before the dread Tribunal of *to come*
> The foremost ... while Rebuke cowers pale and dumb.
> You will see Coleridge – he who sits obscure
> In the exceeding lustre and the pure
> Intense irradiation of a mind
> Which, with its own internal lightning blind,
> Flags wearily through darkness and despair –
> A cloud-encircled meteor of the air,
> A hooded eagle among blinking owls.   (lines 193 ff)

The portraits, affectionate, not uncritical, finely ironic, and studiedly charged with Miltonic evocations, occur in a work which, like *Peter Bell the Third*, is memorable for its literary portraits, in both poems more fastidiously exact than the mushrooming fantastications of the *Dunciad*. Here more than in *Peter Bell the Third* a residue of grandeur is allowed to show itself, but the Miltonic resonances strike one as loose mythologising gestures, not deeply integrated into the poem's essentially conversational fabric (as in *Julian and Maddalo*, Shelley was not always able to sustain his *sermo pedestris* style).

When in *Peter Bell the Third* Shelley secularised and desublimated Hell, his immediate point as we saw was to joke about the Wordsworthian renunciation of the 'supernatural' in poetry, a renunciation Wordsworth makes a point of in the original *Peter Bell* (and related to what Coleridge reports on their respective roles in the *Lyrical Ballads* in chapter xiv of *Biographia Literaria*). And so when the poem gets to the Devil we have the following disclaimers:

> The Devil, I safely can aver,
>   Has neither hoof, nor tail, nor sting;
> Nor is he, as some sages swear,
> A spirit, neither here nor there,
>   In nothing – yet in every thing.
>
> He is – what we are; for sometimes
>   The Devil is a gentleman;
> At others a bard bartering rhymes
> For sack; a statesman spinning crimes;
>   A swindler, living as he can;
>
> A thief, who cometh in the night,
>   With whole boots and net pantaloons,
> Like some one whom it were not right
> To mention; or the luckless wight,
>   From whom he steals nine silver spoons.
>
> But in this case he did appear
>   Like a slop-merchant from Wapping,[15]
> And with smug face, and eye severe
> On every side did perk and peer
>   Till he saw Peter dead or napping.   (ii.i–iv)

It's a graceful patrician put-down, of the sort Byron also liked to make against Lake or Cockney poets: the last stanza belongs to a tradition which includes Swift's jibes at Dissenters or Fielding's at Richardson. (Shelley also capped his jeering by making Peter 'A footman in the Devil's service!' iv.i).

In the entire list of the Devil's guises, each a disreputable real-world type, there is one about whom nothing specific is said: 'sometimes/The Devil is a gentleman'. This is left dangling, where all the other types are specified in more or less contemptible *doings*: 'a stateman spinning crimes', 'A thief, who cometh in the night'. One may speculate that the gentleman is unscathed because, while disreputable in context and in company, there is an ironic hint of what we might call poetic class-loyalty to the type, as though Shelley wouldn't willingly traduce gentlemen when addressing a vulgarian like Wordsworth. There is,

---

[15] For the significance to Augustan satirists of Wapping as a sleazy district with sectarian associations, see John Arbuthnot, *The History of John Bull*, ed. Alan W. Bower and Robert A. Erickson, Oxford, 1976, p.169 n.35.

moreover, an amusing tendency, seen also in Byron's *Vision of Judgment,* to give comic glimpses of the Devil as a figure of patrician grace. The meeting between the Archangel Michael and Satan in Byron's *Vision* is perhaps the *locus classicus:*

> Yet still between his Darkness and his Brightness
> There passed a mutual glance of great politeness.

> The Archangel bowed, not like a modern beau,
>   But with a graceful Oriental bend, ...
> He turned as to an equal, not too low,
>   But kindly; Sathan met his ancient friend
> With more hauteur, as might an old Castilian
> Poor noble meet a mushroom rich civilian. (xxxv–xxxvi)

Such effects include an odd Augustan lordliness, but they are not wholly accounted for as put-downs for the lower poetic orders. There is a disengagement from the kind of harshly targeted hostility you find in the *hauteurs* of Swift or of Pope, and this probably is not only due to the fact that Shelley and Byron are more secure in their patrician standing and more relaxed in their gestures of lordliness. It is partly that they don't take their satirical purposes quite so seriously as Swift and Pope did, because the standard of gentlemanly morality in whose name the lordly accents are mustered has come to seem less absolute. Thus the lordly superiority to turpitude and folly has become culturally less not more secure as an instrument of moral judgment: the uppish urgencies of Swift and Pope are higher in their cultural and lower in their personal sense of lordly certitude.

Notice meanwhile what has become of Satan. He is now neither a titanic villain as in Milton, nor, as in both Milton and Pope, a grovelling 'familiar Toad' (*Epistle to Dr. Arbuthnot,* line 319), but an easy lordly charmer, cousin to Don Juan the 'inveterate Patrician' (*Don Juan,* xi.xlv) with his noble Castilian pride (v.civ) and his 'very graceful bow' (ix.lxxxiii) and also to Lambro, the pirate who has 'such true breeding of a gentleman,/You never could divine his real thought' (iii.xli). This will seem surprising to those who recall the Satanising heroes presented in sublime rebellion in some other works by Shelley or Byron: Prometheus, Cain, Lara, and that whole array of romantic villain–heroes whose creators were labelled the Satanic school by the Laureate Southey.[16] It has often been said that such

---

[16] Robert Southey, Preface to *A Vision of Judgment, Poetical Works,* Longman, etc., London n.d., x.205–6.

heroes of Romantic rebellion derive from Milton's Satan, and build on the perception (especially evident in some Romantic readers including Blake as well as both Shelley and Byron), of a secret Miltonic sympathy for the fallen angel, seen as a courageous and defiant adversary to authority.[17]

If this perception has substance (Dryden's view that Satan was the hero of *Paradise Lost* suggests that it was not wholly a Romantic aberration, though Dryden was probably insisting on Satan's centrality as a protagonist rather than on his moral attraction),[18] the blend of attitudes in Milton is finely balanced, not only between sublimity and mock-heroic ridicule but also between derogation and approval, rejection and admiration. Neither Shelley nor Byron could absorb such a mix. Their rebellious villain–heroes become simplified and unironic projections of the nobility of heroic defiance, including the readiness to carry guilt and endure punishment. They are not touched by humour, which is present in the Miltonic treatment and is radical to the Popeian version. What Shelley and Byron can not do (I think) is regard evil as simultaneously comic and deadly, or as simultaneously comic and noble, so that, while their serious treatments tend to be solemn, their comic treatments hive off into the domain of brilliant hard-edged frivolity which is represented by *Peter Bell the Third, Don Juan*, and the *Vision of Judgment*. If Pope's culture precluded a new Miltonic epic, it nevertheless took that epic seriously enough to adapt it to massive urgencies of satiric perception. Shelley and Byron not only did not take it seriously enough to risk the mixture. They transvaluated Milton's structure of moral authority, and created adversarial counterparts that do not move with enough certainty to contain their own critiques within them, let alone the sense of fun. Fun was to be had, if at all, elsewhere, in contexts where seriousness (whether of the Miltonic or the Dunciadic kind) could not be overtly accommodated.

So Satanic figures in Shelley or Byron can only become sublime rebels or comic charmers, never any genuine blend. This shows strikingly in the one possible exception, that domain of heroic suffering psychologised, where Milton's Satan understands that the limitless geography of hell is in part at least a function of his own mind:

[17] On Milton's influence on Byron's poems, see the good discussion in Jerome J. McGann, *Don Juan in Context*, London, 1976, chs. 2 and 3. For Byron on Milton's Satan, *Letters and Journals*, VIII.115, and Medwin, *Conversations*, pp.77–8, both cited by McGann at pp.24–5; Shelley on Satan, *Defence of Poetry*, in *Poetry and Prose*, p.498; Blake, *Marriage of Heaven and Hell*, Plate 6.

[18] Dryden, *Of Dramatic Poesy and Other Critical Essays*, II.233.

> Which way I flie is Hell; my self am Hell;
> And in the lowest deep a lower deep
> Still threatning to devour me opens wide,
> To which the Hell I suffer seems a Heav'n
>
> *(Paradise Lost* IV.75–8)

and especially:

> The mind is its own place, and in it self
> Can make a Heav'n of Hell, a Hell of Heav'n. (I.254–5)

This is the kind of utterance which we expect to find in Shelleyan or Byronic heroes of the non-satiric kind, and which we might suppose both poets likely to be especially attracted to. It is, of all items in the Miltonic inheritance, the one closest to a frame of mind which both poets could readily internalise, and has been shown to be particularly active in the Byron of *Cain* and *Manfred*.[19] But what Milton had presented as the inescapable ubiquity of damnation, and as a predicament of suffering on a cosmic scale, turns in *Peter Bell the Third* to a narrowed state of mind, confined by parodic purposes and chiefly insisted on in order to harp on Wordsworth's have-it-both-ways anti-supernaturalism and one or two other items of Wordsworthian rhetoric. The idea that hell is everywhere, for example, turns up in the secularising stanzas about the Devil having no 'hoof, nor tail' and being embodied in common human types (II.iff).

A more interesting quasi-sympathetic projection of the idea of turning a Hell into Heaven occurs in a stanza about Coleridge which may be set beside the Miltonising phrases of the 'Letter to Maria Gisborne':

> This was a man who might have turned
>   Hell into Heaven – and so in gladness
> A Heaven unto himself had earned;
> But he in shadows undiscerned
>   Trusted, – and damned himself to madness.   (V.iii)

If the satire seems to turn sentimental and unfocused, this is not mainly because of Shelley's obviously ambivalent feelings about Coleridge. His feelings about Wordsworth were just as ambivalent, but the stanzas about Wordsworth's poems which follow (V.viff.) show an acute sense of strengths and weaknesses in Wordsworth's writings, and are literary criticism of a high order. A likelier cause is

---

[19] For Byron's exploitation of Milton's lines in *Cain* and *Manfred*, see McGann, *Don Juan in Context*, pp.32–3, 36–7.

that the language used about Coleridge here picks up precisely that area in Milton's presentation of Satan to which Shelley (and Byron) would be disposed to respond with particular self-implication. Indeed, an earlier stanza honorifically applies the same Satanic phrases to Shelley himself and the idealistic reformers who were his friends:

> And some few, like we know who,
>   Damned – but God alone knows why –
> To believe their minds are given
> To make this ugly Hell a Heaven;
>   In which faith they live and die. (III.xx)

The appropriation of Satan's predicament teeters between an exalted self-pity and derision of a directionless sort, and 'like we know who' is simperingly sub-Shandean. A fussy gravity invades a satiric idiom whose normal effects tend to be laconic and flattening, and strengthens the suspicion that Shelley, more than Byron, can only be satirical in a wholly externalised mode: where anything of himself is introduced, the result has to be total seriousness or awkward muddle. In *Peter Bell the Third* he generally avoided both, but it is interesting that his collapse into the latter occurs in the one area of Miltonising mock-heroic where the original language of Satan might have felt particularly close to ideals of his own, whether of introspective heroism or of ardour to change the world. For once Milton cannot be confidently joked about, while the immediate context precludes an easy retreat into the high mode of *Prometheus Unbound* or of Byron's non-satiric poems.

To students of mock-heroic it is a further paradox worth pondering that Shelley's critique of Wordsworth as a poet has few moments of grandeur, or mock-grandeur, in the mode of Pope's treatment of Cibber or Blackmore. Unlike Shelley, Pope is never appreciative of his Dunciadic victims. But nothing Shelley says in praise or blame of Wordsworth has the resonance of Pope's majestic tonalities of celebrative rejection, of Cibber's 'brazen, brainless brothers' or 'sonorous Blackmore's strain', let alone the reverberating Miltonic orchestration of Dulness' universal darkness burying all. Shelley's treatment, even at its most jeering, is more complimentary than anything Pope says about these. Mixed feelings come over not as grandeurs collapsing into bathos, but in flip low-key diminutions:

> And these obscure remembrances
> Stirred such harmony in Peter,
> That, whensoever he should please,
> He could speak of rocks and trees
> In poetic metre.   (v.x)

It is partly, and only partly, a matter of Wordsworth's constant insistence on humble subjects and ordinary language, and, if he protested that sublimity might be achieved through these, Shelley's tactic is not so much to mimic this through an inverse grandeur of bombast, as Pope might have done, but instead to flatten it to a muddled banality:

> He had also dim recollections
> Of pedlars tramping on their rounds,
> Milk pans and pails, and odd collections
> Of saws, and proverbs, and reflexions
> Old parsons make in burying-grounds.   (v.xii)

Shelley is jeering at Wordsworth's bids to make the prosaic sublime. It's one of the oddities of literary history that such details only became sublime again much later by what almost seems like an unparodying of the parody, as in the last stanza of Yeats' 'Circus Animals Desertion', where 'masterful images' begin in low places:

> Those masterful images because complete
> Grew in pure mind but out of what began?
> A mound of refuse or the sweepings of a street,
> Old kettles, old bottles, and a broken can,
> Old iron, old bones, old rags, that raving slut
> Who keeps the till. Now that my ladder's gone
> I must lie down where all the ladders start
> In the foul rag and bone shop of the heart,

or in Wallace Stevens' 'Large Red Man Reading':

> There were those that returned to hear him read from the
>   poem of life,
> Of the pans above the stove, the pots on the table, the tulips
>   among them ...
>
> *Poesis, poesis*, the literal characters, the vatic lines ...

It is almost as though Yeats or Stevens had taken Shelley's lines and written in defiance of them. It's unlikely that this happened, but

Yeats especially has been known overtly to pick up an idiom of derision or parody, and *un*parody or rewrite it upwards.

It is instructive in this connection to note that both Byron and Yeats did their own versions of Dryden's famous portrait of Zimri in *Absalom and Achitophel*:

> A man so various, that he seem'd to be
> Not one, but all Mankinds Epitome.
> . . .
> Was Chymist, Fidler, States-Man, and Buffoon:
> Then all for Women, Painting, Rhyming, Drinking;
> Besides ten thousand freaks that dy'd in thinking.
>
> (lines 545ff.)

By coincidence, Dryden's lines have here a peculiarly Byronic cadence, and Byron seems to have remembered the passage, in his portrait of Suwarrow:

> For the man was, we safely may assert,
>   A thing to wonder at beyond most wondering;
> Hero, buffoon, half-demon, and half-dirt,
>   Praying, instructing, desolating, plundering.[20]
>
> (*Don Juan* vii.lv)

Byron retains Dryden's derision, but not the ideal of the Renaissance complete man against which the derision had been played off. When Yeats picked up the passage in 'In Memory of Major Robert Gregory', he discarded derision altogether, and restored the heroic ideal, resublimating Dryden's mockery into the portrait of Gregory, 'Our Sidney and our perfect man':

> Soldier, scholar, horseman, he,
> As 'twere all life's epitome.

This is one of the strangest and least studied mutations of mock-heroic. It begins in the mock-majesties which were valued because they retained a residue of original grandeurs: the classic fruition of this phase is the *Dunciad*. It has connections with the Shandean enterprise of taking Swift's mockery of moderns in *A Tale of a Tub* and outfacing it in self-assertive mimicry which is a recurrent subtheme in this book. But the Yeatsian process seems less commonly noted. In this development original grandeurs are not preserved, but restored, and original

---

[20] See the discussion in A. B. England, *Byron's Don Juan*, pp. 53–5. For another use by Byron of the portrait of Zimri, see Rawson, '"Beppo" and "Absalom and Achitophel": A Parallel', *Notes and Queries*, 209 (1964), 25.

derisions are not outfaced but discarded. A revaluation has taken place, not as in mock-heroic, downwards, but in the opposite direction, upwards, in a species of mock-mock-heroic. The two mocks cancel out, as two negatives do in logic, but as seldom happens in poetry: for, if Drydenian or Dunciadic mock-heroic preserved elements of the old heroic majesty, the Yeatsian mock-version does not preserve the mockery, but resublimates the whole effect. It is an extension, perhaps, of that Shelleyan or Byronic inability to sustain a live and serious ambivalence in those domains where the heroic and the derisive might interact. It took a later age, further removed than they were from Augustan inhibition, to reactivate heroic idiom on unheroic subjects, in the teeth of an accumulated tradition of mockery. In the readiness to assume heroic accents straight, if in nothing else, this may be thought to stretch back before Dryden to Milton himself.

But there is a shorter and more immediate leap to be made, from Milton to Shelley and Byron, where Pope and his generation differ in their own ways from earlier and later stages. This is the area occupied by the subject of war, in two of its guises: the heroic ethos of martial prowess, held up for admiration in traditional military epic, and the awkward fact of war in history, past or present. It is, as I have argued elsewhere, a peculiarity of Augustan mock-heroic that one hardly ever sees any kind of warfare in the major or distinguished examples.[21] This is surprising because the principal heroic originals, and in particular the *Iliad* and the *Aeneid*, have war as their central subject matter. In Boileau's *Lutrin*, or Garth's *Dispensary*, or Swift's *Battle of the Books*, or Pope's *Rape of the Lock*, there are formal simulacra of an unsanguinary kind: learned quarrels among divines, or medics, or men of letters, and a comic battle of the sexes among the flirty *jeunesse dorée* of the Catholic gentry. The *Dunciad* is even more remarkable, since it lacks even this element of ghostly imitation. The poem uses every rhetorical routine associated with classical or Miltonic epics, including an Odyssean or Aenean journey from East to West, a visit to the Underworld, and a parody of heroic sports. But there is no fighting.

As I argued in chapter 3, this military *pudeur* proceeds from an inverse anxiety of influence, timorous of allowing the revered heroic poems to be contaminated by their traditional subject matter, now increasingly felt to be disreputable. Pope declaimed against the

[21] 'Pope's *Waste Land*: Reflections on Mock-Heroic', in *Order from Confusion Sprung*, pp.205–6.

shocking spirit of cruelty in Homer's battles, and he suppressed much of the gory material in his translation. The mock-heroic mode purported not to attack the epic but to pay it homage, by playing its grandeurs off against a lapsed or subheroic modern world. But in pursuing this aim it continually risked self-subversion from reminders of epic's martial values: and especially so in a context of prevailing irony or derision, where cherished positives might pick up a secondary infection from the low life whose company they are made to keep.

The problem of epic and war had already, as is well known, troubled Milton. He was writing not a mock-epic, but a full-scale original, and he was not only the last author of a great classical epic, but also (and the facts are connected) the first major epic writer to have to reconcile his prosecution of a martial genre with a strongly felt dislike of war and of the celebration of war. He met the problem not by omission (as the Augustan mock-heroic writers did), but by a continuous and overt critique of the martial ethos from within: asserting that *his* subject is 'Not less but more heroic' than those of combative epics, than 'the wrauth/ Of Stern *Achilles* ... or rage/Of *Turnus* for *Lavinia* disespous'd' (IX.14–17), and declaring his poor opinion of 'Warrs, hitherto the onely Argument/Heroic deemd' (IX.28–9). But Milton also (unlike the later, mock-heroic writers) offered a major martial episode at the centre of his poem. The war in Heaven is by definition one not open to censure like human wars. But Milton courted difficulties by presenting the military business insistently and graphically, and simultaneously circumvented some of the awkwardness by making sure no one was killed, since the participants were immortal (VI.434). Even Satan's spectacular wound releases not blood but a 'Nectarous humor' (VI.332: an idea Byron played with in *Vision of Judgment*, xxv) and, like Aphrodite's wound in the prototype passage in *Iliad* v.339ff, 416ff, is immediately healed anyway.[22] Both these items of Miltonic precaution were amusingly appropriated in the *Rape of the Lock*, the first at v.43–4, when the battle in which no one will die except in the sexual sense is about to begin:

> No common Weapons in their Hands are found,
> Like Gods they fight, nor dread a mortal Wound,

and the second at III.151–2, when the Sylph guarding Belinda's lock is cut 'in twain,/(But Airy Substance soon unites again)'.

[22] See Rawson, 'Byron's *Vision of Judgment*, xxv, Pope, and Hobbes's Homer', *Byron Journal*, II (1983), 48–51, and *Order from Confusion Sprung*, p.206.

Milton thus has it both ways, presenting a traditional epic subject matter and structure while simultaneously condemning previous treatments; and offering a grim battle that is 'unreal' in human terms and free of the disreputability that normally attends warfare in his eyes. The unrealising effects of this treatment are compounded in the account of gunpowder combat. The spectacular anachronism involved in the portrayal of modern technological warfare in a pre-human battle among celestial beings rests partly on the traditional notion that gunpowder was the invention of the Devil. But the portrayal has a graphic particularity, a species of military realism, which are in dramatic and pictorial effect bizarre beyond Disneyan fantasy. It is paradoxical features of this kind that animate Milton's treatment of war, enabling him to retain the military business and even the martial partisanships of heroic poetry while mounting a massive onslaught on the morality of war and the traditional values of epic. He not only reports on the evil technology where he need not have done, rather than avoiding it as the mock-heroic writers were to do (with minor exceptions, including a passing mention in the *Battle of the Books*)[23] but rubs it in anachronistically and revels in the portrayal. In this sense, though he is writing a straight epic, Milton is less protective of that genre than are the authors of the mock-form. (The more extended discussion of gunpowder in *Gulliver's Travels* is held outside the epic's range of associations, and thus does not arise as a problem). There is no gunpowder combat in the *Rape of the Lock* or the *Dunciad*, or in the *Dispensary* or *Le Lutrin*. But it reemerges in a Miltonic allusion in Byron's *Vision of Judgment*:

> Infernal thunder shook both sea and land
>   In all the planets, and hell's batteries
> Let off the artillery, which Milton mentions
>   As one of Sathan's most sublime inventions.   (lii)

The reminder is jokey, like some of Shelley's flip Miltonisms. But, despite the relatively genial satiric context, there are in Byron's poem and also in Shelley's some very harsh reminders of modern war: the military disreputability of George III's reign erupts as early as Stanza v, with its report of thousands of daily deaths culminating in the 'crowning carnage, Waterloo'. And, just as Byron reminded the

---

[23] See *Battle of the Books*, in *A Tale of a Tub*, ed. A. C. Guthkelch and D. Nichol Smith, 2nd end., Oxford, 1958, p.236 and n.6; there is a chemical explosion in Garth's *Dispensary* (1699), III.232 (*Poems on Affairs of State. Volume 6: 1697–1704*, ed. Frank H. Ellis, New Haven, 1970, p.91). See above, pp. 64–5.

Poet Laureate Southey of the ugly realities of the reign of the monarch he has been celebrating, so Shelley in *Peter Bell the Third* attacks Wordsworth and specifically his celebration of Waterloo in the 'Thanksgiving Ode':

> Then Peter wrote Odes to the Devil; –
> In one of which he meekly said: –
> 'May Carnage and Slaughter,
> Thy niece and thy daughter,
> May Rapine and Famine,
> Thy gorge ever cramming,
> Glut thee with liiving and dead!'   (VI.xxxxvi)

Wordsworth had written rather sanctimoniously of righteous slaughter in God's name: 'Yea, Carnage is thy daughter'. Byron, like Shelley, picked up the phrase in *Don Juan* VIII.ix: '"Carnage" (so Wordsworth tells you) "is God's daughter".' Wordsworth eventually removed the line in 1845.

The fact that some mealy-mouthed texts by Southey or Wordsworth existed to trigger these reactions is almost beside the point. Such a hostile reminder of contemporaneous warfare would be unthinkable in the Augustan mock-heroic writers, whose only historically attested fights are the clerical or medical or learned or flirty imbroglios which are allegorised in their mock-epic productions. Milton had indeed mentioned gunpowder war, but on an unreal and unsanguinary plane, with no strong specific applications from human history past or present. There is an overwhelming sense of 'war-in-general' about the sequence, quite as much as in Gulliver's generalised war-descriptions in Books II and IV. But in the work of Shelley and of Byron it's an insistent theme, very closely interwoven with mock-epic gesturing.

The siege of Ismail is the *locus classicus* in *Don Juan*, with Suwarrow the Russian general 'lecturing on the noble art of killing' (VII.lviii), and with Jonathan-Wild-like ironies about heroes, as when Suwarrow feels a momentary stirring of pity:

> however habit sears
> Men's hearts against whole millions, when their trade
> Is butchery, sometimes a single sorrow
> Will touch even Heroes, and such was Suwarrow.   (VII.lxix)

There is a comic list of combatants, which imitates Homeric enumerations, including Russians with unpronounceable names of 'twelve consonants a-piece' (VII.xiv–xvii) and 'several Englishmen of pith,/ Sixteen called Thomson, and nineteen named Smith' (VII.xviii). When the fighting gets started, there is more Homeric reminder, as when the battle is compared to what it might have been in the *Iliad* had gunpowder been available:

> The work of Glory still went on
>   In preparations for a cannonade
> As terrible as that of Ilion,
>   If Homer had found mortars ready made;
> But now, instead of slaying Priam's son,
>   We only can but talk of escalade,
> Bombs, drums, guns, bastions, batteries, bayonets, bullets,
> Hard words, which stick in the soft Muses' gullets. (VII.lxxviii)

It is a type of entranced listing which we may associate with Gulliver boasting about war-technology to the King of Brobdingnag or Master Houyhnhnm, but there studiously avoiding all epic reminder while Byron rubs it in. The next two stanzas (VII.lxxix–lxxx) repeatedly apostrophise 'eternal Homer':

> Oh, thou eternal Homer! I have now
>   To paint a siege, wherein more men were slain,
> With deadlier engines and a speedier blow,
>   Than in thy Greek gazette of that campaign;
> And yet, like all men else, I must allow,
>   To vie with thee would be about as vain
> As for a brook to cope with Ocean's flood;
> But still we Moderns equal you in blood.   (VII.lxxx)

There is a handsome compliment to Homer, but no more question of a hushed elevation ('thy Greek gazette of that campaign' more or less affectionately downgrades Homer, whereas Swift's parallel piece of mock-heroic and mock-journalese, 'the Full and True Account of the Battel Fought last Friday' serves to mock newspapers and protect Homer).

'Gazette' comes over with reverberations of Scriblerian scorn of journalists: see, for example, *Dunciad* II.314 and the notes of both Scriblerus and Pope. It is a frequent word in *Don Juan*, particularly obsessive in the siege cantos, where Byron accentuates the official Gazettes' special role as necrologies of war. Byron is playfully, but I think insultingly, assimilating Homer to the shoddy ephemera of 'daily scribes', not separating him from these in Swift's manner. It is interesting in this connection that Samuel Johnson thought Joseph

Warton's description of Addison's poem *The Campaign* as a 'Gazette in Rhyme' was particularly contemptuous, 'with harshness not often used by the good-nature of his criticism'.[24]

In the same place, Johnson describes Addison's poem as a departure from the epic habit of celebrating 'personal prowess, and "mighty bone"', and concentrating instead on Marlborough's virtues of cool judgment and tactical generalship. Scott later said 'Addison was the first poet who ventured to celebrate a victorious general for skill and conduct' rather than dealing with the old kind of individual heroic prowess,[25] a procedure held by some to be radically contrary to epic. There seems to have been a belief that modern war was unsuitable for epic treatment precisely because its technologies make strategic expertise more important than personal heroism.[26]

It is interesting at all events to see Addison the Whig celebrant demystifying the heroic in this fashion, while the Tory mock-heroic writers tried to omit mention of war altogether. Steele, in *Tatler* No. 6, amused himself by 'putting the Actions of *Homer's Iliad* into an exact Journal', very much in a contrary spirit to the mock-journalese of Swift's *Battle* five years before.[27] It is of a piece with this kind of readiness to speak of heroic warfare in everyday or journalistic terms that Steele also made a point of noting the military actions performed in the current war 'by Men of private Characters, or Officers of lower Stations' (*Tatler*, No. 56).[28] Byron cheerfully extends this unheroic practice to his epic, with its jeering replacement of Homeric lists of leaders by Byron's own famous lists of common soldiers' names, including the unpronounceable Russian ones and the British Thomsons and Smiths, until he is defeated by sheer numbers. These 'Would form a lengthy lexicon of glory,/And what is worse still, a much longer story' (VIII.xvii), so that the matter has to be resolved journalistically:

> And therefore we must give the greater number
> To the Gazette – which doubtless fairly dealt
> By the deceased, who lie in famous slumber
> In ditches, fields, or wheresoe'er . . .   (VIII.xviii)

---

[24] Samuel Johnson, 'Addison', in *Lives of the English Poets*, ed. G. Birkbeck Hill, Oxford, 1905, II.128–9. See Joseph Warton, *An Essay on the Genius and Writings of Pope*, 4th edn., 1782, I.30.

[25] *The Works of John Dryden*, ed. Walter Scott, 1808, IV.3.

[26] See Dustin Griffin, *Regaining Paradise: Milton and the Eighteenth Century*, Cambridge, 1986, p.50. I have not, however, been able to confirm Griffin's ascription of this view to Goldsmith, his specific reference being evidently incorrect.

[27] *Tatler*, ed. Donald F. Bond, Oxford, 1987, I.56.

[28] *Tatler*, I. 395; cf. also No. 87, II.48ff.

There is no attempt here to protect the hallowed forms of epic from association with the military squalors you read of in the papers, nor any sign of the common Augustan project of separating Homer from history. Homer may not have had the advantage of gunpowder, but when Byron boasts that 'still we Moderns equal you in blood', it is part of his point that Homer was very gory too. As the reflections on the siege continue, we see a readiness not to distinguish between epic deeds and historical horrors, ancient and modern:

> Oh, ye great bulletins of Bonaparte!
>   Oh, ye less grand long lists of killed and wounded!
> Shade of Leonidas, who fought so hearty,
>   When my poor Greece was once, as now, surrounded!
> Oh, Caesar's Commentaries! now impart ye,
>   Shadows of glory! (lest I be confounded)
> A portion of your fading twilight hues,
> So beautiful, so fleeting, to the Muse.
>
> When I call 'fading' martial immortality,
>   I mean, that every age and every year,
> And almost every day, in sad reality,
>   Some sucking hero is compelled to rear,
> Who, when we come to sum up the totality
>   Of deeds to human happiness most dear,
> Turns out to be a butcher in great business,
> Afflicting young folks with a sort of dizziness.
>
> (VII.lxxxii–lxxxiii)

Byron's peculiar brand of jokeyness is painful. But its pain is over human suffering, not the status of epic. Byron may have any amount of affection for Homer's poem, and of acceptance that 'to vie with [him] would be about as vain/ As for a brook to cope with Ocean's flood.' But harsh exposures of war are harsh exposures of Homer, and the joking bruises Homeric dignity without blunting the disparagement of carnage.

Again and again Byron goes out of his way to jeer at sentimental disconnections in which epics are supposed to be one thing and slaughter another:

> Yet I love Glory; – glory's a great thing; –
>   Think what it is to be in your old age
> Maintained at the expense of your good king;
>   A moderate pension shakes full many a sage,
> And heroes are but made for bards to sing,
>   Which is still better; thus in verse to wage

123

> Your wars eternally, besides enjoying
> Half-pay for life, make mankind worth destroying.
>
> (VIII.xiv)

> these rhymes
> A little scorched at present with the blaze
> Of conquest and its consequences, which
> Make Epic poesy so rare and rich   (VIII.xc)

The claim which had been made in the cheerful nonsense of Canto I ('My poem's epic, and is meant to be') is taken up here and at the end of VIII, with all the grim business of the siege ringing in our ears:

> Reader! I have kept my word, – at least so far
> As the first Canto promised. You have now
> Had sketches of love, tempest, travel, war –
> All very accurate, you must allow,
> And *Epic*, if plain truth should prove no bar;
> For I have drawn much less with a long bow
> Than my forerunners. Carelessly I sing,
> But Phoebus lends me now and then a string.
>
> (VIII.cxxxviii)

The carelessness, the easy surface, is, like Shelley's, very insulting where it wants to be, and the Muse of Epic surely ends up with her reputation in tatters, while no intelligent reader would ever be taken in by Byron's protestation that he is courting her. He is not attacking her in the ordinary sense, and he doubtless goes on loving his Homer. But history, ancient and modern, has been allowed to demonstrate that heroic fables are not pretty.

History, fact have played a dual, complementary role in this context. In Milton and more especially in Swift and in Pope, epic is partly kept insulated from the brute facts which would impair its standing. Addison's remark about Homer's Achilles, that he was 'Morally Vicious, and only Poetically Good' (*Spectator*, No. 548), reminds us that the supremacy of epic resided in a distinction between works of art and real-life deeds, and the essential project (for which Byron and Shelley had no use, but which was vital to Swift, Pope or Fielding) was to shield the former from the latter. Hence the silence about war in mock-heroic, or the silence about epic in Swift's attacks on war.

But, if history could release disturbing suspicions of epic, it could also be used to allay them. This is not much in evidence in the time of Byron or Shelley, when the need to shield the standing of epic from

disrepute no longer exerted any significant pressure, but it is powerfully evident in the work of Pope and Fielding. It springs not only from
perceptions like Addison's about Achilles or like Cowley's comment as
early as 1656 that 'a warlike, various, and a tragical age is best to *write
of*, but worst to *write in*'.[29] A large part of the Homer debate in Pope's
day was concerned with the barbarity of the age in which Homer
wrote, or that which he depicted, and with the saving distinctions that
might be made between the greatness of the poetry and the disreputability of the material. This is not quite the simple distinction
between the order of art and the order of fact which it may seem. For
history is a loose concept which may refer both to events, facts, *and* to
the writing which records them. And among those who expressed the
deep uneasy admiration of epic which lies at the heart of Pope's
Homeric translations or the *Dunciad* or Fielding's *Jonathan Wild*, both
these notions of history could be used as lightning conductors,
absorbing and diverting disparagements which would otherwise
strike mortally (as came to happen in Byron) at the edifice of a
cherished loyalty.

Aristotle's famous distinction between poetry and history, according to which poetry was of more universal import than history (*Poetics*,
ix; 1451b), offered a traditional formula for downgrading history
which Fielding made use of in *Joseph Andrews*, III.i, and to which
Wordworth alluded in grander and cloudier terms in the Preface to
the *Lyrical Ballads*.[30] A related distinction, which Wordsworth also
voiced, was between 'Poetry and Matter of Fact, or Science'.
Although there is a logical extension which would, as W. J. B. Owen
expresses it, include 'in general truth . . . what is factually true, merely
because it is true', the impulse to assert the distinction is sustained by a
traditional contempt for mere particulars, and for types of utterance
that aim or are content to report facts for no other reason than that
they are facts.[31]

This partly accounts for the tendency, especially strongly marked
among such Augustan humanists as Swift, Pope, and Fielding, to
despise mere chroniclers and journalists, historians of ephemeral and
day-to-day facts (Byron's 'daily scribes'), and even to identify them
with the essential ephemerality of any historical fact, and therefore of

[29] See above, chapter 3, nn. 43, 89.
[30] See *Prose Works of William Wordsworth*, ed. W. J. B. Owen and Jane Worthington Smyser,
Oxford, 1974, I.139, 179; W. J. B. Owen, *Wordsworth as Critic*, Toronto 1969, pp.88ff.
[31] *Prose Works*, I.135, 140–1, 174, 181–2; *Wordsworth as Critic*, p.96.

history as the written record of such things. Byron turned the tables on this, as we saw, by speaking of Homer's *Iliad* as a gazette and thus downgrading epic writers themselves to gazetteers. A similar irony in inverse form was to say that the claim that *Don Juan* was epic could stand only 'if plain truth should prove no bar' (VIII.cxxxvii). Feeding into this and cutting across the distinction between the order of fact and the order of art is a habit of not distinguishing, linguistically, between history and story (as in Latin *historia*, or French *histoire*): a convergence which C. S. Lewis spoke of as surviving into the Middle Ages, when, he said, 'the very words *story* and *history* had not yet been desynonymised',[32] but which surely lasted longer than that, and which still leads, in our own time, to Lucian's most famous work being translated variously as *True History* or *True Story*, an ironic phenomenon apt to an ironic title.

'Medieval' confusion on such a point is more or less an Augustan synonym for barbarism, directly assimilable to modern duncery, and the full reverberation of scorn for a benighted age occurs in Pope's note in the *Dunciad* on Caxton, one of 'The Classics of an Age that heard of none' (I.148). Caxton's 'rude' English is part of the Gothick decor, but the essential point is that Caxton is identified as 'A Printer [who] . . . translated into prose *Virgil*'s *Aeneis* as a History; of which he speaks in his Proeme in a very singular manner, as of a book hardly known'. 'A Printer' recalls Horace Walpole on Richardson's novels: 'pictures of high life as conceived by a bookseller' (to Sir Horace Mann, 20 December 1764). Translating epic into prose, as a 'history', a daily or journalistic history, is what Swift had done in the *Battle of the Books*, 'A Full and True Account of the Battel Fought last Friday', protectively deflecting parody of epic into parody of journalism. The burden of Pope's charge is that low-class 'medieval' Caxton joins modern dunces in pulling down cherished majesties; this includes the drop into prose, the miscellaneous alleged ignorance of the nature of the *Aeneid*, and the conversion of it into 'history', whether as fact or fiction who can tell, both being in their way disreputable.

The issue becomes further complicated when in Pope's and in Fielding's time novels start to call themselves 'histories', in straight bids for verisimilitude or as ironic travesties of such bids, and when 'history' pretending to truth was therefore openly used to advertise fiction or lies (*histoire*, the history/story confusion, re-entering by the back door of a coy self-awareness). Fielding's practice is to downgrade

---

[32] C. S. Lewis, *The Discarded Image*, Cambridge, 1964, p.179.

'history' in the name of 'epic' or 'comic epic'; to scorn mere chroniclers (in fact or fiction) as 'daily and weekly Historians' (*Tom Jones*, III.i); and yet to put *History* on the title pages of the very novels in which all these takes and double-takes are taking place.

Part of Fielding's subtext is concerned to strike against the phony authentications of fiction, the lies that pass for fact in Grub Street as much as the 'to the moment' immediacies and the pretence of documentary integrity in the Richardsonian novel in letters. If 'history' can't even guarantee to be truthful, what is left? But if it's true, it's even worse. A nasty fact like mass killing is nastier than a poem on the subject. You may say there is inconsistency or even confusion in this cauldron of strongly held views (often held by the same person in varying combinations), but the history of ideas has never been strong on logic. If the siege of Ismail is like Homer, as Byron said, you could, as Byron did, leave it unnervingly at that. But, if you wished to shield Homer from the disrepute, you could attribute the badness to the times or whatever, with Homer's art transcending history. And if this proved hard to sustain in practice, you could divert the focus on heroic deeds from epic to history, from Achilles to Alexander or Aeneas to Caesar.

In the last stages of Augustan mock-heroic, history came to the aid of epic in this way. In Fielding's *Jonathan Wild*, heroic reminder shifts constantly from epic heroes and 'heroic' assertions to the historical Alexander and Caesar, and from the poets Homer and Virgil to historians like Plutarch. The most striking example, which I have cited elsewhere, occurs in Fielding's *Jonathan Wild*, where Fireblood is ironically described as Wild's *fidus Achates*, but where as soon as this Virgilian association is made, Fielding also makes the decisive correction: 'or rather the Hephaestion of our Alexander' (III.iv).[33] By this time, however, there are forces which work to collapse the distinction. When we read that Jonathan Wild 'was a passionate admirer of heroes, particularly of Alexander the Great' (I.iii), we may think we know where we stand. But in the same chapter we also learn that as a schoolboy he loved to hear the epic poets translated and was, for example, 'wonderfully pleased with that passage in the eleventh Iliad where Achilles is said to have bound two sons of Priam upon a mountain, and afterwards to have released them for a sum of money. This was, he said, alone sufficient to refute those who affected a contempt for the wisdom of the ancients' (I.iii). Here, the rot has been

[33] Rawson, *Henry Fielding and the Augustan Ideal under Stress*, pp. 153–4.

allowed in. Wild's love of Homer is not the same as Fielding's, but if Wild can love Homer there must be something wrong: the episodes he admired are, after all, present in the epic poets.

That removal of the difference between ill deeds in epic and in history, which is so harpingly evident in Byron, is already in Fielding rearing its head as a ghastly possibility, and within a few years Fielding was announcing in the Preface to the *Voyage to Lisbon* that 'I must confess I should have honoured and loved Homer more had he written a *true history of his own times in humble prose*, than those noble poems that have so justly collected the praise of all ages' (my italics). Contrast Swift's or Pope's view of the offensiveness of reducing epic to either history *or* humble prose, in the *Battle of the Books* or the note on Caxton, and also Pope's scorn of the indistinguishability of poetry and prose in the work of the dunces (*Dunciad*, 1.189–90, 274): a species of Augustan *hauteur* which survives in Byron's comment on Wordsworth 'Who, both by precept and example, shows/That prose is verse, and verse is merely prose' (*English Bards*, lines 241–2). But Byron is also ready, as Pope or Fielding could not be, to jeer at epic expectation by contaminating it systematically with the 'plain truth' of modern warfare, and *Don Juan* opens with a roll-call of heroes who are precisely of the historical sort, 'the butcher Cumberland' or 'Buonaparté and Dumourier/ Recorded in the Moniteur and Courier' (1.ii), the ruling or conquering thugs who are the modern counterparts of Alexander or Caesar and who regularly come in and out, 'cloying the gazettes with cant' (1.i). Nothing stands in the way of identifying them with epic heroes or of suggesting that the latter differ only in having been lucky enough to get into poems, a distinction which seemed as trivial to Byron as it was important to Pope: 'Brave men were living before Agamemnon/ And since .../ But then they shone not on the poet's page' (1.v).

It would be amusing to think that in Fielding's yearnings for a 'true history . . . in humble prose', Clio was getting some retribution for the humiliations which he and other Augustan writers had been inflicting on her in the great years of mock-heroic. In *Jonathan Wild* we are not only on the way to Byron. We are also half-way to the *Waste Land*'s pervasive suggestion both that the older poems were grander than modern times, *and* also not so very different from them after all. And in *Amelia*, that low-key transposition of the *Aeneid* to modern life, we are, as many have noted, half-way to Joyce.

Pope didn't quite lose his nerve about epic in the way that the

Fielding of the *Voyage of Lisbon* did, though he persistently worried about the 'shocking ... Spirit of Cruelty',[34] and was, like other of his contemporaries, more or less studiously concerned to let military disrepute rub off on historical rather than poetic targets. In Fielding's *Jonathan Wild*, however, an epic and a historical model are more insistently juxtaposed, registering both an unheroic decline *into* history, and the all too 'heroic' continuities *of* history. The distinction between heroic poetry and historical massacres is beginning to wear thin, but Fielding probably never wholly abandoned it, not even in the *Voyage to Lisbon*. Byron did. If Milton retained epic forms and majesties to criticise the heroic from within, Byron effected a radical travesty of this procedure. His 'epic' tells you enough about epics to ensure that no sorrow is felt at the fact that (flaunted assertions notwithstanding) it is not one at all.

[34] Pope, note to translation of *Iliad*, XIII.471, Twickenham Edition, ed. Maynard Mack, VIII, p.129n.

Culture and Catastrophe

· 5 ·

Revolution in the moral wardrobe: mutations of an image from Dryden to Burke

Existence is a covert operation

('Henry Kissinger' in a Feiffer cartoon, 1976)

HEROES AND LAZARS

The title of this chapter comes from Burke's famous passage about Marie Antoinette and the events of October 1789, when the French royal family were forced to leave Versailles and transferred to Paris. Burke saw these incidents as portending the extinction of a culture:

But now all is to be changed ... All the decent drapery of life is to be rudely torn off. All the superadded ideas, furnished from the wardrobe of a moral imagination, which the heart owns, and the understanding ratifies, as necessary to cover the defects of our naked shivering nature ... are to be exploded as a ridiculous, absurd, and antiquated fashion.[1]

Burke's *Reflections on the Revolution in France* were published in 1790. His apocalyptic oratory, which actually spoke of regicide, seemed excessive to many at that time, though some of his forebodings turned out to be prescient.[2] It is said that his account is sometimes taken by

---

[1] *The Writings and Speeches of Edmund Burke. Volume VIII: The French Revolution 1790–1794*, ed. L. G. Mitchell, Oxford, 1989 (hereafter referred to as Mitchell), p. 128; *Reflections on the Revolution in France*, ed. Conor Cruise O'Brien, Harmondsworth 1969, p. 171 (hereafter O'Brien). Quotations are from Mitchell, but in view of the wide currency of the O'Brien edition page-references for the text of the *Reflections* will be given to both, in the form '128/171'. Other writings by Burke, unless otherwise noted, are from *Works*, Bohn's Standard Library, 8 vols., London, 1884–1893.

[2] For 'regicide', see *Reflections*, p. 128/171, and *Correspondence of Edmund Burke*, ed. Thomas W. Copeland and others, 10 vols., Cambridge, 1958–1978, VI.90. For contemporary views of Burke's account of events, viewed on all sides of the political spectrum as inaccurate or exaggerated, see Mitchell, Introduction, esp. pp. 1–28. This account should be supplemented by that in F. P. Lock, *Burke's Reflections on the Revolution in France*, London and Boston, 1985, pp. 132–65, which cites many examples of favourable response, both in private

uninformed readers as referring to the large-scale bloodshed of 1792 and 1793 rather than to the relatively minor convulsions of 1789.[3] More knowing readers see prophetic insight or counter-revolutionary panic, according to taste.

Either way, the note is, as I said, apocalyptic, in a manner which looks back to Augustan imaginings of cultural disintegration like that at the end of Pope's *Dunciad*,[4] and forward to the great twentieth-century master of the catastrophic imagination, W. B. Yeats. Yeats saw Burke as a central figure in his pantheon of Georgian Ireland.[5] A draft of 'The Second Coming' (written in January 1919) shows him to have been deeply exercised by Burke's account of the mob's treatment of the French queen in 1789, which he saw as a prefiguration of the slaughter of the Russian royal family by the Bolsheviks in 1918, when we know Yeats read the *Reflections*.[6] It seems possible that Yeats' draft, which speaks of Marie Antoinette having 'brutally died', involves anachronistic conflation of Burke's account with events later than those the *Reflections* referred to.

It seems likely, too, that Burke's 'all is to be changed' is also evoked in 'All changed, changed utterly' of 'Easter, 1916'.[7] That poem precedes Yeats' reading of the *Reflections* in 1918. But Yeats had already been obsessed with Burke before that time (sometimes adversarially), and whether or not he had previously read the *Reflections*, the passage which opens with these words had acquired freestanding memorability.[8] It was often quoted, its purple jeered at or revelled in from the beginning. The poetry of crisis, the sense of a shocking and momentous transformation, is similar in both writers,

correspondence and in the press (esp. pp. 135ff.) but warns that 'it was mainly those who differed from Burke who set down their opinions at length. Few who agreed with him felt the need to say so in print' (p. 133). Lock also asserts more emphatically than Mitchell that after events in France began to take a more disturbing turn in summer 1791 'public opinion in England slowly began to move towards Burke's interpretation of events' (p. 144). For a modern French view of Burke's European impact at the time, see Gérard Gengembre, 'Burke', in *A Critical Dictionary of the French Revolution*, ed. François Furet and Mona Ozouf, trs. Arthur Goldhammer, Cambridge, MA, and London, 1989, pp. 916–23.

[3] O'Brien, p. 71.   [4] On the work's Dunciadic associations, see below, pp. 153–4, 180–1.
[5] See Donald T. Torchiana, *W. B. Yeats and Georgian Ireland*, Evanston, 1966.
[6] Torchiana, *Yeats and Georgian Ireland*, pp. 171, 214 ff.; Patrick J. Keane, *Yeats' Interactions with Tradition*, Columbia, Missouri, 1987, pp. 17, 64, 76–7; Jon Stallworthy, 'The Second Coming', *Agenda*, 10.1 (1971/2),24–33.
[7] W. B. Yeats, *Poems*, ed. Richard J. Finneran, London, 1984, pp. 180–2; see also Torchiana, *Yeats and Georgian Ireland*, pp. 187, 213, who links this poem with Burke in other ways, and also draws attention to its setting of 'grey/ Eighteenth-century houses' (p. 295).
[8] Torchiana, *Yeats and Georgian Ireland*, pp. 169; 3, 21, 25.

though Yeats in this poem introduces a redemptive turn that is foreign to Burke: 'A terrible beauty is born.'

Burke's opening words appear in the final stanza of 'Coole Park and Ballylee' (1931),

> But all is changed, that high horse riderless,
> Though mounted in that saddle Homer rode,

where a terminal nostalgia for Homeric grandeurs, past all thought of recovery but equally innocent of the Byronic disaffection which has been examined earlier in this book, blends, in a high quixotic gesture, with a nostalgia for 'traditional sanctity and loveliness' which may properly be called Burkeian: it is as though Yeats' nostalgia had conflated the arrogant heroic prowess, and its softening by chivalric codes of courtesy and grace, into a common sense of loss.[9]

The sense of a single convulsive shock which governs 'Easter, 1916' is absent here. Yeats' meditations on the theme of 'old civilisations put to the sword' often come with a sense of the spaciousness of historical cycles, less implicated in the urgencies of present crisis than Burke felt able to be in 1790. He could view them, not with indifference, but with a kind of impassioned serenity:

> No handiwork of Callimachus
> Who handled marble as if it were bronze,
> Made draperies that seemed to rise
> When sea-wind swept the corner, stands.

The sculptor Callimachus was associated in Yeats' mind with a stylised drapery antithetical to 'the naturalistic drapery of Phidias'.[10] 'Drapery' is a topic to which I shall return, in particular to Sir Joshua Reynolds' discriminations between it and the naturalistic portrayal of dress, which are closely related to Burke's political philosophy and to the 'decent drapery of life' of his passage about Marie Antoinette.

---

9 For a discussion of eighteenth-century perceptions of the emergence of a 'knightly class moving out of brutal warrior courage', as part of a 'transition from barbarism to the commerce, intellect, and civilised manners of modern times', see the important introduction to J. G. A. Pocock's edition of Burke's *Reflections*, Indianapolis and Cambridge, 1987, pp. xxxii and liv, nn.75–7. Pocock's discussion suggests that bourgeois elements blended with 'aristocracy' in Burke's conception of this process, rather than being in tension with it (see p. xxii *et passim*): this would not be how Yeats' mythologising viewed either the process or Burke's sympathies on the subject.

10 W. B. Yeats, 'Lapis Lazuli' (1938), in *Poems*, p. 294; 'Certain Noble Plays of Japan' (1916), in *Essays and Introductions*, London, 1961, p. 225; see also A. Norman Jeffares, *A New Commentary on the Poems of W. B. Yeats*, London, 1984, p. 365.

Reynolds praised Phidias for his *anti*-naturalism, and he and Yeats would have differed in most of their individual tastes.[11] But they had in common a quasi-patrician distaste for naturalistic portrayal ('realism is created for the common people'), and a sense that the drift towards it is not unconnected with undesirable political change. Yeats' view that 'art remains at a distance' which 'must be firmly held against a pushing world' has a profound bearing on the writings of Burke as well as of Reynolds.[12] The notion of an honorific connection between realism in art and 'democratic ideas', which enjoyed a wide if patchy circulation in the nineteenth century, and was specifically promoted by the realist painter Gustave Courbet, ran against the cultural sympathies and political outlook of all three.[13]

This discussion is concerned with some aspects of the cultural tradition from which both Burke and Reynolds derived, with some cultural antecedents of Burke's language and imagery, and with the traditional base of certain notions about the nature of civilisation, and about the interactions between art, nature, society, and the constitution of states.

I begin with a well-known passage from Hume's essay 'Of Simplicity and Refinement in Writing':

Sentiments, which are merely natural, affect not the mind with any pleasure, and seem not worthy of our attention. The pleasantries of a waterman, the observations of a peasant, the ribaldry of a porter or hackney coachman, all of these are natural, and disagreeable. What an insipid comedy should we make of the chit-chat of the tea-table, copied faithfully and at full length? Nothing can please persons of taste, but nature drawn with all her graces and ornaments, *la belle nature*; or if we copy low life, the strokes must be strong and remarkable, and must convey a lively image to the mind. The absurd naivety of *Sancho Pancho* is represented in such inimitable colours by CERVANTES that it entertains as much as the picture of the most magnanimous hero or the softest lover.[14]

Hume goes on to argue that excessive refinement is also bad, that one needs a medium between excessive simplicity and refinement, that there is variety and latitude in determining such a medium, that

---

[11] Sir Joshua Reynolds, *Discourses on Art*, ed. Robert R. Wark, 2nd edn., New Haven and London, 1975, pp. 42–3, 45, 128. For Reynolds' anti-naturalism, see especially pp. 232–3.

[12] Yeats, *Essays and Introductions*, pp. 227, 224.

[13] On 'realism' and 'democratic ideas', see Linda Nochlin, *Realism*, Harmondsworth, 1979, pp. 23, 33, 45–50, 111–37; for Courbet's statement that 'le réalisme est par essence l'art démocratique' (1861), see A. Estignard, *Courbet: sa vie, ses oeuvres*, Besançon, 1896, p. 118.

[14] David Hume, *Essays Moral, Political, and Literary*, ed. Eugene F. Miller, rev. edn., Indianapolis, 1987, pp. 191–6.

excessive refinement is '*both less* beautiful, *and more* dangerous' than excessive simplicity, and that 'the justness of the representation' is after all important and risks being lost in stylistic ornament (some degree of tension between the claims of truthful 'representation' and the uneasiness induced by the 'merely natural' is a recurrent feature of most such discussions).

Hume's remark about the 'insipidity' of faithful reproductions of real-life conversation makes two comments. One is about the poor quality of the chit-chat in real life. The other is about faithful portrayals as such, whatever the quality of the real-life original. It is in the latter context especially that 'insipidity', as pertaining for example 'to the minute accidental discriminations of particular and individual objects', became a term of almost obsessive frequency in Reynolds' criticism.[15] What Hume says about 'low life' is not a simple matter of classicising genre-snobbery or genteel squeamishness. The objection is as much to 'the chit-chat of the tea-table' as to the language of watermen and porters. (Hume's casual rejection of this may be contrasted with the immense pains, envisaged as a labour of months, which Flaubert thought right to devote to an accurate notation of such *dialogue trivial* in *Madame Bovary*).[16] Hume does not exclude the 'low', but argues that (like any other factual material) it should be modified, perhaps even in this case *intensified* (its 'strokes' rendered 'strong and remarkable'), into a realm of comic artifice.

The underlying impulse seems to me very similar to that of a statement in Swift's 'Hints towards an Essay on Conversation':

There are some People who think they sufficiently acquit themselves, and entertain their Company with relating of Facts of no Consequence, nor at all out of the Road of such common Incidents as happen every Day: and this I have observed more frequently among the *Scots* than any other Nation, who are very careful not to omit the minutest Circumstances of Time or Place; which Kind of Discourse, if it were not a little relieved by the uncouth Terms and Phrases, as well as Accent and Gesture peculiar to that Country, would be hardly tolerable.[17]

---

[15] Reynolds, *Discourses*, pp. 15–16; *Idler*, No. 79, 20 October 1759 (in Samuel Johnson, *The Idler and the Adventurer*, ed. W. J. Bate and others, New Haven and London, 1963, p. 248, where the term occurs three times on a single page); *Portraits by Sir Joshua Reynolds*, ed. Frederick W. Hilles, London, 1952, pp. 54, 108; also *A Journey to Flanders and Holland, in the year MDCCLXXI*, in *Literary Works*, ed. Edmond Malone, 5th edn., 1819, II.252, 254, 270, 378, 402, 418; 'Notes on The Art of Painting [i.e. the poem by Du Fresnoy, translated by William Mason]', *Literary Works*, III.160, 184.

[16] Gustave Flaubert, letters to Louise Colet, 13 and 19 September 1852, in *Correspondance*, ed. Jean Bruneau, II, Paris, 1980, 156, 159–60.

[17] Swift, *Works*, IV.95.

In its obvious literal sense, the passage is, of course, less close to Hume than it is to Fielding's censure of authors who record 'things and facts of so common a kind' merely because 'they had the honour of having happened to the author'.[18] That Fielding (like Hume) should be talking about writing, and Swift in very similar terms about social conversation, emphasises the intimacy between the two which is presupposed in most Augustan discourse about either. What links Swift's passage with Hume's is the remark about the Scotsmen, whose 'uncouth Terms and Phrases' and peculiar 'Accent and Gesture' help to make tolerable a particularity which would otherwise be quite unacceptable. The Scotsmen, for Swift, turn into stage-comics, whose manner in real life happens to furnish those 'strong and remarkable' strokes which Hume demands of fiction. The thing that relieves the tedium of the conversation is the unprogrammed intrusion of a real-life analogue of comic artifice. Ironically, Hume himself spoke Lowland Scots and 'laboured mightily to eradicate Scotticisms' from his writings.[19] Smollett's novels, with their stage-Scotsmen and Welshmen and other pronounced eccentrics, are perhaps the literary exploitation of what Swift perceived as a case of life imitating art.

Hume's comment about the 'inimitable colours' with which Cervantes presents Sancho Panza puts this treatment of 'low life' paradoxically into the same category as the opposite idealisations of *la belle nature*. Sancho becomes like any hero of epic or romance, not only because he 'entertains as much' in some notional equivalence of aesthetic pleasure, but more precisely because both sorts of character transform the 'merely natural'. Dryden had spoken similarly about the twin-delights of heroic and burlesque: 'the one shows nature beautified', and 'the other shows her deformed', as in the picture 'of a

18 Henry Fielding, *Journal of a Voyage to Lisbon*, ed. Harold E. Pagliaro, New York, 1963, p. 28. Compare Swift, 'Hints', *Works*, IV.88–9.
19 See E. C. Mossner, 'Hume's "Of Criticism"', in *Studies in Criticism and Aesthetics, 1660–1800: Essays in Honor of Samuel Holt Monk*, ed. Howard Anderson and John S. Shea, Minneapolis, 1967, p. 245. For a fuller account, see Mossner, *Life of David Hume*, 2nd edn., Oxford, 1980, pp. 89, 266, 283–4, 299, 373–5, 395–6. Monboddo quipped that Hume 'died confessing, not his sins, but his Scotticisms' (p. 606). Hume drew up 'a list of "Scotticisms" that were rigidly to be excluded from all written works', which was published in various places (p. 373 and n. 2), and drew comment from Boswell and Johnson (Boswell, *Life of Johnson*, ed. G. B. Hill and L. F. Powell, Oxford, 1934–1964, II.72). This linguistic issue exercised many eighteenth-century Scottish writers, including Boswell: see *Life of David Hume*, pp. 370–89, and Pat Rogers, 'Boswell and the Scotticism', in *New Light on Boswell*, ed. Greg Clingham, Cambridge, 1991, pp. 56–71.

lazar, or of a fool with distorted face and antic gestures'.[20] The comment is directly related to a later judgment on *Bartholomew Fair*, where Dryden says Ben Jonson achieved by a proper kind of 'heightening' what

he could never have performed, had he only said or done those very things that are daily spoken or practised in the fair ... he hath made an excellent lazar of it; the copy is of price, though the original be vile.[21]

Dryden's overriding concern, like Hume's, is to remove art from too immediate a correspondence with life. He had just been saying 'that one great reason why prose is not to be used in serious plays is because it is too near the nature of converse: there may be too great a likeness ...' He goes on to say that *Bartholomew Fair* is not a 'serious play' but 'the lowest kind of comedy', that Jonson 'was not there to go out of prose', but that he nevertheless found means of 'heightening' the play away from an undue identity with its real-life original.[22] Dryden's use of the word 'heightening' is a painterly one, meaning intensifying the colour. It's a part-pun, because heightening might be achieved by a stylised form of lowering, the deforming of mere yokels into lazars. But there is nothing unusual in his likening of such lower artistic effects to the procedures of heroic heightening or idealisation. In one sense, heroic idealisations were a normative model for tendencies which were also inherent in the Augustan practice of lower literary kinds. In pastoral, according to the view which Pope derived from Rapin, and which was the more traditional of two prevalent conceptions of the genre, to 'copy Nature' carried the stipulation 'that we are not to describe our shepherds as shepherds at this day really are, but as they may be conceiv'd ... to have been' in the Golden Age, 'when the best of men follow'd the employment'.[23] In the same spirit Reynolds wrote that the Dutch painters who attended 'to literal truth and a minute exactness in the detail' were offering copies not of true nature but 'as I

[20] John Dryden, 'An Account of the Ensuing Poem [*Annus Mirabilis*]' (1667), in Watson, I.101; see also 'A Parallel of Poetry and Painting' (1695), II.190. For some interesting remarks on high and low stylisations, see Françoise Moreux, 'Personnages d'Excentriques dans la Comédie du XVIIIe Siècle', in *L'Excentricité en Grande-Bretagne au 18e Siècle*, ed. Michèle Plaisant, Lille, 1976, pp. 162–3.

[21] Dryden, 'A Defence of *An Essay of Dramatic Poesy*' (1668), in Watson I.114–15.

[22] Watson, I.114–15.

[23] Alexander Pope, 'A Discourse on Pastoral Poetry' (1704?–17), TE, I.25 and n.; for the two views of pastoral poetry, see TE, I.15, and J. E. Congleton, *Theories of Pastoral Poetry in England 1684–1798*, Gainesville, 1952, esp. chs. 2–4.

may say, of nature modified by accident'.[24] One effect or objective of such idealisation was to modify and to distance the raw sense of the actual: the deep impulse may, in fact, have been *not* mainly to 'heighten', but to place at arm's length, to provide a shield against factuality rather than merely to enhance it. It was evidently recognised that procedures other than idealisation, including its opposite, could serve the same purpose. Hence the favourable collocations in Dryden and Hume, and Fielding's contrary (or seemingly contrary) repudiation of heroic romance and of burlesque as twin distortions of honest fact in the Preface to *Joseph Andrews*.

Reynolds was more resistant than Dryden to the attractions of 'deformity', and his conception of correct style narrower in its scope and sympathies. In *Idler* No. 79 he complained in a conventional way of excesses of imagination which produced 'incoherent monsters', but differed from Dryden's or Hume's emphasis by seeing them as comparable with the impoverished imagination which produced the 'lifeless insipidity' of realistic portrayal. In the *Journey to Flanders and Holland* he praised Rubens' *Crucifixion* at Antwerp for portraying Mary Magdalen's 'countenance of great horrour' without any 'grimace or contortion of the features', while praising the 'bold and uncommon' composition and the 'remarkable' quality of its 'colouring'. Elsewhere in the *Journey* he somewhat less guardedly praises 'a Merry-making of Jordaens' for its forceful vitality: 'vulgar, tumultuous merriment was never better expressed: and for colouring and strength, few pictures of Rubens are superior'.[25] In Discourse III he even found a way of accommodating 'deformity' by seeing in it 'a kind of symmetry, or proportion' of its own. Blake scoffed at this as a 'Pretty Foolery': 'Leanness or Fatness is not Deformity, but Reynolds thought Character Itself Extravagance & Deformity.'[26] Blake had a point. Reynolds' remarks show him as less inclusive or more guarded than other writers of broadly similar principles, like Dryden or Hume. But his instinctive concern to view what Hume called 'strong and remarkable' strokes as analogous or related to more exalted stylisations, of 'correctness' as much as of the 'grand style', belongs with theirs.

[24] Reynolds, in *Idler*, ed. Bate p. 247.
[25] Reynolds, in *Idler*, p. 248; *Literary Works*, II. 317–23, 377. In Discourse VI, however, Reynolds spoke slightingly of Jordaens as a servile imitator of Rubens (*Discourses*, pp. 104–5).
[26] Reynolds, *Discourses*, p. 47; William Blake, 'Annotations to *The Works of Sir Joshua Reynolds*', in *Complete Poetry and Prose*, ed. David V. Erdman and Harold Bloom, rev. edn., Berkeley and Los Angeles, 1982, p. 648.

Idealisation and its antic cousins, burlesque exaggeration, comic highlighting, 'strong and remarkable' strokes, connect, in Hume's short essay and elsewhere, with 'elegance of expression, and harmony of numbers', rounded periods and the felicities of rhyme; and also with a habit of applying to these things the traditional image of style as the 'dress of thought'.[27] Dryden's principal concern, as he discusses Jonson's comic 'heightening' in *Bartholomew Fair*, though 'the author was not there to go out of prose', is, in fact, to defend the use of rhyme.[28] His frequently repeated argument in favour of rhyme is based on the notion 'that serious plays ought not to imitate conversation too nearly'.[29] Comedy, being 'the imitation of common persons and ordinary speaking', is different, but Dryden, like Fielding after him, notoriously hedges the issue of comic realism, as the remarks on *Bartholomew Fair* show, whilst his more general prescriptions 'to imitate nature well' inevitably slide, in a familiar Augustan way, from 'resemblance', 'likeness', and 'truth', to 'the best nature ... which is wrought up to a nobler pitch'. This latter wording, from the 'Parallel of Poetry and Painting', is very close to those places in earlier essays where Dryden defends the unrealism of rhyme as suited to heroic poems and plays, which deal with 'nature wrought up to an higher pitch' or 'raised above the life'.[30] In some of Dryden's formulations, as well as in those of others, not only rhyme, but all the stylistic harmonies and graces,

The words, the expressions, the tropes and figures, the versification, and all the other elegancies of sound, as cadences, turns of words upon the thought, and many other things which are all parts of expression,

belong collectively to the project of making nature 'appear more lovely than naturally she is'. Without the colouring or clothing, 'the design of itself is only so many naked lines'.[31]

NAKEDNESS AND THE DRESS OF THOUGHT

'Nakedness' is the significant term, almost obsessively recurrent. This seems logical in a tradition in which language was commonly referred to as the dress of thought, but it carries a peculiar urgency of its own.

---

[27] Hume, *Essays*, p. 195.   [28] Watson, I. 114.
[29] 'Of Heroic Plays' (1672), Watson, I. 157.
[30] 'Parallel', Watson, II. 193–94; *Of Dramatic Poesy: An Essay* (1668), I. 87; 'Of Heroic Plays', I. 157.   [31] 'Parallel', Watson, II. 203.

Positive assertions about the 'garment of style' are frequently concerned with the question of *suitable* clothes, decorum:

> Expression is the *Dress* of *Thought*, and still
> Appears more *decent* as more *suitable*.

The words are Pope's, and his discussion continues in terms of particular garments for particular occasions.[32] Rosemond Tuve has argued that in the sixteenth and seventeenth centuries it is this decorum, variously understood, which is the dominant consideration.[33] But nakedness assumes the lack of garments altogether, and a closer look at the evidence, not only in critical writings, but in the literature of manners and elsewhere, suggests that such terminology, in the late seventeenth century and after, often reflects a primary preoccupation with the 'clothing' of bare fact as such, sometimes in real or apparent contravention of a narrower stylistic decorum; and that this was closely bound up with an anxiety to protect the culture from the menace of some notionally 'naked' pre-civilised or (worse still) post-civilised state.

Such an emphasis does not appear in the few classical instances of the image of the 'garment of style' known to me. The widespread use of the image in any form seems to date from the Renaissance. Classical authors seem to have used anatomical and physiological more often than sartorial images in descriptions of style (healthy, lean, fat, strong, animated, lifeless, lame etc.).[34] Dress images may, however, be found in several classical and medieval authors, including Dionysius of Halicarnassus, Cicero, Seneca, Quintilian, Martianus Capella, and Geoffrey of Vinsauf.[35] Many of these are allusive uses of the metaphor, not especially concerned to enunciate formal principles. They are seldom concerned with the need to clothe nakedness as such: indeed Cicero's *Brutus*, 262, praises Caesar's commentaries for being naked, straight, and beautiful, as if stripped of a garment.[36] Cicero was

---

[32] Pope, *Essay on Criticism* (1711), lines 318ff.

[33] Rosemond Tuve, *Elizabethan and Metaphysical Imagery*, Chicago, 1947, pp. 61–78, 192–247.

[34] A convenient listing of metaphors of bodies and dress in Greek and Latin authors may be found in Larue Van Hook, *The Metaphorical Terminology of Greek Rhetoric and Literary Criticism*, Chicago, 1905, esp. pp. 18–23, 26, 34–7. Images of the body predominate.

[35] Dionysius of Halicarnassus, 'On the Style of Demosthenes', xviii, Cicero, *Brutus*, 262, 274, 327; *De Oratore*, I.142, II.123, III.155; Seneca, *Epistulae Morales*, cxv.2–3; Quintilian, VIII, Pr. 20; Martianus Capella, *Marriage of Philology and Mercury*, v.426; Geoffrey of Vinsauf, *Poetria Nova*, lines 60 ff. The example from Dionysius of Halicarnassus deals with decorum, 'just as certain clothes suit certain bodies, so certain language fits certain thought'.

[36] *Nudi enim sunt, recti et venusti, omni ornatu orationis tamquam veste detracta.*

'probably thinking of the human form as represented in sculpture', rather than of human bodies as such, a fact which may be connected with Reynolds' provisions for a permissible nudity in art.[37]

But a concern with the covering of nudity of the kind displayed by eighteenth-century writers may already be detected in Puttenham. In his discussion 'Of Ornament' in the *Arte of English Poesie* (1588), he invokes the fact that 'custome and ciuilitie haue ordained [ladies] to couer their naked bodies . . . Euen so cannot our vulgar Poesie shew it selfe either gallant or gorgious, if any lymme be left naked and bare and not clad in his kindly clothes and colours' (III.i). The phrase 'kindly clothes' indicates a concern with decorum or *relation*, though the worry about nakedness goes beyond this, and a later discussion, speaks of 'the bare and naked body, which being attired in rich and gorgious apparell, seemeth to the common vsage of th'eye much more comely & bewtifull then the naturall' (III.xx). Tuve is right that Puttenham's discussion is, at least in part, 'about a *relation*, not about the charms of pearls', but the sense of an overriding insufficiency or unacceptability of 'nakedness' is evidently assumed in both places.[38]

This becomes a dominating concern in some later writers, where notions of vulnerability, both social and stylistic, are involved. Thus Chesterfield wrote:

Do not neglect your style, whatever language you speak in, or whomever you speak to, were it your footman. Seek always for the best words and happiest expressions you can find. Do not content yourself with being barely understood; but adorn your thoughts, and dress them as you would your person; which, however well proportioned it might be, it would be very improper and indecent to exhibit naked, or even worse dressed than people of your sort are.[39]

There evidently is, over and above any decorum of particular occasions, a correctness and elegance of style which serves the still more basic purpose of clothing (not necessarily disguising, though that function is not foreign to Chesterfield's thinking) the naked truth. In a comment on Richardson's Clarissa, Lady Mary Wortley Montagu opined that 'Fig leaves are as necessary for our Minds as our

[37] See the note in *Brutus*, ed. A. E. Douglas, Oxford, 1966, p. 191. The Loeb translator, G. L. Hendrickson, translates *nudi enim sunt* as 'they are like nude figures' (in *Brutus and Orator*, London and Cambridge, MA, 1952, p. 227). For Reynolds, see below, p. 164, and n. 104.

[38] George Puttenham, *The Arte of English Poesie*, ed. Gladys Doidge Willcock and Alice Walker, Cambridge, 1936, pp. 137–8, 247–9; Tuve, *Imagery*, p. 66.

[39] Chesterfield, *Letters*, ed. Bonamy Dobrée, London, 1932, IV.1461 (to his son, 12 December O. S., 1749).

Bodies', her point being not so much that the heroine reveals indecent thoughts (though the image of the dress of thought was sometimes used to indicate a decent covering in this sense), as that it was indecent of her to reveal her thoughts at all. As far back as 1689, in his *Treatise of Dreams and Visions*, Thomas Tryon used a similar imagery to describe the discourse of the mad, who have 'no *Covering, Vail,* or *Figg-leaves* before them' but, like children, speak their thoughts 'promiscuously formed into words'. Tryon preferred this to the duplicity of rational people, but his words suggest what is at stake in the vocabulary he shares with Lady Mary. Swift approvingly reported an Irish prelate's view 'that if the wisest man would at any time utter his thoughts, in the crude undigested manner, as they come into his head, he would be looked upon as raving mad', so that 'our thoughts, as they are the seeds of words and actions ... ought to be kept under the strictest regulation'.[40]

The concerns of both Tryon and Swift go deeper than codes of manners, but manners are implicated in the conventions of speech (social as well as rational and grammatical) which both see as distinguishing rational and civilised creatures from madmen and savages. If the formulations of Chesterfield and Lady Mary keep the issue within the narrower terms of a patrician social code, notions (frequently shallow or muddled) of a reversion to savagery have an active force in their thinking. An early poem of Burke's, 'The Muse Divorced', articulates a position which seems to hold the Chesterfieldian and Swiftian perspectives in a single view. Its vocabulary of nakedness, veils, custom, art was to reappear in elaborate orchestration in the *Reflections* forty years later:

> Can we, my friend, with any Conscience bear,
> To show our minds sheer naked as they are,
> Remove each veil of Custom, pride or Art,
> Nor stretch a hand to hide one Shameful part? –
> An equal Share of Scorn and Danger find
> A Naked body, and an open mind.[41]

[40] Lady Mary Wortley Montagu, *Complete Letters*, ed. Robert Halsband, Oxford, 1965–7, III.97 (to Lady Bute, 20 October 1755). For the alternative idea of stylistic dress as a 'modest clothing' for potentially indecent material, see Dryden, Preface to *All for Love* (1678), in Watson, I.223: 'broad obscenities in words ought in good manners to be avoided: expressions therefore are a modest clothing of our thoughts, as breeches and petticoats are of our bodies'. Thomas Tryon, *A Treatise of Dreams and Visions*, 1689, pp. 261–2; Swift, 'Some Thoughts on Free-Thinking', *Works*, IV.49.

[41] *A Note-Book of Edmund Burke*, ed. H. V. F. Somerset, Cambridge, 1957, p. 25.

These are values which Rousseau's whole writing career was dedicated to opposing. In the *Confessions*, he expressly claimed an unprecedented and uncompromising veracity in recording his own character, and declared a lifelong project of stripping naked the heart of man. But as early as 1750, the same year as Burke's poem, his first *Discourse* (1750) had been directed at the 'arts and sciences' and the corrupting effect of 'taste' and 'politeness': at the very same cultural complex which Burke was concerned to vindicate in the *Reflections*.[42]

Rousseau's position represents a quantum leap from prevailing values, though a sense of the necessary duplicity of civilised behaviour, as of the garment of style, was an uneasy undercurrent even among more conformist writers. It is visible in earlier authors, for example Puttenham, writing 'Of Figures and figuratiue speaches' (III.vii).[43] Burke himself had conceded in 'The Muse Divorced' that 'ev'n some friends – that sacred Name – we have/Whom so to keep, 'tis proper to deceive'. Chesterfield is relatively rare in betraying no uneasiness. One of his *Detached Thoughts* makes a similar point to Lady Mary's on the need for not revealing all one's thoughts:

Dissimulation, to a certain degree, is necessary in business as clothes are in the common intercourse of life; and a man would be as impudent who would exhibit his inside naked, as he would be indecent if he produced his outside so.[44]

Chesterfield is reflecting on the conduct of life, but he had similar views to Lady Mary's about Richardson. In a letter recommending that *Clarissa* be abridged in Prévost's French translation, Chesterfield described Richardson as 'un libraire, qui manque de savoir et de style, mais qui connaît le coeur'.[45] Such combinations of contempt and grudging admiration were expressed by other patrician readers of Richardson's novels.[46]

As we might expect, 'style' for Chesterfield is not only a decorous, but also a politic, garment. His words highlight the extent to which 'nakedness', within the highly structured social code to which he subscribed, suggests vulnerability. Among eighteenth-century writers

---

[42] Jean-Jacques Rousseau, *Confessions* (1782–1789), Books x, xii, and viii, in *Oeuvres Complètes*, ed. Bernard Gagnebin and Marcel Raymond, I (1959), 516–17, 656, 388, and introduction pp. xxxff.; *Discours sur les sciences et les arts* (1750), in *Oeuvres Complètes*, iii (1964), 1ff.

[43] Puttenham, *Arte of English Poesie*, III.vii, pp. 154–5. See Lawrence Manley, *Convention 1500–1750*, Cambridge, MA, and London, 1980, pp. 169–70.

[44] Burke, *Note-Book*, p. 25; Chesterfield, *Detached Thoughts*, cited in *Letters*, ed. Dobrée, I.165.

[45] Chesterfield, *Letters*, iv. 1589 (to Madame du Boccage, 13 October O S 1750).

[46] See Rawson, *Order from Confusion Sprung*, pp. 285, 307 n. 46.

with a serious claim to the literary historian's attention, Chesterfield is mercifully unique; and it is characteristic that the issue should crystallise for him in this crude and definite form.

Fielding's writings on social conduct, as I have argued elsewhere, derive from the same tradition, but reflect a more considerate feeling for human behaviour and a morality more sensitively concerned with real human worth.[47] In Fielding's discussions of literary style, where moral issues do not arise in the same overt way, there is a similar preoccupation with the idea of style as the dress of thought, and it also bears a problematic relationship to what is considered by students of literature as the conventional perspective on this idea. When he asserts that 'Diction ... is the Dress of Poetry' in the Preface to *Joseph Andrews*, his active concern is less with a matching of dress to occasion than with the provision of basic stylistic covering for his supposed 'exactest copying of Nature'.[48] The subtextual emphasis is clearly less on the sort of decorum of 'suitable' dress enunciated in the couplet from the *Essay on Criticism*, than on a more general adornment or distancing. To this extent, and with due reservations, he shares something of the more primary motive for 'adorning' one's style which Chesterfield expressed to his son.

Notice, at all events, how Fielding insists on two principles which seem to contravene that concern for decorum which Tuve saw as the basis of the whole business of the 'garment of style'. First, the 'Burlesque' which Fielding says he has introduced into his 'Diction' is said *not* to extend to his 'Sentiments and Characters'. Secondly, he says that the burlesque diction does not turn his novel into a burlesque work, since diction, 'as it is the Dress of Poetry', no more necessarily indicates the nature of the whole work than the 'Dress of Men' does their character.

Another paradoxical fact is that Fielding was ostensibly asserting his 'exactest copying' both against the idealisations of heroic romance and the deformities of burlesque (which is not here distinguished from orthodox mock-heroic, including in this context literary styles as well as caricature in the visual arts). On the other hand, he understood with Dryden the contrary principle that the heroic and the burlesque represented complementary distortions of exactest copying. But unlike Dryden he professes to favour the latter. Fielding tilts his rhetoric by choosing debased examples to score

[47] Rawson, *Henry Fielding and the Augustan Ideal under Stress*, pp. 3–34.
[48] *Joseph Andrews*, Wesleyan edition, ed. Martin C. Battestin, Oxford, 1967, pp. 4–6.

against: heroic romances rather than Homer, low Bartholomew Fair farces (perhaps) rather than Jonson's *Bartholomew Fair*. By comparison with any of these, a claim of 'exactest copying', even for a work as stylised as *Joseph Andrews*, would be sustainable on any common-sense view, as well as in terms of traditional conceptions of comic realism.[49] But the claim would have no standing in comparison with the work of Defoe or Richardson, a truth which Fielding would at all times be more disposed to publicise than to conceal. The claim is, moreover, compromised from within by the fact, ostentatiously avowed in the Preface, that there is a good deal of what he calls burlesque in Fielding's own novel, which he says he introduced for the entertainment of 'the Classical Reader', and the Preface goes on to assert an intrinsic fondness for the genre.

Fielding's objection that he has 'often heard [the] Name' of burlesque given to genuinely 'comic' works (i.e., in the sense of works which perform exact copying) also wears thin in the light of Fielding's later readiness to blur the distinction, in his Preface to the second edition of Sarah Fielding's *David Simple* (1744), where sustained mock-heroic poems like *Le Lutrin* and *The Dunciad* are called comic epics.[50] The critics who think that when Fielding spoke of comic epic in *Joseph Andrews* he meant mock-heroic, although in fact he said the opposite, continue to be mistaken. But one reason why this error dies hard is that Fielding abandoned a distinction he had insisted on, thus bearing a kind of *ex post facto* witness to the substantial presence of mock-heroic in *Joseph Andrews* itself, as though the teller, belatedly and perhaps inadvertently, had caught up with the tale.

Fielding's concern is evidently neither with the notation of bare fact as he pretends, nor with the sort of decorum with which Pope and others demanded that the facts should be 'clothed', but again, ultimately, with the standard cultural project of clothing bareness as such: the bareness of fact, or of naked feeling, which, in the typical scenario, places civilised men in an unguarded posture. What in Chesterfield was a matter of politic defence, or crude social strategy, is in Fielding an expression of instinctive attachment to the role of art and of civilisation as bulwarks against the irrepressible and unruly energies of life.

[49] The best short description of traditional notions of comic realism in relation to Fielding's Preface is W. L. Renwick, 'Comic Epic in Prose', *Essays and Studies*, 32 (1946), 40–3, reprinted in the Penguin Critical Anthology, *Henry Fielding*, ed. Claude Rawson, Harmondsworth, 1973, pp. 464–8.

[50] Sarah Fielding, *The Adventures of David Simple* (1744), ed. Malcolm Kelsall, London and New York, 1969, p. 6.

The two emphases are not mutually exclusive, of course, and at times are hardly distinguishable. They reflect underlying values which were cultural in the widest sense, not merely 'literary'. But the stylistic habits which expressed them were in a state of continuous tension with pressures towards plain unadorned notation which were a familiar part of the history and ideology of writing styles in the seventeenth and eighteenth centuries. These included the calls for a plain style in sermons, chiefly among Puritan preachers reacting against the convoluted eloquence of Donne or Andrewes;[51] and in the language of science and philosophy, Sprat's recommendation of 'a close, naked, natural way of speaking' or Locke's pronouncement that 'if we would speak of Things as they are', all the literary ornaments 'besides Order and Clearness ... are perfect cheat'.[52] The imagery of nakedness and dress, in this as in other contexts, often appears inconsistently and opportunistically. Puritan celebrations of plain style sometimes speak of plain clothing rather than of nakedness.[53] And Sprat's comments in the *History of the Royal Society* may be set

[51] James Sutherland, *On English Prose*, London, 1965, pp. 62–3 cites the Puritan preacher Richard Baxter: 'Truth loves the Light, and is most beautiful when most naked' (*Gildas Salvianus*, 1656, p. 123; *The Practical Works of Richard Baxter*, 1707, IV.358). The passage is often cited: see Harold Fisch, 'The Puritans and the Reform of Prose Style', *ELH*, 19 (1952), 239–40, and Robert Adolph, *The Rise of Modern Prose Style*, Cambridge, MA, and London, 1968, p. 209. Sutherland, p. 63, says 'Baxter clearly thinks of "style" as the dress of thought, a dress that conceals the naked truth.' On Puritan ideas of style, see also Adolph, *Rise of Modern Prose Style*, pp. 16, 163–4, 190–210; Perry Miller, *The New England Mind: The Seventeenth Century*, Cambridge, MA, 1939, pp. 331–61, reprinted in *Seventeenth-Century Prose: Modern Essays in Criticism*, ed. Stanley Fish, New York, 1971, pp. 147–86 (esp. 148, 170, 174–6, 181, including various forms of the image of style as dress).

[52] Thomas Sprat, *History of the Royal Society* (1667), ed. Jackson I. Cope and Harold Whitmore Jones, St Louis and London, 1958, p. 113; see the editors' Introduction, pp. xxvff., for a useful account of Sprat's views on language, which were not confined to scientific discourse, and extended in particular to a plain style in preaching (p. xxvii); John Locke, *An Essay Concerning Human Understanding*, III.x.34, ed. Peter H. Nidditch, Oxford, 1979, p. 508; for Locke's views on language and style in an educational context, see *Some Thoughts Concerning Education*, paragraph 189, in *Educational Writings*, ed. James L. Axtell, Cambridge, 1968, pp. 296–301. For various views on the 'plain style question' (the phrase is taken from Stanley Fish's epilogue in *Self-Consuming Artifacts*, Berkeley, Los Angeles and London, 1972, pp. 374 ff.), and the linguistic doctrines of Sprat, John Wilkins, Locke, and others, see Adolph, *Rise of Modern Prose Style*, passim; Stephen K. Land, *From Signs to Propositions*, London, 1974, pp. 1–20 et passim; Murray Cohen, *Sensible Words: Linguistic Practice in England 1640–1785*, Baltimore and London, 1977, pp. 38–42, 56–63; Ricardo Quintana, *Two Augustans: Locke and Swift*, Madison, 1978, pp. 58 ff.; M. M. Slaughter, *Universal Language and Scientific Taxonomy in the Seventeenth Century*, Cambridge, 1982, pp. 189–219; and more generally, Hans Aarsleff, *From Locke to Saussure*, Minneapolis, 1982, and many of the essays reprinted in *Seventeenth-Century Prose: Modern Essays in Criticism*, ed. Stanley Fish, New York, 1971.

[53] See for example the citations from Joseph Hall, in H. Fisch, 'The Puritans and the Reform of Prose Style', p. 238, or John Saffin and Daniel Gookin in Miller's *New England Mind*, in *Seventeenth-Century Prose*, ed. S. Fish, pp. 176, 181.

beside the 'Account of the Life and Writings of Mr. Abraham Cowley' the following year (1668), where praise of 'Native clearness and shortness, a Domestical plaines' is restricted to private as against public writings: in personal letters like those of Cowley, Sprat insists, 'the Souls of Men should appear undress'd: And in that negligent habit they may be fit to be seen by one or two in a Chamber, but not to go abroad in the street.'[54] It is also of interest in the context of a scientific pursuit of a 'naked' style that scientific exploration was frequently repudiated as a prying into secrets not intended for man to penetrate, an improper lifting of veils. The attitude was widespread in the seventeenth century, and still strongly in evidence in the satire of Swift and Pope.[55]

Swift, for all his own 'conciseness', derisively reduced Sprat's 'so many *things*, almost in an equal number of *words*' to its famous Gulliverian absurdity.[56] The project of Laputian scientists 'for entirely abolishing all Words whatsoever', as visualised by Swift, bears a startling resemblance to his picture of the supposed retreat from language in Puritan worship, as expressed not in formal advocacies of a plain sermon-style, but in a crazed abandonment of all verbal discourse. In the *Mechanical Operation of the Spirit* vocal intercourse not only becomes sexual and orgiastic, but does so by more or less 'abolishing all Words whatsoever', and replacing them by meaningless sounds and incoherences, 'a Hum, a Sigh or a Groan'.[57] The preacher is said to

blow his Nose so powerfully, as to pierce the Hearts of his People, who are disposed to receive the *Excrements* of his Brain with the same Reverence, as the *Issue* of it. Hawking, Spitting, and Belching, the Defects of other Mens Rhetorick, are the Flowers, and Figures, and Ornaments of his.[58]

The issue of the brain are 'words', and this is not the first time Swift used this image in accounts of sub-rational or sub-literate activity. The resemblance to, or coincidence with, the case of the Laputians, is

---

[54] *Critical Essays of the Seventeenth Century*, ed. J. E. Spingarn, Oxford, 1908–1909, II.137.
[55] See the editors' Introduction to Sprat's *History*, pp. xiiff. Compare Swift's satire on scientific dissection in the *Tale of a Tub* (*Works*, I.77, 109–10) or Pope's attack on impious researches in the *Essay on Man*, II.19 ff. (TE III.i. 56ff. and nn.).
[56] Sprat, *History*, p. 113; *Gulliver's Travels*, III.v (*Works*, XI.185–6). On the latter, see further the commentary in *Gulliver's Travels*, World Classics, Oxford, 1986, ed. Paul Turner, pp. 350–1, n. 29. [57] *Mechanical Operation*, II (*Works*, I.189).
[58] *Mechanical Operation*, II (*Works*, I.183); for another example of the distinction between the brain's issue (words) and its excrements, see Swift's early poem, 'Verses wrote in a Lady's Ivory Table-Book' (1698?), *Poems*, I.61.

an illustration of the truism that scientific enquiry and Dissenting religion were viewed as culturally subversive in radically similar ways. It is all the more striking for being inexplicit, showing itself not in pointed innuendoes about the Puritan promotion of scientific as against classical or humanistic studies, or the Royal Society's imputed openness to Puritan influences, but in discrete passages composed more than 20 years apart with no evident notion of signalling any connection between them.

The Laputian 'Expedient ... that since Words are only Names for *Things*, it would be more convenient for all Men to carry about them, such *Things* as were necessary to express the particular Business they are to discourse on', shows the scientific demand for a plain style dissolving into a traffic of bare objects, which defeat human communication in the very effort to make it direct and unmediated.[59] The corresponding passage in the *Mechanical Operation* targets orgiastic excesses rather than plain styles. But it suggests equally unworkable and appalling immediacies, a display of unverbalised feelings parallel to the Laputians' unverbalised facts, both involving modes of expression and experience which the whole tradition of the 'garment of style', with its 'Flowers, and Figures, and Ornaments', was designed to disguise, circumvent or transcend.

The sectaries' substitution of words by 'a Hum, a Sigh or a Groan' would not have seemed absurd to Sterne's Uncle Toby half a century later, any more than scientific objectives of stylistic economy and empirical validation seemed absurd to many of Swift's own contemporaries. The pre-Romantic or Romantic idea that the most genuine expressions of feeling or the most complete experience of sympathy are beyond the power of words to do justice to, was perceived by Swift with uncanny intuition in the miscellaneous inarticulate 'modernisms' he repudiated. There is a deep paradoxical connection, comically exploited by satirists, between cults of wordlessness and the demand for an unadorned factuality which purportedly depended on a plain, bare, and exact use of words. The tension between the inevitability of words in literary expression and the aspiration to escape or transcend them, was to become a major preoccupation among later novelists and poets.

Ideals of bare scientific precision, and of circumstantial and confessional factuality such as novelists were one day to practise, and

[59] *Gulliver's Travels*, III.v (*Works*, XI.185).

such as Lady Mary complained of over the shortage of fig-leaves in Richardson, are interacting strands in the complex history of prose style. Defoe is a writer in whom the two strands combine, but Swift professed not to notice Defoe, let alone read him, though he took strenuous notice of his not taking notice. There existed few novels for Swift to read, and he was doubtless disinclined to read any. The question of whether *Gulliver's Travels* contains parody of *Robinson Crusoe* is contested, both as to fact and as an interpretative issue, though no one doubts that it parodies a style of narrative plainness and particularity. Swift also mocked pretensions to scientific precision in *A Tale of a Tub* as well as in *Gulliver's Travels*, reducing them in the latter especially to a non-verbal incoherence of jostling objects. But the *Tale*, with its appended *Discourse Concerning the Mechanical Operation of the Spirit* (whose 'form', incidentally, is that of a learned communication to a scientific body), brought together even more strikingly the wordy garrulities of self-revelation among 'modern' writers ('Dryden, L'Estrange, *and some others*'),[60] *and* the orgiastic word*less* antics of the sectaries, viewing both as more or less identical forms of indecent exposure: and the terms in which Swift does this, as I suggest in chapters 7 and 9, sound almost as if he were parodying Sterne some sixty-odd years before the event.

The distrust of scientific enquiry as a probing into secrets of nature often runs parallel with, or uses the same vocabulary as, advocacies of reticence in theology, in religious ritual, in social ceremonies and decencies. Swift warned his 'Young Gentleman, Lately Entered into Holy Orders' against attempting to explain 'the Mysteries of the Christian Religion':

And, indeed, since Providence intended there should be Mysteries; I do not see how it can be agreeable to *Piety, Orthodoxy*, or good *Sense*, to go about such a Work. For, to me there seems to be a manifest Dilemma in the Case: If you explain them, they are Mysteries no longer; if you fail, you have laboured to no Purpose.[61]

In 'Several Scattered Hints Concerning Philosophy and Learning' in his *Note-Book* of the 1750s, Burke spoke of the reductive pseudo-realism or misplaced wit of 'authors who talk of the Generation of mankind as getting rid of an excrement'. If we 'hide it in the obscurity of night', it is 'not because it is dishonourable but because it is

---

[60] *Tale of a Tub*, Apology (*Works*, I.3).   [61] Swift, *Works*, IX.77.

mysterious'.[62] Burke is not here expressing the humility of the patristic reminder that *inter urinas et faeces nascimur*, still less a Yeatsian exaltation at the thought that 'Love has pitched his mansion in/ The place of excrement.' His words are a 'serious' counterpart to Swiftian or Popeian jokes about concealing the cloacal mysteries in an appropriate 'temple' of their own.[63] In the same paragraph of his *Note-Book*, Burke had been asserting the value of funeral ceremonies because 'they throw a decent Veil over the weak and dishonourable circumstances of our Nature. What shall we say to that philosophy, that would strip it naked?' The words contain both the thinking and the specific vocabulary (of veils, of the weakness of 'our naked shivering nature') of Burke's central political doctrine, and his most impassioned rhetoric, in the *Reflections*.

Burke's rhetorical question, despite its scorn of 'that philosophy', highlights the fact that such phrases as 'stripping naked' or 'the naked truth', like Fielding's 'exactest copying', are more or less permanently available for honorific use. They may function independently of ideological predisposition, as buzz-words, adaptable to a variety of rhetorical uses, and easily pressed by natural processes of linguistic opportunism into the service of assertions of personal honesty and truthful sobriety, or descriptions of any powerful unadulterated effect (as when Burke's friend Reynolds spoke of 'the naked majesty of Homer'), or repudiations of stylistic extravagance (excesses of 'metaphysical' wit-writing, incredibility of high-flown romances). Fielding's defence of exactest copying is in this sense *ad hoc*, as are one or two pronouncements ostensibly in support of stylistic 'nakedness' in Pope's poems.[64] These are particularly far removed from Sprat's Royal Society ideal of scientific economy. In the *Epistle to a Lady* he

---

[62] Burke, *Note-Book*, pp. 91–2; cf. Gibbon's more ironic version: 'Decency and ignorance cast a veil over the mystery of generations [*sic*], but I may relate that after floating nine months in a liquid element, I was painfully transported into the vital air' (*Autobiographies*, ed. John Murray, London, 1896, p.33).

[63] Yeats, 'Crazy Jane talks with the Bishop', in *Poems*, ed. Finneran, pp. 259–60; Swift, 'A Panegyrick on the Dean', lines 201 ff. (*Poems*, III.893 ff.); see also Gulliver's first act in the converted Lilliputian temple in which he is housed, though he subsequently for hygienic reasons performed 'that Business in open Air' (*Gulliver's Travels*, II.i, *Works*, XI.29); see also the more public rites of Cloacina in *Dunciad*, II.93ff. (TE, v.300 and commentary at v.108–9).

[64] Reynolds, *Discourses*, p.175, Pope *Epistle to a Lady*, lines 187ff, TE III.ii. 65; *Essay on Criticism*, lines 294, 289–336, TE I.271–6; a third example, 'I tell the naked fact without disguise' is satirical (*Dunciad*, IV.433, TE V.383). Pope's significant pronouncements tend to be concerned either with the decorum of suitable styles (*Essay on Criticism*, line 319) or with striking a mean between bareness and overdress (*Epistle to Burlington*, line 52, TE III.ii. 142).

contrasts poets and painters who produce flatteringly decorated portraits of the great with genuine artists whose 'true delight' is 'To draw the Naked', and whose moral integrity shows itself in drawing 'exactest traits' from humble models. Pope is here primarily concerned with moral integrity, as against the sort of stylistic ornament that combines artistic incompetence with self-interested lies. He is not dealing with the proper style for communicating these exactest traits, and does not envisage this style as naked in the sense discussed here.

In an earlier and more characteristic passage, in the *Essay on Criticism*, Pope celebrates the *'naked Nature'* in a more specifically stylistic sense. Here he is opposing not moral untruths, but a 'glitt'ring', 'conceited' style, 'One *glaring Chaos* and *wild Heap* of *Wit*'. He says that it is those (poets and painters) 'unskill'd to trace/ The *naked Nature* and the *living Grace*' who thus 'hide with *Ornaments* their *Want of Art*'. Again 'nakedness' is an *ad hoc* term, serving a local rhetorical purpose, and whatever it precisely suggested in Pope's mind is massively qualified in ensuing lines by a succession of pronouncements on the theme of expression as the dress of thought. The line which immediately follows the passage is the famous '*True Wit* is *Nature* to Advantage drest', after which Pope warns against those who care *excessively* for 'language' (valuing '*Books*, as Women *Men*, for *Dress*'), and goes on to state the ideal of 'true *Expression*':

> But true *Expression*, like th' unchanging *Sun*,
> *Clears*, and *improves* whate'er it shines upon,
> It *gilds* all Objects, but it *alters* none.
> Expression is the *Dress* of *Thought* . . .

and so on to the remarks about 'suitable' styles which have already been noted. Pope's 'nakedness' may remain 'unaltered', but in twenty-odd lines it has also become not only 'improved' and 'gilded', but in fact clothed. The parallel with Fielding protesting exactest copying in the teeth of his own burlesque extravagance is instructive.

It is well known that, during the period covered by this volume, changes were taking place whose discourse not only favoured scientific reporting and various forms of literary introspection, but also drew some of its ideological and rhetorical ammunition from primitivist assertions of the innocence and dignity of naked unaccommodated man. This protracted transformation of 'the mind of Europe' (the phrase is T. S. Eliot's)[65] generated anxieties of cultural extinction

---

[65] T. S. Eliot, 'Tradition and the Individual Talent' (1919), *Selected Essays*, London, 1953, p. 16.

like that of Pope's *Dunciad* (in this and other ways a proleptic *Waste Land*), and it includes among its eventual political consequences the convulsions of the French Revolution itself (an historical event accompanied by an unusually insistent rhetorical preoccupation with images of nakedness and dress: naked reason, naked shivering nature, the decent drapery of life, the coat of prejudice, and, of course, the *sans-culottes*). Hence, no doubt, even at an early stage, some of the fraught protective eloquence expended by conservative thinkers on the dignity and value of ornament and dress. Hence, too, perhaps the possibility of self-deception, when exactest copying or the naked truth are claimed by writers who, in the terms of my argument, manifestly belong to an opposite and older tradition, which would stress how essential it is to cover these things.

Writers in this and earlier periods were content to speak of style as dress and ornament, partly because their critical vocabulary and the available traditions of critical thought were neither inclined nor equipped to deal in a post-Romantic terminology of 'organic' form. But to dismiss such formulations as frivolously concerned with mere decoration is itself inadequate. For one thing, the concern with the integrity of a work of art that went under the complex and multifarious label of decorum, as Rosemond Tuve has argued in the case of poems of an earlier period, shows the issue to be a more serious and sophisticated thing in practice than it has been given credit for; or, for that matter, than some thumbnail sketches (of 'suitable' styles, sound echoing sense, etc.) in the *Essay on Criticism* and older Arts of Poetry might suggest to modern readers. Good poems tend in any case to outpace even those critical theories which they obey or celebrate, and which might be said to animate them: Pope's poems, including the *Essay on Criticism*, are subtler and more exciting successes than the doctrines of the *Essay on Criticism* can altogether account for.

THE PUBLICK BENEFITS OF 'LA BELLE NATURE'

But the Augustan habit of discussing literature in terms of social activities and the social forms, of the dance and the graces of conversation and dress, goes with an actively felt assumption that these social forms represent a high civilised achievement: moral poise, the sociable and public virtues, and social and political stability were ultimately bound up with it. That the triviality of mere dress or ornament, the absurdity of over-dress, the ridiculous insufficiency of mere dancing-skill, or the foppery of beaux and dancing-masters, were widely acknowledged, does not alter the serious respect which was rooted into comparisons of 'True Ease in Writing' with dancing-skill, or of style with dress. Dryden came (temporarily and for certain purposes) to grow 'weary of his long-loved mistress, Rhyme'. But his early celebration of rhyme as resembling a well-contrived dance is alive with a rich feeling for ideas of ceremony, order, and social cohesion.[66] And, if his still grander talk about rhyme being 'more fit for the ends of government' comes over more crudely, it hints at relations between literary practice and matters of restraint and authority which reach beyond the literary into the moral and political spheres.[67] We may feel, too, that Dryden sounds freer and more confident in proclaiming his submission to the 'government' of rhyme, than in a starchy outburst (itself in rhyme) of temporary emancipation: 'Passion's too fierce to be in fetters bound'.[68] We need not take sides in a technical debate about rhyme in 'serious plays' which no longer has much application, in order to recognise in Dryden's best discussions the keen sense, well beyond the ostensible expression of analogy, of intimate relations and interactions between literature and social life.

It is similarly clear that later theorists of *la belle nature*, including Batteux and Reynolds as well as Burke, assume that the question of stylistic dress has social and political implications. For Batteux, writing in 1746, the contemplation of *la belle nature* is 'au profit de la société humaine'; the history of nations shows that humanity, and the civic virtues of which it is the mother, flow from the cultivation of the arts; the civilising properties of taste involve not only a generalised definition of taste as a habitual love of order, or the common parallel between taste and virtue, but a sense of specific relationship between, for example, symmetry of form and good morals.[69]

Burke's early *Note-Book* offers an unusually specific scenario of the process by which poetry exercises a civilising force, over and above any 'preceptive' elements in the poem. The 'great Benefits that result' from poetry and eloquence 'are not in giving precepts but creating habits':

[66] Prologue to *Aureng-Zebe* (1676); Watson, I.192; cf. also Preface to *All for Love* (1678), I.231; *Of Dramatic Poesy*, I.89; for a later celebration of rhyme, see 'To the Earl of Roscommon' (1684), II.15. [67] 'Defence of An Essay', Watson, I.115.
[68] Prologue to *Aureng-Zebe*, Watson, I.192.
[69] Charles Batteux, *Les Beaux Arts Réduits à un même Principe*, new edn., Paris, 1747, pp. 71, 123–8, 130 *et passim*.

For the mind when it is entertained with high fancies, elegant and polite sentiments, beautiful language, and harmonious sounds, is modelled insensibly into a disposition to elegance and humanity. For it is the bias the mind takes that gives direction to our lives; and not any rules or maxims of morals and behaviour. It imitates what is called the natural Temper best; and this is the best guide and guard we can have in every Virtue. For though rules, fear, interest, or other motives may induce us to virtue, it is the virtue of a bad soil, harsh and disagreeable.

Burke's conception of the socialising effects of poetry postulates gradual processes of habituation which prefigure the ideas about custom and nature in the *Reflections* (indeed the 'Several Scattered Hints' go on to speak of a 'general principle operating to produce Customs, that is a more sure guide than our Theories', in a way which encapsulates one of the central anti-revolutionary themes of the later work).[70]

Reynolds, who was to be a close supporter of Burke's antirevolutionary polemics, similarly argued that the pursuit of beauty in the arts extends 'imperceptibly into publick benefits':

refinement of taste ... if it does not lead directly to purity of manners, obviates at least their greatest depravation, by disentangling the mind from appetite, and conducting the thoughts through successive stages of excellence, till that contemplation of universal rectitude and harmony which began by Taste, may, as it is exalted and refined, conclude in Virtue.[71]

This is a generalised expression of a connection which Fielding expressed with a painful and specific immediacy when he told in the *Voyage to Lisbon* of the sailors and watermen who jeered at his crippled state: 'it was a lively picture of that cruelty and inhumanity, in the nature of men' which an English mob reveals in its unadulterated form, and which 'never shews itself in men who are polish'd and refin'd, in such manner as human nature requires, to produce that perfection of which it is susceptible, and to purge away that malevolence of disposition, of which, at our birth we partake in common with the savage creation'[72] ('purge' is a term to which I shall return).

The polishing and refinement are presumed to come from that

---

[70] Burke, *Note-Book*, pp. 88, 90. For a later analogy between poems and states, see *Reflections*, p. 129/172.

[71] Reynolds, *Discourses*, p. 171. For an important discussion of the political subtext of the *Discourses*, see John Barrell, *The Political Theory of Painting from Reynolds to Hazlitt*, New Haven and London, 1986, pp. 69–162.

[72] Fielding, *Journal of a Voyage to Lisbon*, ed. Harold E. Pagliaro, New York, 1963, p. 45 (26 June 1754).

whole gentlemanly or liberal education, which includes a cultivated taste in the arts as well as the lessons of the dancing-master, and about which Fielding speaks more ambiguously elsewhere. Fielding thinks of the potential achievement as more total, and speaks in more absolute terms ('never shews itself', 'that perfection of which it is susceptible', 'purge away') than does Reynolds, whose formulations are somewhat guarded ('if it does not lead directly to purity of manners, obviates at least their greatest depravation'). Fielding's larger claim gains status from the fact that he is speaking from a painful experience of the opposite; as Burke does (writing under a sense of public menace rather than of private pain) when he speaks in the *Reflections* of that 'civil society' without which 'man could not by any possibility arrive at the perfection of which his nature is capable'.[73] Neither Fielding nor Burke, nor for that matter any of the major writers in the conservative Augustan tradition, took an optimistic view of man's nature or the present state of the culture, and it may be that their expression of such ideals is only likely to occur in its most absolute form in contexts of defeated aspiration. The similarity in the cast of thought in the last three statements will seem the more remarkable when one recognises that one is speaking of personal experience, the second of a theory of the arts, and the third of affairs of state.

Fielding, Reynolds and Burke all make their claims with an urgency of eloquence which, it may be felt, depends partly on their choosing in context not to use those more trivialising images of clothes or of dancing-skill which they feel able to invoke in less painful or exalted contexts. And the dress of thought, the ornaments of art, the outward forms, are deeply germane to the whole issue of the social and political import of *la belle nature*. The metaphor of dress, potentially trivialising, sometimes acquires eloquence when rephrased in terms of its opposite, the naked, the unadorned, that natural state of unaccommodated man, on whose splendours and squalors almost every Augustan writer has something to say. It is the 'naked shivering nature' more than the 'decent drapery of life' that gives Burke's famous passage its strongest rhetorical charge. Even in the *Reflections*, the celebration of that 'wardrobe of a moral imagination' which is 'to be exploded' by the Revolution, is offset by a later comment that the new régime had taken 'an old huge full-bottomed perriwig out of the wardrobe of the antiquated frippery of Louis XIV. to cover the

[73] *Reflections*, p. 148/196.

premature baldness of the national assembly'. When he chose to show up the 'pretenders to liberty' in a 'servile imitation of one of the poorest resources of doting despotism', it was this satirical example that Burke found handiest for ridicule, even though it ran counter to the idiom and tendency of his purplest celebration of French royalty.[74] He was specifically exploiting an old anti-French stereotype: '*France*', as Gay had said sarcastically in 1713, 'may as properly be called *the Fountain of Dress*, as *Greece* was of literature'.[75] The primitive unpoliced state, even when it is thought of as 'solitary, poor, nasty, brutish, and short',[76] often acquires something of the dignity which comes fully into its own with Romantic assertions of the grandeur of unaccommodated man. In pity or even contempt the image tends to be freer of bathos or ridicule than its opposite image of overdress: the Yahoos may be disgusting, but they are never ludicrous like their modern incarnation or *alter ego*, the beau.

Speaking of the primitive, unpoliced condition as one of 'nakedness' has always been commonplace, and it has followed from this that the image of 'dress' (despite its almost built-in tendency to reduce the dignity of the issue) could readily be used to describe the achievements of civilisation, becoming in the process more than a matter of mere surface, whether in a good, bad, or neutral sense:

> The whole World without *Art*, and *Dress*,
> Would be but one great *Wilderness*.
> And mankind but a Savage Heard,
> For all that Nature had Conferd.
> That do's but *Rough-hew*, and *Design*,
> Leave *Art* to *Polish*, and *Refine*.[77]

So the Lady tells Hudibras. We are reminded that for some, notably Swift, Puritans were modern manifestations of unregenerate man, a form of primitive Yahoo obeying his unrestrained instincts and disowning the civil and religious authority of state and church, tradition, and rule. (Paul Fussell has noted a different analogy

---

[74] *Reflections*, pp. 128/171, 277/356. See also the remarks on the 'perfect despotism' of Louis XIV, in Burke's Speech on the Army Estimates, 9 February 1790, *Works*, III.272: 'Though that despotism was proudly arrayed in manners, gallantry, splendour, magnificence, and even covered over with the imposing robes of science, literature, and arts, it was, in government, nothing better than a painted and gilded tyranny ...'

[75] *Guardian*, No. 149, 1 September 1713, in John Gay, *Poetry and Prose*, ed. Vinton A. Dearing and Charles E. Beckwith, Oxford, 1974, II.462.

[76] Thomas Hobbes, *Leviathan*, I.xiii, ed. Michael Oakeshott, Oxford, (nd), p. 82.

[77] Samuel Butler, *Hudibras* (1663–78), Third Part, 'The Ladies Answer to the Knight', lines 233–8, ed. John Wilders, Oxford, 1967, p. 317.

concerning Puritan individualism in language and in dress: their prose style was deemed to be 'as novel and eccentric as their dress and demeanour: both betray the distance of the Puritan from the centre of general human nature').[78] The reverse valuation of the same image is epitomised by Tom Paine, at the beginning of *Common Sense* (1776), where he is arguing that 'government, even in its best state, is but a necessary evil', and adds: 'Government, like dress, is the badge of lost innocence; the palaces of kings are built upon the ruins of the bowers of paradise'[79] (the passage illustrates, incidentally, what Fussell never quite pressed to its full implications, how close the metaphor of dress is to that other common metaphor of civilised achievement, the building, in eighteenth-century thought).[80]

Here, even the negative valuation is stated with great splendour. More often, the hostility of radical thinkers would take a more dismissive form, connoting mere surface and inessential accretion. It is this dismissive usage that Burke revalidates, defiantly making respectable the contemptuous phrases of revolutionary rhetoric, when he says that it is unwise 'to cast away the coat of prejudice, and to leave nothing but the naked reason'.[81] Burke reinstates the value of 'prejudice' in politics in much the same way, and at much the same time, as his friend Reynolds was doing so in the arts.[82]

In this passage, 'the naked reason' is associated not with unaccommodated man, but with the inhumane pedantry of abstract principle. In another passage, Burke said: 'I cannot stand forward, and give praise or blame to any thing which relates to human actions, and human concerns, on a simple view of the object, as it stands stripped of every relation, in all the nakedness and solitude of metaphysical abstraction.' The 'coat of prejudice', which covers the naked abstraction, is the same as that which covers what, in the most famous of Burke's statements, is called 'our naked shivering nature'.[83] The

---

[78] Paul Fussell, *The Rhetorical World of Augustan Humanism*, Oxford, 1965, p. 219.
[79] Thomas Paine, *Complete Writings*, ed. Philip S. Foner, New York, 1969, 1.4–5.
[80] See Fussell, *Rhetorical World*, pp. 218–25, for some discussion of this.
[81] *Reflections*, p. 138/183.
[82] Reynolds' *Discourses* were delivered between 1769 and 1790. His 'Ironical Discourse' was written in 1791, and was triggered by Burke's *Reflections*. See *Portraits by Sir Joshua Reynolds*, ed. Frederick W. Hilles, London, 1952, pp. 123–46. On 'prejudice' see especially the parallel passages on pp. 136–7. Also pp. 157–8 for Reynolds' note 'On Prejudice' preserved, like the 'Ironical Discourse', among the Boswell papers at Yale, and a note to Du Fresnoy's *Art of Painting*, in Reynolds, *Literary Works*, 5th edn., 1819, III.168–70. For some qualifications, see Irène Simon, 'Reynolds on Custom and Prejudice', *English Studies*, 65 (1984), 226–36.
[83] *Reflections*, pp. 58/89–90; 128/171.

difference, at least superficially, is in the thing which is being covered. 'Our naked shivering nature' needs covering because it is too dangerously 'natural', animal, human, 'the naked reason' because it is not 'natural', animal or human enough. When he talks about the latter, he opposes the warm and natural sentiments of human beings to revolutionary dummies, 'filled, like stuffed birds in a museum, with chaff and rags, and paltry, blurred shreds of paper about the rights of man'. *The Rights of Man* became the title of Paine's famous reply to Burke, and where Burke saw the revolutionaries as birds not live but 'stuffed', Paine saw the *ancien régime* as a bird not live but 'dying'. Burke, he said, in a famous phrase that returns us strikingly to an 'organic' variant of the metaphor of dress, 'pities the plumage, but forgets the dying bird'.[84]

THE DECENT DRAPERY OF LIFE

The best-known of Burke's images of civilisation as clothing, with which this discussion began, opposes it to the nakedness not of abstract reason, but of man's primitive state. The full paragraph reads as follows:

But now all is to be changed. All the pleasing illusions, which made power gentle, and obedience liberal, which harmonized the different shades of life, and which, by a bland assimilation, incorporated into politics the sentiments which beautify and soften private society, are to be dissolved by this new conquering empire of light and reason. All the decent drapery of life is to be rudely torn off. All the superadded ideas, furnished from the wardrobe of a moral imagination, which the heart owns, and the understanding ratifies, as necessary to cover the defects of our naked shivering nature, and to raise it to dignity in our own estimation, are to be exploded as a ridiculous, absurd, and antiquated fashion.

It is the climax of Burke's account of Marie Antoinette and the October days, which has been both greatly admired and widely derided.[85] It begins a few pages earlier with a passage whose lurid details are often contested, and in which there is a horrified glimpse of the queen with just enough time to flee 'almost naked'. It has been said that the queen was almost certainly fully dressed and anyway unlikely to have been seen in her flight to the king.[86] The previous

---

[84] *Reflections*, pp. 137/182; Paine, *Rights of Man*, in *Complete Writings*, 1.260.

[85] For some examples of both, see F. P. Lock, *Burke's Reflections on the Revolution in France*, Unwin Critical Library, London and Boston, 1985, pp. 110–11, 141–3.

[86] *Reflections*, pp. 122/164. For expressions of scepticism of Burke's account, see Mitchell, p. 122 n., and Isaac Kramnick, *The Rage of Edmund Burke*, New York, 1977, pp. 152–3.

year, in his indictment of Warren Hastings, Burke had written with similar passion of the maltreatment by Hastings and his men of Indian women, some of whom were 'stripped naked' and some 'of the first rank'.[87] Isaac Kramnick has suggested that both passages share the same obsessive fantasy of the 'defiling of feminine rank by sexually aggressive upstarts', a 'preoccupation with naked women' which caused derision in the House of Commons, and the same configuration of political anxieties: 'the treatment of these princesses becomes the grand metaphor for all that India represented for Burke just as the treatment of Marie Antoinette on the night of 6 October 1789 would symbolise the passing of chivalry and the old order'.[88]

Kramnick's psychobiographical reading has been shown to be vulnerable on several points of detail,[89] but the last observation has particular force. From the present perspective, the passage is of interest less as an expression of personal apprehensions than as a thickly woven tapestry of classic eighteenth-century attitudes. The 'pleasing illusions, which made power gentle, and obedience liberal ... and ... incorporated into politics the sentiments which beautify and soften private society' are the larger, political counterpart of the effect of a liberal gentlemanly education as seen by Fielding in the passage about the sailors and watermen, whose heartless jeering would never be heard from 'men who are polish'd and refin'd, in such manner as human nature requires, to produce that perfection of which it is susceptible, and to purge away that malevolence of disposition, of which, at our birth we partake in common with the savage creation'. The view of 'our naked shivering nature' combines a Hobbesian realism or even a Swiftian contempt for Yahoos, with a Johnsonian compassion ready to identify itself *personally* with the general lot: '*our* naked shivering nature'.[90]

It is interesting that what Burke imagines this naked nature to be covered with, in this passage, is *drapery*, not dress. Too much should not be made of this: only a few pages later, he speaks honorifically, as we saw, of the '*coat* of prejudice'.[91] But drapery is the painter's and sculptor's term for a stylised formal design, sometimes specifically distinguishable from clothes actually worn in real life. When Rey-

---

[87] Burke, Speeches in the Impeachment of Warren Hastings, 18 and 19 February 1788, in *Works*, VII.189, 229, cited by Kramnick, pp. 136–7.

[88] Kramnick, *Rage of Edmund Burke*, pp. 137–8; also 152–3.

[89] See F. P. Lock, *Burke's Reflections*, pp. 197–8, 215 nn. 97–9.

[90] *Journal of a Voyage to Lisbon*, p. 45, *Reflections*, p. 128/171.

[91] *Reflections*, p. 138/183, italics mine.

nolds spoke of it, he frequently had in mind a classicising or Romanised stylisation, especially in sculpture, evoking an ironic symmetry with the wedding-cake Latinism of French revolutionary art. As Marx pointed out, the French Revolution 'draped itself alternately as the Roman republic and the Roman empire ... in Roman costume and with Roman phrases'.[92]

Fielding spoke in *Joseph Andrews*, III.i, of 'the Drapery of a Picture' as something relatively inessential, which 'Fashion varies at different Times'.[93] What Reynolds required from it was, on the contrary, what distinguished it from both the fashion-governed changeability and the demeaning 'naturalness' of a realistically pictured modern (or 'period') dress. He complained that Lairesse's *Death of Cleopatra* was (for a 'heroick' picture) 'degraded by the naturalness of the white sattin, which is thrown over her ... this of Lairesse is not drapery, it is white sattin'.[94] In Discourse IV he had said:

In the same manner as the historical Painter never enters into the detail of colours, so neither does he debase his conceptions with minute attention to the discriminations of Drapery. It is the inferior stile that marks the variety of stuffs. With him, the cloathing is neither woollen, nor linen, nor silk, sattin, or velvet: it is drapery; it is nothing more. The art of disposing the foldings of the drapery makes a very considerable part of the painter's study. To make it merely natural is a mechanical operation.[95]

This identification of the 'merely natural' with 'mechanical operation' is a constant theme of Reynolds. It has Swiftian reverberations, and the fact reminds us of the degenerately 'natural' spontaneities of the sectaries, stimulated by 'mechanical operation' from the preacher, and the paradoxical unhealthy transitions 'from *Art* into *Nature*' and vice-versa in Swift's satirical *Discourse* on the subject.[96] Reynolds differs in his emphasis, distinguishing the 'mechanical trade' of mere ornamental accomplishment from the 'liberal art' of serious painting.[97] The artist worthy of the name becomes identified with the truly gentlemanly in a manner which is rather beside Swift's point. But phrases like 'mechanical operation' cannot escape Swiftian

---

[92] Reynolds, *Discourses*, p. 138; Karl Marx, *The Eighteenth Brumaire of Louis Bonaparte* (1852), in Marx and Engels, *Selected Works*, London, 1968, p. 96, and see p. 97; see also Ronald Paulson, *Representations of Revolution (1789–1820)*, New Haven and London, 1983, pp. 10–11.

[93] *Joseph Andrews*, III.i, pp. 189–90.

[94] Reynolds, *A Journey into Flanders and Holland, in the Year MDCCLXXXI*, in *Literary Works*, II.361, 364.

[95] Reynolds, *Discourses*, p. 62; for the 'ironical' version, see 'Ironical Discourse', *Portraits*, p. 140.

[96] Swift, *Works*, I.176.   [97] Reynolds, *Discourses*, p. 57.

association. When Reynolds repeatedly speaks of the lower kind of artist as a 'mere mechanick', the pretension of gentlemanly uppishness is close to a familiar hauteur of Swift's.[98] The mechanic is 'mob' ('excuse the term', Burke explained to the 'Gentleman in Paris' to whom the *Reflections* is addressed 'it is still in use here'), and mob, for Swift as for Burke, is a collective form of the 'natural' man (though Swift complained of the word as a vulgar neologism). Two paragraphs after the passage about 'our naked shivering nature' Burke spoke of the revolutionary creed as 'this mechanic philosophy'.[99]

Reynolds' aesthetic theories, as well as his vocabulary, bear a close relation to Burke's political views. The two men were very close, and influenced one another's thinking, notably so at the time when the *Reflections* were written. Reynolds shared with Burke and Malone a loathing of the French Revolution, as well as a deep conservatism in art and a dislike of new artists like Blake, radical in both politics and art. (Blake, as is well known, returned the compliment.) Reynolds' defences of 'prejudice' in the 'Ironical Discourse' as well as in the straight discourses are full of interacting echoes with Burke's.[100] The following passage from the 'Ironical Discourse'is Burkeian not only in sentiment but in the most detailed elements of its vocabulary and imagery:

Destroy every trace that remains of ancient taste. Let us pull the whole fabric down at once, root it up even to its foundation. Let us begin the art again upon this solid ground of nature and of reason. The world will then see what naked art is, in its uneducated, unprejudiced, unadulterated state.[101]

The passage follows immediately upon a scornful mimicry of the imputedly revolutionary requirement that paintings should be realistic, so that a man might 'recognise his neighbour's face' or 'mistake the drapery ... for real stuff ... silk, satin, or velvet', materials which (in an extension of Swiftian sarcasm) are deemed the proper province of the tailor. The nineteenth-century 'realist' insistence on contemporary personalities and dress, 'the derbies, the black dress-coats, the polished shoes or the peasants' sabots' demanded by Champfleury, who was Courbet's 'major supporter in the "*bataille realiste*"', was the

[98] Reynolds, *Dicourses*, p. 43.
[99] *Reflections*, pp. 135/179; 129/172; Swift, *Works*, II.175–7; IV.113.
[100] See Reynolds, *Portraits*, pp. 123 ff. and see above, n. 82. For Blake, see below pp. 166–7 and n.116, and Reynolds, *Portraits*, pp. 123 and n. 125.
[101] Reynolds, *Portraits*, pp. 140–2.

total antithesis of Reynolds' outlook.[102] Courbet's declaration in 1861 that 'le réalisme est par essence l'art démocratique' would have been all too self-evident to Reynolds, who had affirmed in Discourse XIII (1786) that art 'is, and ought to be, in many points of view, and strictly speaking, no imitation at all of external nature. Perhaps it ought to be as far removed from the vulgar idea of imitation, as the refined civilised state in which we live, is removed from a gross state of nature.'[103]

The 'decent drapery', in art as in life, for both Reynolds and Burke, provides the appropriate cover. Reynolds' theory actually allowed for nude figures as well as for drapery, as against the portrayal of contemporaneous clothes which 'an individual ... himself wore'.[104] This nudity is conceived, however, as a formalised and ideal state, stripped of individual peculiarities and blemishes (these being not nature 'but an accidental deviation from her accustomed practice'). In Discourse VII, which contains some of the main statements on dress and drapery, Dutch painters are faulted for introducing 'into their historical pictures exact representations of individual objects with all their imperfections'. By contrast, Reynolds notes with approval the practice, modelled on ancient statuary, 'of dressing statues of modern heroes or senators in the fashion of the Roman armour or peaceful robe; we go so far as hardly to bear a statue in any other drapery'. The predisposing factors, in addition to the 'veneration' which Greece and Rome 'have a right to claim', are the 'simplicity' of ancient dress, 'consisting of little more than one single piece of drapery', and the fact that 'the old has that great advantage of having custom and prejudice on its side'. These principles, as John Barrell says, apply especially to sculpture, which 'according to Reynolds ... admits of no styles or genre except the grand style'.[105]

Discourse VII exemplifies these points, citing a case of unacceptable nudity, the statue of Voltaire by Pigalle, 'which the sculptor, not having that respect for the prejudices of mankind which he ought to have had, made entirely naked, and as meagre and emaciated as the original is said to be', and which, though 'intended as a publick

---

[102] Reynolds, *Portraits*, pp. 140–4; Linda Nochlin, *Realism*, p. 28; see p. 33 for the politico-aesthetic principle, formulated by Duranty: 'In reality nothing is shocking; in the sun, rags are as good as imperial vestments.'

[103] A. Estignard, *Courbet*, p. 118; Reynolds, *Discourses*, pp.232–3.

[104] *Discourses*, pp. 127–8; Fussell, *Rhetorical World*, p. 217; Barrell, *Political Theory of Painting*, pp. 128, 144, 154.

[105] *Discourses*, pp. 124, 138–9, 175–88; Barrell, *Political Theory of Painting*, pp. 53–4.

ornament and a publick honour', remained unsold. Reynolds goes on to enunciate a principle of change in the arts which is an exact counterpart of Burke's gradualism in politics:

Whoever would reform a nation, supposing a bad taste to prevail in it, will not accomplish his purpose by going directly against the stream of their prejudices. Men's minds must be prepared to receive what is new to them. Reformation is a work of time. A national taste, however wrong it may be, cannot be totally changed at once; we must yield a little to the prepossession which has taken hold on the mind, and we may then bring people to adopt what would offend them, if endeavoured to be introduced by violence.[106]

This concession 'to the prepossession which has taken hold on the mind' rests on a psychological first principle, which Reynolds shared with Burke, that men are by nature indolent and resistant to change (their opposite liking for novelty and innovation being, Reynolds says, a secondary force, soon spent).[107] Burke made nationalist use of this point, proudly distinguishing the English from the French for their sluggish preservation of an ancient 'generosity and dignity': 'Thanks to our sullen resistance to innovation, thanks to the cold sluggishness of our national character, we still bear the stamp of our forefathers.'[108]

In this, Burke resembles and perhaps remembers Swift. In *A Tale of a Tub* (1704), and in the *Project for the Advancement of Religion* (1709), Swift had paid a similar but flatter compliment to English indolence. Defending the argument that a hypocritical virtue is better than 'open Infidelity and Vice' because it 'wears the Livery of Religion', acknowledges its authority, pays tribute to it, and 'is cautious of giving Scandal', he adds in the *Project* that in religion as in love pretence often induces a settled habit and from 'Dissembling, at last grows real'. Why? Because

a long continued Disguise is too great a Constraint upon human Nature, especially an *English* Disposition. Men would leave off their Vices out of meer Weariness.[109]

Swift's rhetoric is less exalted than Reynolds' or Burke's, as we should expect, and he keeps his praise of the natural indolence in a low and somewhat grubby key. Burke's early *Note-Book* has some interesting sentences in support of settled custom and against an excessive

---

[106] *Discourses*, pp. 140–1.

[107] *Discourses*, pp. 139, 146–7, 257. On novelty see also pp. 84–5. Reynolds' objection to novelty is not absolute: see Barrell, *Political Theory of Painting*, pp. 156–7.

[108] *Reflections*, p. 137/181; see also p. 106/145.   [109] Swift, *Works*, II.57.

pursuit of innovative and subtilising 'refinements of reasoning' (also a strong Swiftian antipathy), adding the oddly worded comment that 'I never would have our reasoning too much dephlegmatic'. Here one detects an almost Swiftian testiness, and perhaps even an evocation of the *Tale*'s Martin, 'extremely flegmatick and sedate', maintaining Anglican composure and stability beside his unruly brothers.[110] Both Swift and Burke show the same dislike of 'innovation', and the same impulse to harness the facts of human psychology as they saw them to the preservation of established morality and institutionalised religion. 'Is not Religion a *Cloak*?'[111] Yes, but cloaks are better than nudity, as Burke's defence of the 'coat of prejudice' was to proclaim, standing Swift's irony on its head.[112]

The difference even here should not be exaggerated. Swift was a harsher thinker, likelier to call a spade a spade, a phrase, incidentally, which he used in ambivalent jeering at the lowered perspectives that Strephon and Chloe are forced into by the stripping of Strephon's rosy illusions about the female body.[113] What Burke will call 'pleasing illusions' and 'the decent drapery of life', Swift will sometimes call hypocrisy. But if the cloak of pretended religion is repudiated in the more absolute satire of the *Tale of a Tub*, it is given its practical political value in the *Project*'s world of practical political preoccupation. In the latter work a bad coat turns into a good coat which then turns into second nature, as 'habits' tend to do. Because we are too lazy to keep taking our coats off, they eventually accommodate themselves to our bodies. Burke similarly says the old evolving British constitution 'is a vestment, which accommodates itself to the body', thereby also potentially imposing its shape on,[114] or 'moulding', the body politic: the French, who 'had the elements of a constitution very nearly as good as could be wished' chose disastrously instead 'to act as if [they] had never been moulded into civil society'.[115]

To Blake, who as an artist had no fear of the plasticity of natural or naked contours, who asserted against Reynolds that 'the Drapery is formed alone by the Shape of the Naked', and whose political attitudes were entirely opposite to Reynolds', the closeness of Reynolds' ideas to those of Burke, and the political implications of

[110] Burke, *Note-Book*, p. 90; Swift, *Tale*, VI (*Works*, 1.87).   [111] Swift, *Tale*, II (*Works*, 1.47).
[112] *Reflections*, p. 138/183.
[113] Swift, 'Strephon and Chloe', line 204, in *Poems*, ed. Harold Williams, 2nd edn., Oxford, 1958, II.590.
[114] Burke, 'Speech on a Motion Made in the House of Commons', 7 May 1782, in *Works*, VI.147.
[115] *Reflections*, p. 86/122.

Reynolds' views on art, were depressingly apparent. In response to Malone's praise of Reynolds' endorsement of Burke's *Reflections*, and Malone's satisfaction that Reynolds 'did not live to participate of the gloom' of recent revolutionary times, Blake said of Reynolds' *Discourses:* 'This Whole Book was Written to Serve Political Purposes.' His annotations begin with the words: 'This Man was Hired to Depress Art.'[116] As to Marie Antoinette and 'decent drapery', Blake wrote *c.* 1792: 'The Queen of France just touchd this Globe/ And the Pestilence darted from her Robe.'[117]

For Burke the 'decent drapery' is valuable because it conceals rather than reveals the naked form, or because it moulds it to its own decorous outlines instead of being shaped to the natural contours of the body, as Blake would have required. (It is interesting that eighteenth-century fashions in dress changed progressively from stylised garments that concealed or repressed the body to more flowing designs and fabrics, a transition Rousseau is said to have helped to influence).[118] It would, however, be misleading to see in Burke a simple advocacy of superimposed covering, in some heightened version of Chesterfieldian 'dissimulation'. His language characteristically oscillated between 'drapery' and the organic plasticity implied by images of 'moulding' and growth. In the passage about Marie Antoinette, Burke chooses to stress the most 'artificial' form of clothing, in order to oppose it to the pitiful 'naturalness' of man's 'naked' state. When the 'nakedness' which Burke repudiates is that of abstract principle, Burke stresses its inhumanity and *un*naturalness, and the civilised garment which is contrasted with the nakedness is chosen among those which men wear, like a 'coat'.[119] Paradoxically, the garment serves the same function in both cases, both variants occurring within a short space of one another, and both comprehending the same complex of ideas about the civilised state, just as the two

---

[116] William Blake, 'Annotations to *The Works of Sir Joshua Reynolds*, edited by Edmond Malone. London, 1798', in *Complete Poetry and Prose*, pp. 650, 641, 635. (In the first quotation, the next word after 'Naked' was 'cut away in binding'). The passages in Malone's edition of Reynolds are respectively I.90; I.civ; and I. title-page. This pagination corresponds to that of the 5th edn., 1819, normally cited here.

[117] Blake, 'Let the Brothels of Paris be opened', lines 17–18, *Complete Poetry and Prose*, p. 500.

[118] I owe this information to an unpublished lecture by Richard Martin of the Fashion Institute of Technology, New York, and to *Revolution in Fashion. European Clothing, 1715–1815*, New York, 1989, the catalogue of an exhibition held at the Institute. See the remarks by Jean Starobinski on Rousseau's role (p. 16) and by other contributors on the changes in clothing style in general in the later years of the century (pp. 114, 116, 133 and *passim*).

[119] *Reflections*, pp. 218/282 (on 'plasticity') and 138/183.

'nakednesses', the one inhuman and inhumane, the other inhumane but all too human, are linked by their uncivilised character, and by the fact that the ideology of abstraction tends to extol a reality which Burke considers to be not only miserable and pitiable, but also nasty and brutish, if not short.

THE AUGUST FABRIC OF STATES

Oscillations of this kind have the effect of enforcing the idea that the imagery of drapery and dress is not concerned with mere surfaces, but with the substance of the whole civilised inheritance. The contribution to this of the organic strand in Burke's rhetoric can only be fully understood, however, in the context of another set of interacting metaphors, those of dress and architecture I mentioned earlier, through which concepts of covering also merge into concepts of structure and substance. Here is Burke speaking in defence of that 'first of our prejudices', that 'church establishment' which is a prominent part of the civilised inheritance often alluded to as dress:

For, taking ground on that religious system, of which we are now in possession, we continue to act on the early received, and uniformly continued sense of mankind. That sense not only, like a wise architect, hath built up the august fabric of states, but like a provident proprietor, to preserve the structure from prophanation and ruin, as a sacred temple, purged from all the impurities of fraud, and violence, and injustice, and tyranny, hath solemnly and for ever consecrated the commonwealth, and all that officiate in it.

Only a page or so earlier Burke had warned against what would happen if 'we should uncover our nakedness by throwing off that Christian religion which has hitherto been our boast and our comfort, and one great source of civilization amongst us'.[120]

This image of religion as clothing may be seen as a startling reversal of Swift's famous rhetorical question: 'Is not Religion a *Cloak*?' to which, as I suggested, Burke's answer is a defiant yes, not because he values the hypocrisy which Swift is exposing, but because he is prepared to risk the paradox in order to proclaim the value and the rightness of covering the naked man within. Swift, in this sense, would have agreed with him: 'The want of belief is a defect that ought to be concealed when it cannot be overcome.'[121] Swift also used the metaphor of a building to denote the necessary and vulnerable

---

[120] *Reflections*, pp. 142–43/187–89.   [121] Swift, *Works*, I.47, IX.261.

structure of church and state, notably at the end of the *Project for the Advancement of Religion*, a passage which anticipates Burke's admonition to the French that they possessed, in their constitution, 'in some parts the walls, and in all the foundations of a noble and venerable castle', which though impaired and dilapidated, should be 'built on' rather than pulled down. There is a corresponding boast about 'that old-fashioned constitution, under which we have long prospered', and it is apposite to remember that 'constitution' is also a term with bodily connotations.[122]

In the analogy between dress and buildings, 'fabric' is a link-word: the dress connotation is mainly subtextual in Burke, but it was in the second half of the century that the word's application to cloth or textiles became well-established.[123] It is easy to see that the analogy in general tends not only to add ideas of solidity to those of superficial cover, but to confer on the rhetoric a dignity which the imagery of dress rarely achieves, except, as I suggested, through the potential sublime of its opposite.

Poor naked wretches need both clothes and roofs to cover or protect them, habitations as well as habits. Buildings also have foundations, and the image attaches itself to the idea of religion as 'the basis of civil society' taken up soon after, in the reference to 'taking ground', in the passage about the 'august fabric of states'. 'Taking ground' may also evoke rootedness, and the image of a plant or tree as an emblem of traditional government and ancient stabilities is recurrent in Burke, culminating in the *Reflections* in the passage about the 'British oak', which triggered Yeats' line about 'haughtier-headed Burke that

---

[122] Swift, *Works*, ii.63; *Reflections*, pp. 85–6/121–2, 107/146. For an excellent account of Burke's attachment to the traditional doctrine, probably older than 1600, of an 'ancient constitution', with a body of 'immemorial law' but constantly evolving through 'experience', see J. G. A. Pocock, 'Burke and the Ancient Constitution: A Problem in the History of Ideas', in his *Politics, Language, and Time*, Chicago and London, 1989, pp. 202–32.

[123] The sense of 'A building; an edifice' is much the oldest, and is given in all early editions of Johnson's *Dictionary*, which does not record the sense of 'cloth' or 'textile'. But *OED*, 2nd edn., 1989, s.v. Fabric, sb., 4 and 6b, gives citations for 1753, 1764 and 1791, the earliest of which is from Jonas Hanway, *An Historical Account of the British Trade over the Caspian Sea*, 1753, ii.56. The second example, from Thomas Harmer, *Observations on Divers Passages of Scripture* (1764), 2nd edn., 1776, i. 139, discusses tents in the Holy Land: 'curtains of goats-hair were directed for the Tabernacle ... we may naturally conjecture, that the tents of the Patriarchs ... were of the *same fabric*', which happens, fortuitously in this instance, to bring together the ideas of dwelling and dress. Subtextual punning of a kind similar to Burke's, and doubtless more self-aware, is found in Carlyle, *Sartor Resartus* (1836), i.ix: 'the whole fabric of Government', in *Works of Thomas Carlyle*, London, 1896–1899, i.48. The non-architectural senses of the term seem to have been more available in Burke's or Johnson's time than is suggested by Fussell, *Rhetorical World*, p. 186.

proved the State a tree' (and also Wordsworth's description of Burke himself standing 'like an oak' in his old age).[124] The image was not new, and had been used by both loyalists and revolutionaries at the time of the American Revolution: the 'Tree of Liberty', a 'young oak', is the best-known alternative emblem.[125] (J. G. A. Pocock comments on one of the many ironic reciprocities of the history of the revolutionary debate: 'it is curious to see modern paperback editions of Burke whose cover designs, in fact, glorify revolution, planting the Tree of Liberty where he praised the British Oak').[126] Paine activated both uses in his passage about blossoming and rotten trees at the end of Part Second of the *Rights of Man* (1792). For the rotten kind he associated with Burke he had already proposed in Part First that one should 'Lay then the axe to the root', an idea parodied in advance in Reynolds' 'Ironical Discourse': 'This tree of knowledge . . . is fastened by strong roots to ancient rocks, and is the slow growth of ages . . . Let us pull the whole fabric down at once, root it up even to its foundation', an ironical version, transposing Burke's political rhetoric to the sphere of art, which seizes on Burke's characteristic merging of ideas of architecture and vegetation.[127]

Burke's 'august fabric of states', at all events, evokes not merely earth and stone, but rootedness and growth, and the fact brings us to the central paradox of his use of the images of both dress and buildings, which is that they blend, in a peculiar and characteristically Burkeian symbiosis, with images of natural feeling and organic growth. In political debate, 'organic' imagery has usually been concerned with animal rather than vegetable metaphors, and particularly with the human body and constitution. The oldest and most usual metaphor has been that of the body politic, in its many applications, and this seems to have been the prevalent model

[124] *Reflections*, pp. 186–9/141–3, 136/181; see *Correspondence*, II.377; Yeats, 'Blood and the Moon' (1928), line 22, in *Poems*, ed. Finneran, p. 238 (for this image in Yeats, see also Torchiana, *W. B. Yeats and Georgian Ireland*, pp. 191 ff.; Jeffares, *New Commentary*, p. 274); Wordsworth, *Prelude*, 1850 version, VII.519–22. Wordsworth's lines on Burke, VII.512–43, 'appear in their earliest form in 1832' (*The Prelude, 1799, 1805, 1850*, ed. Jonathan Wordsworth, M. H. Abrams and Stephen Gill, New York and London, 1979, p. 255).

[125] For earlier uses of trees as emblems, positive or negative, of government and tradition, see Howard Erskine-Hill, *The Social Milieu of Alexander Pope*, New Haven and London, 1975, pp. 268–9, 288. For widespread use during the revolutionary period, see Paulson, *Representations of Revolution*, pp. 60, 73–9.

[126] *Reflections*, ed. Pocock, pp. xl, lv: the cover of O'Brien's edition depicts the planting of the liberty tree.

[127] Paine, *Complete Writings*, I.453–4, 266, 256, 257, 288. In passages about laying the axe, Paine was recalling Matthew, 3.10. Reynolds, 'Ironical Discourse', in *Portraits*, pp. 128, 142.

throughout the Renaissance and in the seventeenth century.[128] For all his calling the state a tree, this is also the main tendency of Burke's imagery, highly individual though his treatment is. The paragraph about the clothing of religion actually begins:

We know, and it is our pride to know, that man is by his constitution a religious animal; that atheism is against, not only our reason but our instincts.[129]

The religious clothing, the need and the craving for it, are thus spoken of as involving fundamental instinct, a deep part of our basic animal nature. The dress imagery is represented not only as a matter of 'covering', but as an intrinsic and instinctual part of the 'naked shivering nature' it is supposed to cover. The example helps us to see that not only religion, but all the other elements of 'the decent drapery of life', the whole political, social, and cultural tradition which has been built around 'our naked shivering nature', are themselves a matter of deep instinctive aspirations, loyalties, and habits. The dress whose artifice was openly and proudly indicated in the term 'drapery' is simultaneously seen as natural too. And the argument which unfolds from this celebrated paragraph about the treatment of Marie Antoinette is charged with a passional and instinctual vocabulary and a reiterative emphasis on natural feeling.

THE DRESS OF THOUGHT AND THE BODY OF THOUGHT

The distinctive feature of Burke's organicism is precisely his fusion into it of an ornamentalist mode of thinking, with all its sartorial accoutrements. The 'decent drapery of life' is simultaneously spoken of as part of a process of 'incorporation' and as a matter of cultural increment or 'superadded ideas'. In an earlier paragraph[130] he cited the Bill of Rights of 1689, to the effect that it declared 'the legal prerogatives of the crown ... "*intirely* invested, incorporated, united, and annexed"' in their majesties William and Mary. The juxtapo-

---

[128] See David George Hale, *The Body Politic: A Political Metaphor in Renaissance English Literature*, The Hague and Paris, 1971; Michael Walzer, *The Revolution of the Saints: A Study in the Origins of Radical Politics*, Cambridge, MA, 1965, pp. 171–7.

[129] *Reflections*, p. 142/187.

[130] *Reflections*, pp. 128/171; 70/103; for the text of the Bill of Rights, 1689, see *English Historical Documents 1660–1714*, ed. Andrew Browning, New York, 1953, pp. 126, 122–8. The Declaration of Rights enacted as part of the Bill, had been drafted under the leadership of John, later Lord, Somers, whom Burke cited approvingly (*Reflections*, pp. 69–71/102–4) and to whom Swift dedicated *A Tale of a Tub* (*Works*, 1.13–16), though Swift later became a political opponent of his.

sition 'invested, incorporated', whether originally set down as a rhetorical escalation or as units in a series of legislative discriminations, leaps out of Burke's text, in a way the original document would hardly have prepared one for, as consecrating his own deep habit of assimilating images of clothing and embodiment. When Burke, introducing the quotation, himself speaks of parliament 'vesting' the prerogatives in the monarchs, the term picks up suggestions of 'incorporation'. It is in this very paragraph, dealing with the implications of the English Revolution of 1688, that the Houses of Parliament are seen not as asserting 'a right to choose their own governors', like the French, but instead as throwing 'a politic, well-wrought veil over every circumstance tending to weaken the rights, which in the meliorated order of succession they meant to perpetuate'.[131]

This is a mode of political thinking which Rousseau would be quick to call 'hypocrisy', of a kind which neither Burke, nor Swift, was inclined to disavow, as a matter of principle. But what would be equally inconceivable in Swift on the one side or Rousseau on the other is the intense interaction throughout Burke's discourse of ideas of disguise and organic process, clothing and 'moulding', 'vesting', and 'incorporating'. It is as close as the imagery of the 'garment of style' can get, without losing its identity, to the Romantic notion, whose first English formulation is apparently by Wordsworth, that words are 'an incarnation of the thought' rather than 'only a clothing for it'; a notion anticipated by some German critics and later prominent in Flaubert as well as common among English writers.[132]

Burke's enforcing of the symbiosis, at all events, calls to mind the way in which, on the plane of stylistic definitions, the image of the dress of thought ran parallel with the other ancient image, in which style and content were represented as the body and soul of thought. In older formulations of the latter, the two sets of metaphor are closely parallel in function and imply a similar broadly 'ornamentalist' perspective (as in the words from Vives which Ben Jonson incorpor-

---

[131] *Reflections*, pp. 137/182; 69/103.
[132] William Wordsworth, *Essays upon Epitaphs*, III, in *Prose Works*, ed. W. J. B. Owen and J. W. Smyser, Oxford, 1974, II.84; also M. H. Abrams, *The Mirror and the Lamp: Romantic Theory and the Critical Tradition*, London, 1960, pp. 290–1; for earlier German and later English examples, see Abrams, *Mirror*, p. 385 nn. 89–90; for Flaubert, see *Correspondance*, ed. Bruneau, II.286, 785 (and see 372).

ated into *Timber: or, Discoveries:* 'words and sense, are as the body and the soule').[133] Burke's way with images of dress may have been a predisposing influence in the shift to an emphatically organic use of the body/soul metaphor, which made it an antithesis rather than an analogue of the dress metaphor as traditionally conceived. This is a paradoxical consequence of Burke's intensification of the parallels and interactions to the point where the ornamental concept itself acquired organic force, leaving it open to a more fundamental rethinking to place the honorific value on the organic dimension alone.

Wordsworth offers a striking illustration. He was steeped in Burke's writings and closely affected by the texture of his thought.[134] He praised Burke in the 1850 *Prelude* for 'Exploding upstart Theory' (vii. 529), and it is not surprising to find him using, in an attack of *c.* 1798 on the radical rationalism of Godwin and others, some variations on Burke's imagery of naked abstraction: 'These moralists attempt to strip the mind of all its old clothing when their object ought to be to furnish it with new ... these bald & naked reasonings are impotent over our habits ...', setting against them a Burkeian vocabulary of

---

[133] See *Ben Jonson*, ed. C. H. Herford and Percy and Evelyn Simpson, Oxford, 1925–1952, viii.621; Jonson is translating Juan Luis Vives, *De Ratione Dicendi* (Cologne, 1537), p.4: 'In sermone omni sunt uerba & sensa tamquam corpus & animus' (cited *Ben Jonson*, xi.265). Abrams notes Jonson's formulation, distinguishing it from the organicist version because it is plainly 'compatible with the matter-and-ornament concept of language' (*Mirror*, p. 385 n. 89). Two Shakespearean examples invite comment in this context. The famous lines in *Midsummer Night's Dream*, v.i. 14ff., 'as imagination bodies forth/ The forms of things unknown, the poet's pen/ Turns them to shapes, and gives to airy nothing/ A local habitation and a name' stop short of full organicist implication: it appears that what is 'bodied forth' are not words but pre-verbal imagined 'forms', mental pictures; where the poet translates this into writing, the image that accrues is that of 'habitation' rather than 'habit', interesting in the light of Burke's traffic between the two concepts, but meaning mainly that what the poet says contains rather than clothes his thoughts. In *Troilus and Cressida*, i.iii. 16–17, 'that unbodied figure of the thought/ That gave't surmised shape', 'unbodied' means 'unenacted' rather than 'unverbalised'. There is, however, a tradition of metaphors of conception and some examples are given in Jay L. Halio, 'The Metaphor of Conception and Elizabethan Theories of the Imagination', *Neophilologus*, 50 (1966), 454–61; and Louis L. Martz, *The Paradise Within: Studies in Vaughan, Traherne, and Milton*, New Haven and London, 1964, pp. 48–9. The idea of the word made flesh (John, 1. 27) is the reverse of the Wordsworthian idea of 'incarnation' since the end-product is literally the physical presence rather than the verbal sign, though the processes of verbal expression were sometimes seen as analogues 'to the Word of God, whose outward sign is not the word but the world' (see Tzvetan Todorov, *Theories of the Symbol*, trs. Catherine Porter, Ithaca, 1982, p. 44, on Augustine).

[134] On Burke's influence on Wordsworth see especially James K. Chandler, *Wordsworth's Second Nature: A Study of the Poetry and Politics*, Chicago and London, 1984, *passim*. Wordsworth originally disliked Burke and the *Reflections*: see his *Letter to the Bishop of Llandaff*, 1793, *Prose Works*, i. 48–9.

'incorporation', of 'blood & vital juices of our minds', of 'old habit'.[135] It is especially interesting that a page or so before the passage in which, in the third 'Essay upon Epitaphs' (*c.* 1810), he spoke of words as the *incarnation* of thought, rejecting the image of dress or 'garb', Wordsworth had originally used that image in the manuscript and then changed his mind. The textual note to line 125 shows that a phrasing which in the final text reads 'uttered after a different manner' had originally been written down as '*clothed in* a different manner' (my italics). The idea of incarnation on the next page, which strongly establishes an antithesis to the image of dress, seems, in fact, to have been arrived at as an afterthought, since Wordsworth had originally been content in the earlier passage to use the dress metaphor in the traditional way.[136] The textual change seems to show Wordsworth in the very act of discovering the limitations of the conventional dress metaphor for his conception of poetry. It also illustrates the process by which Burke's writings, having brought that metaphor to the brink of its organicist opposite, helped to create a mood hospitable to the Wordsworthian reformulation.

That Burke would not cross that brink is to be expected, though he eased the transition for others. The dress metaphor and its ramifying associations (of covering and protection and 'investing', of stylistic adornment or fitness, of habit or custom) were too deeply and intricately involved in the fabric of his thought. Too much of his outlook, of his cultural anxieties, aspirations, and loyalties, was indeed invested in the mode of thinking which depended on, and followed from, it. When he used words like 'invest' and 'incorporate' more or less interchangeably, he seems to have been positing connections more radical than those of the old quasi-ornamentalist identifications of style and content with body and soul, though short of what Wordsworth claimed when he spoke of 'expressions which are not what the garb is to the body but what the body is to the soul ... an incarnation'.[137] Paine was perhaps instinctively responding to those

---

[135] Wordsworth, *Prose Works*, I. 103. For some discussion of this fragment, now called an 'Essay on Morals', see Chandler, pp. 81ff.

[136] Wordsworth, *Prose Works*, II.83–5, textual note to p. 83, line 125, and commentary at pp. 114–15.

[137] Wordsworth, *Prose Works*, II.84–5. By the end of his discussion, Wordsworth has moved towards the view that words which are merely a 'garb' are pernicious, like one of 'those poisoned vestments, read of in the stories of superstitious times, which had power to consume and to alienate from his right mind the victim who put them on. Language, if it do not uphold, and feed, and leave in quiet, like the power of gravitation or the air we breathe, is a counter-spirit, unremittingly and noiselessly at work to 'derange, to subvert, to lay waste, to

elements in Burke's discourse which tended to collapse distinctions between body and dress, when he said Burke pitied the *plumage* and forgot the dying bird. But it was Carlyle, in many ways the heir of Swift and Burke in the exploitation of 'clothes philosophies', who most explicitly reformulated the 'dress of thought' in the light both of Burke's symbiosis, and of its Romantic extension: 'Language is called the Garment of Thought: however, it should rather be, Language is the Flesh-Garment, the Body of Thought.'[138]

Why, Burke asks, does he feel so anguished about the downfall of the French monarchy?

For this plain reason – because it is *natural* I should; because we are so made as to be affected at such spectacles with melancholy sentiments upon the unstable condition of mortal prosperity, and the tremendous uncertainty of human greatness; because in those natural feelings we learn great lessons; because in events like these our passions instruct our reason; because when kings are hurl'd from their thrones by the Supreme Director of this great drama, and become the objects of insult to the base, and of pity to the good, we behold such disasters in the moral, as we should behold a miracle in the physical order of things.[139]

The reference to miracles proclaims the unnaturalness of revolution quite as much as it concedes God's power to use the unnaturalness of men in order to bring about miracles. And this unnaturalness is reinforced by the naturalness claimed for Burke's own reactions of indignation, against the cold rationality of pedantic purveyors of revolutionary abstractions about 'the rights of man':

In England we have not yet been completely embowelled of our natural entrails; we still feel within us, and we cherish and cultivate, those inbred sentiments which are the faithful guardians, the active monitors of our duty, the true supporters of all liberal and manly morals. We have not been drawn and trussed, in order that we may be filled, like stuffed birds in a museum, with chaff and rags, and paltry, blurred shreds of paper about the rights of man. We preserve the whole of our feelings still native and entire, unsophisticated by pedantry and infidelity. We have real hearts of flesh and blood beating in our bosoms. We fear God; we look up with awe to kings; with affection to parliaments; with duty to magistrates; with reverence to priests;

---

vitiate, and dissolve', Even here, in the insistence on unforced and natural processes of influence and penetration ('like the power of gravitation or the air we breathe'), and his assertion that 'the taste, intellectual Power, and morals of a Country are inseparably linked in mutual dependence', Wordsworth seems manifestly to have assimilated the substance and texture of Burke's thought.   [138] Carlyle, *Sartor Resartus*, I.xi, in *Works*, I.57.
[139] *Reflections*, p. 131/175.

and with respect to nobility. Why? Because when such ideas are brought before our minds, it is *natural* to be affected; because all other feelings are false and spurious . . .

You see, Sir, that in this enlightened age I am bold enough to confess, that we are generally men of untaught feelings; that instead of casting away all our old prejudices . . . we cherish them because they are prejudices . . . [italics are Burke's].[140]

By the time we get back to the defence of the 'coat of prejudice' we see it to have been conducted in a sustained crescendo of passional terms: 'naturalness', 'inbred sentiments', 'feelings . . . native and entire', 'real hearts of flesh and blood', 'untaught feelings'.

This sense of a deep interplay between natural impulse and the accretions of civilisation makes of the latter something more than a mechanical superimposition. In the very place where he champions 'the decent drapery of life' and the 'coat of prejudice' against the scorn of radicals, Burke moves the goalposts by saying that it is the radicals who 'think that government may vary like modes of dress, and with as little effect'. One implication of this is that Burke in politics, like Reynolds in art, wants a mode of dress that does not vary with every turn of fashion: hence the predilection for a more unvarying and classical 'drapery'. Another implication is that Burke finds the radicals' notion of dress offensive precisely because it is 'mechanical' or, to use today's or perhaps yesterday's, term, 'inorganic', in a way that his is not.

Burke is, throughout, determined to sustain a paradoxical identity between 'natural' or 'native' or 'primary' or 'untaught' aspirations or feelings, and the civilised arrangements and educational processes which are normally alleged to be imposed upon them as restraints. The phrase 'inbred sentiments' has an ambiguity which illustrates the point, because while 'inbred' means mainly 'innate, native', it seems to hint at overtones of 'bred into', absorbed by a deep process of breeding, 'those natural feelings [from which] we learn great lessons' in a comparable interplay of instinct and cultural accretion. Put in day-to-day terms, the matter can partly be described as one of acquiring *habits*, a term with a punning etymological relation with 'dress'. Carlyle was to make the pun with more ostentation than Burke normally indulged in. He described France in 1793, under a

---

[140] *Reflections*, pp. 137-8/182-3; see also pp. 145/192-3. For Reynolds' dislike of reflecting changing fashions of dress in art, see *Discourses*, pp. 127-8, and 'Ironical Discourse', *Portraits*, pp. 142-4.

'Dominant Sansculottism', as 'A nation of men, full of wants and void of habits! The old habits are gone to wreck because they were old.'[141] The notion of habit or custom (whose etymological dress-counterpart is 'costume') as second nature is an old one. An approximate form is cited in Aristotle, and it reappears in European letters in Cicero, Erasmus, Montaigne, and numerous English authors.[142] It has an old proverbial status in most European languages, sometimes without the punning connection with dress, which Burke seems to be exploiting in his defence of the 'coat of prejudice' when he says, 'Prejudice renders a man's virtue his habit . . . Through just prejudice, his duty becomes a part of his nature.' The idea of habit as second nature is recurrent in Burke's writings, before and after the *Reflections*.[143]

This process is the one recognised, more negatively, by Swift, when he traced the progress of 'enthusiasm' from '*Art* into *Nature*' in the *Mechanical Operation of the Spirit*: 'there is many an Operation, which in its Original, was purely an Artifice, but through a long Succession of Ages, hath grown to be natural'. As in the history of civilisations, so in the lives of individuals: what begins as a mechanically operated delusion turns into a natural way of life, growing at last sincere, in this case with a vicious sincerity. An opposite process, in which (as in Burke) it is virtue and not vice which is acquired through habit is Swift's famous advocacy of hypocrisy in the *Project for the Advancement of Religion*: 'it is often with Religion as it is with Love; which, by much Dissembling, at last grows real'.[144] This psychological principle, puzzling to modern readers of Swift, was in fact widely accepted among moralists at the time. Reynolds, following James Harris,

---

[141] Thomas Carlyle, *The French Revolution* (1837), III.v. 1, in *Works*, IV.206.

[142] Aristotle, *Nicomachean Ethics*, VII.x. 4; Cicero, *De Finibus*, v.xxv; Erasmus, *Adagia* 3794 and 3825, *Opera Omnia*, Leyden, 1703–1706, II. 1143, 1149 (the second adage is *Usus est altera natura*); Montaigne, III.x. For some Renaissance English uses, see Lawrence Manley, *Convention 1500–1750*, pp. 90ff., 110–11, 188, 199ff., and Morris P. Tilley, *A Dictionary of Proverbs in England in the Sixteenth and Seventeenth Centuries*, Ann Arbor, 1950, C. 932; a useful broader listing may be found in Burton Stevenson, *The Home Book of Proverbs, Maxims and Familiar Phrases*, New York, 1948, pp. 475–6.

[143] *Reflections*, p. 138/183; for Burke's variations on this idea, see *Reflections*, pp. 146/193; 148/197; 231/299. See also *A Philosophical Enquiry into the Origin of our Ideas of the Sublime and Beautiful* (1757, 2nd edn., 1759), III.v, ed. James T. Boulton, Oxford, 1968, p. 104; *Speeches in the Impeachment of Warren Hastings*, 7th day of Reply, 12 June 1794, *Works*, VIII.274. For comparisons between Burke and Rousseau on this, see David Cameron, *The Social Thought of Rousseau and Burke*, Toronto and Buffalo, 1973, pp. 82–95, esp. 89, 94, and Chandler, *Wordsworth's Second Nature*, pp. xviii, 62–74; for 'second nature' in a discussion of Reynolds, Johnson and Burke, see Barrell, *Political Theory of Painting*, p. 138.

[144] Swift, *Works*, I.175–6: II.57.

applied it to the acquisition of aesthetic taste.[145] But it is in Burke's *Appeal from the New to the Old Whigs* (1791), a work said to have been Yeats' 'political bible', that one finds the most comprehensive celebration of this principle, applied to the workings of a 'true natural aristocracy' over the entire spectrum of human activity.[146] This 'natural aristocracy' is the opposite of Paine's 'noble of nature' precisely in the sense that its 'naturalness' is the product of a protracted process of breeding (whose elements are very specifically enumerated in the *Appeal*), a 'second nature' that has assimilated civilisation and politeness rather than the Rousseauist nature that has escaped or transcended them:[147]

The state of civil society, which necessarily generates this aristocracy, is a state of nature; and much more truly so than a savage and incoherent mode of life. For man is by nature reasonable; and he is never perfectly in his natural state, but when he is placed where reason may be best cultivated, and most predominates. Art is man's nature.[148]

Set against this, Swift's transitions from '*Art* into *Nature*' will seem a minimalist activity. Burke differs from Swift in many ways. He lacks the tartness. His eye is trained on the positive aspects of the issue. Swift writes as a disenchanted pragmatist, unhopeful of any state in which viciousness is not a primary and ineradicable fact, which has to be harnessed to good use because it cannot simply be replaced by an uncontaminated virtue. His first example, as we saw, was negative, dealing with an artificially induced vice turning into a natural habit of vice. In the second, the acquired habit is, as in Burke, a virtue, but it is acquired in the first place through the practice of a vice, hypocrisy. Even in his positive formulation in the *Project*, Swift is settling, flatly, for small mercies, a piecemeal self-conquest by grubby means. Burke is aglow with the feeling that the whole richness of a culture is at stake, this richness still visible, in England if not in France: 'In England we have not yet been completely embowelled of our natural entrails; we

---

[145] Reynolds, *Discourses*, pp. 277–8, and quotations from Harris, *Philological Inquiries*, ii.xii, in Harris' *Works*, 1801, ii.411: 'if, while we peruse some Author of high rank, we perceive we don't instantly relish him, let us not be disheartened – let us even FEIGN *a Relish, till we find a Relish come*'.

[146] Burke, *Works*, iii.85–6; Torchiana, *W. B. Yeats and Georgian Ireland*, p. 169. For Burke, as perhaps not for Yeats, this ideal of 'natural aristocracy' was blended with a strong sense of the value and civilising properties of commerce (see *Reflections*, ed. Pocock, pp. xxii, xxxi, xxxii, xlvii, etc.).

[147] See Paine, *Rights of Man*, in *Complete Writings*, i.289; for a qualification to this contrast between Burke and Rousseau, see Cameron, *Social Thought of Rousseau and Burke*, p. 94.

[148] Burke, *Works*, iii.86.

still feel within us, and we cherish and cultivate, those inbred sentiments.'[149] Swift, too, had felt the culture to be at stake, and his ideological affinities with Burke have been recognised by many, and most eloquently by Yeats. But there is not the Burkeian hopefulness, the sense that goodness is still richly present, the warmth and the grandeur of utterance, the slightly overblown and perhaps proleptically Yeatsian vocabulary of 'cherishing' and of 'real hearts of flesh and blood beating in our bosoms'.

This vocabulary, which brings the bodily processes themselves into the debate, emphasises how much the issue was felt by Burke to involve the whole nature of the human organism, biological as well as psychological. We should guard against taking such a passionate rhetoric too literally. But, when the civilised accretions are spoken of as 'our natural entrails' within a page of being proudly identified with the 'coat of prejudice',[150] we must assume either confusion or a defiant proclamation of paradox: it is as though the inside of Swift's flayed woman, and her fair outside, with its clothes and cosmetics, were not only one inseparable whole, but a valued and 'cherished' whole. The degree of reiterative emphasis on both types of image, of natural or bodily process and of dress, suggest that the connections Burke was making were studied ones.

At times, the imagery of bodily process is commonplace and unhighlighted, as when 'the sentiments which beautify and soften private society' are beneficently '*incorporated* into politics' (my italics), or when 'the august fabric of states' is seen 'as a sacred temple, purged from all the impurities of fraud, and violence, and injustice, and tyranny.'[151] Many such terms, in so far as they are more than simply idiomatic, may ultimately be referable to the ancient punning commonplace of the body politic. And 'purgation' has spiritual as well as physiological overtones. But these overtones, which convey both a training or refinement of the sensibility and an inner cleansing of the body, are apt to my argument, and imply something of that interaction of concepts of body and soul to which we used to like to give the word 'organic' and to which Yeats responded warmly in Burke. Burke's image of 'purging' brings to mind once again that passage of Fielding's *Voyage to Lisbon* in which the refinements of a liberal upbringing help 'to produce that perfection of which [human nature] is susceptible, and to purge away that malevolence of

[149] *Reflections*, p. 137/182.   [150] *Reflections*, p. 138/183.
[151] *Reflections*, pp. 128/171; 143/189.

disposition, of which, at our birth we partake in common with the savage creation.'[152] 'Purging' here too is not just a medical operation. Nor is it merely a matter of evacuation. Its cleansing activity fosters an inner growth and, as in Burke, does so with the help of civilising influences from without. I have argued elsewhere that such blendings of learnt courtesy with a feeling of natural growth made Fielding (unlike Chesterfield, whose conception of courtesy was more crudely low-key and unillusioned) comparable to Yeats. It is certain that they are part of what Yeats admired in Burke.[153]

REVOLUTION AND HYPOCRISY

The metaphor of dress as covering the nakedness of the body politic, and signifying the ascendancy of civilisation over barbarism, was not new. The main feeling of a large-scale threat to the civilised order was itself a commonplace among Augustan writers of conservative cast for almost a century: it is everywhere implicit in Swift, and spectacularly articulated in the finale of Pope's *Dunciad*. Burke seems from the start to have thought of the Revolution in terms of Dunciadic apocalypse. In the letter to Depont of November 1789 he saw France as undergoing a 'progress thro' Chaos and darkness', and the previous month he had written of Mirabeau in Miltonic–Dunciadic idiom as a presiding 'Grand Anarch'.[154] Contemporaries seemed to sense other Dunciadic or Scriblerian parallels. Horace Walpole speaks of Burke's female adversaries as likely to 'return to Fleet Ditch, more fortunate in being forgotten than their predecessors immortalized in the *Dunciad*'.[155] In France, the *Moniteur* found the *Reflections* 'un pauvre ouvrage', if one excepts 'quelques traits d'imagination déparés même par un style digne de Lycophron ou des Scriblerus'.[156] Carlyle, saluting 'Great Burke ... eloquently demonstrating that the end of an Epoch is come, to all appearance the end of Civilised Time', himself adopted accents of a Miltonising Dunciadic gloom as though by

---

[152] Fielding, *Journal of a Voyage to Lisbon*, p. 45.
[153] Rawson, *Henry Fielding and the Augustan Ideal under Stress*, pp. 3–34.
[154] Burke, *Correspondence*, VI.46, 30.
[155] Walpole, *Correspondence*, XI.170 (to Mary Berry, 20 December 1790).
[156] *Le Moniteur*, 14 December 1790, cited Mitchell, p. 14. It may seem surprising that the Scriblerus family or Scriblerian authors were known to a French journalist writing in 1790. The Catalogue of the Bibliothèque Nationale (Pope, 27 and 175) shows that the *Memoirs of Martinus Scriblerus*, as well as Scriblerus' notes to the *Dunciad*, were included in the French translation of Pope's *Oeuvres Poétiques*, Paris, 1779, vols. V and VI, and a French translation of the *Memoirs* appeared in London in 1755. The Scriblerus name would be familiar from several works by members of the group as well as from those Fielding plays purporting to be annotated by H. Scriblerus Secundus.

osmosis, speaking of France surrounded by a 'troublous Cimmerian Night'.[157]

The French Revolution naturally appeared to some as a distressingly visible realisation of this menace, enacted on a political and social, rather than an imaginative, plane, and it gave an enhanced immediacy to a traditional scenario of crisis. That there was a feverishly intensified rhetoric of nakedness and dress in the writings not only of Reynolds and Burke, but in those of Paine and others on the opposite side, is perhaps a consequence of this. Burke's *Reflections* came very early in the Revolution, but their imagery is a manifest exploitation of modes of political discourse which were current in the long ideological run-up to it. The imagery is visible in such pre-Revolutionary texts as Rousseau's first *Discourse* (1750), in which the arts of civilisation and 'ce voile ... perfide de politesse' (contrast Burke's 'politic, well-wrought veil') are presented as the sugared adjuncts of tyranny, and as enervating and corrupting to the nature of man.[158] Primitivist images of the virtue and vigour of naked savages, and of disguising wickedness under a dangerous cloak of hypocrisy, were already quite prominent there, and they are ringingly reiterated and compounded with claims of unadorned truthfulness in Book VIII of the *Confessions*: 'I dared to strip bare the nature of men' (*j'osois devoiler à nud leur nature*) and to show the superiority of *l'homme naturel* over *l'homme de l'homme*.[159] This is almost as far removed from Popeian declarations in favour of tracing 'the *naked Nature* and the *living Grace*' examined earlier in this discussion, as Rousseau's repudiation of the maxim that hypocrisy is a friend to virtue was from the principle it repudiates.[160]

Burke is said to have introduced into England the idea of Rousseau as the animating influence on the French Revolution, though he is mentioned only briefly, and as an unstable and lightweight character, in the *Reflections*.[161] It is only after the National Assembly resolved in

---

[157] Carlyle, *French Revolution*, II.v. 5, in *Works* III.227–8; there is much imagery of Cimmerian gloom, chaos and primeval night in Carlyle's *French Revolution*.

[158] Rousseau, *Oeuvres Complètes*, III.8; *Reflections*, p. 69/103.

[159] Rousseau, *Discours sur les sciences et les arts*, *Oeuvres Complètes* III.8, 52, 61; *Confessions*, VIII, in *Oeuvres Complètes*, I.388.

[160] Pope, *Essay on Criticism*, line 294, TE, I.272; Rousseau, *Oeuvres Complètes*, III.51–2.

[161] Edward Duffy, *Rousseau in England: The Context for Shelley's Critique of the Enlightenment*, Berkeley and Los Angeles, 1979, pp. 38–9; *Reflections*, pp. 137/181–2; 219/283–4. For other references to Rousseau, see *Correspondence*, VI. 81, 214, 252–3; 270; VIII.242; Mitchell, p. 438, and see next note. Burke reviewed the English translations of the *Lettre à d'Alembert sur les Spectacles* and *Emile* in *Annual Register*, 1759, pp. 479–84, and 1762, pp. 227–39 (second pagination).

December 1790 to erect a commemorative statue to Rousseau that Burke wrote the *Letter to a Member of the National Assembly* (1791), with its extended portrait of him as the Assembly's ideological mentor and model of personal conduct, their 'canon of holy writ' and 'standard figure of perfection', which established Rousseau as the principal bogeyman of English counter-revolutionary polemics.[162] Burke's diatribe against Rousseau was more concerned with his personal character than with his political theories, and the two works he specifically alludes to are the *Nouvelle Héloïse* ('his famous work of philosophic gallantry'), and the *Confessions* with what he saw as its appalling revelation of a vicious life.[163] Hypocrisy of a sort is imputed to Rousseau as one of the vices which came under the perverse scope of Rousseau's overwhelming vanity, but it is clear that it is Rousseau's unabashed and uncensored recording of 'a life not . . . distinguished by a single good action' which is the object of Burke's criticism. For the chief characteristic of this vanity is that it 'is fond to talk even of its own faults and vices, as what will excite surprize and draw attention, and what will pass at worst for openness and candour', hypocrisy being itself a paradoxical item, to which Rousseau did not strictly admit. To the question whether he would wish to see a social order in which vice revealed itself openly Rousseau once replied that indeed he would, *assurément je le voudrois*. His worst offence, in Burke's account in the *Letter to a Member of the National Assembly*, was that he chose to record his depravities for the 'attention of mankind'. Burke adds that Rousseau flung his confessions 'with a wild defiance . . . in the face of his Creator', which sounds even more opprobrious, but what really exercised Burke was the subversive potential in human affairs.[164]

---

[162] *Letter to a Member of the National Assembly*, in Mitchell, pp. 312–18. Plans for the statue did not materialise: see James A. Leith, *The Idea of Art as Propaganda in France 1750–1799*, Toronto, 1965, p. 103. Horace Walpole found Burke's 'invective against Rousseau . . . admirable, just and new' (*Correspondence*, XI.277; to Mary Berry, 26 May 1791).

[163] Mitchell, pp. 317, 314. See Duffy, *Rousseau in England*, p. 39; Cameron, *Social Thought of Rousseau and Burke*, p. 142; Kramnick, *Rage of Edmund Burke*, pp. 153–6, characteristically stresses the element of sexual depravity in Burke's account of Rousseau's evil influence, which may be an overspecialised view, but most commentators concur that Burke did not enter into specific ideological argument with Rousseau. In focusing on Rousseau's morals, Burke claimed to be meeting him on his own terms: 'Rousseau is a moralist, or he is nothing' (Mitchell, p. 313). See *Correspondence*, VI.81: 'I have read long since the *Contrat Social*. It has left very few traces upon my mind' (January, 1790).

[164] Mitchell, p. 314; Rousseau, *Oeuvres Complète*, III.51. For Rousseau on his project of total sincerity, see *Confessions*, Foreword and Books, I, X, and XII (*Oeuvres Complètes*, I.3, 5, 516–17, 656, 1230–3nn.). In Book X, he distinguishes himself from Montaigne, whose frankness consisted of ascribing only amiable vices to himself (I. 516–17, and on Montaigne as heading a list of the 'falsely sincere', 1524–5 n.). Rousseau's habit of disclosing his shortcomings, or

Whatever role is to be attached to Rousseau in the Revolutionary phenomenon, 'hypocrisy' and its unmasking became a political issue of exceptional and perhaps unprecedented prominence during the French revolutionary period. Hannah Arendt has indeed argued that it was then that hypocrisy came to be seen, for the first time in history, as the chief political crime.[165] She argues that in earlier political thought, from Socrates to Machiavelli and after, hypocrisy was not normally considered a very serious offence in the realm of state affairs, if it did not involve 'wilful deception and ... false witness', or the concealment of a 'criminal act'.[166] Inner motives were less important, provided the public actions were right. Judith Shklar makes the point that to Franklin or Hume 'the politics of persuasion required hypocrisy', and that both would have taken for granted 'that "the common Duties of Society usually require it" and that it was "impossible to pass thro the World" without it'.[167] The notion of hypocrisy, the pretence to virtue, as a 'compliment to virtue', preferable to open vice, was common (it is present in Swift and Pascal, as well as in the famous maxim by La Rochefoucauld which Rousseau repudiated early).[168]

Such thinking was based on the conviction that the human heart was a dark place, that 'nobody but God can see (and, perhaps, can bear to see) the nakedness of a human heart' (including 'one's own self'), and that the murky and tortuous domain of inner motive *should be kept dark*. (You see its post-revolutionary traces in a number of later writers, notably Conrad.) The moment you insist on the publishing of motives, 'hypocrisy begins to poison all human relations.'[169]

Arendt says that this is what happened when Rousseau's baring of

even boasting of them as indulged on principle, began early: see, for example, the 'Dernière Résponse' (1752) concerning the first *Discours*: 'Je suis grossier, maussade, impoli par principes, et ne veux point de prôneurs; ainsi je vais dire la vérité tout à mon aise' (*Oeuvres Complètes*, III.75 n).

[165] Hannah Arendt, *On Revolution*, Harmondsworth, 1973, pp. 95ff.; see also Judith Shklar, 'Let Us Not Be Hypocritical', *Daedalus*, 108, 3 (Summer, 1979), 1–25, esp. 7–8; and Lionel Trilling, *Sincerity and Authenticity*, Cambridge, MA, 1973, *passim*.

[166] Arendt, *On Revolution*, pp. 102, 101–3. See also some remarks in Arendt's 'Lying in Politics', *Crises of the Republic*, Harmondsworth, 1973, pp. 10–11 and her wider treatment of the questions of 'Turth and Politics', *Between Past and Future*, rev. edn., New York, 1968, rptd. 1976, pp. 227–64. [167] Shklar, 'Let Us Not Be Hypocritical', p. 16; David Hume, letter to J. Edmonstoune, April 1764, *New Letters*, ed. R. Klibansky and E. C. Mossner, Oxford, 1954, p. 83.

[168] Arendt, *On Revolution*, pp. 101–5; La Rochefoucauld, *Reflexions ou Sentences et Maximes Morales*, 1678, No. 218 (this first appeared in the 2nd edn., 1666), *Oeuvres Complètes*, ed. L. Martin-Chauffier and others, Paris, 1964, p. 432: Blaise Pascal, *Pensées*, No. 418 ('Infini rien'), in *Oeuvres Complètes*, ed. Louis Lafuma, Paris, 1963, p. 551; Swift, *Project for the Advancement of Religion*, in *Works*, II. 56–7; Rousseau, 'Observations' on *Discours sur les Sciences et les Arts*, in *Oeuvres Complètes*, III. 51–2, 1264 n.). [169] Arendt, *On Revolution*, pp. 96, 98.

his *âme dechirée* was carried, by Robespierre, into politics. There, 'the conflicts of the soul ... became murderous because they were insoluble'. She adds:

If, in the words of Robespierre, 'patriotism was a thing of the heart', then the reign of virtue was bound to be at worst the rule of hypocrisy, and at best the never-ending fight to ferret out the hypocrites, a fight which could only end in defeat because of the simple fact that it was impossible to distinguish between true and false patriots.[170]

Robespierre has recently been described as committed 'to a single strategy: the uncompromising repudiation of duplicity erected into a political art'. Mirabeau had said 'he will go far; he believes everything he says'.[171] Carlyle's portrayal of him as Seagreen Incorruptible, 'most consistent, incorruptible of thin acrid men' (seagreen comes from his 'complexion of a multiplex atrabiliar colour, the final shade of which may be the pale sea-green') calls to mind those Dissenting fanatics on whose unhealthy sincerities Swift and Burke showered their contempt. (Carlyle's portrait of Rousseau, incidentally, evokes a Swiftian idiom of a variant kind, when he speaks of the '*Contrat Social*; explaining the whole mystery of Government, and how it is *contracted* and bargained for, – to Universal satisfaction').[172]

Arendt remarks that 'It was the war upon hypocrisy that transformed Robespierre's dictatorship into the Reign of Terror, and the outstanding characteristic of this period was the self-purging of the rulers', and thence the purges and show-trials of the Bolsheviks, which were, at least in theory, 'originally modelled upon, and justified by reference to' those of the French Revolution: 'it was always a question of uncovering what had been hidden, of unmasking the disguises, of exposing duplicity and mendacity'.[173] Yeats was one of those who perceived, through Burke's account, a relation between the French Revolution and Bolshevik regicide.[174] The idea of a 'purgation' through confession is an old one, but it may be that the emphasis has shifted, if only notionally, from a theatre of humiliation or penance to one of self-authentication. If so the distinction is probably not universally evident to either victims or spectators. Although show-trials have a long history, it is also possible that the character of the

---

[170] Arendt, *On Revolution*, p. 97.
[171] See *Critical Dictionary of the French Revolution*, ed. Furet and Ozouf, pp. 300, 301.
[172] Carlyle, *The French Revolution*, II.iii. 3; I.iv. 4; I.ii. 7 (*Works*, III.114; II.141; II.54).
[173] Arendt, *On Revolution*, pp. 99–100. For discriminations between the French and Bolshevik Terrors, see p. 100.   [174] See above, p. 134 and n. 6.

autocritiques exacted by some later revolutionary regimes was not unconnected with the accentuated predilection for confessional exposure which is one of the features of European Romanticism. Equally it seems difficult to imagine that they would not otherwise have taken place.

It is, however, interesting to note the different use of the metaphor of 'purging' from that seen in Burke and in Fielding. There, the operation was conducted by, rather than against, the agencies of civilised concealment. At worst, concealment prevented the naked nastiness from coming to the surface, which is where the later purges wished to force it. At best, as envisaged in Fielding and Burke, concealment was transcended, and the purges effected a cleansing (precisely that *épuration* of our manners that Rousseau said the arts and sciences and the refining influence of polite manners had no power to achieve) as distinct from an unmasking: either the nastiness within remained wholesomely hidden, or it was eradicated from within (what Yeats called recovering 'radical innocence')[175] in both cases by means, or at least with the help, of the civilised cover. And what, if anything, was eradicated, of course, was the nastiness and not, as in some Revolutionary Terrors, the person in whom it existed.

Eliminating the person may be an extreme implication of Romantic notions of the integrity of the self. Burke and many of his predecessors had no strongly held notion of a primal uncorrupted core of inner being. Not only, in their view, could good conduct more usefully and surely be insisted on than purity of motive, but their acceptance of man as a flawed and infinitely various animal made it easier for them to speak in terms of piecemeal improvements and the purging of individual ugly features. Reynolds' advocacy of an art in which accidental blemishes and imperfections are removed from the

[175] Yeats, 'A Prayer for my Daughter' (1919), lines 65ff., *Poems*, ed. Finneran, p. 189: 'all hatred driven hence,/ The soul recovers radical innocence.' The words seem to imply not an innate innocence, but one which through culture penetrates to the roots. Yeats' lines in the same poem, 'How but in custom and in ceremony/ Are innocence and beauty born?' (lines 77–8), which similarly assert natural processes as deriving from social acculturation, may be compared with a passage in Burke's early *Note-Book*, p. 90 (which Yeats presumably did not see) about 'Custom' and 'forms and ceremonies' as 'suitable to our nature', rather than as mere external 'fopperies'. In Yeats' poem (written near the time of his reading of Burke's *Reflections* and almost contemporary with 'The Second Coming', whose draft contains references to Burke and Marie Antoinette) the 'courtesy' which drives away hatred is identified with 'a flourishing hidden tree' (line 41) in a way which shows Burke's influence, and also with a decorous house. The purging of evil instincts ('hatred') through a process of acculturation is that envisaged by Fielding in the *Voyage to Lisbon* and elsewhere, as well as by Burke: for Yeats and Fielding on this, see Rawson, *Henry Fielding and the Augustan Ideal under Stress*, pp. 22–5, 33–4.

portraiture is the ideal expression of this cast of mind, and suggests that it is only in art that the unillusioned pragmatism of Burke or Johnson or perhaps Swift would entertain notions of perfectibility. Where a more total (totalitarian?) view is taken of the wholeness or integrity of the self, the inner corrosion created by hypocrisy may seem to justify a radical solution which purges the world of the 'hypocrite' himself.[176] Arendt writes that the special ugliness ascribed to hypocrisy derives from the fact that, 'psychologically speaking', the hypocrite not only wants 'to appear virtuous before others, he wants to convince himself', though this is only one of several ways of giving hypocrisy a special or unique status among vices. Hazlitt said, for example, that 'the only vice that cannot be forgiven is hypocrisy. The repentance of a hypocrite is itself hypocrisy.' It seems, if Rousseau and Hazlitt are representative, to have become a habit of the Romantic mentality to think of hypocrisy as the worst of vices, and especially ineradicable: a view which Burke, in his attack on Rousseau, applied to the opposite vice of 'vanity', whose impulse of comprehensive and egocentric display extended to, and subsumed, hypocrisy itself.[177]

The self-legitimation derived from 'convincing oneself', and the hideous sincerities to which this gives rise in both the private and the public spheres, were anatomised as evils more repellent than any politic pretence of virtue in Swift's Digression on Madness and in the *Mechanical Operation of the Spirit*.[178] The radical sectaries portrayed in the latter work are not condemned for professing beliefs they do not have, but for the orgiastic spontaneities that issue from their all too genuine conversion to them. It has been observed that Burke's portrayal of the Parisian mob bears strong resemblance to Swift's account of the sectaries.[179] Hypocrisy, the public falsification of the

---

[176] Arendt, *On Revolution*, p. 103; see also p. 107, 'what made the hypocrite so odious was that he claimed not only sincerity but naturalness', and p. 108 on hypocrisy and deception.

[177] Rousseau, rebutting La Rochefoucauld's maxim 218, said that hypocrisy compounded other vices and blocked forever any return to probity. One of his arguments about hypocrisy's special status, in a follow-up to the first *Discours*, was that no hypocrite has ever turned into a good man, and that where other crimes are compatible with a *je ne sçai quoi de fier et de généreux*, which appertains to great souls (*les belles âmes*), 'l'ame vile et rampante de l'hypocrite est semblable à un cadavre, où l'on ne trouve plus ni feu, ni chaleur, ni ressource à la vie' (Rousseau, *Oeuvres Complètes*, III.51–2; see La Rochefoucauld, *Oeuvres Complètes*, p. 828). William Hazlitt, *Characteristics: In the Manner of Rochefoucault's Maxims* (1823), no. CCLVI, in *Complete Works*, ed. P. P. Howe, London and Toronto, 1930–4, IX.204. For another Hazlittean perspective on hypocrisy, see David Bromwich, 'Master of Regret', *New York Review of Books*, 11 April 1991, p.53.

[178] Swift, *A Tale of a Tub*, IX, and *Mechanical Operation*, in *Works*, I.108, 171–90 *passim*.

[179] Paulson, *Representations of Revolution*, pp. 58–9, 61, 69.

self, could only seem an evil of the magnitude claimed for it by Rousseau or Robespierre at a time when the idea of the inviolate integrity of the self assumed an overriding cultural importance. For Swift, as for Burke, the uglier features of the self must indeed be falsified for the sake of decency and public order, and individual self-expression had no privileged status. The sectaries and their secular avatars of the Revolution represented all the dangers of individualism in a multiplied or collective form.

Hypocrite means play-actor in Greek. It is not irrelevant in this connection that Rousseau had a distrust of the theatre whose fullest expression is to be found in the *Lettre à d'Alembert sur les spectacles* (1758), a work whose English translation Burke reviewed, critically, but with some grudging admiration, in the *Annual Register* for 1759.[180] Rousseau's condemnation of play-acting, as Trilling pointed out, is based not on the Platonic idea that an actor's personality deteriorates through the impersonation of inferior characters, but on a more absolute objection to assuming any character other than one's own.[181] Robespierre, in a famous speech of 1794, denounced the Pharisee as a hypocrite, or actor.[182] According to Arendt, revolutionary ideologues tended to see the *ancien régime* as theatrical, a pantomime of over-dressed luxury and of moral and political duplicity, and their object was to tear off the actor's mask.[183] (Burke thought the National Assembly, under Rousseau's influence, was creating something 'false and theatric').[184] Arendt notes that where some commentators, usually later ones, speak of revolution in what she calls the 'organic metaphor' (she cites Marx on the 'birth-pangs of revolutions'), 'the men who enacted the [French] Revolution preferred to draw their images from the language of the theatre.'[185]

This may be a simplification. Organic imagery was at all events widely used, in the 1790s and earlier, both by revolutionary apologists and by their opponents, as the image of the tree of liberty or references to the nakedness of natural man make clear. And damaging comparisons between government and the theatre, which derive from ancient analogies of the world as a play or of man as a puppet of the gods, had

---

[180] *Annual Register*, 1759, pp. 479–84.   [181] Trilling, *Sincerity and Authenticity*, p. 64.
[182] J. M. Thompson, *Robespierre*, New York, 1936, II.179–80.
[183] Arendt, *On Revolution*, pp. 105–8. See also Trilling, *Sincerity and Authenticity*, pp. 69ff., commenting on Arendt.
[184] *Letter to a Member of the National Assembly*, in Mitchell, p. 315.
[185] Arendt, *On Revolution*, p. 106.

a strong currency in pre-Revolutionary times.[186] They were, for example, much in evidence in anti-Walpole polemics from the 1720s to the early 1740s, and powerfully exploited by Fielding in particular,[187] who would certainly have sided with Burke rather than with the Jacobins. But Arendt's point has emblematic force, and she has a suggestive discussion of how the distinction between the private individual and his legal *persona* as a citizen in the sense understood in Roman law, was ignored in Revolutionary theory, and collapsed under the Terror (the concept of the persona is itself drawn from the masked actor or *dramatis persona* of the classical stage):

They believed that they had ... liberated the natural man in all men, and given him the Rights of Man to which each was entitled, not by virtue of the body politic to which he belonged but by virtue of being born. In other words, by the unending hunt for hypocrites and through the passion for unmasking society, they had, albeit unknowingly, torn away the mask of the *persona* as well, so that the Reign of Terror eventually spelled the exact opposite of true liberation and true equality; it equalized because it left all inhabitants equally without the protecting mask of a legal personality.[188]

At all events, the revolutionary war against hypocrisy, directed at the court and at the institutions and privileges of the *ancien régime*, took on the ideological contours of a drama in which 'natural man' broke through the accumulated artifice of a rotten society. It was seen, in Arendt's sketch of the prevailing self-image, as the 'explosion of an uncorrupted and incorruptible inner core through an outward shell of decay':

When the *malheureux* appeared on the streets of Paris it must have seemed as if Rousseau's 'natural man' with his 'real wants' in his 'original state' had suddenly materialized ... No hypocrisy distorted their faces and no legal personality protected them ... When this force was let loose, when everybody had become convinced that only naked need and interest were without hypocrisy, the *malheureux* changed into the *enragés*, for rage is indeed the only form in which misfortune can become active.[189]

The notion of an uncorrupted primitive man unspoilt by civilisation is much older than Rousseau or Robespierre. Until the Revolution, he was normally imagined by those who idealised him as a creature of peaceable, and even passive, innocence, rather than of a

---

[186] Ernst Robert Curtius, *European Literature and the Latin Middle Ages*, trs. Willard R. Trask, New York, 1953, pp. 138ff.

[187] See Rawson, *Henry Fielding and the Augustan Ideal under Stress*, pp. 113, 121–2, 126–7, 144 n. 54.

[188] Arendt, *On Revolution*, p. 108.   [189] Arendt, *On Revolution*, pp. 105–6, 109–10.

purity so explosive, so aggressive, and so disenchanted. The rhetoric of celebration of poor naked wretches was raised to new levels of grandeur and intensity, both within and outside the context of direct political action, by Romantic conceptions of 'the native and naked dignity of man' as not just unspotted, but sublime.[190] Those conservative thinkers who took the alternative view of human nature in the raw state would regard the unleashings of revolutionary violence as the fulfilment of time-honoured fears, and specifically as the predictable consequence of any move to release natural impulse from the restraints and deceptions, and what Burke honorifically called the 'pleasing illusions', of civilisation.

The language of Swift, of Fielding, of Chesterfield, and of Burke makes it evident that the 'pleasing illusions' are being cherished as more than an escapist holiday or a protection for the aristocratic or the genteel sensibility. The stripping away of the 'politic, well-wrought veil' might strike a blow against 'hypocrisy', but the moral satisfactions of that had to be set against the terrors of the naked truth, of naked vice and naked virtue, in all their splendid and destructive integrity. The events of the French Revolution seemed to confirm the point. They account not only for the unexampled urgency and passion with which Burke asserted the counter-revolutionary position, but also his willingness to use an imagery of 'illusions' and of 'clothes' which carried considerable rhetorical risks. The jargon of dress, after all, ran against instinctive predilections in favour of the naked truth, and the dislike of disguise and the superficial. It was open to imputations of being sympathetic to mendacity, and courted the ridicule traditionally directed (by Swift and Burke among others) at the over-dressed and fashion-minded figures of the beau and dancing-master. That Burke was not only ready to run these risks, but made himself additionally vulnerable by devoting some of his most powerful eloquence to the exercise, is more remarkable than it may seem to those for whom the *Reflections* are a collection of gorgeous anthology pieces.

CANNIBALS AND 'SANS-CULOTTES'

I conclude this study of the political use of metaphors of nakedness, dress, and unmasking at the time of the French Revolution with some

---

[190] Wordsworth, Preface to *Lyrical Ballads* (1802), *Prose Works*, 1.140. See 1.139: 'there is no necessity to trick out or to elevate nature'.

notes on the verbal phenomenon of the *sans-culottes*. The appellation seems to date back to 1790, but achieved currency a year or two later.[191] It may seem to evoke the natural unaccommodated man, naked with the grace of poverty and the openness of truth. The *sans-culottes*, many of them followers of Rousseau, were particularly identified with the radical repudiation of hypocrisy: 'it was hard for the *sans-culotte* to believe that a man could be moral in public and dishonest in private'.[192]

The name, if understood with a simple connotation of undress, might seem to be an apt embodiment of revolutionary purity, and a fit, if surprising, reminder of the continuing vitality of the symbolism of dress, confuting all reactionary talk of decent drapery and pleasing veils. In fact, of course, it didn't imply nakedness, or was perceived to do so mainly, if not exclusively, for rhetorical or satirical purposes. Carlyle harped on absolute deprivation, both the literal poverty of those for whose 'indigent Patriotism' the word was taken to stand, and in associated metaphorical senses: 'The nation is for the present, figuratively speaking, *naked*; it has no rule or vesture; but is naked, – a Sansculottic Nation.' Satirists often focused on naked savagery.[193] The real point of the term was to suggest not deprivation but the conscientious substitution of trousers (*pantalons*) for breeches (*culottes*), deemed as an aristocratic garment. Deprivation was an associated idea, and the *sans-culottes* were sometimes identified with the very poor and with a radicalised mob. But their social composition is now understood to have been 'fairly representative of the Parisian population'. The leadership included a substantial proportion of rentiers, and 'the typical sans-culotte' was neither an indigent nor a factory-worker 'but an artisan, journeyman, or owner of a small business'.[194] Even symbolically, there's an imperfect fit, since the 'pantalons longs', which they wore instead, may be thought a more comprehen-

---

[191] Paul Robert, *Dictionnaire Alphabétique et Analogique de la Langue Française* (Le Grand Robert), 2nd edn., Paris, 1989, and *OED*, 2nd edn., 1989, give 1790 for the first recorded occurrences in French and English. For a possible earlier usage, see below, n. 195. For the term's wider circulation at the time of the Legislative Assembly, see the useful article in Larousse's *Grande Encyclopédie*, Paris, 1971–81, XVII, s.v. 'sans culottes'. For examples of Burke's use of the term, see *Remarks on the Policy of the Allies* (1793), Mitchell, p.460, and *Preface to Brissot's Address to his Constituents* (1794), Mitchell, p.513.

[192] Patrice Higonnet, in *Critical Dictionary of the French Revolution*, p. 395.

[193] Carlyle, *French Revolution*, II.iii. 4; III.ii. 1 (Works, III.123; IV.67). For satirical versions, see below, p. 193 and n. 204.

[194] Higonnet, *Critical Dictionary*, p. 394; see also Gwyn A. Williams, *Artisans and Sans-Culottes*, New York, 1969, pp. 4, 19–20.

sive garment than breeches, which only came down to the knees: the idea of the Jacobins was to have a 'costume national' specifically distinguished from the aristocratic *culotte*, and which 'se composait d'un pantalon à pont retenu par des bretelles, d'une courte veste, la *carmagnole* . . .', fairly elaborate clothing, remote from nakedness.[195]

The wearing of breeches (*culottes* or *haut-de-chausses*) seems long to have been a sign of polite or civilised status. This is the point of Montaigne's sarcasm at the end of 'Des Cannibales' (I.xxxi), when reporting on the three Amerindians at Rouen who made wise and telling points about French civilisation and their own, that they wore no breeches (*haut-de-chausses*). Burke did not have Montaigne's high opinion of Amerindians. He compared the revolutionary mob to 'American savages' with 'cannibal appetites', and cited a member of the National Assembly describing that body as a *'caverne d'Antropophages'*.[196] (Rousseau, not at all times an unqualified admirer of Montaigne, praised the passage about the breechless Indians in his first *Discourse*, and was ready in subsequent debate to allow that those who go naked may have decency (*pudeur*), and that cannibals may be virtuous.)[197] The idea of revolutionary conflict and civil strife as cannibal activities became commonplace. The iconography of this is

[195] See Michèle Beaulieu, *Le Costume moderne et contemporain* Paris, 1951, p. 82. See also *Grande Encyclopédie*, Paris, 1886–1902, XXIX.447 (s.v. 'sans-culotte'). See also XII.1169, s.v. 'costume', for an account of the debate over the 'costume national'. It seems that before the adoption of the term 'sans-culotte' by the democrat groups and the project for a 'costume national', the phrase had been used as an expression of contempt from above: for alternative versions of this scenario, see Pierre Larousse, *Grand Dictionnaire Universel du XIXe Siècle*, 1866–79, XIV.189, which says that the democrats took over the phrase 'que l'insolence aristocratique leur avait donné par Mépris'; the entry in Littré's *Dictionnaire*, Paris, 1962, VI. 1891–92, cites a reported episode in the Constituent Assembly when the Abbé Maury, angered by noisy women, exclaimed: 'faites taire ce tas de sans-culottes'. The *Grand Dictionnaire Universel* (XIV.189–90) notes that in his *Nouveau Paris* (1798) Louis-Sébastien Mercier claimed, rightly or wrongly, that the term was used before the Revolution in a satire entitled *Le Sans-culotte*, mocking the reportedly indigent poet Gilbert, presumably Nicolas-Joseph-Laurent Gilbert (1750–80), author of *Le Génie aux prises avec la fortune, ou le poète malheureux*, 1772; that the usage was adoped by the rich to mock ill-dressed poets, and that it was resuscitated at the Revolution (Sébastien Mercier, *Paris pendant la Révolution (1789–1798) ou le Nouveau Paris*, new edn., 1862, I.425–6: see the whole chapter, XCIX, entitled 'Sans-culottes'; also Carlyle, *French Revolution*, II.iii. 4, *Works*, III.123). For an interesting discussion of French revolutionary costume, see Jennifer Harris, 'The Red Cap of Liberty: A Study of Dress worn by French Revolutionary Partisans 1789–94', *Eighteenth-Century Studies*, 14 (1981), 283–312.
[196] *Reflections*, pp. 117/159; 191/249; 124/167. See also pp. 123/165; 259/333. Most of these are figurative usages. Mitchell, p. 4, suggests that Burke believed literally that the revolutionaries 'had practised cannibalism'. See below n. 200.
[197] Rousseau, *Discours sur les sciences et les arts*, in *Oeuvres Complètes*, III.11–12n., 61. For reservations on Montaigne, see for example *Confessions*, x, in *Oeuvres Complètes*, I.516 and 1524–5n.

abundant: Gillray and Goya were only two of its best-known exponents, the latter's work belonging to the French Revolution's Spanish after-life.[198] Burke reverted to it in the *Letters on a Regicide Peace*, adding even that cannibalism was something of which 'with the greatest truth, their several factions accuse each other'.[199]

Burke had in mind literally anthropophagous acts of a ritual kind as well as 'nameless, unmanly, and abominable insults on the bodies of those they slaughter', a category of unspecified horrors which was to become naturalised into nineteenth-century fiction in such phrases as 'unspeakable rites': phrases designed to suggest cannibalism without saying so, or alternatively to suggest something so appalling that only metaphors of cannibalism can give an appropriate idea of its horror. Most of Burke's usages are metaphorical in more conventional ways, but the present passage makes clear that he came to believe the imputations (or boasts) literally, as did others: he wrote 'cannibalism' in the margin of an account of an alleged atrocity in 1791.[200] Mitchell speaks superciliously of Burke's belief and notes that his 'interest in cannibalism was noted by his critics'. But cannibal acts were reported by others than Burke, and seem generally to occur in situations of war, civil disturbance and mass-hunger, on a scale which we have an instinct to ignore or play down.

Imputations of cannibalism, both literal and figurative, were in any case a prominent part of the propaganda of the Revolution, on all sides of the question. This is in line with a long tradition of reciprocal imputation, of which the Amerindian debate and its famous 'liberal' paradox (most widely known through Montaigne's essay) that the civilised conqueror or tyrant is more cannibal than the cannibals are a late example. The ancient topos which sees tyranny as a reversion to barbarism equal to or greater than the alleged barbarism of the alleged cannibals, or savages, or mob over whom it is exercised, is, as I have shown elsewhere, adumbrated in the *Iliad*, where Achilles calls Agamemnon a 'people-devouring king' (*demoboros basileus*: the phrase was later applied to other tyrants), and more fully articulated by political thinkers from Plato and Aristotle onwards.[201] It here receives

---

[198] See Paulson, *Representations of Revolution*, pp. 24, 73, 120, 200, 206, 373, 363–78, *et passim*.

[199] Burke, *Letters on a Regicide Peace* (1796), I, in *Works*, V.212.

[200] Mitchell, pp. 4, 191–2n. See the copy ('with MS. remarks by the Right Honourable Edmd. Burke') of *Situation politique d'Avignon et du Comtat*, 1791, in Bodleian Library, 8° Jur. Z. 491, p. 38. The passage occurs in an 'Exposé' which contains several underlinings and handwritten marginalia. Mitchell's account, like much else in his edition, contains inaccuracies of detail.

[201] *Iliad*, I.231; see H. G. Liddell and R. Scott, *Greek–English Lexicon*, rev. H. S. Jones and others,

a further twist. For now it is the mob itself that is the tyrant, thus appropriating to itself both sides of the cannibal equation. The most remarkable turn of all is that the *sans-culottes* proudly appropriated the description to themselves. Paulson reports a Jacobin cartoon which shows 'the giant sans-culotte Hercules roasting the king over a fire and preparing to eat him': the picture's title is 'Le Peuple Mangeur de Rois', a pointed reversal of Homer's 'people-devouring king'.[202] Burke said, 'the sufferings of monarchs make a delicious repast to some sort of palates'.[203]

Nakedness and 'savagery' traditionally go together, and satirical prints of the *sans-culottes* sometimes represented them as not only unbreeched but trouserless. In Gillray's 'Un petit Souper a la Parisienne: – or – A Family of Sans Culotts refreshing after the fatigues of the day' (1792), which shows them feasting on a guillotined head, the Sans Culotts are shown not only breechless but naked from the waist down.[204] You might say in their case that breeches, though intended as 'a Cover for Lewdness as well as Nastiness', are indeed, in a revolutionary parody of Swift's clothes' philosophy, 'easily slipt down for the Service of both'.[205]

Oxford, 1978, p. 386, for an application to Caligula. Thomas More's reference to *Lestrigonas populiuoros* (people-devouring Laestrigonians) is a Latin literalisation of the Homeric metaphor: see *Utopia*, ed. Edward Surtz, S. J., and J. H. Hexter, New Haven and London, 1965, p. 52, and commentary, pp. 306–7, with citations from Erasmus. Erasmus used the Homeric phrase to describe a tyrant in the *Institutio principis christiani*, Basle, 1516, sig. g2v (*Education of a Christian Prince*, trs. Cheshire and Heath, *Collected Works*, xxvii.229); and both the Greek and a Latin translation *populi devoratores* in the *Adages* (*Opera*, Leyden, 1703–6, ii.21). For the association of tyrants with cannibalism or cannibal propensities of a literal or metaphorical kind, see Plato, *Republic*, ix.i (571A–D) and Aristotle, *Nicomachean Ethics*, vii.v. 2–7 (1148B–1149A). I have discussed this question more extensively in 'Narrative and the Proscribed Act: Homer, Euripides and the Literature of Cannibalism', in *Literary Theory and Criticism: Festschrift Presented to René Wellek*, ed. Joseph P. Strelka, New York, 1984, ii.1159–87, esp. 1162, 1178–9, and 1187nn.

[202] See Paulson, *Representations of Revolution*, pp. 363–7; the print appeared in the paper *Révolutions de Paris*, xvii, No. 217 (10–18 frimaire, an ii); also Paulson, p. 206, to the effect that revolutionary propaganda 'sometimes spoke of having an aristocrat for breakfast'; contemporary mythology spoke of blood-drinkers (*buveurs de sang: Critical Dictionary*, p. 393, Paulson p. 19).   [203] Burke, *Reflections*, p. 123/165.

[204] Reproduced in Paulson, *Representations of Revolution*, p. 201; for a description, see Mary Dorothy George, *Catalogue of Political and Personal Satires ... in ... the British Museum. Volume VI: 1784–1792*, London, 1978, No. 8122, pp. 927–8. This work was a satire on the massacres of 2–6 September 1792. See also No. 8087, p. 904, Isaac Cruikshank's 'Mad Tom's First Practical Essay on the Rights of Man', 14 May 1792, where the *sans-culottes* Paine, Sheridan and Whitbread are barelegged. George's *Catalogue* has the words 'Political [not Practical] Essay', but copies of the print at the British Museum, the Lewis Walpole Library at Farmington, Connecticut, the Yale Center for British Art, and the Huntington Library all agree on 'Practical'.   [205] Swift, *Tale of a Tub*, ii, in *Works*, 1.47.

The *sans-culottes* were a many-sided and complex phenomenon, whose real-life contours are only partly assimilable to the preoccupations of intellectual history which I have been examining. But the imagery of nakedness and dress which permeates the political and cultural discourse of the *ancien régime* is present also in the language of revolutionary times, and figures naturally in the hagiography, as well as the demonology, of *sans-culottism*. Arendt speaks of an ideological shift in Robespierre in which relief of poverty came to take precedence over the pursuit of liberty, the 'rights of the Sans-Culottes' over the more abstractly conceived 'rights of man' (Robespierre's friend Boisset even proposed a 'Declaration of the Rights of *Sansculottes*').[206] These rights were depicted by Boisset as including 'dress, food and the reproduction of the species', a formulation which ideologues of an opposite persuasion might equally readily have put to contemptuous use, and the reference to reproduction actually raised laughter at the Jacobin club.[207] No one set much practical, as distinct from rhetorical, store by nakedness, especially not the naked or their advocates, whether in a literal or a figurative sense: Paine, though he plumed himself on the discovery that Burke pitied the plumage but forgot the dying bird, also proclaimed that revolutionary France had 'outgrown the babyclothes of *count* and *duke*, and breeched itself in manhood' – the rights of man being reconceived so that 'the NOBLE of Nature', before whom 'the artificial NOBLE shrinks into a dwarf', may be clothed in metaphors appropriate to his station.[208]

While Paine conferred *culottes* of their own on those who rejected them as a badge of caste, Mary Wollstonecraft, in her retort to Burke's decent drapery passage, had stressed the obfuscatory quality of such imagery: 'a *gentleman* of lively imagination must borrow some drapery from fancy before he can love or pity a *man*'. Thus Burke's tears on 'the downfall of queens' derive from the fact that their rank 'throws a graceful veil over vices that degrade humanity', while the 'vulgar sorrows' of 'industrious mothers' and their 'helpless babes' left him unmoved. Wollstonecraft is engaged in a critique of the whole figurative habit in which both sides seem equally implicated. Burke's tenderness over queens rather than humble mothers is not seen merely as a predilection for rank. Burke's response involves a derealising of suffering which is placed on a level with his imagined reaction to 'the

---

[206] Arendt, *On Revolution*, p. 60; J. M. Thompson, *Robespierre*, New York, 1936, ii. 53n.
[207] Thompson, *Robespierre*, ii. 53n.
[208] Paine, *Rights of Man*, in *Complete Writings*, ed. Foner, i.260, 286, 289.

declamation of the theatre', and Wollstonecraft appeals to a tart demystification of such things by the author of the *Lettre à d'Alembert sur les spectacles*: '"The tears that are shed for fictitious sorrow are admirably adapted", says Rousseau, "to make us proud of all the virtues which we do not possess".'[209]

Burke had himself expressed contempt in the *Reflections* for those who could weep in the theatre at events that left them indifferent in real life, but he nevertheless believed that the theatre might be 'a better school of moral sentiments than churches, where the feelings of humanity are thus outraged', if they had the effect of sensitising people to real-life disasters.[210] As to Wollstonecraft's argument about 'the downfall of queens', Burke had already commented on that issue in February 1790, in a letter to Philip Francis, who had seen a draft of the *Reflections*: '"Whats Hecuba to him or he to Hecuba that he should weep for her?" Why because she was Hecuba, the Queen of Troy, the Wife of Priam, and sufferd in the close of Life a thousand Calamities. I felt too for Hecuba when I read the fine Tragedy of Euripides upon her Story: and I never enquired into the Anecdotes of the Court or City of Troy before I gave way to the Sentiments which the author wished to inspire; nor do I remember that he ever said one word of her Virtues.'[211]

The principle which Wollstonecraft was deriding when she jeeringly accused him of suggesting that a queen's rank threw 'a graceful veil over vices that degrade humanity' was one which Burke would probably assent to as put. Slurs on Marie Antoinette's virtue were a commonplace of anti-royalists polemics. Burns was to call her 'an unprincipled Prostitute', and this is one of the implications of Blake's lines about the pestilence darting from her robe. Blake's brutally reductive unveiling corresponds on a satirical plane to the project Rousseau adopted in the *Confessions* in the mode of self-exposing

---

[209] Mary Wollstonecraft, *A Vindication of the Rights of Men*, 1790, in *The Works of Mary Wollstonecraft*, ed. Janet Todd and Marilyn Butler, New York, 1989, v.15–16. The editors cite Rousseau's *Lettre à d'Alembert sur les spectacles*, 1758, p. 31–2: ' En donnant des pleurs à ces fictions, nous avons satisfait à tous les droits de l'humanité, sans avoir plus rien à mettre du nôtre.' Only the opening words match Wollstonecraft's quotation. The last part seems to correspond more closely to the remark about 'les apparences de toutes les vertus sans en avoir aucune' in the *Discours sur les sciences et les arts*, in *Oeuvres Complètes*, III.7). There may be a third statement by Rousseau combining both elements and corresponding more closely to what Wollstonecraft says.

[210] *Reflections*, pp. 131–3/175–7. He also scorned the new French system of government as 'false and theatric', while Paine called the *Reflections* a 'dramatic performance': such *tu quoques* were common in revolutionary polemics, on both sides (*Letter to a Member of the National Assembly*, in Mitchell, p. 315; Paine, *Complete Writings*, I.268). [211] *Correspondence*, VI.90.

autobiography. Burke would find both repellent, not because he thought them 'untrue', but because they blew the cover. For all his rhapsodic romancing about the French queen and the chivalry due to her, his social and political doctrines were grounded on the conviction of a 'pestilence' within, and he indicated to Francis that he would not find it necessary to retract his celebration if it were demonstrated that the queen was personally vicious. This had something to do with her royal status, as Wollstonecraft said, and with that civilising 'veneration for Women of condition and Beauty' which chivalry had contributed to the manners of Europe.[212] But the underlying sentiment is not that queens don't have faults, but that the decent drapery is necessary because they do. That is the unsentimental fact which the rhetorical pathos about 'the defects of our naked shivering nature' is designed to express. Burke recognised, as Rousseau and Wollstonecraft did, that the institutions of royal power and the arts of civilisation were fictions of concealment and of self-deception ('pleasing illusions'), as well as conspiracies of containment; and that they shared these functions with the sanitised dissimulations and decencies of quotidian social intercourse. Whether Wollstonecraft, or Rousseau, were themselves free of the mystifications which attend the rhetoric of nakedness and dress would be an interesting question.

The later idiomatic history of the term *sans-culotte* continues to show the same see-sawing between the connotation of garments deliberately deficient in lordliness, and the looser but semantically more logical suggestion of absolute deprivation. The latter surfaced in *The Times* of 18 July 1955, which described the celebrations of 14 July that year, with a 'crowd of *sans autos* – the modern *sans-culottes*? – who are left to swarm over the streets' where there were only buses with Tricolor flags, and taxis. The passage carries echoes of a frequently cited document of 1793: 'What is a sans-culotte? ... He is a person who always travels on foot ...' though its absolute use of 'sans' is its own.[213] The second edition of the *OED*, where I found the citation from *The Times*, also provides a counter-example from Shaw, who said in 1927 that 'Mozart ... was a court flunkey in breeches whilst Beethoven was a Sansculotte.'[214]

---

[212] Wollstonecraft, *Works*, v 15; Robert Burns, *Letters*, ed. G. Ross Roy, 2nd edn., Oxford, 1985, II. 334; Burke, *Correspondence*, VI.90; and see the whole discussion, 89–91; *Reflections*, p. 69/103.

[213] Cited, among other places, in Gwyn A. Williams, *Artisans and Sans-Culottes*, pp. 19, 120 n.1, and *Critical Dictionary*, p. 393.

[214] *OED*, 2nd edn., 1989, s.v. 'sansculotte, 1'; George Bernard Shaw, *The Great Composers: Reviews and Bombardments*, Berkeley, Los Angeles and London, 1978, p. 18 (from *Radio Times*, 18 March 1927).

Sentiment

· 6 ·

The 'Tatler' *and* 'Spectator'

Steele and Addison are the two most important figures in the early history of English periodical journalism. Steele's *Englishman* (1713–14) and Addison's *Freeholder* (1715–16) were substantial presences in the party-political press of the time, and Steele created several other journals, including the *Lover* (1714) and the *Theatre* (1720), to some of which Addison contributed. But their decisive importance rests on the three periodicals in which both collaborated most fully, the *Tatler*, *Spectator*, and *Guardian*, which between them ran to well over a thousand issues from April 1709 to December 1714. All three bequeathed their names to journalistic tradition, providing the titles of several later papers and indeed helping to establish a standard type of newspaper title.

This is merely an outward sign of more substantial things. They virtually created the genre of the 'periodical essay', exercising in the process an important influence on the early English novel and playing a large part in the formation of English manners and taste in the eighteenth century and beyond. With their mixture of social, cultural, and (more mutedly or intermittently) political commentary, of literary and theatrical criticism, original poetry and fiction, and correspondence from readers (often genuine, sometimes invented), they contributed more than any other early periodical to the kind of general intellectual journalism nowadays provided by a wide range of weeklies and by some Sunday papers. Among their contributors were Swift, Pope, Gay, Berkeley, and a host of lesser writers.

But Addison and Steele were the principal personalities, Addison as the most distinguished regular essayist, Steele as editor and activist and contributor (erratic in all these roles and usually second-rate in the last), though Addison had an important role in the editorial direction of the *Spectator's* main series as well as being the editor of the second series of 1714, which had no contributions from Steele. The collaboration was a complex and many-sided affair, and the names go together, like Rodgers and Hammerstein and Tweedledum and Tweedledee. But it was not always so. Addison was in Ireland when the *Tatler* began appearing, and only guessed Steele to be the author when he stumbled, in No. 6, on one of the early *Tatler's* rare moments of perceptive literary criticism, recognising it as one of his own insights, which he remembered having 'communicated to his friend'. In later years, their activities were more separate. Both men continued their journalistic activities after the termination of the *Guardian* in 1713, Steele in the highly political *Englishman* and in several other ventures both serious and frivolous, and Addison in the *Freeholder*, and both led active careers in Whig politics (both were MPs and Addison held high office). Both men became personally and politically estranged in varying degrees from former literary associates with Tory sympathies, like Swift and Pope (Steele's estrangement from Swift began as far back as the *Tatler*, which Swift had helped to inaugurate). Steele and Addison were finally estranged from each other over Sunderland's Peerage Bill not long before Addison's death in 1719.

The *Tatler* and *Spectator* are now little read. The decline in their reputation goes back a long time, and has been understood by their most perceptive critics as a measure of their success. In his life of Addison, Johnson remarked of the Renaissance courtesy books which he saw as precursors of the periodical essays that 'if they are now less read' it is 'only because they have effected that reformation which their authors intended'. Of Addison himself he added that he 'is now despised by some who perhaps would never have seen his defects, but by the lights which he afforded them'. More than a century and a half later, in 1945, C. S. Lewis similarly wondered 'whether the very degree of [Steele's and Addison's] success does not conceal from us the greatness of [their] undertaking':

[Addison] appears to be ... the source of a quite astonishing number of mental habits which were still prevalent when men now living were born ... If he is not at present the most hated of our writers, that can only be because he is so little read. Everything the moderns detest, all that they call *smugness*, *complacency*, and *bourgeois ideology*, is brought together in his work and given its most perfect expression.

The rejection reported by both Johnson and Lewis is the end-product of a deep assimilation. The built-in obsolescence it reflects can be seen as a quintessential triumph of journalism, a high fulfilment, played out in slow motion, of that 'ephemerality' which is the defining characteristic of the kind.

The *Tatler* appeared thrice weekly, the *Spectator* daily. They were not (except marginally in the *Tatler's* earlier numbers) concerned with 'news', but with what Geoffrey Hartman, in an essay recently reprinted in his book *Minor Prophecies* (Cambridge, MA., 1991), has described as the 'dailiness of life' in a sense which links them both with the early novelists, and more far-reachingly with 'Bouvard and Pécuchet generating endless copy'. The material, which combines both 'dailiness' and cliché, was indeed Flaubertian, the beginning of a long phase in the history of print in which combinations of the immediate and the commonplace have permeated the culture as mechanisms of intellectual evasion. Steele and Addison not only projected or furthered this phenomenon, but sometimes imply a muted or self-conscious critique of it, as though some simpering authorial ghost had entered *Bouvard et Pécuchet* with wholly unFlaubertian accents of affable self-mockery. Steele was especially coy and jumpy in this self-depreciating mode, and Swift, who helped to found the *Tatler*, but found that it 'grew cruel dull and dry', was both before and after one of the most blistering critics of the modern preoccupation with the quotidian.

One declared purpose of the periodical essayists was the healing of political differences between 'Whig and Tory, or Puritan and Papist', and a programmed fostering of evasion seems present from the start. Addison claimed that the *Spectator* 'draws Mens Minds off from the Bitterness of Party, and furnishes them with Subjects of Discourse that may be treated without Warmth or Passion' and went on to compare it to the Royal Society's project for pacifying political passions at the Restoration: 'the Air-Pump, the Barometer, the Quadrant, and the like Inventions, were thrown out to ... busy Spirits, as Tubs and Barrels are to a Whale'. As a way of not taking science seriously, whether as a progressive force (as Whigs were sometimes supposed to do) or as a cultural menace (in the manner of some Tory divines and satirists), the remark may seem to reflect the *Spectator's* political neutrality at its most genially trivialising. Addison was similarly tickled with the idea that Richelieu had founded the French Academy in order 'to divert the Men of Genius from meddling with Politicks'.

The connection between generating conversation and redirecting political energies was one which Swift (the only critic comparable to

Flaubert in such matters) had perceived as one of the modes of modern inanity several years before the *Tatler* and *Spectator*. It was he who had most recently and influentially reactivated, in the Preface to *A Tale of a Tub* (1704), the traditional image of the tub and the whale, which was repeated by Steele and Addison in both periodicals. It is a measure of Swift's distance from them that the very essay in which Addison was to adopt Swift's image of the tub was one in which he prided himself on not indulging in satire. This is not the only occasion when Swift's jeering was assimilated by others to cosier or more benign purposes. The neutralised or agreeably self-exalting appropriation of Swiftian material which reached its fullest development in Sterne was one of the *Tatler's* and *Spectator's* less recognised legacies to the eighteenth-century novel. But it is another characteristic paradox that the Swift who was in essential ways the polar antithesis of the periodical essayists, was also a participant in their enterprise, actively helping to initiate the *Tatler* and contributing to it and probably also to the *Spectator*.

The Bouvardiste idea of 'generating endless copy' is one which Swift entertained more negatively than his periodical colleagues, not only in the guise of the *Tale's* narrator determined to write on indefinitely, after his ostensible 'Subject is utterly exhausted', but as one who claimed to have spent several decades compiling *A Complete Collection of Genteel and Ingenious Conversation*. This Flaubertian labour, evidently begun well before the *Tatler* and *Spectator*, and not completed until long after the deaths of both Addison and Steele, nevertheless had its own signposted relationship to the *Tatler*. It was pseudonymously published in 1738 as the work of Simon Wagstaff, whose name identified him as a scion of the *Tatler's* illustrious family of Staffs and thus as a kinsman of Isaac Bickerstaff, 'author' of the *Tatler*, whose name Swift had also invented for another purpose and subsequently bequeathed to Steele; and as an even closer kinsman of Humphrey Wagstaff, a subsidiary pseudonym of Swift himself in the *Tatler*.

By the time of the *Complete Collection* such associations were registering parody of, rather than solidarity with, the *Tatlerian* enterprise. But Swift was still using the pre-*Tatlerian* accents of the *Tale* to mock the periodicals' fixation ('novelistic' *avant la lettre*) on the quotidian, the immediate, the inanely particular, and the complacent political opportunism which he associated with such things. Thus Wagstaff describes his research into the speech of the most polite families:

only changing as the Masters or Ladies died, or left the Town, or grew out of Vogue, or sunk in their Fortunes, or (which to me was of the highest Moment) became disaffected to the Government: Which Practice I have followed ever since, to this very Day; except, when I happened ... to be sick, or in the Spleen upon cloudy Weather ...,

a startlingly reductive endorsement by Swift of the now fashionable truism that apolitical discourse is political.

By that time Addison and Steele were both dead, and Swift had long been estranged from Steele especially. Nevertheless the *Tatler* retained a positive, as well as a negative, role in the Bouvardian evolution of the *Complete Collection*. Nos. 31 and 230 include contributions by Swift on the subject of current social jargon, and what appears to be a specific prefiguration of the *Complete Collection* itself. No. 12 records a typical conversation supposedly overheard at White's Chocolate-House, and several other numbers contain mini-anthologies of the absurdities of modern conversation, in a genre which had considerable vogue throughout the eighteenth century. No. 36 has a dialogue about 'Some People' and 'Other People', who 'give themselves Airs' or 'go abroad in Other People's Coaches', which must certainly have been the inspiration for the 'smart Dialogue between some People, and some Folks' in Fielding's *Joseph Andrews*.

Such things are a circumstantial aspect of the deep relation between the periodical essays and the fiction of the immediately succeeding period. The social coverage is wide, ranging from servant and demotic speech to that of drawing rooms and coffee-houses. Swift's *Complete Collection* undertook the 'polite' end of the social spectrum, and when he defied 'all the Clubs and Coffee-Houses in this Town' to invent any new phrases to match the excellence of his own list, he was pointing to social institutions which provided distinctive fictional frames for both *Tatler* and *Spectator*, as well as a substantial section of their readership. Swift's linguistic anthologising elsewhere extended brilliantly to lower social groups, as in the poems 'Mrs. Harris's Petition' and 'Mary the Cook-Maid's Letter', while his uncompleted *Directions to Servants*, related to the *Complete Collection* in conception and date, is a satirical tabulation of types of servant behaviour.

This anthologising habit, a pervasive and inadequately recognised feature of eighteenth-century writing, was particularly suited to the periodical essay, whose length and format encouraged summary encapsulations of manners and speech. But it reflects a broader self-consciousness about linguistic usage which is expressed more formally in the debate, to which both Swift and the *Spectator* contributed, as to whether there ought to be, as in France, an academy for regulating the language, and in the development of lexicography from Bailey in the 1720s and 1730s to Johnson's great and conscientiously regulatory *Dictionary* (1755). Other manifestations include the obsessively frequent use of nervous verbal qualifiers like 'as they call it' in most forms of eighteenth-century writing, notably, but not exclusively, in fictional dialogue and in diaries and correspondence; and the monitory lists of incorrect or socially unacceptable usages in Chesterfield's letters and other courtesy literature, which are a practical and didactic counterpart of the satirical or quasi-fictional lists in the periodical essays and in fiction. The *Tatler* and *Spectator* did not invent these, but they absorbed and developed the cultural predisposition and helped to promote the mini-anthology into a standard and almost instinctive stylistic routine.

The ultimate affinities with Flaubert's activity are real, but complex. They are modified by historical change as well as by individual factors, and the case of Swift both helps to clarify differences and to define the link. The mini-anthologies in Fielding's fiction or in the *Tatler*, including Swift's contributions to the latter, differ from the *Complete Collection* or Flaubert's two posthumous works of satiric accumulation, *Bouvard et Pécuchet* and the *Dictionnaire des idées reçues*, not only in size but in kind: 'complete collections' are strictly speaking the opposite of anthologies, whose essential character is selective rather than exhaustive. The satirical lists inserted in the *Tatler* or in Fielding's narratives tend towards the set-piece, with a circumscribed autonomy which suggests that the material is contained within boundaries of the author's choosing, and projects his confidence in the curative efficacy of diagnosis and definition.

'Complete collections', by contrast, paradoxically suggest the unlimited (and incurable). Neither of Flaubert's works in that mode was ever completed, and this is true also of Swift's *Directions to Servants*, which Swift said he worked on over the same long period as the *Complete Collection*, and once thought of publishing in the same year. The *Collection* itself, despite Wagstaff's protestations to the contrary, only became 'complete' as a convenience of publication: ending like the *Tale* because any discourse must rather than because the talking has been exhausted, since, as the *Tale*'s author says, one can '*write upon*

Nothing . . . [and] let the Pen still move on'. There is in all his parodies of 'compleat Systems' a jeering negation of any such possibility, a sense of the projector's insane aspiration to an unattainable ordering of life's centrifugal excesses. Each of his lists inevitably implies a longer one, replaying within the satirist's own performance the satirised projector's defeated quest for completeness, and reflecting an enumerative obsessiveness and an unappeasable *jusqu'au-boutisme* comparable to Flaubert's. It was not any radical difference of plan, but contingencies of publication and mortality, that secured the ironic outcome whereby Flaubert carried the project to its logical conclusion, which is non-conclusion.

The frankly selective lists of Steele or Fielding suggest a completeness of typification, a sufficiency to the purpose paradoxically absent from the 'complete' projects. Neither Steele, nor Addison, nor any eighteenth-century novelist, had the aggressive stamina to pursue such projects for whole lifetimes, nor the absolute sense of human fatuity and the misanthropic stubbornness to track it down to its last expression or detail. The deep similarity of Swift and Flaubert as good haters of their kind (*les bourgeois, c'est-à-dire tout le monde*) is hardly concealed by Flaubert's ambition of transcending 'satire' in a dispassionate author-excluding novelistic notation. In their enumerative works, both authors sport a posture of deadpan tabulation which is actually the expression of billowing energies of rejection, by comparison with which the signposted satirical commentary of the periodical essays is so bland as to seem non-judgmental. As if to emphasise this, Swift allows into Wagstaff's ostensibly sober prose a sense of activist force expended on inert matter, evocations of mechanical energy, a vocabulary of 'Materials' supplied or redistributed, of 'Fuel', of interchangeably phrasal matter made available in modular parts, of service to the nation on what might be described as an industrial scale. The ballet of compulsive conversational inanities, enhanced by an appropriate accompaniment of bodily gestures, is enacted on a hard metallic grid, in which social comedy has become rigidified into a critique of which the *Tatler* and *Spectator* would have been incapable, though, as Hartman may be implying, they provided the raw materials.

If Swift prefigures *Bouvard et Pécuchet* in his anatomy of modern culture, it was Addison and Steele who were the immediate and pervasive influences on eighteenth-century writing and manners. This is evident in the way Johnson accepted Addison's claims about the power of 'conversation' to effect political healing. He wrote of the *Tatler* and *Spectator*:

to minds heated with political contest they supplied cooler and more inoffensive reflections; and it is said by Addison ... that they had a perceptible influence upon the conversation of the time, and taught the frolick and the gay to unite merriment with decency ... they continue to be among the first books by which both sexes are initiated in the elegances of knowledge.

'Conversation' is an elastic term often stretching to a broader meaning than the verbal. Johnson saw the periodical essays as belonging with the great conduct books of Castiglione, della Casa, and La Bruyère. He regarded Steele and Addison as 'masters of common life' who undertook the first large-scale reform of manners in England, and did so in a new journalistic medium ('the frequent publication of short papers') which Johnson considered particularly suited to such an enterprise. And the word 'conversation' readily applied to the entire project which introduced not only the politically mollifying geniality of Sir Roger de Coverley, but also the correction of Restoration scurrility and the *Tatler's* crusades against gambling and duelling. Even when the word was used in the more specifically verbal sense in which we use it today, it is within the context of a broader concern with manners: 'To teach the minuter decencies and inferior duties, to regulate the practice of daily conversation.' The manner, not just the matter, of conversational exchanges is included in the regulation. Nevertheless Johnson also perceived the periodical essays as a supply of conversational copy: 'That general knowledge which now circulates in common talk was in his time rarely to be found.' This is observed in a benign way, and with a fairly precise sense of how it might contribute to political healing, for example by introducing 'subjects on which faction had produced no diversity of sentiments; such as literature, morality, and familiar life'. The notion that 'literature, morality, and familiar life' do not produce 'diversity of sentiments' has a certain period charm (for which Hartman incidentally experiences a momentary nostalgia, when he speaks of Addison's and Steele's style, 'so different, in its energy and humor, from that of modern conversational critics who try to perpetuate the mode'. Who they?).

Swift's *Complete Collection*, by contrast, is of 'conversation' in the narrower sense. The poor quality of this is an implicit reflection of *mœurs*, but the lists are of talk: the 'endless copy' supplied consists of phrases in a pure state, empty of thought or content. They have no concern with what Johnson called 'that general knowledge which now circulates', and they are free also of the 'novelistic' dimension for which the periodical essays, with their rudimentary interest in character, narrative, and social portraiture helped to prepare the way. What Hartman calls their 'journalistic stream of conversation' is part of the process by which 'the very dailiness of life now enters consciousness more thoroughly' not only in the periodicals, but 'by way of the novels of Defoe, and then Richardson and Sterne'. In this sense *Bouvard et Pécuchet* belongs with them, not mainly because the commonplaces it tabulates emanate from personages who have a certain fictional solidity, but because they are clichés of received opinion and superficial knowledge rather than of empty phrase. Unlike Swift's ghostly speakers, who exchange meaningless phrases and know nothing, Bouvard and Pécuchet possess considerable stocks of knowledge on a wide variety of subjects. If their conversational banalities are therefore more 'substantial', it is because they have been unceasingly exposed to a journalism and other products of print culture whose supply of packaged fact and opinion, 'that general knowledge which now circulates', has expanded on a scale undreamt of when the *Tatler* and *Spectator* helped to generate the phenomenon in European letters. Flaubert's novel could not have been conceived without this evolution, while Swift's distillation of pure conversational vacuity pulls away from the novelistic, even in the sketchy forms fostered by the periodical essays. But Flaubert's critique of the journalistic void, his sense of its ubiquitous and limitless encroachment, is neither Addisonian nor Johnsonian, but Swiftian.

The genial satire which the *Tatler* and *Spectator* applied to the modes of modern speech and behaviour are as nothing to the scale on which they created or perpetuated those modes: the satire, and its very geniality, may suggest not confidence, as is sometimes supposed, but a self-reassuring nervousness. For all their enormous importance, the periodical essays are undermined by a persistent sense of their own triviality. Their very titles reflect this, especially the *Tatler* and its constant signposting of its essays as 'lucubrations'. The *Spectator* and *Guardian* (Steele's and Addison's third important collaborative periodical) may suggest a progression in 'seriousness' and even in confidence, though Steele divided his subsequent journalistic efforts between the patriotic gravity of the *Englishman* and productions with such *Tatler*-derived titles as the *Lover* ('By Marmaduke Myrtle,

Gent.'), *Town-Talk, Chit-Chat*, and possibly the *Tea-Table* (now lost). That the titles are sometimes more frivolous than the content is significant in itself. The *Tatler* idiom certainly caught on. In addition to several continuations with the same title, there was from the start a flood of answers and imitations (Addison complained of some hostile ones in No. 229), with titles like *Female Tatler, Tatling Harlot, Whisperer, Titt for Tatt*, and many variants throughout the century: *Parrott, Prattler, Prater, Busy-Body*. The *Spectator*-derived titles (not all of them new) tended to be more sober: *Monitor, Mirror, Observer, Looker-On* (but a *Peeper* section appeared in the *European Magazine* in 1788–91). They doubtless varied in tone, but the self-undercutting tendency of the genre must have been strong for Johnson to have given the names of *Rambler* and *Idler* (both of which had been used before) to enterprises of considerable substance and gravity. Boswell thought ' "The Rambler" ... not suited to a series of grave and moral discourses', but Johnson had difficulty in finding a title and 'The Rambler seemed the best that occurred'. It is interesting that what thus 'occurred' struck a note more evocative of Steele and Addison than of the content or style of Johnson's own periodical.

The *Tatler* was experimental and uncertain of its direction. It aimed at a miscellaneous coverage of entertainment, poetry, learning, and foreign and domestic news. Its formula was that each item emanated from a particular coffee-house or 'From my own Apartment'. The miscellaneity of individual numbers gives a jumpy impression. Under Addison's influence the *Tatler* gradually moved towards the 'unified single essay' format eventually perfected in the *Spectator*, and thus acquired whatever *gravitas* Addison could confer upon it. The *Spectator's* breadth of coverage showed itself not within single numbers, but from number to number. The device of a Spectator Club, each of whose members represented a different walk of life, was only intermittently activated.

But the early *Tatler's* chief weakness was a matter not of formal framework, but of tone, a strained sprightliness, both apologetic and nudging. The jokes are awful. If you want to know the worst of all Irish jokes, it is in No. 58. Steele may not have invented it, which makes his putting it there all the more remarkable. There are puppyish self-castigations: 'Mr. *Greenhat* [who may have been Swift] has convinc'd me that I have writ Nonsense; yet am I not at all offended at him.' The literary and theatrical criticism is limply facetious at its own expense. Some passable critical observations in

No. 6, including the one Steele stole from Addison's conversation, are underminingly ascribed to a giddy 'Fine Lady' called Sappho and 'a Gentleman playing the Critick': they are, it is true, mixed with silliness, and we are told about it in case we have not noticed, but that is Steele's doing too.

Even the *Tatler's* favourite moral crusades are coyly deflated: 'never Hero in Romance was carried away with a more furious Ambition to conquer Giants and Tyrants, than I have been in extirpating Gamesters and Duellists'. But the failure of nerve is most visible in the reporting of news, where the contemporary contempt for 'daily Historians' exercised an uneasy pressure. The column of 'Foreign *and* Domestick News ... *from St.* James's Coffee-house' typically has a facetious get-it-over-with briskness, sometimes laced with defensive comments about 'our Brother Newsmongers'. Facts and dates sometimes read like Swift's famous piece of mock-journalese, 'A Full and True Account of the Battel Fought last Friday.' Eventually, and mercifully, the news column was abandoned.

Erich Auerbach might well, as Hartman says, 'have interpreted the gentle humor and temperate didacticism of Mr. Spectator as evidence that the quotidian did not yet seem entirely newsworthy'. If so, then the *Tatler* makes the uneasiness look like something close to panic. In fact, it contrives to make out of the uneasiness about the quotidian merely another expression of the quotidian. It does so by shamelessly appropriating the critique of newsmongering, as found in Swift and many others, and melting it into the 'elegant trifling' of its own self-cherishing enterprise. You could say that it made an *idée reçue* of the critique itself, and that (true to its character of proleptic *bouvardisme*) it passed the idiom on. It is found, in its primary form, wittily authentic and without the Tatlerian simper, not only in Swift, but also in Fielding and as late as Byron mocking 'daily scribes'. But there is a secondary transmission, not of the critique as such, but of its assimilation in cosy forms of self-acceptance, and that is the Shandean habit.

The self-trivialising is, however, most striking in the treatment of women. The *Tatler* was partly addressed 'to the Fair Sex, in Honour of whom I have invented the Title of this Paper'. Two years later Steele wrote in the *Spectator* that he would 'take it for the greatest Glory of my Work, if among reasonable Women this Paper may furnish *Tea-Table Talk*'. It is hard to believe today that such things were not only meant, but accepted as compliments. The mixture of hyperbole and limitation (greatest Glory/*Tea-Table Talk*) was a standard feature, a cultural nervous tic, simultaneously gallant and coercive: 'the utmost of a Woman's Character is contained in Domestick Life'. Together with phrases like 'Fair Sex' and 'better half of the World', it is part of a burgherly appropriation of courtly compliment which still survives today with minor mutations.

Tea-table talk, spectatorially furnished in 'endless copy', was not meant to be trivial. It referred to serious things, 'Domestick Life', 'the becoming Duties of Virginity, Marriage, and Widowhood', the social and moral aspects of relations between the sexes. It takes in the assumption that women have by 'Nature and Instinct' a greater 'Subtilty of Spirit' in the portrayal of love. The comment was made in relation to Susanna Centlivre's play *The Busie Body*, and there is a sense in which 'tattling' in Steele has much the same status as 'scribbling' in Richardson. Both bring out a supposed female superiority in matters of sentiment of a sort that properly raises hackles in feminist quarters. But Richardson is nowadays a feminist hero, which suggests that the willingness to accept compliments may have undergone changes since the eighteenth century, but has not disappeared. Perhaps the progression from 'tattling' to 'scribbling' marks a shift from an oral to a printed conception of public feminine expression and should pass as an improvement.

Richardson said he wrote to 'exalt the Sex', which may be set beside the *Spectator's* assertion that in aiming at 'a Stile and Air suitable to [Women's] Understanding' he would 'not lower but exalt' what he wrote about. It is a feature of all such overdetermined gallantries, including the habit of calling women the 'fairer' and the 'better' sex, that they are a polite way of saying they're not equal. This may appear more insulting now than it did then. But it seems clear that any contempt involved in the exaltation of tattling and scribbling was, in Steele's case as in Richardson's, inwardly as much as outwardly directed. Richardson was always identifying or comparing himself with the fair scribblers who are his correspondents and his heroines, and the eponymous Tatler was not any lady but Steele himself.

The proclaiming of a female audience and self-identification with the fair sex protected both authors from the risk of being taken too seriously, while leaving plenty of room for the reassuring complacencies of compliment. It provided a kind of polite pariah status, both celebrative and self-abasing. Steele's 'fair-sex [ing] it to the world's end' (as Swift described the *Spectator*) has less to do with women than with the luxuries of self-depreciation which made him refer to his crusade against gambling and duelling as a quixotic extravagance, or undermine some critical perceptions by ascribing them to 'a Fine Lady' and 'a Gentleman ... Critick'. This even-handed allocation reinforces the impression that the belittling is not directed at either sex so much as at the author's own belief in what he has to say.

· 7 ·
Richardson, alas

Richardson is the *Hugo, hélas*! of the eighteenth-century novel, as
Coleridge might have said:

I confess that it has cost & still costs my philosophy some exertion not to be
vexed that I admire – aye, greatly, very greatly, admire *Richardson* his mind is
so very vile a mind – so oozy, hypocritical, praise-mad, canting, envious,
concupiscent.

These sentences of 1805 echo and reverberate through Coleridge's
Notebooks and *Marginalia* and *Table Talk*, as well as the *Biographia
Literaria*, to the closing weeks of his life in July 1834. He brooded with
fascinated revulsion on 'the loaded sensibility, the minute detail, the
morbid consciousness of every thought and feeling ... the self-
involution and dreamlike continuity', like 'a sick room heated by
stoves' contrasted with Fielding, who resembles 'an open lawn, on a
breezy day in May'.

Most of the themes of Richardson criticism, before and since, are
contained in Coleridge's comments, and the blend of admiration and
repugnance belonged to the case from the start. Contemptuous
adversaries, like Fielding himself, paid glowing tributes to *Clarissa*.
Johnson, a devoted admirer, derided Richardson's self-importance,
remarking that he 'died merely for want of change among his
flatterers': Johnson meant that his own praises 'would have added two
or three years to his life' had Richardson lived 'till *I* came out',
implying presumably that Johnson had not yet become famous
enough for his praises to please. Such ambivalence was no simple
separation of the man from the books. Johnson praised the novels
almost unstintingly, but said that 'if you were to read Richardson for
the story, your impatience would be so much fretted that you would
hang yourself'. Fielding, who might be expected to be personally

hostile, probably did not know who the author of *Pamela* was when he wrote *Shamela*, but did know when he praised *Clarissa*. When Lady Mary Wortley Montagu said 'I heartily despise [Richardson] and eagerly read him, nay, sob over his works in a most scandalous manner', she was responding simultaneously to the power of the novels and to a personality felt through the work to be repugnant. For her, as for Coleridge, Richardson was the most 'despised' of 'admired' writers. Either way, he has always been someone people love to hate, or vice versa.

Perhaps this explains how it comes about that this self-righteous burgherly patriarch, presiding unctuously over his little senate of admiring ladies, has been adopted as an adversarial hero by some campus ideologues both Marxist and feminist. He does not, on the face of it, seem the type. It is a merit of Jocelyn Harris' *Samuel Richardson* nevertheless to demonstrate sensitively and without pretentious haranguing that Richardson 'speaks ... to feminist concerns' and played an honourable part in 'the "fair sex debate" ' (the phrase suggests how anachronistic it is, as Harris concedes, to use the word 'feminist' in this context). He expressed views on education and marriage close to those of Mary Astell, who may have been a model for Clarissa. Astell has been called 'England's first feminist' in a good recent book by Ruth Perry, where she is also shown to have been (like Richardson) generally conservative in religion and politics.

Like some other critics, Harris reads Richardson's novels in the context of Locke's rebuttal of Filmer's theories of government, and of traditional extensions of constitutional debate to the sphere of domestic life. Both Astell and Richardson liked to apply principles of Lockeian liberalism to personal and family relations, and the male villains in Richardson's novels tend to be associated with a Filmerian authoritarian–patriarchal outlook. Harris sometimes seems unduly specific on the point, as when she says that 'Lovelace the Filmerian maintains that the female sex "is made to bear pain" ' as a consequence of Eve's transgression, and 'that women love those best who pain them most'. Such male mythologising seems pretty timeless, more folkloric than Filmerian. But it is true that the male characters, and especially Lovelace, make use of the terminology of government (king, emperor, throne, rebel, authority, bestowal of preferments, prerogative), as well as of military conquest (a traditional source of metaphors in transactions between the sexes), in their exercises or boasts of sexual tyranny, in ways which sometimes go beyond the idiomatic or poetic commonplace and acquire an air of formal ideologising. Richardson was driven by a relentless over-explicitness which sometimes builds into the novels themselves the kind of 'thematic' gloss normally practised, on another plane, by academic explicators. Harris is too good a critic to write like a bad one, but too generous to her author to acknowledge that he has pedantries of his own.

Richardson's 'feminism' is summed up in the tone, as well as the substance, of comments like 'You must see that the Tendency of all I have written is to exalt the Sex.' In this, as I suggested in the last chapter, he writes like Steele or Addison. He also urges young ladies to write him letters, precisely because that is what 'young ladies, delicate by sex, by education', are 'qualified by genius and imagination to excell in'. When he intimates equality of relationship, it is only after condescending to lower himself to a coyly assumed role of 'undesigning scribbler', a specialised counterpart of his relegation of the women to an equally specialised sphere of the feeling heart and sensitive pen. Within these limits, fantasies of sympathetic rapport may flourish, usually through the mediation of his fictional heroines, whom he and his correspondents endlessly discuss, feel for, and relate to themselves and each other. As Harris says, his correspondence with women 'intersected excitingly with his fictional worlds', though 'excitingly' suggests, perhaps more than she intends, excitation rather than excitement. The ladies are, for the most part, urged to write only to other ladies, men being (as the novels demonstrate) 'hardly ever void of design' – except himself, since he is older, of good character, already married, and wholly 'paternal in my views'. The heroines, in these heavily hedged transactions, offer an additional protective element, acting as invisible chaperones, as texts for the elaboration of fine sentiments, and as derealising agents, as if to say it is only a story, a scribble engendering more scribbling.

Richardson might claim to enter into the hearts of his fair correspondents much as he entered into those of the scribbler-heroines of the novels. His sympathy with the sex is less that of an equal than of 'a sincere well-wisher'. Equality yields to the customary hyperbolic gallantries, which hold that women are 'the fairer and *better Sex*': a tried way, as in Steele, of enforcing the idea that they're not equal while absolving the speaker of churlishness (the emphasis, though, is Richardson's: he emphasised everything). When Richardson says that in the special field of letter-writing, a delicate lady 'cannot set pen to paper but a beauty must follow it', he is adapting to fair scribblers the kind of courtly turn which Pope excelled at simultaneously executing and subverting: 'If to her share some Female Errors fall,/ Look on her Face, and you'll forget 'em all.' The irony disappears from Richardson's use of the formula at precisely the time when good poets were variously registering its bankruptcy, in accents of witty disengagement or (as in Swift) of radical rejection. The uncourtly Richardson's way with the courtly forms is to reinstate them with a bald literalness. What is shed is not the 'sexism', but any critical awareness of its fatuity.

'If there were Sex in Heaven, good Women would be angels *there*, as they are *here*.' This was written to Sophia Westcomb in 1746, when Richardson was well into the writing of *Clarissa*, the novel in which the image of the beloved mistress as angel is given imaginative revalidation in the figure of a heroine martyred to virtue. Here too the clichés of poetic gallantry, which Swift probed even in his tenderest declarations:

> Now, this is Stella's Case in Fact;
> An Angel's Face, a little crack't;
> (Could Poets or could Painters fix
> How Angels look at thirty-six)
> This drew us in at first to find
> In such a Form an Angel's mind ...

are in Richardson upwardly reformulated or *un*parodied. The courtly compliment to a mistress is given a bourgeois consolation and applied to all good women. Richardson had a low opinion of Swift's low opinion of women, though some intelligent feminists understand Swift's position differently. In this passage, at all events, Swift's play with the 'angel' cliché reflects his usual deep distaste for the routines of love poets, but it is not a means of insulting the lady. For once Swift treats love-poetry as Augustan mock-heroic treats epic: not mainly as a mode to be derided, but as a reflection or repository of respected values from which moderns have lapsed, here with the one exception of Stella. The ironic gesture is a way of enforcing Stella's right to the compliment, despite its customary abuse and in the only sense that matters: 'an Angel's mind'.

The idea that Clarissa has 'an Angel's mind' is also subjected to an attempted deconstruction, as Harris shows: 'Lovelace's plan is to make her mortal by making her sexual. There are people who remember that she was born, he exults, "that she came not from above, all at once an angel!" ... he reasons that "*matrimonial* or *equal* intimacies" will make her less an angel.' Lovelace fails, but he begins by serving Richardson as irony served Swift, to preempt the scepticism of readers resistant to the excesses of amatory hyperbole. It is a way, perhaps for both authors, of having it both ways. Like Swift's, Lovelace's image has its origins in the love poets. He had been a lovelorn sonneteer, who 'must have a Cynthia, a Stella, a Sacharissa' of his own, but discovered that ladies are not as pure as sonnets claim, much as Swift's swain discovers that his Celia shits.

Besides, Lovelace has been jilted by one of them. He is committed to vengeance on all women, and in particular to exposing the angelic pretensions he once proclaimed. Clarissa is to be his spectacular exhibit, and the novel proves him wrong. Clarissa's angelic status is unremittingly asserted and Lovelace in particular in his dying moments speaks of her as 'dear angel ... Divine Creature ... blessed Spirit'. His deconstruction fails, because he has been *re*constructed, and the challenge it posed has the effect of containing or neutralising objections, not of exploding a myth. The angelic metaphor is indeed asserted in terms so emphatic that it acquires literal pretensions, and the non-fictional letter to Miss Westcomb shows that Richardson did not shrink from these. We witness in the novel a peculiar species of overkill, which works not merely through inordinate accretion or repetition, but through a prosiness which finally boils things down to their prose sense. It is as though Richardson were atoning for his use of figurative language by a dogged determination to prove it true.

Richardson's manner may be seen as an overturning of Augustan ironies in Swift or in Pope's *Rape of the Lock* (which *Clarissa* evokes in various ways, including the name of its heroine). Such overturning is hostile, but underisive, for the mocking graces of Augustan wit, the glancing obliquity of Pope's critique of gallantry, are themselves the objects of his hostility, along with Lovelace's high-born arrogance and patrician profligacy.

Richardson's literalness, like that of his friend Johnson, naturally shrank from ironic utterance. But it differed from Johnson's in both its mechanics and motivation. Johnson seems to have avoided irony because it distorted plain truth and specifically because, in its aggressive forms, it hid from view those aspects of the case which made possible a completer and more charitable understanding: this is the positive sense in which he is sometimes spoken of as a satirist *manqué*. But, for all his specific reservations over Swift or Pope, Johnson was rooted in the same tradition of classical learning and polite letters, which Richardson viewed with resentment and a touch of class-envy. He was consistently censorious of the Scriblerian circle (deploring the 'Dunciad, and its Scriblerus-Prolegomena-Stuff'), not least, one supposes, because Fielding had early assumed the mantle of Scriblerus Secundus. From *Shamela* onwards, Fielding submitted Richardson to a form of patrician put-down which earlier wits had applied to cits, and which the Scriblerians transferred to the burghers and scribblers of the *Dunciad* or *A Tale of a Tub*.

It rankled, as though the Scriblerian enterprise had been designed to ridicule him in advance. Richardson's fond references to his own 'scribbling' are not simply assimilations to his heroine-authoresses. Sometimes ('myself, the Scribbler,' 'a low-classed scribbler') they read like a self-conscious, as well as self-approving, acceptance of Scriblerian slurs in the teeth of their proleptic derision.

Both assimilations, to sentimental scribblers and derided ones, are in turn proleptically Shandean. Tristram Shandy, who thought his book should 'swim down the gutter of Time' with *A Tale of a Tub*, had a clear sense of being derided in advance. He outfaced the derision by, so to speak, outdoing it, by feats of jokey digressiveness and egotistic self-indulgence which exceeded anything Swift's *Tale* might have invented in repudiation: characteristically, when the time came, Richardson disapproved of *Tristram Shandy*, partly because Sterne answered derision with derision and, worse still, self-derision. Sullen harping on his low-classed scribbling was as far as Richardson was prepared to go in sarcastic response, and the spectacle of Sterne committing his whole enterprise to mimicry of Scriblerian mimicry was calculated to displease him.

By a sad irony the very letter in which he reproves Sterne's book is one in which, as often in his later years, he was 'sensible of failure in my fingers'. The Shandean autonomy of the scribbling pen has gone into reverse, like phalluses in Rochester which rise and fall independently of their owners: 'Too, too often my Pen will not touch the Paper, – nor stay in my Fingers.' The intrusion of physical infirmity was the result of aging. But it had long been part of his epistolary mythology that he was endlessly engaged in quasi-adversarial dealings with his headstrong pen, in tones which range from the Shandean whimsical (he would have written 'sooner ... had I not quarrelled with my Pen') to the Shandean pathetick ('Another there was whom his soul loved; but with a reverence – Hush! – Pen, lie thee down!').

These examples help to remind us how much Shandeism was the heir to Richardsonian 'sentiment' as well as to that alternative and antagonistic tradition of 'learned wit' which came to Sterne by way of Fielding and Swift. But the Richardsonian topos of the self-willed and self-propelling pen had itself already come up for derision long before Richardson, when the scribbler-author of *A Tale of a Tub* announced that he was 'trying an Experiment very frequent among Modern Authors . . . When the Subject is utterly exhausted, to let the Pen still move on.' And when that same scribbler declared that what he wrote was 'literally true this Minute I am writing' he was pre-parodying the ideal of 'to the Moment' writing in its primary Richardsonian form as well as its Shandean self-ironic transformation. What Sterne went on to outparody, Richardson was content to unparody.

That Swift's parody is perhaps closer to these later writers than to any he was actually attacking (Dryden, among others), implies that these forms of modern self-consciousness were a matter of deep tendency before they attained overt fruition, and early available for exposure or expression by hostile and sympathetic figures alike. A feature of them was the blurring of judgmental demarcations between the hostile and the sympathetic, in a domain where disclosure of the disreputable might be cherished for its sincerity or acumen, or as evidence of an enhanced valuation of confession and self-expression as such. The disreputabilities which Swift exposes in his modern spokesmen are things which they for their part take pride in reporting, and it is clear that Swift dislikes the confessional gusto as much as the things confessed, much as Sterne's narrators cherish both.

Richardson was somewhere in between, as can be seen from a letter of 1748 in which he urges Susanna Highmore to come to Tunbridge Wells, where she might see the aged Mr Nash and Mr Cibber 'hunting after new beauties, and with faces of high importance traversing the walks', and goes on to describe himself:

And if you do, I will shew you a still more grotesque figure than either. A sly sinner, creeping along the very edges of the walks, getting behind benches: one hand in his bosom, the other held up to his chin, as if to keep it in its place: afraid of being seen, as a thief of detection. The people of fashion, if he happen to cross a walk (which he always does with precipitation) *unsmiling* their faces, as if they thought him in their way; and he as sensible of so being, stealing in and out of the bookseller's shop, as if he had one of their glass-cases under his coat. Come and see this odd figure! You never *will* see him, unless *I* shew him to you.

Sterne could never have written this. It reminds us of a sometimes neglected feature of Richardson's writing, that his set-pieces sometimes attain the strong obsessive power of the great nineteenth-century masters. The 'sly sinner, creeping along the very edges of the walks, getting behind benches', has the unctuous surreptitiousness of a Dickensian villain. The furtive grimness seems surprising in a self-portrait. It is evidently meant as affectionately self-depreciating, but reveals a degree of self-contempt, which nevertheless quickly dissolves into, or coexists with, a more indulgent portraiture. Although Sterne could not have written it, it is indeed Shandean in its fond sense of its own eccentricity ('this odd figure') and its mock-mystification ('you never *will* see him, unless *I* shew him to you'). The use of the third person belongs with this, though also superficially unlike Sterne. There is a kind of self-consciousness that luxuriates in third-person presentations, which set Number One into relief and provide a mock-distance for effects of exhibition close in spirit to Shandy's coy aplomb. The specialist in our time of this species of histrionic self-foregrounding, with its teasing delusion of enhanced objectivity and its opportunities for a smirking inwardly directed irony, is Norman Mailer.

Richardson would not have relished Mailer and did not like Sterne. He was incapable of the flippancy with which they expressed their egos, though there is an attempt at comedy in his self-portrait. And neither Mailer nor Sterne shows the peculiar class-consciousness of Richardson's writing, though Sterne had his own way of loving a lord. Richardson's way of loving a lord is to believe he doesn't, an almost statutory ambivalence of the British bourgeois. His avoidance of the 'people of fashion ... *unsmiling* their faces, as if they thought him in their way' is both sheepishly 'sensible of so being' and sourly offended by the imagined slight. The hurt accents of the excluded tradesman against 'that upper life [which] is low enough to despise the metropolis, which furnishes them with all their beloved luxury' is a steady undercurrent in his writing. On the other hand he saw his acquisition of a female little senate as a form of social advancement, a penetration of the gentry, so to speak, through its soft underbelly: he expressed satisfaction at being 'envied ... for the Favour I stand in with near a Score of very admirable Women, some of them of Condition'.

The fictional expression of these mixed feelings is to be found in his treatment of Lovelace and his family in *Clarissa*, and indeed in the portrayals of the nobility and upper gentry in all the novels. His fascinated fixation on these social strata and his outsider's lack of knowledge of them were a matter for early comment. Horace Walpole called the novels 'pictures of high life as conceived by a bookseller', and the sentiment was echoed in softer or more considered forms by friend and foe alike. Richardson repeatedly excused himself by appealing to his early 'narrowness of fortune', his temperament 'naturally shy and sheepish' (he seems to have made a habit of calling himself sheepish), and similar obstacles: 'How, I say, shall such a man pretend to describe and enter into characters in upper life?' It is characteristic of him not to notice that what called for explanation was not his ignorance of 'high life' but his determination to write about it.

Richardson was fond of calling high people low when they behaved uppishly: 'upper life is low enough to despise the metropolis'. It is a form of the classic put-down discussed in earlier sections of this book, readily available in a lordly culture, and found in quasi-aristocrats like Fielding as well as in a commoner like Pope (both of whom did however 'despise the metropolis' in their own way). Richardson sometimes sports their grandee manner, as when, responding to some remarks against him in Fulke Greville's *Maxims, Characters, and Reflections* (1756), he works himself into a veritable lather of gentle-manly wit-writing, to the effect 'that Mr. G. was perhaps as much too high-bred, as the other was too low: But that, with his Superior Advantages, it is as much a Wonder, that he wrote no better, as that the other wrote no worse'. 'The other', 'a *certain Author*' (Greville had used the phrase, but again the emphasis is Richardson's) is himself, and the third person here is fraught with all the haughty indignation of a Mrs Honour even as he strains to mimic the uppish accents of her creator.

About Fielding himself he said this:

Poor Fielding! I could not help telling his sister, that I was equally surprised at and concerned for his continued lowness. Had your brother, said I, been born in a stable, or been a runner at a sponging-house, we should have thought him a genius, and wished he had had the advantage of a liberal education, and of being admitted into good company.

It is one of the unwitting symmetries of literary history that another now famous private letter, by Fielding's cousin Lady Mary Wortley Montagu, expresses the conviction that Richardson 'was never admitted into higher Company, and should confine his Pen to the

Amours of Housemaids', just as her surmise in the same letter that 'Richardson never had (probably) money enough to purchase ... a Ticket for a Masquerade', echoes his own account of the 'narrowness of fortune' which prevented his frequenting 'public entertainments' and other haunts of 'upper life'.

Richardson had a great readiness to condemn Fielding's work in the most specific detail while pretending not to have had time to read it. There is a Leavisian flavour in the sour haughtiness with which he disliked admitting that he had bestowed his attention on a book he was simultaneously willing to vilify, as well as in the tortuous explanations, always involving third parties, of how he came to know about it.

He was similarly 'inclined to deny that he had read' other authors, perhaps truthfully, as his biographers Eaves and Kimpel report. If lack of time was the problem, he could have read many books in the time that it took him to write the letters in which he complained of lack of time, or penned the acidulous dissertations explaining his dislike of the books and his reasons for not reading them. In this way he acted out in his own life comments made by readers of his novels, to the effect that his characters' letters were so long that they hardly left time for the events they described. Richardson actually went one better: his own longest letters are frequently about his characters' letters, enlarging upon them, citing them as authorities on points of wisdom or conduct.

Richardson comes nearest of all great writers to enacting his friend Johnson's *mot* about the dramatist Hugh Kelly, that he had 'written more than he has read'. He was, sometimes quite movingly, conscious of this. He found writing easier than reading, and spoke of this as a neurotic disability: 'my nervous disorders will permit me to write with more impunity than to read'. If 'impunity' suggests that reading induced 'guilt', as a passive or idle activity, that attitude in turn induced its own form of guilt. He wrote in October 1753: 'Now I have done Writing, if Life be lent me, I must endeavour to recover the Power of Reading: Yet, what will be the End of it, if I do, but to shew me that I ought to have read more, and writt less?'

· 8 ·

Boswell's life and journals[1]

Boswell's life was one of unfulfilled ambitions. Neither in politics, nor in the law, nor even in letters did he, in his own lifetime, fulfil his expectations or rise to the level of his distinguished friends. When, at the beginning of his literary career, he published *An Account of Corsica* (1768), he became an international celebrity, better known for a time than Johnson himself. At the end, his *Life of Samuel Johnson* (1791) became a landmark in the history of biography, but he died too soon to see its fame consolidated. In between there was frenetic activity, amorous, social, and convivial, as well as legal, political, and literary; but also dispersal of effort, dissipation of life, and a painful conscious-ness of career failure. 'I have an ardent ambition for literary fame', he had said in the Corsica book: but despite the book's notoriety, he was never quite taken seriously as a writer. Among the members of The Club (to which he was elected after some opposition) he never achieved the weight of Johnson, Goldsmith, Burke, Reynolds, Gibbon, or Sheridan. The two friends have become posthumous rivals. Some have said that Boswell's *Life* created Johnson for posterity, others that Johnson provided the material for Boswell to write the book without which he would not be remembered.

The mountain of private papers now at Yale, which provides the basis for the excellent two-volume biography by Frederick Pottle and Frank Brady, must be one of the completest self-portraits ever left by a writer. Everything public or private, important or unimportant, is included: legal work in Edinburgh, literary friendships in London,

---

[1] It seems appropriate to indicate that the two pieces which make up this chapter were written before I became editorially associated with the Yale editions of the Private Papers of James Boswell.

travels in Europe, drinking (heavy, but as Johnson said, 'without skill in inebriation'), sexual exploits. The latter have become notorious, especially after the publication some forty years ago of the *London Journal*. They are also very dull, except as expressions of a personality whose dulness is itself a fascinating phenomenon. The diaries, whose publication in thirteen volumes was completed recently, record women of all ages, shapes, and sizes, from adolescent girls to women of sixty, whores, maids, widows, other men's mistresses, wives and daughters, just as they list the various beverages consumed on his drunken sprees: port, sherry, claret, hock, burgundy. Some copulations are signalled by the Greek letter π: an 'uncommon act' gets π upside down. The mere fact of occurrence (*any* occurrence, even of non-occurrence) qualified it for writing-down: hence a Greek letter, by itself, is sufficient. States of mind are occurrences too, of course, and where these befall him they are duly noted: broodings about his wife (her goodness, her limitations in bed), sundry appreciations of other ladies, some biblical fantasies of 'Asiatic' concubinage and corresponding religiose prickings of conscience. One night with a lady of the town he records '*Three* then. Insisted she should repeat LORD's prayer. Strange mixture. Wondrous fondness.' Solemnity broke in on dalliance, and dalliance on solemnity. When his mother died, he rushed to a brothel. When his father died, he tried π but checked himself. When Johnson died, he did not check himself. His regular habit of attending public hangings was frequently followed by a bout of whoring. Death and sex coexisted in his mind in a mixture quite overt and unrepressed. There is poetic symmetry in the fact that his own death seems to have been caused by a 'postgonorrheal urethral stricture'.

As a lawyer and social thinker he was in principle hard-line, though generous and compassionate by impulse. He believed that the duty of the poor 'is to work and not aspire above their station', but defended men whose poverty drove them to crime. Like Fielding, he upheld an ideology and a legal system which seem harsh by modern standards, but often acted and felt with a humanity that went against his harsher principles. Boswell acted (without a fee) for a Negro slave from Jamaica who claimed freedom on the grounds that slavery was illegal in Scotland, but he himself supported slavery as a status sanctioned by God and regarded abolitionists as subversive (Johnson, by contrast, drank 'to the next insurrection of the Negroes'). Late in life, he wrote a bizarre poem called *No Abolition of Slavery; or the Universal Empire of*

Love, in which he compared Negro slaves to lovers who are happy to be the slaves of their 'beauteous tyrant'. In such states of exaltation, Boswell's ideological, religious, and erotic sentiments readily converge in extravagant and guileless fatuity: his addiction to public hangings, spiced by his solemn broodings and consolatory copulations, enact a similar mixture on another plane.

The idea of a 'happiness in slavery', which slaves and lovers cherish, partly derives from the traditional metaphors of love-poetry, and is sometimes adopted more or less literally by bookish erotomanes. Jean Paulhan's preface to *Histoire d'O*, the novel of chains and torture by 'Pauline Réage', is entitled 'Le Bonheur dans l'esclavage', and opens with an account of some freed Barbadian slaves in 1838 asking to be taken back by their master. The pseudonymous author herself does not deal in such Boswellian silliness, but in *O m'a dit*, a remarkable series of conversations with Régine Deforges, she points out that she is herself terrified of torture, and that her torture scenes have the unreality of detective story fights. She insists throughout on bookish origins (lives of saints, Gothick dungeons): *je suis bourrée de littérature comme d'autres de religion.* Her story, like Boswell's poem, literalises the *façons de parler* of amatory verse, enslavement, chains and the rest, but with a witty distance and a clarity of self-awareness which distinguish her treatment from the outlandish reductiveness of Boswell or of her own patron Paulhan. Even within the novel it is clear that what is being presented are not the Boswellian analogies in a raw state, but the mind of a heroine who herself cherishes second-remove experiences: the 'idea' of torture, the subsequent happiness of having undergone it, the abnegation and self-surrender, the devotional and martyrological fantasies.

Perhaps all erotomania is bookish, bordering on pedantry, aspiring to the condition of a Barthesian *jouissance* and other forms of textual intercourse, perhaps even harassment. This may be a secularised variant of being *bourré de religion*, as Rochester came to be at the end. But somehow one does not quite see Boswell in that light. Intensities of spiritual or learned excitation do not seem to have provided intellectual structuring, or even functioned as displacements or substitutes, for his sexual doings. He was, in his way, *bourré* with religion as well as with literature, but both were bread and butter adjuncts to, rather than transcendences of, quotidian activity. He seems to have done most of the things others wrote about. He wrote about them too, but only in the way he wrote about everything else. There is no fascinated dwelling on detail: indeed, shorthand of the barest kind would usually do. Perhaps 'exaltation' is the wrong word, even in the lowered sense of the French *exalté*, though a genial febrility is everywhere evident.

He was what might be called a complaisant neurasthenic. He enjoyed his febrile states and liked to record them. His compulsion to record was itself febrile. He lived for it, sometimes thinking, as Frank Brady says, 'that a man should not live more than he can record' and regretting 'that there is no invention for getting an immediate and exact transcript of the mind'. This makes clear that writing was not a substitute for experience, but an unceasing lust to do it justice. No mere magical psycho-copier would in fact have suited him. He liked to arrange and to stage-manage not only the events he wrote about, but his writing of them. He readily saw himself as 'the hero of a romance or novel', and sometimes even as a 'heroine'. This, in the private papers, is not an example of 'literary art', but the compulsive showmanship of a self-regardingly bookish temperament. In the *Life of Johnson*, 'art' does come into play, with publication in view. Selection and crafting here take on a new dimension, and Brady offers a few glimpses into this, but what comes through most in his account of the *Life of Johnson* are the forms of Boswellian self-expression which make the *Life* an extension, rather than an artistic transformation, of the journals. Those combinations of vanity and abasement, for example, which in the journals make him note that he 'was brilliant' on a particular occasion and elsewhere show him as the victim of a Johnsonian snub, appear in more muted form throughout the *Life*, along with the stage-managed meetings, the prepared conversations, the posturing indiscretions. In some ways the *Life*, as a published work, permitted forms of self-expression denied to the private diary. For example, although Boswell shrank puppyishly from angry or aggressive behaviour, he discovered in himself an oblique talent for 'nettling people' by reporting hurtful things said by one friend about another: Johnson about Mrs Thrale or about Burke, for example. Boswell could, and did, put these things down in his diaries, but they could only realise themselves as aggressions by emerging from privacy. The *Life* drew blood, and it was said more generally that Boswell's company was shunned by many who feared that their private conversations would be recorded.

The authoritative biography of Boswell was begun by Frederick Pottle in *James Boswell: The Earlier Years (1740–1769)*, which appeared in 1966. Frank Brady's *The Later Years (1769–1795)* completes the undertaking with a fine thoroughness, and the two volumes are now published together in a handsome format. Both authors do their best to be wholly truthful without becoming swamped by the mass of petty detail which that silly little genius left behind. It is a double achievement of high authority and notable grace, which enables us to understand Boswell more clearly and more fully than his own raw data by themselves ever could.

BOSWELL AND HIS JOURNALS

Boswell struts on. *Boswell: The English Experiment, 1785–1789* is the twelfth volume of his private papers to appear in the Yale Edition in the 37 years since the *London Journal 1762–1763* created its little sensation. (A final volume, *The Great Biographer, 1789–1795*, completes the series and takes us to his death in 1795, aged 54.) Perhaps the strut is becoming a waddle. He is showing signs of age. The self-absorption and mediocrity of mind remain unabated, but he says that he is 'not so greedy of great people as I used to be'. This did not mean passing up the particular social opportunity then on offer. Later, when Mr Ramus the king's page invited him to St James', he noted: 'Formerly I should have jumped at such an opening. I am now too far advanced. Yet I may go.' It is like Crusoe feeling he can't use the ship-wrecked money, but then deciding to keep it, accelerated to the tempo of farce. One is not sure whether the social climbing has abated or whether a need to say so has developed: the distinction may be a fine one. Sometimes flagging energies merely take the form of talking about flagging energies.

Another change which has been coming over him in these later years is that his acts of 'conjugal intercourse' are now usually signalled by a dash, which began to replace the Greek letter π after May 1780. In this volume he also obtains solace of a less π-ious kind with 'M. C.', an adventuress called Margaret Caroline Rudd, whom he had sought out nine years earlier when 'she had been acquitted of a charge of forgery when she turned King's evidence', while her accomplices were sent to the gallows. Boswell's sexuality was frequently roused by the scabrous situations to which his legal interests, as well as his insatiable quasi-voyeuristic curiosity, drew him. Hangings, as I noted, created a need for sexual outlets, but an acquitted accomplice was perhaps special.

Boswell's habit of frequenting the gallows seems to have declined in this late volume, perhaps another index of flagging powers, and the febrile priapism that used to accompany the deaths of others seems also to have receded. But the affair with M. C., which had been triggered by the forensic frisson of a criminal trial, ended in a deliciously morbid amalgam of guilty nightmare (for him) and imprisonment (for her). On 29 May 1787 Boswell reports having 'dreamt of M. M. [Mrs Boswell] and M. C. contending for me'. 'This heated my fancy, and the flame being increased by wine', he guiltily went to M. C.'s residence, where he 'fortunately' did not find her, for she was 'now in the Fleet Prison'. He left word '(absurdly enough) . . . that Mr. *Parr* had called', an odd subconscious aggression, perhaps, against Samuel Parr, 'the Whig Dr. Johnson', with whom as it happens he dined later in the volume, and who spoke of writing a life of Johnson himself. Boswell apparently never saw M. C. again and the callous frivolity both of his behaviour and of his report is capped with brutal economy in an editorial note: 'This is the last mention of Mrs. Rudd in the journal. She lived until 1797.' Another footnote intended for this passage is missing, signalling an unusual loss of editorial cool. But Boswell, reporting nightmare, guilt, arousal, inebriation, relief, and disappointment, loses no cool, his prose, at such times, readily freezing to a kind of morbid anaesthesia.

The self-absorption, the proneness to erotomanic bizarreries, the display of young doggishness demanding to be loved, the simultaneous apathy towards the feelings of others are reminiscent of Dylan Thomas, that other priapic show-off descending on London from an Anglo-Celtic metropolis, except that the earlier incarnation seems to have consummated his amours more often than the later, and did not to his credit go in very much for 'portraying' himself as an 'artist'. But his critics and editors do it for him, though the editors of *The English Experiment* seem prepared to confine the claim to his published writings (in particular the *Life of Johnson*, on which Boswell was working in these years), where it belongs if at all. The tendency to assimilate Boswell's personal writings to the art of the novelist or playwright or to the conventions of formally crafted rhetoric, is here subdued. But the volume shares with the rest of the series a straining to impose a quasi-novelistic 'artistry' on what Boswell mainly rendered as a daily flow of circumstance. The titles unwittingly enforce the impression: *Boswell in Search of a Wife*, *The Ominous Years*, *Boswell in Extremes*. *The English Experiment* gets its name from the fact that Boswell was in these years 'committing himself in mid-life to the most significant decision of his career: a permanent removal from the Scottish to the English bar'. But in fact the 'commitment' is throughout this period blurred by almost daily vacillations, and London was, in any case, 'where since early manhood he had wished to centre his existence, preferably as a Member of Parliament', so that he can be thought to have been engaged for most of his adult life on his 'English experiment'.

The title-page's terminal years 1785–9 are also not as tidy as they look. The volume actually runs from 12 November 1785 to 3 July 1789, a grouping which reflects, not any dispassionate chronological subdivision, but an editorial hankering for narrative climaxes and closures. The volume ends with an important death, that of Mrs Boswell, as the two preceding volumes reached their climaxes with the deaths of Boswell's father and of Johnson respectively. Lord Kames, another great man whose biography Boswell was planning to write, died near the beginning of the preceding volume (*The Applause of the Jury*), so that it has the additional imposed symmetry of beginning and ending with the death of a potential biographee.

Although the editors begin or end a volume in mid-year or even in mid-month, they operate differently *within the volume*, where each year is typographically displayed on a fresh page and as a fresh start, whatever the actual course of events seems to call for. Paradoxically this works towards the same effect of 'form' where none exists, with typography and layout suggesting the opening of a chapter or a story, whereas what is happening is merely Boswell's next day. Thus 1788 begins:

It was a very wet day. So we only went through the house. When he came into my room, which had once been his own, 'Here', said he ...

One can imagine a novel beginning like this, and this is precisely what is misleading about the presentation, in a critical climate in which claims of artistry are being made. For this is not a beginning at all. Neither Boswell nor anyone else would ever have begun a journal, or even a fresh section of one, in this way, without for example formally identifying the 'he', even though only writing to himself. 'He' is here the gracelessly bossy Earl of Lonsdale, with whom Boswell is staying at Whitehaven, and the entry, far from making any sort of start, merely picks up (on the same page of Boswell's manuscript at Yale) from the previous day's 'He dragged me on so slowly along the quays ... We dined tolerably and had tea and supper.'

If the story-like layout is editorial, however, the last phrase may remind us more substantially of *Pamela* or even of *Shamela*, and critics have sometimes gone in for comparing Boswell's style with that of epistolary heroines. Boswell's diet is frequently reported on with Shamelaic gusto mingled with Pamelian solemnity: 'went... and had tea and dry toast and butter'. Even Bruce Redford, who in his excellent book *The Converse of the Pen* disclaims any attempt 'to trace connections between letter-writing in "real life" and the development of epistolary fiction', likes to speak of Boswell the letter-writer as 'heir of Richardson and Sterne' in his 'writing to the moment'. Piquancies of self-consciousness, as when Boswell, like Pamela, broods fondly over his scribbling or worries about detection, or when he speaks of himself in ways that evoke a heroine in a flutter at the prospect of an exciting social encounter (his election to the Club, for example, or a meeting with the king), or describes the king approaching towards him as a sort of beaming incarnation of Squire Allworthy, are products of his novel-reading only in so far as novels provide a rhetoric or a situational model, only partly unconscious, for dramatising himself to himself: he more than once compared himself explicitly with novel-heroes, or with Aeneas or Macheath. It would perhaps be excessive to say that there is no more 'artistry' in such things than there is in the fact that the manuscript sometimes breaks off in mid-entry, in a superficial resemblance to the Shandean prototype. But not very excessive, and there probably was a self-conscious awareness of such resemblance anyway. Perhaps, on second thoughts, that should be thought of as artistry, in one of its trivial forms.

Boswell's ego easily matched Sterne's or Shandy's. The fact that they wrote for an audience and he only for himself is less of a difference than it might seem, for he was his own audience and liked to stage himself in framed postures. He was a widely read man and his self-dramatising was thus often literary, whether by instinct or design. But these were modes of self-projection, not means of organisation. The idea was not to exercise technical mastery, but to tickle up the display of self. Significantly his instinct in such cases is to liken himself, not to the writer, but to the hero or heroine. So little did he think of himself as an artist that even when he could legitimately present himself as one, as in reporting his work on the *Life of Johnson*, he tended to dwell on the factual or circumstantial aspects (soliciting information, collecting papers, sorting) rather than on processes of composition or considerations of technique. Once or twice writing the *Life* is seen, not as an activity of any sort, but as the happy cause of social invitations which would not otherwise have been forthcoming (for example 'The occasion of my being at length invited to his house was my being engaged in writing Dr. Johnson's *Life*').

If writing the *Life* had any interior dimension, it seems on the evidence of these diaries to have been confined to such satisfactions, or to statements of feeling about rival biographers: Hawkins, with whom he met 'in perfect good humour', or Mrs Thrale, whose correspondence with Johnson bruised his self-esteem. Wilkes took 'a mischievous pleasure' in pointing out the offending passages, and Malone 'thought better' of the Johnson–Thrale letters than Boswell hoped, with the result that eventually 'they improved upon me'. He was easily influenced, and his resentments did not run very deep (that is part of what is sometimes described as his charm).

But on the whole, reading his account of his Johnsonian labours, we learn more of the facts than of the feelings, and the facts often belong to the same order of banality as his shorthand reports of 'conjugal intercourse' or drinking bouts. He worked on the *Life* some days, and on others did not. If you are lucky, you might be given a reason: 'I grew so much hipped that I could not write any *Life*.' A lot of energy went into recording non-events: 'Did not get drunk' is a typical entry. One day at Lancaster Assizes some legal wags tricked Boswell by leaving a 'feigned brief' at his lodgings. Boswell records the humiliation, though briefly (perhaps, the editors surmise, from shame). A later account by a participant reports that the prank was executed after Boswell had been found lying drunk on the pavement. The editors doubt this partly because the journal had not specifically recorded drunkenness on the night in question. This might suggest a naive conception of the nature of evidence, except that in Boswell's case the inference seems right. And anyway he virtually *did* say he was sober: 'Dined at the mess moderately', an elegant variation on 'not drunk'. Even not making journal-entries called for journal-entries, as in the section headed 'View of My Life till 1 November 1786 When No Diary'.

In the journals, as in the published writings, including the *Life*, Boswell's gift was for the situational *mise-en-scène*: he created happenings, triggered confrontations, engineered conversations. It is the event and not primarily the writing up that brought 'artistry' into play. He could do it brilliantly, as in an earlier volume, where an opportunity is seized of eliciting an account of Johnson's sexuality from Mrs Desmoulins. If the account reads stylishly, this seems partly to be because the event was stylishly manufactured, a matter more fully discussed in the next chapter. A good deal of editing and even of crafting went into the transmission of an episode from private journal to published biography, so that it is possible to talk of the artistry of the *Life* without seeming to have abandoned one's sense of reality, though many of the episodes in the *Life* were themselves first created by Boswell as happenings.

There was a variant and seemingly opposite process in which Boswell might re-imagine an event so as to bring Johnson out in a more central or impressive role. In an interesting book, *Printing Technology, Letters & Samuel Johnson*, recently republished as *Samuel Johnson and the Impact of Print*, Alvin Kernan compares two treatments, familiar to specialists, of the scene in the King's Library, where, according to Boswell's *Life*, George III went up to Johnson and, after hearing his opinions on various matters, pressed him to write 'the literary biography of this country'. The other account, known as the Caldwell Minute, 'probably dictated by Johnson to a copyist shortly after the event', offers a less spectacular version. Instead of going straight to Johnson, the king first ' "talked for some time to other persons" ':

And instead of Boswell's magnificent conclusion in which the King withdraws leaving the great cham in serene possession of the library and of English letters, the Minute tells us that '. . . a visit from the Princess Dowager put an end to the Conversation'.

Boswell used this account, rewriting the record not with a view to making the narrative clearer, tidier or more vivid, but in order to convert the event itself into what he would have wished it to be, had he had the planning and management of the situation. It is, if you like, a 'true' report of *that*.

Kernan goes too far in insisting that Boswell 'created' Johnson out of his own 'needs and art', though he builds on a fine observation by Hugo Reichard in an article of 1980 about Johnson's need to be 'started': 'in conversation, on journeys, to dinners, and on writing'. Towering personality though Johnson was, there was in him a strain of indolence and passivity that made him strangely manipulable by his friends, and especially adaptable to the inspired productions of a gadfly social impresario like Boswell. The force and individuality of his character could be relied on to generate a good show, and

Boswellian 'veracity' was presumably assisted by the fact that Johnson's 'language was so accurate, and his sentences so neatly constructed, that his conversation might have been all printed without any correction'. This was not said by Boswell, as Kernan thought, but by one of his informants. But it was a widely held view, shared by Fanny Burney and others.

Boswell's belief in his own scrupulous and carefully researched truthfulness contained an element of wishful thinking, as well as obscuring the fact, which scholars have since uncovered, that the *Life* was as much a work of shaping and interpretation as of reportage. He took trouble to check out his facts, but he had a point of view and also a large capacity for self-deception. If an episode did not wholly conform to what he might more or less consciously have planned for it, his 'veracity' might take the form of a precise imagining of what was meant to have happened, and the temptation to operate in this way might proceed all the more freely in the case of episodes (like the one in the King's Library) at which he was not present. The Johnson of the *Life* is partly the product of situations Boswell had created and partly of other situations as he would have created them if he could.

Boswell planned his scenes, whether or not they might enter into his literary projects. His whole life, in its public, social or private dimensions, was a continuous stage-management. As in earlier diaries, for example, we see him here resolving 'to be seen well received at Court'. Like Johnson, he gets spoken to by the king, though this time Boswell does not say he is 'in a flutter'. Not all the stagings went according to plan or were fully worked out in advance. But there was a continuous feeling for situations likely to eventuate as set-pieces, and 'literary' stylisation in the writing up was a more or less instinctive formalisation of the arranged quality of the event or of an *ex post facto* view of it.

His amour with M. C. was as likely to have its stage-managed aspects as were his dealings with more noble persons. His social voyeurism was easily converted into self-voyeurism, and he took a prurient interest in submitting the underworld of his own love-life to the witting or unwitting gaze of others, turning it into a spectacle of which he formed part of the audience. He engineered an elaborate conversational manœuvre designed to trick Lord Rawdon, an aristocratic kinsman of the lady, into acknowledging a family connection with her. He was very pleased with his 'great address' and the fact that it 'had a fine effect' when he told her about it. A day or two later, however, he was less successful, 'raving' about M. C. to Mrs Stuart, whose husband 'said he would think of her only as a w—re. I was shocked by his hardness.'

Perhaps in this too he was losing his touch. Or perhaps being embarrassed was merely an inverse way of creating a 'fine effect', with the gusto rerouted rather than reduced. Entries like 'It was observed I was quite dull', or 'unable to make a good figure', or simply 'Was awkward', are not rare. Discomfitures may be just as much of a spectacle as social triumphs, and have the same power to make a person feel centre-stage. Exposure to embarrassment is a natural consequence of Boswell's search for *éclat*, and the frequency of the experience suggests that he may not have been above courting it. He would go to almost any lengths to be the centre of attention, even if this entailed the opposite of 'being seen': he once left a room in which he sensed that people were talking about him, merely in order that they might not stop.

His guileless effrontery and his vast capacity for *gaucherie* seem related to this. When all his other efforts to ingratiate himself with Lord Chancellor Thurlow were met with sardonic gruffness, Boswell resorted to retailing a Johnsonian compliment to the senior judge, in case 'I may die or your Lordship may die before my *Life of Dr Johnson* is published'. He seemed surprised that Lord Monboddo, the anthropological writer, did not return his greeting, although Boswell had recently described him in print as a 'grotesque philosopher, whom ludicrous *fable* represents as going about avowing his hunger, and wagging his tail, fain to become cannibal, and eat his deceased brethren'. Such obtuseness must have been sustained by a positive appetite for rebuff. Common self-esteem might blunt a normal awareness of the oddity of his own reactions, but there seems to have been a connoisseurship in the courting of ridicule which reflects a quite schizoid detachment from himself as an object of self-observation.

An anaesthetised penchant for self-scrutiny extends to his most intimate and tenderest feelings. Twice in less than a week he reports: 'found a ... letter from my dear wife. I adored her'; 'I came home and found two ... letters from her. I worshipped her.' The past tense of 'adored' and 'worshipped' is striking, as if he had momentarily activated a continuous state which at other times maintained its existence in some kind of suspension from himself. He cannot mean that he no longer 'adores' her, or did not previously, or that these feelings are discrete events of the same order as finding the letters. But he writes as though he can call them up whenever appropriate, framed in a *tableau* which abstracts them from their own hidden continuity, rather like scenes described in some modern photograph poems. Genuine and durable and loving though these feelings are, they come up on almost equal terms with any other state that happened to be in play, and are instantly relinquishable. Thus the second passage goes on: '. . . I worshipped her. The General being to dine abroad, I was unsettled and uneasy where to dine.'

To move around one's own emotional life with such unselective freedom presupposes, as I have suggested, a certain cool detachment from one's strongest and one's most trivial sentiments alike. Many of Boswell's 'novelistic' self-portrayals are extensions on another plane of the same predisposition to observe himself from the outside. It seemed necessary in various ways for him to think of himself as an outsider, even where (in some cases especially where) this entailed a sense of rejection or incomplete acceptance. His social climbing appears to be aimed at being treated less as an equal than as a sort of accredited upstart, so that he might retain an outsider's role even when received as an insider. When Burke was 'quite easy and polite' to him, Boswell '*felt* that I was now wonderfully up in the scale of literary and intellectual society': a remark which shows the extent to which, as late as 1788, after years of association with the entire Johnson circle, Boswell clearly still thought of himself not as belonging, but as having arrived. One gets the same impression when he records his social, rather than his literary, progress: though 'fluttered somewhat', he proudly announces to his wife that his guests include 'an earl and a bishop' as well as literary and artistic luminaries, but he reflects that he '*must* have an English [servant]'.

Being a Scotsman in England provided the most effective and continuous framework for feeling simultaneously outside and in. 'My English connection must be *jealously* cultivated.' He meant this at every level, professional, social, and personal, and was prepared to sacrifice his private affections in the cause. He never got over the wonder of being accepted. 'I . . . could not but think within myself how wonderful it was that I was now so easy and even confidential in an English town', he says in *The English Experiment*, just as several years earlier he had reported feeling 'quite as I could wish: an agreeable Scotch gentleman creditably received by an English judge'.

English accents were an obsession with him. From friendly voices, they usually made him feel that he was accepted, but also that he could never *pass*, and he sometimes even 'felt as if I could not contend [professionally] with those whom I heard speaking with a perfect English accent'. He resented it when the Recorder of Durham, 'by way of being on Johnsonian familiarity ... called me (in northern broad dialect) *Bozzy*', but when talking with a pretty girl in White-haven he 'took a fancy to the *Coomberland* pronunciation'. In Kent, 'I liked to catch the smart pronunciation *Medstone*, and was in good spirits'. There were particular factors in each episode, but each shows him mesmerised by English speech of one or other region, whose charm included a persistently delicious reminder of his own otherness.

9

Boswell's 'Life of Johnson'

SHINING

One of the preoccupations of the *Life of Johnson*, as of all Boswell's writings, is with *shining* in company, cutting a figure (or, as Chesterfield would say, making a figure, since *cutting* a figure is 'the very lowest vulgarism in the English language', perhaps because cutting is what tailors do), impressing not only by acts and words, but through social rank and status.

This is apparent in the presentation not only of Boswell himself and of Johnson, but also in accounts of third parties. It included Johnson's 'talking for victory', as well as other people's failures to win such victories, and the snubs and discomfitures which follow, of which Boswell is a reporter and connoisseur.

On 7 May 1773 at dinner at the house of the booksellers Edward and Charles Dilly, Boswell 'introduced the subject of [religious] toleration' and a long and animated conversation got under way. Several people were present including Goldsmith, Langton, Boswell's friend William Temple, Dr Henry Mayo ('a dissenting minister'), and The Revd Augustus Toplady, the hymn writer. Goldsmith was on the fringes of the conversation and, as usual, was trying to get noticed:

During this argument, Goldsmith sat in restless agitation, from a wish to get in and *shine*. Finding himself excluded, he had taken his hat to go away, but remained for some time with it in his hand, like a gamester, who at the close of a long night, lingers for a little while, to see if he can have a favourable opening to finish with success. Once when he was beginning to speak, he found himself overpowered by the loud voice of Johnson, who was at the opposite end of the table, and did not perceive Goldsmith's attempt. Thus disappointed of his wish to obtain the attention of the company, Goldsmith in a passion threw down his hat, looking angrily at Johnson, and exclaiming in a bitter tone, '*Take it*'.

Evidently, even this dramatic behaviour failed to attract notice, and Boswell's account continues:

When Toplady was going to speak, Johnson uttered some sound, which led Goldsmith to think that he was beginning again, and taking the words from Toplady. Upon which, he seized this opportunity of venting his own envy and spleen, under the pretext of supporting another person: 'Sir, (said he to Johnson,) the gentleman has heard you patiently for an hour; pray allow us now to hear him.' JOHNSON (sternly,) 'Sir, I was not interrupting the gentleman. I was only giving him a signal of my attention. Sir, you are impertinent.' Goldsmith made no reply, but continued in the company for some time.

Goldsmith's biographer Forster suggests that there may have been a specific reason for Goldsmith to leave early that particular day, so that he originally picked up his hat not, as Boswell thought, out of pique, but because he needed to be at Covent-Garden. If that is so, it makes Boswell's account sound even more accurate in spirit, and Goldsmith's eventual decision to remain in the company 'for some time' is even more pregnant with masochistic stubbornness than Boswell guessed.

It is a shrewd portrayal which sharply brings out Goldsmith's social gaucherie and that masochistic stubbornness. His huffy and dramatic gestures are portrayed with an economy and vividness that are almost cinematic. A little later, the scene shifts to the Club. After dinner,

[Johnson] and Mr. Langton and I went together to THE CLUB, where we found Mr. Burke, Mr. Garrick, and some other members, and amongst them our friend Goldsmith, who sat silently brooding over Johnson's reprimand to him after dinner. Johnson perceived this, and said aside to some of us, 'I'll make Goldsmith forgive me;' and then called to him in a loud voice, 'Dr. Goldsmith, – something passed to-day where you and I dined; I ask your pardon.' Goldsmith answered placidly, 'It must be much from you, Sir, that I take ill.' And so at once the difference was over, and they were on as easy terms as ever, and Goldsmith rattled away as usual.

These two complementary scenes seem to me to hold in almost perfect balance the blend of affection, malice, and insight which is a characteristic but intermittent attraction of the *Life of Johnson*. They are also impressively crafted in a way that is distinct from (but sometimes confused with) *another* kind of Boswellian crafting, which derives less from what might be thought of as writerly accomplishment than from a successful staging of the situation itself: his well-known contriving of meetings, his planting of a deliberate conversational cue, his cunning or mischievous flair for the fraught topic that will trigger an argument or display of wit, an embarrassment or a disclosure.

An example is the episode marked *Tacenda* (to be kept silent), which was almost wholly edited out of the *Life*, but appeared for the first time in full in the volume of the journals called *The Applause of the Jury*, in which, when Johnson had retired after dinner, on 20 April 1783, Boswell and the painter Mauritius Lowe prise out of Mrs Desmoulins some scraps of sexual information about Johnson. The account, it has been suggested 'could be a scene from Restoration comedy', but, as I argued in another place, 'in so far as the passage suggests careful plotting', this plotting is not mainly 'in the setting down of the episode, but in the instinctive management' of the real-life conversation. Once 'Lowe and Boswell ... perceived that there was lively information to be extracted from the lady', the scene developed its own situational momentum. There was something about Boswell both of the stage-manager and the voyeur, as everyone knows. By *voyeur* I do not merely mean the prurience of this particular episode, or Boswell's bizarre predilection elsewhere, for example, for witnessing public hangings. I mean a capacity or predilection for entranced eyewitnessing, quite apart from any sexual or necrological interests, which has both social and introspective manifestations: introspective, in those many passages in the journals in which Boswell sets himself up almost as a separate creature for himself to contemplate, sometimes in assumed roles of a literary kind, as the hero of a novel or play; and social, in the many scenes, in both the journals and the *Life of Johnson*, which he engineered, stimulated or viewed with a quite peculiar combination of witness and participant.

Consider an example from the *Life*, a conversation about *catharsis* in tragedy, recorded in the entry for 12 (actually 13) April 1776. Here the product is not the unfolding of a satisfactorily plotted social drama, but an eloquent disquisition by Johnson. It happens that Boswell was dissatisfied on this occasion with his own writing-up: 'My record upon this occasion does great injustice to Johnson's expression, which was so forcible and brilliant, that Mr. Cradock whispered me, "O that his words were written in a book!" '. I do not know whether Boswell knew that Cradock was quoting Job 19.23, 'Oh that my words were now written! oh that they were printed in a book!', which may give a quizzical turn to the comment. But the thing to notice in what Boswell says is that though he may be dissatisfied with his own verbal powers, with the writing-up of his scene, he clearly regards the scene itself, considered as an event, as a success. As so often, it was he who started the conversation, but not, apparently, in the fairly neutral or unstructured way in which he started the discussion of toleration in which poor Goldsmith came to grief. There the plotting is more precise, and involves a programmed manipulation of the chief personality. The beginnings are similar: 'I introduced the subject of toleration', 'I introduced Aristotle's doctrine' of *catharsis*. Now read on:

'But how are the passions to be purged by terrour and pity?' (said I, with an assumed air of ignorance, to incite him to talk, for which it was often necessary to employ some address).

In what sense Boswell's ignorance was feigned is not clear. But he was conscious of feigning something, and two things stand out. The engineering of the social happening; and, oddly related to this, Boswell's adoption of a coy girlish role, like a wheedling heroine in a novel, a variation on the heroine-in-a-flutter role I noted earlier. My object is not to suggest some sinister sexual paradox. I take Boswell's virility at face value, and we can probably all agree that it has a pretty broad face. The heroine-complex functions less as an expression of sexual pathology than as a self-stylisation that enables him to view himself in a partly prefabricated literary frame. He is as likely to turn himself into a novel-*hero* as into a heroine, and as likely to view another person in a novelistic frame as he is himself. Thus in another organisational coup, concerned with luring Johnson to the famous dinner-party at which he was going to meet Wilkes, Boswell compares himself to 'a fortune-hunter who has got an heiress into a post-chaise with him to set out for Gretna-Green'. In this case the eloping heroine in the post-chaise is Johnson, not Boswell. I assume that the erotic content of this passage is approximately zero, even in the most elastic subtextual sense, but the literary self-mythologising and self-contemplation are obvious. In the passage which produced Johnson's remarks on catharsis, Boswell has studiously designed a scene or planned a happening, and also, perhaps more instinctively than studiously, adopted a fictional stereotype as his role within it. As we read, he seems very much on the outside, looking at both.

The complementary scenes about Goldsmith differ from these episodes in that their peculiar excellence seems to reside more in the telling of the story than in the staging of the event. The two are never separable in Boswell, and even the Goldsmith scenes are the product of stage-management to the extent that it was Boswell who started the conversation about religious freedom of which they were an accidental consequence. As so often, things took care of themselves, providing quotable material for the journals and (eventually) the *Life*. But these consequences could not in themselves be predicted, and the power is here that of a consummate narration and not that of an arranged outcome in the events narrated. They have, as we saw, a vitality of social notation, a sharp penetration of character, a fine sense of climax and anticlimax, and a graphic economy of portraiture. What they reveal about Goldsmith, both damaging and endearing, comes over sufficient and complete. They are Boswell at his writerly best.

That is the good news. The bad news is, of course, that he won't leave it alone. For four ensuing paragraphs, he takes it up, turns it over, pushes it this way and that, like a hyperactive puppy on a benzedrine diet. The fuss, the condescension, the definitions and redefinitions, the rubbing in and in and in, the reports 'that Goldsmith would, upon every occasion, endeavour to shine, by which he often exposed himself', his 'incessant desire of being conspicuous in company, [which] was the occasion of his sometimes appearing to such disadvantage as one should hardly have supposed possible in a man of his genius', his jealousy 'of the extraordinary attention which was every where paid to Johnson', his intermittent good-humoured acceptance of 'easy familiarity' and his intermittent displeasure at the same, and, in case you hadn't got the point, some elaborations and reprises of these, with examples, themselves quite funny.

A similar example of going on and on, long after the point has been disposed of, and telling you he is doing or has done so, and in this way doing it over again, occurs in a long conversation about Garrick. Boswell 'presumed to animadvert on [Johnson's] eulogy on Garrick' in the *Life of Edmund Smith*, thinking it hyperbolic to say 'his death eclipsed the gaiety of nations'; Johnson said 'I could not have said more nor less', adding that he had after all said '*eclipsed*, not *extinguished*'. 'BOSWELL: "But why nations?" ... JOHNSON. "Why, Sir, some exaggeration must be allowed ..."' After more toing and froing and some attempt by Beauclerk to change the subject, or to redirect it to the evidently less contentious terrain of Scots-baiting, we learn from Boswell that 'I, however, continued to think the compliment to Garrick hyperbolically untrue', and moreover that the ensuing remark about Garrick's death having 'diminished the publick stock of *harmless pleasure'* was *tame.* 'JOHNSON. "Nay, Sir, harmless pleasure is the highest praise."' Reasons given. End of conversation. But end of paragraph? No. 'This was, perhaps, as ingenious a defence as could be made; still, however, [have you guessed, reader?] I was not satisfied.'

This type of curt conclusion (the only kind of curtness or conclusion you are likely to find) will usually occur only when the conversation has run out of words or Boswell has run out of afterthoughts. It may appear to resemble those bossy Swiftian speakers who, when they run out of steam, will say something like 'I will tell you the Reason some other time' or who, after noting a pretended gap in the manuscript, might add 'And this I take to be a clear Solution of the Matter.' I have already suggested that the genial torrents of egomania in Swift's speakers resemble such later writers as Boswell or Sterne even more than those, like Dryden, whom Swift was knowingly parodying, so that the *Tale of a Tub* stands as a proleptic anatomy of a modern self-consciousness which runs, in progressive escalation, from Swift's dunces through Sterne and Boswell and Lamb to Norman Mailer's *Advertisements for Myself*.

Boswell is Shandean not as the Sterne who invented Shandy and structured his doings was Shandean, but in the sense of being an expression of the modes of modern self-consciousness which Swift perceived and derided before Sterne was born, and which Sterne also derided, partly by Swiftian means. Sterne's derision was self-cherishing rather than, like Swift's, aggressive, and his appropriation of the style internalised the derision and made it part of an inclusive imaginative expression, a mythologising crystallisation that lent its name to the phenomenon through a classic fictional text. That the manner of Boswell's self-reporting may itself have been coloured by Sterne's novel, merely means that *Tristram Shandy* had popularised an idiom which answered to the culture, not that Boswell was engaged in the stylistic craftings which had given that idiom its peculiar representative status.

Sterne's patenting of the idiom had a powerful ironic charge, which self-consciously defied the proleptic derision of Swift's *Tale*, but this neither resembles Boswell nor implicates him significantly. Sterne turned Swift's derision inward and made it benign, but the derided self-consciousness existed even before Swift's *Tale* had detected the drive towards it. Boswell's version evokes Sterne merely because the full-scale model had become available. He has none of the manic energy of Shandean involution, just as he has none of Swift's implacable irony of rejection. He is neither arrogant nor overbearing in his advertisements for himself. If he does not agree with, or remains unconvinced by, Johnson, he tells you so as a fact of nature; and, if the fact continues after he has reported it, he repeats the report.

This is the atmosphere of the *explanatory* afterthoughts about Goldsmith, or, to take another of his past obsessions, of those recurrent waves of painstaking pointing-out that Mrs Thrale had a tendency to get her facts slightly wrong: he waits for her to get something wrong, corrects her ('Now, Madam, (said I,) give me leave to catch you in the fact: it was not an old *woman*, but an old *man*, whom I mentioned as having told me this'), then explains that he did all this and why: 'I presumed to take an opportunity, in presence of Johnson, of shewing this lively lady how ready she was, unintentionally, to deviate from exact authenticity of narration.' It seems likely that what goes on, in *both* the repetitions *and* the explanations, is really a guileless act of reporting, as innocent from conceit about himself as of any assumption that the reader must be a half-wit who cannot understand. I suspect that Boswell would not be capable of understanding anything that he thought a reader could not understand, but also that he is genuinely incapable of understanding that a reader's interest in anything he reported might be exhaustible. Both the repetitions, and the explanations, are, above all, accounts of his own flow of mind. There is an element of deadpan factuality about it.

This does not inhibit a ballooning absurdity from taking over from time to time. Connoisseurs of the more eccentric modes of dramatic irony should study the conversation with Johnson on 10 October 1779 about conjugal infidelity, and the relative culpability of adulterous wives and husbands, in which Boswell the daily adulterer blames the husbands, while the chaste Johnson says that 'between a man and his wife, a husband's infidelity is nothing' and that adulterous wives are more culpable. (I owe to Gordon Turnbull a suggestion that Johnson's attitude on this question may have been conditioned by Richard Savage's account of Lady Macclesfield's behaviour.) When the conversation pauses, the usual afterthoughts pour out. 'Here it may be questioned whether Johnson was entirely in the right. I suppose . . . but still . . . because . . . Johnson probably at another time would have admitted . . . And let it be kept in remembrance . . .' Let it also be kept in remembrance that Boswell, like Johnson, sometimes argued cases against his own beliefs, or practices, and even against himself. He got snubbed, and loved it. If Johnson, in such cases, always 'talked for victory', Boswell sometimes chose to 'talk for defeat'. But the after-thoughts kept coming up for air, like the clown who rises with a straight face every time he is knocked down, and, in Boswell's case, rising by force of habit even after his adversary has departed. On this occasion, however, Boswell was embarrassed about parts of the conversation getting into print, and got some of it (dealing with the wives of both men) cancelled as late as February 1791. He wrote to Malone: 'I wonder how you and I admitted this to the publick eye, for Windham etc. were struck with the *indelicacy*, and it might have hurt the book much. It is, however, mighty good stuff.'

LORDLY ACCENTS

In 1765 Johnson was introduced to the Thrale family. Boswell describes Mr Thrale as 'one of the most eminent brewers in England, and Member of Parliament for the borough of Southwark'. He adds:

Foreigners are not a little amazed, when they hear of brewers, distillers, and men in similar departments of trade, held forth as persons of considerable consequence. In this great commercial country it is natural that a situation which produces much wealth should be considered as very respectable; and, no doubt, honest industry is entitled to esteem.

As you might expect, there is a but: 'But, perhaps, the too rapid advance of men of low extraction tends to lessen the value of that distinction by birth and gentility, which has ever been found beneficial to the grand scheme of subordination.' This will sound unattractive to some present-day readers. To single out Boswell for the sentiment itself would be largely anachronistic. Anxieties about the loosening of hierarchic divisions, through rapid fortunes made in trade or gaming (a principal objection to gambling was that it threatened distinctions of rank), or through professional distinction in the army or navy, the law or the church, or through marriage, were frequently voiced in this time of social mobility. All times are times of social mobility, but the anxieties seem to have been especially frequently voiced in Boswell's lifetime. They survived as late as Jane Austen (partly, but only partly, to be satirised there). The 'grand scheme of subordination' is a throw-back to old ideas of order and degree, which have a more prestigious ancestry than anything Boswell could boast of in the domain of either talent or birth. Johnson believed in it, more in its social and political implications than in its cosmological resonances, but this social and political dimension is what (as a matter of live allegiance) the scheme had shrunk to by the eighteenth century – even, I believe, for Pope, notwithstanding the overt declarations to the contrary in the *Essay on Man*. Boswell meant no more by it. Any contempt felt for him on this score might just as properly be extended to others, for whom we do not normally feel it; unless the unpleasantness we may feel in Boswell is a matter of style rather than the thing said. There may also be a suggestion, quite often implicit in Boswell, that any contempt you cared to feel for him would be gratefully received. That, too, I suppose, is a matter of style, perhaps even of 'life-style'. I am not referring to his morals in the accepted sense, but to his persistent courting of snubs.

After introducing these reflections on trade and subordination, Boswell gives a graphic summary report of Johnson's account of the Thrale family history. Johnson is sympathetic to the Thrales, and is faithfully reported as such by Boswell, despite the strain in Boswell's feelings towards the Thrales and Mrs Thrale in particular. We read of Thrale's father working 'at six shillings a week in the great brewery', which he was helped to buy after the owner's death, the latter's daughter having married a nobleman and it being 'not fit that a peer should continue the business'. Within 11 years, old Mr Thrale paid off the loan, 'acquired a large fortune, and lived to be Member of Parliament for Southwark'. Johnson's account to Boswell continues:

But what was most remarkable was the liberality with which he used his riches. He gave his son and daughters the best education. The esteem which his good conduct procured him from the nobleman who had married his master's daughter, made him be treated with much attention; and his son, both at school and at the University of Oxford, associated with young men of the first rank.

If this were an interpolated narrative in a novel, one of those exemplary stories told by one of the characters to enforce some monitory or edifying point (and Boswell's narrative, as has often been remarked, often picks up the narrative routines and atmosphere of fiction-writers), or part of a *Rambler* essay, a genre whose moralised fictions were similar in structure and style to such interpolated narratives (the reciprocal traffic between fiction and periodical essays in this regard is also well recognised), you might well expect, after such a build-up, to hear of wealth squandered, of dissipation among the idle rich, and of the fruits of industry wasted by an improvident progeny. Boswell was reporting Johnson, but one presumes he was arranging his rhetoric, and the crafting of the account is manifestly literary, conscious of climaxes and of impressive points of rest.

After Boswell's preamble about the questionable desirability of trade as a subverter of 'distinction by birth and gentility', you might also expect him to deflate his build-up if it was not going to be deflated from within. As we shall see, it is ultimately in his mind to do some such thing. But it is a remarkable feature of his particular kind of honesty that he should not only render the spirit of Johnson's sympathetic account as fairly as possible, but also that *in the first instance* he should himself enter into the spirit of the thing in his own name. Here Boswell continues:

The son [Henry Thrale], though in affluent circumstances, had good sense enough to carry on his father's trade, which was of such extent, that I remember he once told me, he would not quit it for an annuity of ten thousand a year; 'Not (said he,) that I get ten thousand a year by it, but it is an estate to a family.' Having left daughters only, the property was sold for the immense sum of one hundred and thirty-five thousand pounds; a magnificent proof of what may be done by fair trade in no long period of time.

Two important Boswellian qualities are evident here. The ostentatious concern to report faithfully and sympathetically, and the ability to work himself up into an enthusiasm of his own about it, even when this enthusiasm was against his own announced feelings. In giving Johnson's perspective, and throwing in his own bit of extra commitment, he is in a peculiarly self-conscious and unsophisticated way enacting a style of sympathetic imagination which was to find an absolute and ostensibly *unselfconscious* form in the Keatsian idea of the 'chameleon poet', or the Flaubertian enterprise of entering so fully into his characters that he could say 'Madame Bovary, c'est moi'. The difference is in the self-consciousness. Flaubert said such things in conversation or in letters: you cannot, by Flaubert's rules, say 'Madame Bovary, c'est moi' inside the novel *Madame Bovary*, because once you do this you breach the illusion both for yourself and your reader, and establish precisely the distinction between author and character that the phrase ostensibly denies. Boswell is always saying 'c'est moi', but the unguarded candour with which he throws himself into the moods of those he reports is in its way all the more striking for that fact.

Equally striking is the thoroughness and abruptness with which the *moi* returns from this to its sole self. Having talked himself into an

entranced contemplation of the 'magnificent proof' of the achievements of 'fair trade', he characteristically stands back. The Boswell of
reportorial and more-than-reportorial empathy rapidly reverts to the
Boswell of irrepressible Boswellian afterthoughts, the endlessly
opinionated chatterbox we all know and some people love. Here is the
paragraph which follows the panegyric on trade:

There may be some who think that a new system of gentility might be
established, upon principles totally different from what have hitherto
prevailed. Our present heraldry, it may be said, is suited to the barbarous
times in which it had its origin. It is chiefly founded upon ferocious merit,
upon military excellence. Why, in civilised times, we may be asked, should
there not be rank and honours, upon principles, which, independent of long
custom, are certainly not less worthy, and which, when once allowed to be
connected with elevation and precedency, would obtain the same dignity in
our imagination? Why should not the knowledge, the skill, the expertness,
the assiduity, and the spirited hazards of trade and commerce, when
crowned with success, be entitled to give those flattering distinctions by
which mankind are so universally captivated?

I've called Boswell a chatterbox, but this does not do justice to the
extraordinary interest of this passage. It offers a compelling scenario
of the possible relations between distinction of rank and the heroic
ethos, and especially of that softening of manners from the roughness
of the old admired heroic codes, which forms a context for some of the
mutations of heroic and mock-heroic expression studied elsewhere in
this book. I would call this a bourgeois account, as distinct from a
patrician one, both in the part which praises trade and which Boswell
will distance himself from, and in any part of it he would endorse. This
is partly because trade is so overtly described as the softening or
civilising force in the transition from heroic ferocity to polite ways.
You would certainly not hear it put in this way by an older generation
of aristocratic Augustans, the mob of gentlemen who wrote with ease,
or their literary hangers-on, or for that matter by their non-patrician
Scriblerian successors. Burke, a direct descendant of these, and a
contemporary of Boswell whose relations with him were also somewhat prickly, would have offered an analysis which similarly did not
exclude trade, but which gave patrician susceptibilities something to
hold on to, by dwelling on chivalry and its codes of consideration and
courtesy as the agents of change, softening the old martial roughness
without loss of hierarchy. The issue was much pondered over, by
Robertson and Burke as by Boswell and Johnson himself.

There is nothing silly about Boswell's formulation, which he sets out with his characteristically scrupulous regard for a fair statement of the argument *except* that you know *he* is not taking it seriously – either as something to agree with or disagree with. The reflections, though interesting in themselves, seem top-heavy for the case in hand. There is a jumpy self-consciousness, perhaps deriving from the disproportion between the magnitude of the historical reflections and the particular personal case. We witness for a second time Boswell's readiness to give the full argument against himself, but this time he is really setting it up for deflation, as patently and inexorably as those mounting rhetorical routines in mock-heroic poems, which can only conclude in a total collapse. And, as in such places, the collapse, when it comes, is abrupt, calculated, and complete:

Such are the specious, but false, arguments for a proposition which will always find numerous advocates, in a nation where men are every day starting up from obscurity to wealth. To refute them is needless. The general sense of mankind cries out, with irresistible force, '*Un gentilhomme est toujours un gentilhomme*'.

I think that in this passage we are again witnessing a spectacle, not as rare as I used to think, of Boswell running out of steam. Having driven himself into a corner by his exercise of sympathetic imagining of the adversary's argument, he is suddenly without answers. Boswell with nothing to say. 'To refute them is needless': *that* has never been a reason for Boswell not to undertake the refutation. The more obvious the answers, the more likely he usually is to spell them all out, and it seems bizarre for him to peter out in this way.

It is tempting to set Boswell's bombinations against a simple forthright Johnsonian remark that 'There is, indeed, this in trade: – it gives men an opportunity of improving their situation. If there were no trade, many who are poor would always remain poor.' We should not overstate the difference. The conversation in which this occurred is one in which Johnson is 'talking for victory', knocking Boswell down with a series of paradoxes: trade does not bring money, 'commodities come from commodities; but trade produces no capital accession of wealth'; trade brings pleasure, because we enjoy foreign goods; and so on. When he gets to trade giving men 'an opportunity of improving their situation', it is in context a way of saying, perversely, that this is the only good thing that might really be said for it ('There is, indeed, this in trade'). Also he obviously knows that this is just what Boswell *does not* like, so he is talking for yet *another* victory, and the remark, glowing with all the force of wise and thoughtful aphorism, teaches us once again how dangerous it is to infer Johnson's opinions from things forcefully said in the momentum of particular conversations. Moreover, what Johnson actually said was 'if there were no trade, many who are poor would always remain poor'. He does *not* praise trade for removing distinctions of rank, only for reducing poverty and making some people rich.

Johnson should not be sentimentalised. He praised the Indian caste system precisely because it blocked mobility of social rank. 'As for an estate newly acquired by trade, you may give it, if you will, to the dog *Towser*, and let him keep his *own* name.' Notice the aggressive patrician uppishness, not a tone usually associated with Johnson. Another example, from the reminiscences Boswell cites from the Reverend Dr Maxwell: 'Being solicited to compose a funeral sermon for the daughter of a tradesman, he [Johnson] naturally inquired into the character of the deceased; and being told she was remarkable for her humility and condescension to her inferiours, he observed, that those were very laudable qualities, but it might not be easy to discover who the lady's inferiours were.' Again it is unwise to draw inferences without a knowledge of context, which in this case we do not possess: the specific flavour of such *bons mots* depends on the atmosphere of a conversation, and it is sometimes a mistake to infer some real conviction in what might only have been a display of conversational prowess.

The retort bears an interesting relation to another famous Johnsonian *hauteur*, on the subject of Lord Chesterfield's *Letters*, to the effect that they taught 'the morals of a whore, and the manners of a dancing master'. This is a jumbo version of an authentically Chesterfieldian idiom, turning the tables on his lordship with an odd burgherly thud. It belongs to a well-established line of Augustan put-downs of lords by commoners assuming lordly accents, like Pope's: 'And who unknown defame me, let them be/ Scriblers or Peers, alike are *Mob* to me.' In these cases, the principal concern is with moral turpitude. The transgressions of lords are characterised as being of low *rank*, as though the only insult which can be expected to penetrate such people is one which could be perceived as a social solecism. Lords, it is implied, do not mind being called debauchees or liars, but can't stand being thought of as resembling scribblers or dancing-masters. A particular sting about Johnson's dancing-masters, is that Chesterfield's letters

248

are specifically concerned with the inculcation of good manners, and with the fine distinction that a gentleman learns his graceful bearing from a dancing-master, but should never be mistaken for one. The wider point is that the nobleman's concern with caste and good manners is itself bad manners; and when Swift or Fielding suggest that the snobbery of courtiers is the behaviour of pedants, they are not only saying it is low as well as immoral, but also low *because* it is immoral. Behind this lies a myth, or assumption, or working fiction, of *ideal* congruence between virtue and rank. Swift, Pope, and Johnson were all conscious of their own lack of caste, and (in varying degrees, but Johnson most of all) proclaimed it openly. But in all three there is a surviving assumption that distinction of rank and an aristocratic culture are, in their animating ideal, embodiments of social order and moral rectitude, as well as cultural grace, and that the misconduct of real-life lords proves not the wrongness of the ideal, but a failure to live up to it. (Fielding differs from the other three in that *he* did have caste, but like them cared strongly for the ideal).

These lordly put-downs of lords thus differ from the way some lords liked to put down writers. Lord Hervey referred to the *Beggar's Opera* as by 'one Gay, a poet', and the many remarks by Chesterfield, Horace Walpole, Lady Mary Wortley Montagu, and others variously referring to Richardson's novels as a bookseller's view of high life are well known. Such gesturing was replicated on a lower social scale, and Grub Street hacks played this game with as much vigour in real life as Fielding's Slipslop and Mrs Grave-airs, or Mrs Honour and Mrs Western's maid, did in fiction. And there were odd unwitting reciprocities: Chesterfield patronisingly saying Richardson would have deserved 'a higher education than he has had', Richardson telling Fielding's sister that if Fielding had 'been born in a stable' one would have 'wished he had had the advantage of a liberal education, and of being admitted into better company'; Johnson repeating a version of this ('Richardson used to say, that had he not known who Fielding was, he should have believed he was an ostler'); the Earl of Eglintoune expressing regret, as reported by Boswell, 'that Johnson had not been educated with more refinement, and lived more in polished society'. Baretti answered on that occasion, ' "do with him what you would, [Johnson] would always have been a bear." "True, (answered the Earl, with a smile,) but he would have been a *dancing* bear." ' '

It is, incidentally, remarkable how frequently such *tu quoques* occur in the chain of gossip, the network of mythology and anecdote, about Augustan writers, usually without the knowledge of the other party, and how frequently Boswell's *Life of Johnson* acts as a point of intersection. Gray and Smart disliked each other as much as Fielding and Richardson. Gray's correspondence thrills with lofty disapproval of Smart's disreputable escapades; Smart reports that 'Gray *walks* as if he had fould his small-clothes, and *looks* as if he smelt it'; Johnson, presumably unaware of this, reported that Smart was often shunned for 'not lov[ing] clean linen', adding loyally that he had 'no passion for it' himself. Johnson was always (or almost always) loyal to Smart. Mrs Thrale, noting Smart's growing symptoms of derangement, said that he took '*au pied de la lettre* our Saviour's injunction *to pray without ceasing*' and would rouse his friends from dinner or sleep to join him. Smart's account in *Jubilate Agno*, '*For I blessed God in St. James's Park till I routed all the company*' makes it sound like drinking everyone under the table. People wanted Smart locked up, but, reporting that 'He insisted on people praying with him', Johnson said finely 'I'd as lief pray with Kit Smart as any one else.' This did not prevent him, on another occasion, when asked to say whether Smart or Samuel Derrick was a better poet, from answering that he did not bother to distinguish between 'a louse and a flea'.

These comments on Smart bring out a greatness in Johnson's personality. They display not just fair-mindedness or sympathy, but an actual gusto for sheer human worth, even when an element of real contempt can be assumed to be competing with it. In this context the important issue is not whether he should have liked Smart's poetry better than he did, but the fact that he did not, and was able to keep this separate from an affectionate and generous acceptance of the person, including the indignities about his linen and the eccentric devotional habits. Where others (Gray, Mrs Thrale, and so on) looked down on Smart, Johnson asserted not sympathy, but equality: having no passion for clean linen himself, being as willing to pray with Smart as with anyone else, as nobody else evidently was. Part of this comes from a literal-mindedness that won't mistake one fault for another or all others. This worked even when his dominant feeling was not of fondness (as for Smart), but of dislike (as for Sterne). Boswell reports Goldsmith toadying up to Johnson, in a conversation on Sterne, by saying 'And a very dull fellow': Johnson replied 'Why, no, sir.' Fact.

Johnson, as well as Swift and Pope, sometimes spoke of other writers in the accents of Lords Hervey or Chesterfield. But it is also the case that Johnson's view of worth, notably in other writers, was larger than Swift's or Pope's, though he shared their attachment to social rank, their loftiness about trade, their disposition to be uppish to and about others, especially authors, of lower caste or alternative cultural allegiance. Take his treatment of Defoe, a test case, for writers of genteel pretensions, of a successful author of low degree, and a classic target of the earlier Augustan masters. Johnson was able to enumerate most of Defoe's works, no mean feat in itself, and allowed 'a considerable share of merit to a man, who, bred a tradesman, had written so variously and so well. Indeed, his "Robinson Crusoe" is enough of itself to establish his reputation.' The reference to trade will seem patronising to modern readers, and my point is precisely that the 'prejudice' exists and is not allowed to block recognition of a great writer. The note is far removed from Swift's passing reference, in 1709, to 'the Fellow that was *pilloryed*, I have forgot his Name', which we know Swift did not forget, because in 1735, when reprinting his works, he added Defoe's name in a footnote without deleting the remark about having forgotten it. You might say that the reference was to Defoe the pamphleteer and author of the *Shortest-Way with the Dissenters*, not that of *Robinson Crusoe*, though this could no longer be so in 1735. As to *Robinson Crusoe*, Swift left no overt sign that he knew of its existence, except that it might be parodied tacitly, in part of *Gulliver's Travels*. Or might not. The uncertainty is itself significant, since it rests on the fact that any clear sign of acquaintance with, or interest in, the book itself is withheld.

A more impressive example in Johnson's conversation occurred on 20 March 1776, when Boswell patronisingly opined that someone should write a biography of the bookseller Robert Dodsley, who had begun as a footman:

I said, Mr. Robert Dodsley's life should be written, as he had been so much connected with the wits of his time, and by his literary merit had raised himself from the station of a footman. Mr. Warton said, he had published a little volume under the title of 'The Muse in Livery.' JOHNSON. 'I doubt whether Dodsley's brother would thank a man who should write his life: yet Dodsley himself was not unwilling that his original low condition should be recollected. When Lord Lyttelton's "Dialogues of the Dead" came out, one of which is between Apicius, an ancient epicure, and Dartineuf, a modern epicure, Dodsley said to me, "I knew Dartineuf well, for I was once his footman."'

For Boswell, Dodsley deserves to be remembered because he had risen from a footman. For Johnson he was splendid because he freely admitted having been one. This appears to reverse the positions of the two men, since we saw that Boswell did not like social mobility, while Johnson thought trade had the advantage of making poor men rich. This is deceptive. Dodsley 'raised himself' by 'literary merit', which is a special kind of case, and Boswell does not mention the part played by the trade of bookselling in Dodsley's rise. But, above all, he is concerned to praise the prowess, not to approve of the process. Johnson is not concerned with the prowess *or* the process, but the human decency of the product.

Like Boswell, he believed in distinctions of rank. But he made no pretensions to rank himself. Boswell 'heard him once say, "I have great merit in being zealous for subordination and the honours of birth; for I can hardly tell who was my grandfather." ' In this regard again he resembles earlier spokesmen of an Augustan ethos, including most of the great satirists of the preceding hundred years, whose lordly accents came without any necessary pretension to lordly rank. 'I can hardly tell who was my grandfather' is sturdier and blunter than any parallel statement by, for example, Pope, but it is evident that the open acknowledgement of his own low origins not only did not diminish his zeal 'for the honours of birth', but carried with it something very close to the mystique expressed in Boswell's *un gentilhomme est toujours un gentilhomme*. Among the collectanea of The Revd Dr Maxwell of Falkland in Ireland, Boswell cited: 'Though of no high extraction himself, he had much respect for birth and family, especially among ladies. He said "adventitious accomplishments may be possessed by all ranks; but one may easily distinguish the *born gentlewoman*".' In a conversation of 6 April 1772 he thought Lord Cardross 'did right to refuse to go Secretary of the Embassy to Spain, when Sir James Gray, a man of inferiour rank, went Ambassadour . . . perhaps in point of interest he did wrong; but in point of dignity he did well . . . Sir, had he gone Secretary . . . he would have been a traitor to his rank and family.'

On some of the badges of caste to which the patrician literary culture of the eighteenth century was especially attached, we find Johnson the curmudgeonly commoner more insistent than Boswell the gentleman born. They discussed the Horatian precept of *Nil admirari* (do not marvel or show unguarded enthusiasm), which Creech rendered in words that reverberate in many a lordly accent from Pope to Byron, and of which Pope's version is the best known: 'Not to Admire, is all the Art I know,/ To make men happy, and to keep them so.' Byron commented more ambivalently that 'rash Enthusiasm in good society/ Were nothing but a moral Inebriety', on the whole preferring those who release the solecism. His words might be applied to Boswell, who indeed enthuses about enthusing, 'one of the most agreeable of all our feelings', resembling love, which is 'like being enlivened with champagne', rather than friendship, which is merely like 'being comfortably filled with roast beef'. Despite the low-pitched fatuity with which he makes the point, he is here expressing a kind of Romantic openness to unguarded strong feelings, and the Hill–Powell edition is not wrong, if a bit heavy-handed, to cite Wordsworth's 'We live by Admiration, Hope, and Love.' Indeed, as Boswell notes that his capacity for 'admiration' has diminished with age, he is enacting a desublimated or parlour version of those crises of the life of feeling which were to become a major theme of Romantic and post-Romantic introspection, in the Dejection and Immortality Odes and their numerous progeny.

Although *Nil admirari* had become an Augustan slogan for the maintenance of a patrician cool or poise, it was capable of extension, like most aspects of the gentlemanly code, to more substantive matters of mind and morals. Pope's 'Fools *Admire*, but Men of Sense *Approve*' also derives ultimately from Horace, through specific English word-ings in Creech's translation, but a more immediate source is a passage from La Bruyère's 'Des ouvrages de l'esprit', where the phrase for 'Men of Sense' is *personnes d'esprit*: a concept quite closely related to the ideal of urbane civility and lightly borne wisdom usually implied by the phrase *honnêtes gens*. Pope's wording (also apparently anticipated by a line in an early unpublished satire by Thomas Parnell, 'A letter to a friend. On poets', which Pope may or may not have seen) projects an ideal of restrained thoughtfulness, though it also has a curtness and uppishness which enact the 'urbanity' it is simultaneously advocat-ing.

Johnson is more prosaic in such things, as might be expected, and his reply in the conversation had more to do with ideas of judicious steadiness than Pope's line did, with urbanity dropping lower on the scale: 'Sir, as a man advances in life, he gets what is better than admiration, – judgement, to estimate things at their true value.' Readers do not, you might say, spontaneously think of Johnson as an exponent of drawing-room urbanity, the Bear adopting the style of the dancing-master. But, for all the personal resentment Johnson felt for Chesterfield over the *Dictionary*, and his disapproval of the profligacy implied in his *Letters* to his son, he insisted that the book was an excellent guide to manners: 'Take out the immorality, and it should be put into the hands of every young gentleman.' Boswell adds that 'no man was a more attentive and nice observer of behaviour in those in whose company he happened to be, than Johnson.' He once 'surprized the company' by saying 'Every man of any education would rather be called a rascal, than accused of deficiency in *the graces*', that famous Chesterfieldian acquisition: 'Gibbon, who was present', asked, 'looking towards Johnson', whether there might not be *one* exception, but Johnson was not meant to notice and evidently did not. Criticising Soame Jenyns' *View of the Internal Evidence of the Christian Religion* (1776), Johnson said 'there seems to be an affectation of ease and carelessness, as if it were not suitable to his character to be very serious about the matter'.

Ease is one of the pivotal terms in the discourse of urbanity, and has the usual slipperiness of such terms. Johnson is using it more in the sense of Pope's rebuke to 'the Mob of Gentlemen who wrote with Ease', than as the more honorific concept which Pope celebrated in the couplet 'True Ease in Writing comes from Art, not Chance,/ As those move easiest who have learn'd to dance'. But there is something of the latter sense, as of an aspiration gone wrong: 'an affectation of ease and carelessness' suggests that Jenyns was trying too hard or being ostentatious. On an earlier occasion, Johnson focused on another and similarly coded term, 'wit', to define an unseriousness in Jenyns' book: what Jenyns said about the springs of benevolence 'is not to be minded; he is a wit'. The term expresses a similar mood to the one Pope expressed about the ease of the mob of gentlemen, pointing to wit in the lowest of its forms on the scale of Popeian usages (as in a parallel reference to Restoration frivolity, 'when . . . *Wits* had *Pensions*, and *young Lords* had *Wit*'). Johnson's censure sounds mainly like the contempt of a man of sense for a witling, but, as in the case of Jenyns' 'ease', he is also reminding us that an excess of 'urbanity' is also a failure of urbanity.

This has an interesting connection with Johnson's preference for being called Mister rather than Doctor (a preference he shares with the higher echelons of the medical profession in Britain, and with learned men in some distinguished universities on both sides of the Atlantic). Boswell insisted on calling him Doctor, as Donald Greene has frequently pointed out, though Boswell certainly was not the only one. Dr Greene seems to think this was because of the 'proliferation of doctorates' for political hangers-on, but Boswell tells a highly revealing story in a note appended to his account of Johnson's receipt of his honorary doctorate in 1775:

It is remarkable that he never, so far as I know, assumed his title of *Doctor*, but called himself *Mr.* Johnson, as appears from many of his cards or notes to myself, and I have seen many from him to other persons, in which he uniformly takes that designation. – I once observed on his table a letter directed to him with the addition of *Esquire*, and objected to it as being a designation inferiour to that of Doctor; but he checked me, and seemed pleased with it, because, as I conjectured, he liked to be sometimes taken out of the class of literary men, and to be merely *genteel, – un gentilhomme com[m]e un autre*.

I do not know what this tells us about English medical men or American professors, or even, having called the anecdote instructive, whether it tells us more about Boswell or about Johnson. But it bears a relation to the story Voltaire tells about visiting Congreve, who told him he wanted to be visited not as a playwright, but as a gentleman. Voltaire replied, in the very words Boswell came to use, that if Congreve had merely been *un gentilhomme comme un autre*, Voltaire would not have bothered to visit him at all. This is a story Ford Madox Ford was exercised by, as illustrating the fact that English writers preferred to be thought gentlemen rather than authors, while French writers had professional pride, so that the anecdote has picked up resonances which are not my concern here. Johnson, at all events, thought Congreve's attitude a 'despicable foppery'. But Boswell's story, which has the ring of truth, nevertheless glimpses at a strange unwitting convergence, a point of charged susceptibility, between two writers, Congreve and Johnson, whom we hardly think of as resembling each other in any strong way. And if after Johnson's death, Boswell, as Donald Greene writes, promoted 'all the "Misters" in the MS of his *Journal of a Tour to the Hebrides* ... to "Doctors" – from what motivation one can [Greene darkly hints] only speculate', might it just possibly be that the Laird of Auchinleck, in the remoter recesses of his lairdly soul, was scoring a posthumous point?

We shall never know, and *that* I assume, was not what Greene meant anyway. The story is less simple than he says, because in fact others than Boswell, including Fanny Burney and Mrs Thrale, freely called Johnson Doctor in his lifetime, and Johnson indeed did so himself, orally and in writing. Issues arise as to whether, before he got his Oxford doctorate and only had the one from Trinity College, Dublin, he might have preferred to acknowledge his honorary Oxford MA rather than the Dublin LL D, and the suggestions in Hawkins and others that he did not like to be called Doctor have been questioned. Johnson certainly felt that a medical doctor had no business to feel slighted if the title were used of him, as he opined in the context of a bizarre suit brought by an aggrieved Dr Memis, over which Boswell's father presided and which he dismissed. The plaintiff appealed to the Court of Session, which also turned it down. Boswell thought the court had judged wrong, and wrote to Johnson:

The defendants were *in malâ fide*, to persist in a way that he disliked. You remember poor Goldsmith, when he grew important, and wished to appear *Doctor Major*, could not bear your calling him *Goldy*. Would it not have been wrong to have named him so in your 'Preface to Shakespeare', or in any serious permanent writing of any sort?

In conversation, Johnson certainly sometimes called Goldsmith Dr Goldsmith, notably in the scene at the Club where he wished to make peace for having snubbed him, and is unlikely to have wanted this to sound offensive, especially as that was what Goldsmith preferred. That would not, I suppose, prove anything about Johnson's own position, since a preference on his part for appearing *un gentilhomme comme un autre* might perfectly well go with a sense that others did not. Such a gentleman might well feel that Doctor was a compliment to Goldy, but beneath himself. Goldsmith addressed Johnson as Doctor too, without any sign of this being proffered or received as offensive, though one can never wholly rule out the possibility that on given occasions a Dr from either source may have been partly put in to put down.

If anything, however, Goldsmith's real distress, as Boswell loved to emphasise, came from being cast as Dr Minor to Johnson's Dr Major, and Johnson was not free of a corresponding triumphalism on the same point. An anecdote reported in the *Tour to the Hebrides* on 24 August 1773 illustrates this with particular piquancy in the manuscript version, where Boswell follows Johnson's wish that Boswell should speak of him as Mr, while Johnson's own story presupposes that he enjoyed situations in which others did the opposite:

He told me a good story of Dr. Goldsmith. 'Telemachus' Graham was sitting one night with him and Mr. Johnson, and was half drunk. He rattled away, and told Mr. Johnson, 'You're a clever fellow, but you can't write an essay like Addison or verses like *The Rape of the Lock.*' At last he said, 'Doctor, I will be happy to see you at Eton.' 'I shall be glad to wait on you', answered Goldsmith. 'No', said Graham, ''tis not you I meant, Dr. Minor. 'Tis Dr. Major there.' Goldsmith was prodigiously hurt with this. He spoke of it himself. Said he: 'Graham is a fellow to make one commit suicide.'

Johnson's pleasure was here competitive, and perhaps for the occasion willing to disregard social nuances. Most revealing of all is perhaps the paragraph immediately preceding this, in the same entry:

Breakfasted at Ellon. The landlady said to me, 'Is not this the great Doctor that is going about through the country?' I said, 'Yes.' 'Ay', said she, 'we heard of him. I made an errand into the room on purpose to see him. There's something great in his appearance. It is a pleasure to have such a man in one's house; a man who does so much good. If I had thought, I would have shown him a child of mine who has had a lump on his throat for some time.' 'But', said I, 'he's not a Doctor of Physic'. 'Is he an oculist?' said the landlord. 'No', said I, 'he's just a very learned man'. Said the landlord: 'They say he's the greatest man in England except Lord Mansfield.' Mr. Johnson was highly entertained with this, and I do think he was pleased too. He said he liked the exception, for that in Scotland it must be Lord Mansfield or Sir John Pringle.

It shows 'Mr' Johnson was not, after all, above being delighted to be called Doctor, and precisely not in the sense of 'Doctor of Physic' which he thought physicians should not feel slighted by, but in the more gratuitous sense of 'a very learned man'.

10

Dining out in Paris and London: Thomas Moore's journal

Thomas Moore was born in 1779 in Dublin, and spent most of his life harping not through Tara's halls, but English noble houses. At twenty he was in London, ostensibly to read for the Bar, got a foothold in the musical and theatrical worlds, and published his *Odes of Anacreon* (1800), which he dedicated to the Prince of Wales. More especially he became what Wilfred S. Dowden, the editor of his *Journal*, uncharmingly but accurately calls a 'diner outer', and soon this Dublin grocer's son was a favourite guest of lords and ladies, delighting in his success with a kind of guileless gusto which recalls Boswell's, whom he resembled in other ways. He charmed his hosts with renderings of his own songs, but succeeded in coming over as something more than an entertainer or pet Irishman. He was absorbed into the intellectual circle of Whig grandees, frequenting Holland House, settling near Lord Lansdowne's home in Wiltshire in 1817, and forming a lifelong friendship with Lord John Russell, the future Prime Minister and first editor of his *Journal*. He was a friend of Byron, who entrusted him with his ill-fated *Memoirs*, and whose life he eventually wrote.

It has been said that today he would have been in television, and it is easy to imagine him running a chat show, a Terry Wogan of the book world. His geniality and friendly limpness of intellectual muscle were suited to this role, and he used his Hibernian charm with unerring professional instinct. It is here that the paradoxes start. For he was also an Irish patriot of serious standing, not a revolutionary, but firm in his own principled position, an active publicist in his writings, frequently standing up on Irish issues to his highly placed friends in the English political establishment.

He was also the feeblest poet ever to be taken seriously by serious men of letters and by a highly literate political élite. Poe called Moore 'the most skilful literary artist of his day' and thought *Lalla Rookh*

(1817) a work of surpassing brilliance. Poe was perhaps the only poet of any reputation who regularly wrote worse poems than Moore himself, but the fact is that this unreadable masterpiece *was* widely read. Jeffrey called it 'the finest Orientalism we have had yet'. Fanny Burney's son knew it by heart. Stendhal wrote to Moore announcing his *fifth* reading (but he wanted to palm off three copies of his own *Histoire de la peinture* on Moore and any likely friends). Longman's, who paid him £3,000, still thought of it twenty years later as the 'cream of the copyrights', though Moore thought the lush slurpings of *Irish Melodies* would do even better with posterity.

Or rather, as he put it, 'these little ponies, the "Melodies", will beat the mare, Lalla, hollow'. Not exactly hymning harmonious Houyhnhnm through the nose, you might think, but the Melodies were much sung. Moore frequently performed them himself, like a drawing-room Bob Dylan, blending lovelorn balladry with the melodious celebration of political good causes. The *Journal* offers many glimpses of him as a literary pop-hero, both through his connection with Byron (as when he received a request for a lock of the late lord's hair to save a Miss Sophie 'from the grave'), and in his own right. An unknown Mrs A. writes 'offering me her house as a place of concealment, if I found it necessary', but asking him to reply in such a way that her husband will not guess; an 'unknown Poetess' entreats him 'to call upon her any day between three & nine', warning him not to 'expect to find her a Blue-Stocking; for that she is "only a curly-headed little mortal &c. &c."'.

The *Journal* also records a lot of conversations, anecdotes and *bons mots*, about absent third parties like Wilberforce and Godwin and proverbial men who came to dinner. Moore's aristocratic friends were clearly undeterred by Chesterfieldian injunctions against retailing anecdotes in company, and a latter-day Bennett Cerf would find material for a small (or not so small) anthology from these volumes alone. There are many well-captured glimpses: of the 'curmudgeonly' Samuel Rogers, always 'ready to extinguish one's little agreeable vanities' (Moore took a Boswellian pleasure in recording his own humiliations); of Thomas Campbell 'in the bar of the White Hart, dictating to a waiter . . . his ideas of the true Sublime in Poetry – never was there such a Parson Adams, since the real one'. Wordsworth, in high oracular mood in Paris, delivers a string of sour *ex cathedra* judgments on other writers, and there are vivid extended reports of visits to Byron in Italy and to Scott at Abbotsford.

This *Journal*, which Moore kept from 1818 to 1847, was first published in bowdlerised form by Lord John Russell (8 volumes, 1852–56). Selections have appeared from time to time, including an attractive abridgement by Peter Quennell (1964). The original manuscript was discovered by W. S. Dowden in Longman's archives in 1967, and this new edition gives an uncensored text, with typographical indication of passages deleted by Russell. As with Boswell (whose greatest gift, like Moore's, was to make himself agreeable to his more talented friends and to record their lives and conversations), a posthumous hoard of private papers has been thudding its way into print volume by massive volume. The Boswellian archive does not usually rise to the level of the more finished publications of his lifetime, whereas Moore's *Journal* is an improvement on almost every poem he ever wrote.

Moore suddenly began his journal on 18 August 1818. If you first read it in Quennell's popular selection, you would be struck by the directness, vivacity and economy of portraiture of its opening entries:

August 18 – Went to Bath, on my way to Leamington Spa, for the purpose of consulting Mrs Lefanu, the only surviving sister of Sheridan, on the subject of her brother's life [which Moore was writing]: meant to call also upon Dr Parr, with whom I had had a correspondence on the same subject.

20th – Breakfast in the coffee-room. Found Mrs Lefanu – the very image of Sheridan, having his features without his carbuncles, and all the light of his eyes without the illumination of his nose. Her daughter, who has written novels, seems amiable, and looked up to by father and mother. While I was there, and talking of Sheridan, Dr Parr entered in full wig and apron (which he wears as prebendary of St. Paul's, and not unwilling, of course, to look like a bishop). I had written to him to say Mrs L. was in his neighbourhood, and he came thus promptly and kindly to visit the sister of his friend; a powerful old man both in body and mind. Though it was then morning, he drank two glasses and a half of wine; and over that, when he was going away, a tumbler of the spa.

A reader reeling from the latest flood of Boswellian confession might cheer this conciseness, the selection of detail, the plunging *in medias res*. There is nothing of the endless Boswellian rundown of dinner guests and drinking-companions, of their aunts and uncles, nieces and nephews, of liquor consumed and any headaches or coughs that happened to be going. The cheer might be tempered by the suspicion that our debt was really to Quennell's editing; an abridgement of what was already an abridgement. Now that we can get behind Russell's curtailments and streamlinings in the name of style and morality and concern for the sensibilities of survivors, how, we may suspiciously ask, does that first impression survive direct exposure to what Moore really wrote?

The answer is, rather well. The immediacy, the vivid sense of the detail worth reporting, are Moore's own: even that setting off to Leamington, without preamble and *in medias res*, is how the whole vast thirty-year diary freshly opens. Some students of Boswell have developed a habit of celebrating the 'art' of his private journals which is an object-lesson in how not to talk about diaries. But any compensating feeling that the artistry of Moore might be due to Quennell's gifted editing can be dismissed in this instance (which makes Quennell's editing appear even more gifted). Boswell's 'art', outside his published works, went into arranging situations, as we have seen; Moore really had a natural artistry in writing them up. What Quennell unknowingly left out because Russell did is mainly an entry for 19 August, with a highly comic account of the coach-ride from Bath in which a Tory gentleman attacked the politics of 'Anacreon Moore', not knowing he was actually speaking to him, followed by a girl who also spoke 'behind-my-back-before-my-face', and another amusing episode involving a deaf man. Russell also cut out some additional details about Miss Lefanu, 'a lively, mincing & precious little Blue Stocking'. What Quennell *knowingly* left out, in the paragraph as I quoted it, were a few tiny details, though he does go on to abridge a good deal, and Moore sometimes reads the better for it. But it seems clear that even without Quennell's help, Moore's diary-writing, as compared with Boswell's, is managed with an instinctive writerly discipline.

There is a real novelistic gift. The coach-ride back *from* Leamington is worthy of Fielding or Smollett. The gallery of eccentrics thrown together for the journey includes a 'quaker lady ... who had been poisoned by applying a nightshade to her arm for the tic douloureux', and a 'cloddish beau, who could not speak a word of decent English ... with a little footman in gaudy livery, of whom he seemed to be more careful than if it had been his wife'. This beau 'proved to be the son of ... the extraordinary man, alluded to by Southey ... who had a museum of the ropes in which various malefactors had been hanged, all ticketted & hung in order round his room ... Southey says *his own* ought to have completed the collection'. Boswell, with his addiction to public executions, would have understood the bizarre taste of this 'rope-virtuoso', whom Moore knew a little, saying he was, 'notwithstanding this ferocious taste, a poor weak, squeaking, unmanly-mannered old creature'. The situation is real-life, but the energetic feeling for human oddity is Smollettian.

This Boswell could not match, though critics like to find novelistic elements in the presentational strategies of his diary entries. These, I argued earlier, are half-inadvertent, more like nervous tics than a natural stylistic predisposition, as when he describes himself as 'in a flutter' before meeting the king, like a heroine in a delicious expectation of courtship, or when the king himself, in the same entry, comes over as a complacently beaming Squire Allworthy. When Moore has scenes of this sort (Lord Holland coming down to breakfast 'full of sunshine', for example), they tend to be redeemed by irony. And there are moments of a simperingly Shandean kind, but they are rare.

Moore seems to have been nervously conscious of Boswell. He enjoyed recapturing echoes of Johnson's world, taking the *Lives of the Poets* on a walk through the fields, visiting Mrs Piozzi at Bath. He even reports having once been taken to be writing a life of Johnson. Moore's real Johnson was of course Byron. He knew, in so many words, that Byron had more than one Boswell recording his talk and his doings, and he, like Boswell, had other biographees. But it was to Moore that Byron entrusted his *Memoirs*, and Moore who wrote his life. Byron sometimes Johnsonised Moore shamelessly ('What do you think of Shakespeare, Moore? I think him a damned humbug'). It is piquant to think that when Byron first met Moore, it was Moore who was the better-known writer, as Corsica Boswell was for a time more famous than Johnson.

Moore had Boswell's mixture of pushiness and geniality, his ever-renewed wonder at being *accepted* by the English or finding himself in the company of 'Sir Robert This & Sir John That'. On such matters he spontaneously said of himself in the diaries what others said in scorn behind his back. Byron was right that 'Tommy loves a lord', but as W. S. Dowden says the lords loved Tommy too.

By an odd coincidence of fate, Moore's journals, like Boswell's, suffered censorship at the hands of an officious posterity. Like Lord John Russell, Boswell's descendants blotted out passages which 'might shock Victorian tastes'. In both cases, scholarship has had to retrieve and reconstitute, though on the evidence of the first two volumes of Moore, no spectacular profligacies seem to have lurked beneath the printable residue. He seems to have had little of Boswell's erotomania, though he was sometimes thought of, and liked to be thought of, as a bit of a rake.

This seems to have been due more to his poems than to his real-life conduct. Two of his early collections, the coyly pseudonymous *Poetical Works* of 'Thomas Little' (1801, and much reprinted) and the *Epistles, Odes and other Poems* (1806), acquired deliciously libertine reputations. Coleridge was scandalised by the first (in 1802) and Byron attacked it in a bizarre and extended fit of Calvinistic censoriousness in *English Bards and Scotch Reviewers* (1809). The other volume was reviewed by Jeffrey in the *Edinburgh Review* and found to be more dangerous than Rochester and Dryden, because less openly diabolical in its profligacy. Specimens from this 'most licentious of modern versifiers' might include Little's 'Where I love, I must not marry;/ Where I marry, cannot love' and, from *Epistles, Odes*, in what a recent biographer describes as the pose of an 'emotionally exhausted rake', veteran of 'many a maid': 'With some I wanton'd wild and vain,/ While some I truly, dearly lov'd' (compare Rochester's 'Ive swived more whores more ways than Sodoms walls/ Ere knew' for some idea of the difference). Moore issued duelling challenges to both Jeffrey and Byron, but these both eventuated in nothing worse than a cementing of friendship between the parties. These outcomes are piquantly symbolic of the fact that Moore was not too radically displeased by the slur. As late as 1821 he was gleefully reporting as 'not amiss' a rhyme about *Lalla Rookh* being a book

> By Thomas Moore
> Who has written four,
> Each warmer
> Than the former,
> So that the most recent
> Is the least decent.

What bawdinesses were there for Russell to delete? Parr once mentioned 'the Siphylis [*sic?*] of Fracastorius', and Russell substituted 'poem'. Russell also deleted two interesting passages of 1818 reporting that Moore and his companions 'Talked of the infamous novel of Justine – written by the Marquis de Sade, who had acted himself with Servant-maids &c. all the cruelties he describes', and that one of Moore's cronies 'mentioned that there is at present a society of Debaucheries in Paris founded upon the principles contained in Justine, & so on, which they call Sadism – There is another book,

called Juliette, a sort of set-off to Justine of quite the opposite tack –
Les bonheurs du Vice instead of les malheurs de la vertue [*sic?*]'.

A fact not reported in this modern scholarly edition is that Moore's
use of the word 'Sadism' in 1818 antedates the *OED*'s first recording
(1888) by seventy years, and is also sixteen years earlier than the first
French usage (1834) recorded in any of the French dictionaries (at
least that I have been able to consult). Such are the unexpected effects
on scholarly knowledge (in this case of lexicography and perhaps also
of cultural history) of a casual moralistic deletion in the 1850s, and
such (one is sorry to add) is the scholarly shoddiness of the present
edition that no attempt was made to annotate either the word, or
(what I suppose might not have been too difficult either) the reference
to the Parisian society of debaucheries. If the incorrect 'vertue' is
Moore's, moreover, the error is repeated in the meagre note identifying Sade's books which Dowden does give.

It is amusing to see the erstwhile author of 'Thomas Little' and his
fellow *beaux-esprits* astir at Parisian carry-ons in the name of the divine
marquis. They were probably responding to the Sadean myth more
than to the books. If Moore did read *Justine* or *Juliette*, as Byron may
have done, it is as well that his comments have not survived, for he
found even *Joseph Andrews* a bit over the top: 'had forgot how
gratuitously gross many of the scenes are'. He went on reading it to his
wife, however, though he was relieved when they finished and could
move on to *The Vicar of Wakefield* ('we both enjoyed it so much more').
One of the attractive things in the journals are these conjugal reading
sessions. Moore's critical comments on the books are of great banality,
but the feeling for his dear Bessy, whether he is in her company or
thinking about her while dining out in Paris and London, makes the
pages come to life with sheer affection and warmth, wholly free of
Boswell's contrite brooding and maudlin protestation.

Moore's remarks about *Joseph Andrews*, his ambiguous pleasure in
Fielding, show a mixture not unlike Thackeray's, with the elements of
admiration and recoil blended in slightly different proportions. They
confirm the truism that Victorian respectability, both in its simple
and its self-questioning manifestations, precedes Victoria's reign by
two decades or more. Byron's strictures on 'Thomas Little' came to be
reciprocated (how consciously is not clear) by Moore's own titillated
censoriousness on the subject of *Don Juan*, as well as by the whole
collective panic that culminated in the burning of Byron's *Memoirs*

(which Moore tried to prevent, while admitting they had some 'very coarse things').

Moore's account of the latter episode was felt by Russell to be unfit even for abridgement, so he gave a brief summary of it in his own words. At least he did not destroy this document about the destruction of a document. But one of life's little ironies has seen to it that what Russell spared, nature has chosen to disfigure. The volume containing the account is tantalisingly there, but irrecoverably damaged by damp. It includes not only the day of the burning, 17 May 1824, but apparently the whole period from 1 September 1822 to 19 October 1825, or about half of volume II, which therefore comes to us in Russell's adulterated text.

Satire and sensibility

· 11 ·

Satire, sensibility and innovation in Jane Austen
Persuasion *and the minor works*

Persuasion is Jane Austen's last completed novel. It was written between 8 August 1815 and 6 August 1816. The last three weeks of this period were probably devoted to revising the ending. The two final chapters of the original ending are the only portion from any of her published novels to have survived in manuscript. Austen died on 18 July 1817, and *Persuasion* was published posthumously in December, together with *Northanger Abbey*, whose publication had been long delayed. Ironically, her last and mellowest novel, conspicuous for its tender and underisive treatment of its heroine's affections, appeared side by side with one of her earliest full-length satires of sentimental romances and their readers.

The contrast might be taken to highlight a reversal neatly and finally consummated after a graduated progress in her intervening works, but it would be more accurate to speak of an enlargement of sympathies rather than radical change. The accentuated 'romantic' sympathies of *Persuasion* do not signal any abandonment of satire, although fashionable persons of sentiment distrusted the satirical: a character in *Sense and Sensibility*, Austen's first published novel and one which derided the modish cult of fine feelings, objected to persons she

The following abbreviations for works by Jane Austen are used in this chapter. Page references, unless otherwise noted, are to the World's Classics editions of Jane Austen's novels (numerical page references without indication of title are to *Persuasion*):

E	*Emma*:
G	*Jane Austen's 'Sir Charles Grandison'*, ed. Brian Southam, Oxford, 1980;
L	*Jane Austen's Letters*, ed. R. W. Chapman, 2nd. edn., Oxford, 1952;
MP	*Mansfield Park*;
MW	*Minor Works*, ed. R. W. Chapman, Oxford, 1954;
NA	*Northanger Abbey*;
P and P	*Pride and Prejudice*;
S	*Sanditon* (as included in *NA* above);
S and S	*Sense and Sensibility*

I have retained the uncorrected title of *Love and Freindship*, despite recent practice.

thought satirical, 'without exactly knowing what it was to be satirical', but aware that 'it was censure in common use' (*S and S* 215). *Persuasion's* heroine Anne Elliot is valued for a warmth of feeling and an attitude to love on which Austen would have cast a colder eye in her earlier work. And the vindication of Anne's first love for Wentworth, against the prudential considerations which forced her to break off their engagement, represents a reversal, or at least a change of emphasis, from the treatment of Marianne in *Sense and Sensibility*. Nevertheless *Persuasion* is in places a sharply satirical book, and even its stylistic innovations may be seen as developments of some old-fashioned satirical ploys.

After finishing *Persuasion*, Austen began *Sanditon*, a work which contained some of her funniest satire of the cult of sensibility in its most extravagant high Romantic phase. The late novel whose heroine 'learned romance as she grew older', having been unhappily 'forced into prudence in her youth' (33), was followed by an unfinished tale in which a sober-minded heroine is portrayed as properly resistant to the influence of novels and 'any spirit of Romance' (*S* 346), while its absurd hero Sir Edward, 'very sentimental, very full of some Feelings or other', is satirised for his taste in fictions which 'exhibit the progress of strong Passion from the first Germ of incipient Susceptibility to the utmost Energies of Reason half-dethroned' (*S* 353, 357). Austen, then in her final illness, abandoned *Sanditon* on 18 March 1817, two months after she began it and four months before she died. It seems to announce some variations in her customary range, and might have developed in new directions, more 'experimental' and less concerned with realistic depiction, than either *Persuasion* or the early anti-'sentimental' novels, *Sense and Sensibility* and *Northanger Abbey*. But its satirical sequences show considerable continuity with these early works and even more perhaps with the youthful burlesques: the best-known of these, *Love and Freindship* (1790), even has a sentimental hero called Edward, 'son of an English Baronet', who sometimes speaks the same novelistic gibberish as his namesake in *Sanditon* (*MW* 8off.).

Persuasion also shows change, prefiguring *Sanditon* in some ways, but its innovations similarly look forward and backward. Its accentuated 'romantic' emphasis does not signal any abandonment of satire, and some traditional satiric routines are closely bound up with what is often regarded as one of the innovative features of Austen's style, her use of 'free indirect speech'. This narrative mode has been much studied since the early years of this century, when Charles Bally and then Proust described its versatile workings in Flaubert. It combines the ostensibly factual reporting of speech and thought with complex and shifting intimations of judgmental perspective: of the attitudes or point of view, for example, not only of a first- or second-hand reporter, or of a narrator (whether 'personalised' or 'authorial'), but also of participants in the reported conversation, and even those of the notional reader. Recent criticism has stressed Austen's role in the evolution (not, of course, the invention) of this technical resource, especially in her later novels: 'it is *Persuasion*', says Norman Page in his good book on Austen's language, 'that offers the fullest and most important use of free indirect speech in Jane Austen's work, and represents a remarkable and fascinating step towards technical experimentation at the end of the novelist's life'. An example, cited by Page as showing 'the power of free indirect speech to embody dramatic elements within the flow of the narrative', can also be seen as a reversion to a stylised Augustan satirical mode.[1] Sir Walter has to be persuaded to rent Kellynch-hall:

How Anne's more rigid requisitions might have been taken, is of little consequence. Lady Russell's had no success at all – could not be put up with – were not to be borne. 'What! Every comfort of life knocked off! Journeys, London, servants, horses, table, – contractions and restrictions every where. To live no longer with the decencies even of a private gentleman! No, he would sooner quit Kellynch-hall at once, than remain in it on such disgraceful terms.' (18)

The trick is to report actual phrases used, but 'indirectly', so that the narration combines the voice and moral perspective of the original speaker with those of one or more reporting or narrating agents. The words within quotation marks are broadly to be taken as Sir Walter's, though the syntax and grammar (verb tenses, the pronoun 'he', etc.) indicate that he is not being quoted directly, but through the reporting voice of Lady Russell (as we shall see, however, the matter is less simple than this suggests). The same might be said of the two immediately preceding phrases, 'could not be put up with – were not to be borne', which are not in quotation marks. They are not very different from what follows and suggest mimicry by a reporting voice: the quotation marks might well have begun earlier so as to include them. But it is not true of the words preceding *them*, 'Lady Russell's had no success at all', which do not mimic Sir Walter's exclamations,

[1] Norman Page, *The Language of Jane Austen*, Oxford, 1972, pp. 127, 135–36.

but sound like a report by the narrator of what Lady Russell said in her own name. Though the various statements have various sources, however, all report Lady Russell's difficulties with Sir Walter, and they are grouped in a formal set of three, comically highlighting the rush of activity and denial: 'had no success at all – could not be put up with – were not be be borne'.

Formal triadic arrangements were a feature of eighteenth-century prose, much practised by Johnson. His famous letter to Chesterfiled of 7 February 1754, quoted in Boswell's *Life*, is a classic example. His Lordship is accused of treating Johnson 'without one act of assistance, one word of encouragement, or one smile of favour', and of delaying his patronage 'till I am indifferent, and cannot enjoy it; till I am solitary, and cannot impart it; till I am known, and do not want it.' Johnson brought the manner to unusual heights of marmorial dignity, but playful or ironic applications were also possible. They are common in Austen's novels and a familiar feature of eighteenth-century satiric style.[2] They almost invariably signal a retreat from strictly 'realistic' representation. People do not usually talk in triads, and there is a suggestion that absurdities are being anthologised. In Fielding's satiric allegory *Jonathan Wild* (1743), a similar effect is created when the depraved Snap family discover that the young Theodosia is pregnant. Their hypocritical indignation takes the form of a catalogue of the cant of moral outrage: 'An Injury never to be repaired. A Blot never to be wiped out. A Sore never to be healed' (III.xiii).[3] In both Austen and Fielding the impression emerges not of an actual conversation faithfully recorded by a self-effacing narrator, but of a stylised anecdotal performance, bringing out the preposterous and the comically habitual, knowingly aware that the usual sentiments were uttered in the usual phrases.

A further complexity is involved. This does not usually cause difficulties for readers, but it is useful to understand its nature. As we have seen, 'Lady Russell's [requisitions] had no success at all' can naturally be read in the context of the triad as the narrator's report of Lady Russell's phrases, alongside Lady Russell's report of Sir Walter's. But it is equally possible to take the words as the narrator's

---

[2] On triadic groupings, see Page, *Language of Jane Austen*, pp. 109ff. (also 93, 99, 104). For Johnson's letter, see Boswell, *Life of Johnson*, ed. G. B. Hill and L. F. Powell, Oxford, 1934–64, I.261–2.

[3] Henry Fielding, *Jonathan Wild*, III.xiii. For a discussion of this passage and of satirical forms of free indirect speech in Fielding and others, see Rawson, *Order from Confusion Sprung*; pp. 288, 261–310.

factual account of Lady Russell's failure, without implication of reported speech. A slight indeterminacy exists as to who is saying what. In the phrases in quotation-marks we know the words to be Sir Walter's, as reported by Lady Russell, and the same is true of the last two phrases in the triad: 'could not be put up with – were not to be borne'. The report is a satirical one, but Lady Russell is not normally satirical in this manner in her own direct speech, and there is a sense that her report is itself reported by a subtly interfering authorial voice. The punctuation reinforces this indeterminacy. While those of Sir Walter's phrases which are outside quotation marks are effectively linked to Lady Russell's voice, the presence of the quotation marks around the phrases officially punctuated as his does not preclude Lady Russell's input from being felt. The movement between the three main voices, Sir Walter's, Lady Russell's, and the author-narrator's throughout the entire report is more fluid than the punctuation suggests. And if the punctuation fails to indicate a formal division of voices, it seems unlikely in this passage that any alternative punctuation would provide unambiguous clarification.[4]

These fluidities and indeterminacies are manifestly under control. The essential distinction, between Sir Walter's utterances and the judgmental ironies projected on to them by a reporting consciousness, is secure and sharply realised. What we are neither able, nor invited, to discriminate between at this particular point are the perspectives of Lady Russell and the narrating author. The effect of this, however, is to convey not confusion, but consensual interplay. In some later novelists, in James or Ford, and perhaps elsewhere in Austen, such discriminations are essential to an exact apprehension of important nuances in the text. Even here, the consensus is hardly habitual. *Persuasion* is full of instances in which authorial sympathies and values are at variance with Lady Russell's. The incentive to distinguish between them in this passage is withheld not from any sense that there are no differences, but because the satirical description of Sir Walter is most effectively projected through an assumption of shared judgment as to its absurdity. The passage is less concerned with capturing elusive perceptions or with the shifting interplay between perceiver and perceived than with a more traditional mode of satiric typifica-

---

[4] *Persuasion* appeared posthumously, and its punctuation was not verified by Jane Austen. (See Chapman's 'Introductory Note' to *Northanger Abbey and Persuasion*, in his edition of the Novels of Jane Austen, Oxford, 1923–54, v, p. xiii, which reports that nevertheless 'the text is good'). As the ensuing discussion suggests, a different punctuation would not have been likely to alter the main drift of the present argument.

tion. Satiric effects require, or at least flourish in, an atmosphere of fixed standards and normative certainties. They are also character-istically, in some classic eighteenth-century forms, concerned with follies or transgressions that are habitual to a type or a social group rather than to individuals. Just as Sir Walter's ritual exclamations enact a comic stereotype of imprisoning pretensions of rank, so the ironies of disapproval are of a kind, common in the rhetoric of Augustan satire, which assume broad agreement among all sensible parties, rather than emanating from the private perspective of an individual character. Although Lady Russell, as a character, is described only a page earlier as having herself 'a value for rank and consequence, which blinded her a little to the faults of those who possessed them' (17), she functions here, without any marked feeling of inconsistency, as part of the consensus.

Seemingly disjointed sequences like 'had no success at all – could not be put up with – were not to be borne' give an impression of abbreviated notation, as though salient phrases had been jotted down for later elaboration. Brian Southam has identified a similar feature in the manuscript of *Sanditon*, begun a few months after *Persuasion* was finished, and he argues that the disjointed note-like effect was a calculated one: where we 'expect much of [the] briskness and concentration to disappear in revision ... the effect of the alterations to the manuscript is in the opposite direction'.[5] He seems to regard this as part of a broader innovative quality in *Sanditon*, but the specific tendency is visible in the published novels at least as early as *Emma*: 'Was she a horse-woman? – Pleasant rides? – Pleasant walks? – Had they a large neighbourhood?' (*E* 171). Such fragmented impression-ism appears especially arresting in a style more often remembered for its 'Augustan' qualities of firmly orchestrated patterning and closure. Southam describes some interesting interactions between the two manners in the *Sanditon* manuscript, and other critics like to stress in *Persuasion* a less formal, 'more relaxed and conversational manner' as well as a more 'personal and dramatic form'.[6] In the instances I have cited, the 'disjointed' lists are traditional routines of satiric summar-ising, coexisting and collaborating with formal Augustan sentence-structures, not at all antithetical to that style. 'No success at all – could not be put up with – were not to be borne' has more in common with Fielding's itemising of the Snap family's moral indignations than with

---

[5] Brian Southam, *Jane Austen's Literary Manuscripts*, Oxford, 1964, p. 108.
[6] Southam, *ibid.*; Page, *Language of Jane Austen*, pp. 49, 52.

any later experiments in dislocated syntax. The buoyant enumerative disposition, the predilection for triadic groupings, the anthologising of stock phrases and attitudes in abstraction from syntax or meaning, as well as from their natural conversational context, project a definitional command, rather than tentative explorations of consciousness or any pressing sense of incomprehensible disconnection.

There are places, perhaps increasingly frequent in *Persuasion*, in which, as Page says, 'the abrupt phrases and the absence of coordination' are as far from 'the Johnsonian model' as they could be. An interesting example occurs in the important scene where Anne Elliot first sees Wentworth at Uppercross Cottage, almost 8 years after their engagement had been broken off because her father and Lady Russell thought the match unsuitable. Wentworth is now prosperous, and a successful naval officer, and, having returned to the neighbourhood, visits the cottage where Anne's married sister Mary Musgrove lives:

Mary, very much gratified by this attention, was delighted to receive him; while a thousand feelings rushed on Anne, of which this was the most consoling, that it would soon be over. And it was soon over. In two minutes after Charles's preparation, the others appeared; they were in the drawing-room. Her eye half met Captain Wentworth's; a bow, a curtsey passed; she heard his voice – he talked to Mary, said all that was right; said something to the Miss Musgroves, enough to mark an easy footing: the room seemed full – full of persons and voices – but a few minutes ended it. Charles shewed himself at the window, all was ready, their visitor had bowed and was gone; the Miss Musgroves were gone too, suddenly resolving to walk to the end of the village with the sportsmen: the room was cleared, and Anne might finish her breakfast as she could. (60)

This beautifully executed scene has elements of the manner which Southam noted in *Sanditon*, and one sees what Page means when he says that it seems 'much closer to *Mrs. Dalloway* than to *The Rambler*.'[7] This is sensitively observed. The passage has a delicate particularity, a vivid immediacy in its projection of Anne's observations and feelings, which are seldom found in the eighteenth-century novelists who were Austen's predecessors and models. Its prose-rhythms are not of the formal symmetrically structured kind which is characteristic of much of Austen's writing, and which derives variously from Augustan satire, from the satirical novels of Fielding, and from the moral discourses of Samuel Johnson, whom Austen deeply admired. It has a

[7] Page, in *The Jane Austen Companion*, ed. J. David Grey and others, New York and London, 1986, pp. 262–3 (hereafter referred to as *Companion*).

directness in both observation and style which looks forward to some later women novelists.

At the same time, however, the rush of perception, the kaleidoscopic impressionism of the scene, are conveyed in an idiom of quick summarising despatch which resembles the ironic knowingness of Austen's more traditional satirical manner, stripped only of part of its sting: 'he talked to Mary, said all that was right; said something to the Miss Musgroves, enough to mark an easy footing'. The vivid fluidities of perception which seem to anticipate the stream-of-consciousness writing of a hundred years later blend curiously with these sharply efficient summations. As we read them, we are not always able to determine how much they represent Anne's awareness, sensitised and accelerated by flustered embarrassment, and how much is to be attributed to the more comprehensive and summarising perspective of the author or narrator herself. An interplay between the two is sensed throughout the passage. Anne's feelings and perceptions are conveyed not directly in her own words or thoughts, but through an approximate report of these, selective and knowledgeable, from a remoter narrative voice disengaged from the action. If parts of the scene at Uppercross Cottage resemble Austen's more usual satirical idiom, stripped, as I suggest, of part of its sting, much of the writing of *Persuasion* preserves all the sting, and this is especially true of passages sometimes singled out for their innovative qualities, like the passage about Sir Walter's reluctance to move out of Kellynch-hall.

The earlier passage, with its summary anthologising and its notation of cant-phrases, also has more fully developed modern analogues not considered by Page. These are perhaps to be found, at an opposite extreme of extensive elaboration, in Flaubert's *Bouvard et Pécuchet* or, at an opposite extreme of staccato selectiveness, in Mr Deasy's letter to the paper, as glimpsed by Stephen Dedalus: 'May I trespass on your valuable space. That doctrine of *laisser faire* which so often in our history. Our cattle trade . . . Pardoned a classical allusion . . . By a woman who was no better than she should be. To come to the point at issue . . . Dictates of common sense. Allimportant question . . .'[8] The latter is in fact a satirical boiling-down of a pompous cliché-letter of the kind Mr Collins writes out in full in *Pride and Prejudice*, I.xiii (*P and P* 55–6). In this pair of examples the stylised satiric selectiveness occurs in the modern stream-of-consciousness writer rather than in the Augustan prototype, and Page's view that Austen's syncopated

[8] James Joyce, *Ulysses*, London, 1955, p. 30.

syntax 'sometimes anticipates the stream-of-consciousness fiction of a hundred years later' acquires an unexpected literalness.[9] It seems that in such places the 'moderns' whom Austen most resembles may be those who, like Flaubert and Joyce, were closest to the anthologising habits of the eighteenth-century satirical masters, principally Swift. Swift, as I suggested in chapter 6, looks forward to Flaubert in an enumerative exhaustiveness, an obsessive *jusqu'auboutisme*, which Austen cannot be said to have shared. Her manner derives from a variant style of selective knowingness, popularised in the early eighteenth century in the *Tatler* and *Spectator*, and sharpened by Fielding for novelistic use. In this matter she displays a greater affinity with Fielding than with either Richardson or Johnson, and greater than she might altogether have cared to admit. Perhaps Johnson offers no more reliable a norm for the traditional elements in Austen than Woolf does of her modernity.

Both Fielding and Austen were exuberant cataloguers of dialogue and 'received ideas'. Fielding tended to signpost them, with varying degrees of explicitness, as set-pieces, both within and outside the novels, as in the 'smart Dialogue between some People, and some Folks' and the 'Dissertation concerning high People and low People' in *Joseph Andrews* (ii.v, xiii), or the 'Scenes of Altercation, of no very uncommon Kind' between Mrs Honour and Mrs Western's maid in *Tom Jones* (vii.viii), or the 'modern Glossary' in his periodical the *Covent-Garden Journal* (No. 4, 14 January 1752): the latter in some ways a mini-prefiguration of Flaubert's uncompleted *Dictionnaire des idées reçues*, but characteristically compact and selective rather than exhaustive. Austen is less given to such bumptious procedures, at least in her novels, though her habit of assimilating dialogue to a satirical list belongs to the same narrative mode. Her unpublished burlesques, on the other hand, from the earliest juvenilia to her very last fiction, *Sanditon*, are remarkable for the tearaway buoyancy of their satire. They often tend, with or without labelling, towards the satirical catalogue, the *sottisier* of the cant of 'sensibility' and the fatuities of what she called 'novel slang' (*L* 404). The two are unusually congruent. There was in Austen's time, as not in Fielding's, a direct correspondence between the conversational clichés of novels and the real-life affectations of passionate feeling or refined sensibility by devotees of the cult of sentiment, because novels had become the prime literary expression and favourite reading-matter of that

[9] Page, in *Companion*, p. 267.

fashionable cult. In this Austen's burlesques differ from Fielding's *Shamela*, which they otherwise resemble in their quick-paced zaniness and their surreal stylishness of parodic reduction.

Austen had an exceptionally strong grasp of these verbal affectations, including the affectation by which proponents of fashionable cant professed themselves to be fashionably hostile to cant. This fastidiousness over 'jargon' and 'hackneyed metaphor' was derided in Marianne Dashwood (*S and S* 83, 285; also 38), presumably from social observation, but an underided self-consciousness on the matter is displayed as early as 1767 by the hero of Hugh Kelly's novel *Memoirs of a Magdalen*.[10] *Sanditon's* Sir Edward Denham, who was 'very sentimental ... and very much addicted to all the newest-fashioned hard words', and who 'had read more sentimental Novels than agreed with him', finds it necessary in turn to declare his contempt for 'the mere Trash of the common Circulating Library' (*S* 353, 357–8). Real-life analogues for *Sanditon's* 'wild and strange' characters, including Sir Edward, are a matter of record.[11] Austen's anthologising habit was not confined to conversations or to fashionable cant. It naturally extended to typical novelistic situations, and there are several summary-treatments, of which the late 'Plan of a Novel' (*MW* 428–30) is the best known. Among the juvenilia, 'The Beautiful Cassandra' is 'a novel in twelve chapters' which runs to three pages (*MW* 44–7) and 'Amelia Webster' an epistolary novel telescoped into two pages (*MW* 47–9).

But the main survival of the enumerative-summarising style in the mature novels is found, much subdued by comparison with these extravagant exercises, in dialogue, with its tendency to the free indirect form. Behind these enumerative dialogues lie traditions of fictional rhetoric which are still imperfectly understood. Two modes of enumeration are involved, one implying exhaustiveness, the other intimating satirical selection. In fact, both are satirical *and* selective. The first, which includes Rabelaisian as well as Swiftian lists, tends to hint at indefinite extension, but may in practice be as brief as the second, concluding in a Swiftian 'or the like',

a Lawyer, a Pick-pocket, a Colonel, a Fool, a Lord, a Gamester, a Politician, a Whoremunger, a Physician, an Evidence, a Suborner, an Attorney, a Traytor, or the like ... [*Gulliver's Travels*, IV.xii],

[10] Hugh Kelly, *Memoirs of a Magdalen, or the History of Louisa Mildmay* (1767), Cooke's Edition, n.d. 1. 20 (letter 3): 'I will not address you in the hacknied forms of commonplace courtship', he says, before going on to do just that.
[11] Southam, *Jane Austen's Literary Manuscripts*, p. 110.

or some other rhetorical *et cetera*. The underlying paradox is that, given unlimited time, a complete catalogue might be compiled, and Swift's *Complete Collection of Genteel and Ingenious Conversation* (1738) is a book-length enactment of this rhetorical tease. The *Collection* is presented as direct dialogue, in 'dramatic' form, and the 'exhaustive' mode seems to encourage unmediated reporting and a pretence of bare factuality, though the case of Flaubert, the other great master of the exhaustive mode, shows that these correlations are not simple. *Bouvard et Pécuchet*, perhaps the purest and most extensive *novelistic* (non-dramatic as well as non-discursive) catalogue of conversational inanity, frequently uses a deadpan mode of free indirect style. It gives off a paradoxical 'summary-effect',[12] based on suggestions of predictable automatism and of a running true to type, even as the sheer mass of the compilation, and the years of labour which he, like Swift, devoted to its assembly, register the ambition of exhaustiveness. In this sense, Flaubert may appear also as a master of the alternative rhetorical mode, that of Fielding and Austen, with its overt tendency to a summarising typicality and an interventionist narration hospitable to the satirical indirect style. Flaubert's doctrine of authorial non-intervention reveals a deep ambivalence on this matter. One might say, alternatively, that it reflects the inclusiveness of his absorption of the whole range of fictional traditions.

It suggests also that the two rhetorical modes are, like all such things, essentially 'untruthful'. They are indeed distinguishable from one another, but as expressions of deep differences of style and outlook which are outside the range of the actual rhetorical claims. If the summarising appearance of free indirect style subverts a sense of the exhaustiveness of the account, the mechanics of its operation may in turn be such as to belie the impression of a summary. The summarising mode may, in fact, be more exhaustive than apparently complete reports in a more unmediated or less ostentatious notation. In the dialogue between Joseph and Parson Barnabas in *Joseph Andrews*, I.xiii, the content suggests a complete record even as the style tends the opposite way: one can learn more of what purports to have been 'actually said' than in Moll Flanders' report, in a more conventional and self-effacing form of *oratio obliqua*, in a parallel scene between herself and the Ordinary of Newgate, despite the greater particularity we have been taught to expect from Defoe.[13] The summary style may

---

[12] Page's useful phrase, *Language of Jane Austen*, p. 129.
[13] Defoe, *Moll Flanders*, ed. G. A. Starr, London and Oxford, 1976, pp. 277–8. See *Order from Confusion Sprung*, pp. 292ff.

even invite a suspicion that it is in excess of what might actually have been said, as Austen's triadic repetitions are open to a suspicion that the anthologising is a *raconteur*'s exaggeration. They display the anecdotal embellishments of a knowing narrator, and the suggestion of summary in such cases tells us not that a selection has taken place, but that the discourse is being managed: not only the creation of consensual feeling of broad agreement between all sensible parties on essential standards of morals and social behaviour, but also the play of irony which reinforces this, implying a complicity among wise judges in uppish mockery of the foolish and the bad.

Fielding provided the model for such management in a way that Austen's favourite Richardson did not. In his 'Biographical Notice', Austen's brother Henry makes clear that Richardson's powers of characterisation, especially in *Sir Charles Grandison*, 'gratified the natural discrimination of her mind', although she avoided 'the errors of his prolix style and tedious narrative'. He adds that 'she did not rank any work of Fielding quite so high' because 'she recoiled from everything gross. Neither nature, wit, nor humour, could make her amends for so very low a scale of morals' (5). These comments, simplified and simplifying though they are, indicate that her admiration for Richardson and her reservations about Fielding were both dominated by moral, rather than technical, considerations, though 'Richardson's power of creating, and preserving the consistency of his characters' naturally has technical implications too. The strongest sign of Richardson's influence on Austen is the fact that all her male heroes are Grandisonian figures. This is especially true of the later heroes, Edmund Bertram, Knightley, and Wentworth, with their somewhat burgherly chivalric uprightness, but it applies also to the reconstructed Darcy and even to Henry Tilney and the unglamorous Colonel Brandon.

Austen was also more broadly fascinated by Richardson, and notably by the main technical feature of his narrative style, his use of an epistolary format. She seems to have experimented with it, but to have been inclined from an early stage to be sceptical of its virtues. The first version of *Sense and Sensibility*, and probably also of *Pride and Prejudice*, were in letter-form, and may have been satirical of it. She abandoned this method in the finalised versions, and did not use it in her other full-scale novels, perhaps concurring with Fielding's opinion, in his preface to Sarah Fielding's *Familiar Letters between the Principal Characters in David Simple* (1747), that it is not the style 'most proper to a Novelist, or ... used by the best writers of this Kind'. Earlier still she had parodied the genre in a series of burlesques of which 'Amelia Webster' is the briefest, and *Love and Freindship* the best known. These are partly directed against Richardson's imitators, but mockery or criticism of Richardson, not invariably affectionate, is found from the earliest juvenilia to her last work, *Sanditon*. Austen did not have Fielding's intense distaste for Richardsonian morality: on the contrary, she shared Richardson's view of Fielding's novels as morally 'very low'. But *Sanditon* is explicitly about the 'exceptionable parts' of Richardson's novels and their corrupting effect (*S* 358), and it has been suggested that Lucy Steele in *Sense and Sensibility* was partly modelled on Pamela.[14] If this suggestion is correct, Austen must have shared something of Fielding's Shamelaic view of Richardson's first heroine. She may not have known *Shamela* itself, or not known it to be by Fielding. But the essentials of that conception of Pamela may be found in *Joseph Andrews* and were, in any case, in wide circulation.

If Austen's epistolary parodies share *Shamela's* accelerated tempo, as I suggested earlier, the fact does not presuppose a reading of Fielding's pamphlet, and has less to do with Austen's moral view of Richardson than with her artistic instincts about the representation of reality. In stylistic matters, in her technical habits and presentational strategies, her deepest affinities were with Fielding. Like him, she seems to have been resistant to Richardson's pretensions as to the superior authenticity of the novel-in-letters and the immediacy of its 'to the Moment' narration. She probably disliked the idea of such immediacy anyway, and seems to have found uncongenial a narrative arrangement which left the story to the actors, and in which the author remained invisible as in a play. She would have sympathised with Fielding's jeering at the Shamelaic boast that 'You see I write in the present Tense' (Letter vi). Precision timing and clockwork reaction in both behaviour and repartee in *Shamela* are a stylish farcical response to Richardson's pseudo-instantaneities. They are matched in Austen's burlesques by a comedy of instant fainting-fits, accelerated deaths, and love at (or before) first sight, followed within moments by marriage (*MW* 80–2, 99–102, etc.; '*First-sight* Love' was incidentally something of a Richardsonian issue: all his novels contain solemn admonitions against the idea, and one of his essays is ridiculed in *Northanger Abbey* for asserting 'that no young lady can be justified in falling in love before the gentleman's love is declared', *NA* 15).

[14] F. W. Bradbrook, *Jane Austen and her Predecessors*, Cambridge, 1966, pp. 84–6.

The clockwork rhythms of farce accelerate time into a species of lunatic and supercharged immediacy which subverts the credibility of all 'to the Moment' pretensions. It also neutralises the related immediacy which surrenders the story-telling to a non-authorial participant. The importance of authorial mediation, guaranteeing a presiding wisdom and a protective filter against the invasiveness of raw experience, was deeply inscribed in an Augustan cultural code of which Fielding was a (sometimes rather loud) spokesman, and to which Austen paid an instinctive allegiance in a modified and subtler form. Richardson's novels were in their nature subversive of this. Parodying him in a format which excluded overt intervention called for stylisations from within which visibly reflected the knowing operations and ironic perspectives of a controlling intelligence. The farcical precisions and surreal coincidences in such narratives are effectively, if not formally, interventionist. Their outrageousness discredits the ostensible narrator, and signals the tacit presence of a satirical raconteur-mimic. Anecdotal routines and automatisms of the 'I said/he said' type, habitual in both *Shamela* and Austen's epistolary burlesques, are readily transferred in the reader's mind from the ostensible speaker to that mimicking presence, especially when the narrative is deadpan in a way that defies an expected or appropriate response. This seems a direct consequence of planting suggestions of farce within a purportedly realistic genre. Although author-figures are not normally visible in stage-compositions, the importation of stage-effects into fictional narratives tends to increase, rather than diminish, a consciousness of authorial presence.

This has particular pertinence because the epistolary genre is 'dramatic' not only in its 'to the Moment' elements, but also in the sense that the narration is left to the actors and the author is notionally invisible as in a play. Richardson was proud of these dramatic features, sometimes accentuating them by introducing dialogue in play-script form. That such effacement of the author was no more congenial to Austen than to Fielding seems amusingly confirmed by a dramatic adaptation of *Sir Charles Grandison*, once attributed to a niece, but now shown to be probably by Austen herself.[15] This work (a good-humoured travesty rather than an attack, and perhaps as much directed at popular abridgements and adaptations of Richardson's novel as at the novel itself) was composed intermittently between the early 1790s and 1800. It resembles some of the early burlesques in its

[15] See *Jane Austen's 'Sir Charles Grandison'*, ed. Brian Southam, Oxford, 1980.

comic telescoping of a huge novel into a short space (as *Shamela* boils *Pamela* down to a brief pamphlet) and in its speeded-up action and dialogue. It is also especially insistent in its stage-directions, the one area where an author can intervene directly in a play's written text. Southam says these leave 'little to chance or to the player's uncertainty' (*G* 12) and speaks of this as a practical matter, concerned with managing inexperienced players in family productions, but the directions sometimes hint at the same accelerated zaniness as the burlesque narratives: 'She gets half-way through the door and he, in shutting it, squeezes her. She screams and faints. He carries her away in his arms to a chair and rings the bell violently. Enter MRS. AWBERRY ...' (*G* 43). Southam stresses the difference between this slight family piece and the major published works, but like the burlesques it displays, in unsubdued and unprocessed form, characteristics which Austen refashioned and transformed in the mature novels.

It has long been recognised that Austen's novels, like Fielding's, contained 'dramatic' or at least theatrical elements of their own. Fielding had been a professional playwright, and had written over twenty plays before he began writing novels. The genres he practised were stylised ones: dramatic burlesques, comedies of witty repartee, *Rehearsal*-plays which contain a playwright-character producing a play-within-the-play (in some ways the prototype of authorial figures in the novels who comment not only on the action, but also on the writing of the story). Austen's stage-experience was not on this scale, but there was a strong tradition of private theatricals in her family, partly reflected in a well-known episode in *Mansfield Park*; and, in addition to the *Grandison* play, she wrote some dramatic sketches, scraps of which survive among the juvenilia (*MW* 49–57, 172–5). The novels of both authors show many marks of this experience: a keen sense of plot; chapters or episodes framed as set-pieces, analogous in shape and length to a scene in a play; comic reversals and resolutions; semi-autonomous *tableaux*; a sharp ear for dialogue and especially a highly-developed feeling for character-revealing stylisations in dialogue; the 'playfulness and epigrammatism' (*L* 300) in *Pride and Prejudice*, often reminiscent of repartee in wit-comedy; a whole repertoire of stage-routines, including well-timed coincidences, contrived meetings, comic misunderstandings, conversations overheard at cross-purposes. Such theatrical elements were the opposite of those through which Richardson might claim to have achieved dramatic illusion. What they took from the drama were its artifices rather than its immediacies, and they contain further examples of the way in which a pointed importation of stage-effects into narrative tends to maximise, rather than reduce, the impression of authorial management.

In Austen's mature novels, such things are less ostentatiously paraded than they are in Fielding, and we can sometimes sense a specific instinct to moderate them. An important difference between the manuscript draft and the final version of the last chapters of *Persuasion*, finely discussed by Southam, shows a drawing away from stereotyped comic contrivance to a more natural account of the clarification between Wentworth and Anne.[16] This is a particularly impressive late development, but in this as in other respects *Persuasion* extends, rather than departs from, the other novels. Her stylised self-projections, 'dramatic' and other, are on a smaller scale than Fielding's. Her novels have no 'introductory' chapters of the kind Fielding prefixed to each of the eighteen books of *Tom Jones*, only occasional overt appearances, 'brisk and ironic', which, as Page says, anticipate George Eliot and E. M. Forster more than they recall Fielding.[17] At times, as I shall argue, one even senses a momentary withdrawal of authorial certainty very unlike Fielding's parade of bossy assurance.

The subordination of both conversation and incident to authorial performance and satirical perspective is, in Fielding, sustained over large tracts of narrative, and seldom gives way to underisive particularities of observation or the sober analysis of situation and motive. This is not so in Austen. The indirectly reported account of Sir Walter's refusal to leave Kellynch-hall is quickly followed, as it would not be in Fielding, by paragraphs of lucid, low-key analysis: 'There had been three alternatives, London, Bath, or another house in the country. All Anne's wishes had been for the latter ...' (19). Satiric triumphalism gradually gives way to a respect for the factuality of fact and motive, whereas Fielding's modulations are normally in an opposite direction, into a massive flow of explanatory sarcasm or an extended mock-heroic elaboration. Even a deliberate drop into the real, like the portrait of the heroine in *Tom Jones*, iv.ii: '*Sophia* then, the only Daughter of Mr. *Western*, was a middle-sized Woman; but rather inclining to tall', comes over less as a concession to fact than as a pointedly contrastive gesture, trumpeting its difference from the surrounding burlesque rant. The performative set-pieces in Austen

---

[16] Southam, *Jane Austen's Literary Manuscripts*, pp. 88ff.; Marilyn Butler, *Jane Austen and the War of Ideas*, rev. edn., Oxford, 1987, pp. 281ff.   [17] Page, in *Companion*, p. 228.

are not only more subdued. They come in waves, more intermittent, but with certain perceptible rhythms. Sir Walter's refusal to leave Kellynch-hall had, in the emphatic nature of its report, been comically set up for reversal. He changes his mind in less than a page, even before the analysis of alternatives. The next comparable orchestration of dialogue occurs in the following chapter, where a renewed and more elaborate pattern of reversal is unfolded.

The lawyer Shepherd reports to Sir Walter his discovery of a suitable tenant:

Mr. Shepherd hastened to assure him, that Admiral Croft was a very hale, hearty, well-looking man, a little weather-beaten, to be sure, but not much; and quite the gentleman in all his notions and behaviour; – not likely to make the smallest difficulty about terms; – only wanted a comfortable home, and to get into it as soon as possible; – knew he must pay for his convenience; – knew what rent a ready-furnished house of that consequence might fetch; – should not have been surprised if Sir Walter had asked more; – had inquired about the manor; – would be glad of the deputation, certainly, but made no great point of it; – said he sometimes took out a gun, but never killed; – quite the gentleman. (26–7)

As in the earlier example, there is a degree of indeterminacy as to who is saying what: where Croft's speeches end and Shepherd's gloss begins, and where authorial mimicry is travestying either or both. Punctuation offers no guide here, not even the faintly confusing signal whereby, in the earlier passage, some of Sir Walter's phrases but not others are given within quotation-marks. Another difference is that in the earlier passage a sympathetic character was reporting an unsympathetic one, thus inducing an impression of solidarity between the reporter and the overall narrator. Here, the process is reversed. The reporter is repellent, and it is the reportee who generates sympathy, though this has to work its way through the distorting medium of the report. The automatism imputed to Admiral Croft's statements by Shepherd's narration reflects discredit on Shepherd, not Croft. It is Shepherd's nastiness that presents Croft's accommodating and good-natured phrases as mechanical routines, though to the extent that it comes naturally to Croft to say good-natured things the automatism itself, unusually, becomes a sign of grace.

The detail about the Admiral's gun, that he sometimes took one out 'but never killed', may strike some present-day readers as more of a bizarrerie than it really is. It involves the issue of blood-sports, more quotidian then than now, but it has an odd eruptive force in the otherwise banal catalogue of the Admiral's easy-going concessions, and the word 'killed', without suggesting anything that gentlemen do not often do, disturbs the insipid surface of the lawyer's recital. Even in its negative form, since the Admiral *does not* kill, it announces a small sudden violence within that 'little bit (two Inches wide) of Ivory' (*L* 469) to which Austen compared her fictional world, much as, on another plane, some stinging acerbities of her own violate the decorous idiom of that world.

The main point of the detail is the Admiral's moral soundness. The 'never killing' vouches for that, as Willoughby's being 'a very decent shot' (*S and S* 37) perhaps hints at the opposite; while the Admiral's having the gun at all presumably assures us, as it assures Mr Shepherd, that he could pass for a country gentleman. 'Quite the gentleman', says the lawyer twice, toadyingly ironic, suggesting an 'it will do' gentility, better than one might expect, but not enough to take *him* in. Shepherd's cheap lazy phrasing, and his whole get-it-over-with summary of the Admiral's attitudes, are a staple of the satirical repertoire of free indirect reporting (compare the it-will-do laxities of Parson Barnabas in *Joseph Andrews*, i.xiii). They establish the lawyer as sanctimoniously complicitous and irredeemably low: he is treated *de haut en bas* by Austen, even as she derides the uppish pretensions of himself and Sir Walter (another standard satiric ploy, habitual in Fielding and others). The Admiral emerges as an honest, heart-of-the-matter figure, generously eccentric in a social milieu whose accepted forms of behaviour might seem suspect by comparison. He represents an ideal of unrefined decency against the self-importance and fetid politeness of Sir Walter and his hangers-on.

The portrait comes as a local climax in an extended debate about the social acceptability of Navy officers, regarded by Sir Walter as a coarse species with unseemly weather-beaten features. The Navy is one of the few intrusions from the wider world which Jane Austen allows into the two inches of ivory, and in *Persuasion* it is especially prominent. It brings hints of distant places and reminders of foreign wars. Its hardships, as weathered by Mrs Croft, are a focus for the novel's insistence on the rightness of taking risks for the sake of love, though Wentworth's opposition to the idea of letting women live on board ship suggests that Austen's endorsement of Mrs Croft has its limits, as least on the specific point. Two of Austen's brothers were naval officers and became admirals, so she had, as we are often reminded, a soft spot for the service. *Persuasion* is one of the two novels (*Mansfield Park* is the other) where the professions, specifically the

naval and the clerical professions, play an important part, and where
professional duty is held up as an especially important value. In both
novels, the idea is entertained that what you do is more important
than who you are. Again, one suspects some ambivalence. By the time
Anne marries Wentworth, he is not only a successful naval officer but
has a substantial fortune. The Crofts, warm-hearted, forthright and
lovable, are nevertheless 'character parts', marginalised by their
amiable eccentricities. The Navy is presented as disconcertingly
outside the customary divisions of rank, and even as a challenge to
them, especially offensive to Sir Walter 'as being the means of
bringing persons of obscure birth into undue distinction, and raising
men to honours which their fathers and grandfathers never dreamt of'
(24). In any contest with Sir Walter for the reader's sympathies, the
Crofts cannot lose.

The decision to vacate the house and to lease it to the Crofts, much
fussed and agonised over, suddenly becomes a matter of quick
summarising despatch: 'The house and grounds, and furniture, were
approved, the Crofts were approved, terms, time, every thing, and
every body, was right; and Mr. Shepherd's clerks were set to work,
without there having been a single preliminary difference to modify of
all that "This indenture sheweth"' (35). It is as if the narrator had
wearied of the details, and is in fact the expression of a long-standing
Augustan *pudeur* over retailing events merely because they occurred: a
pudeur which Defoe and Richardson did not share, which was in its
way contrary to the essential character of the novel-form, but which
acted as a vitalising constraint in the work of novelists who, like
Fielding and Austen, retained a commitment to older canons of
'polite' style. The rule, as Fielding put it in the Preface to the *Voyage to
Lisbon*, that you should not mention a 'merely common incident . . . for
its own sake, but for some observations and reflections naturally
resulting from it', was for many writers a matter of deep cultural
predisposition (it had a non-literary counterpart in the rules for
conversation propounded in courtesy books). It was not a demand for
conciseness as such, and was sometimes the occasion for self-conscious
and even prolix disclaimers or mock-disclaimers of mere particularity, in Swift, Fielding, and others. Breaches of the rule implied
vulgarity and an unhealthy and unregulated surrender to the flow of
events. A prolixity which resulted from this was especially culpable.
Richardson's novels seemed to Fielding and others a paradigm-case of
stylistic solecism in this matter.

Whatever Austen's view of Fielding, she too disliked 'the errors of

[Richardson's] prolix style' (5). The summarising account of the agreement to lease Kellynch-hall is uniquely Austenian, but it has much in common with Fielding's summary ironies and has no counterpart in Richardson. Its blend of circumstantial reticence and amused critical irony declares the account to be under selective and discriminating management. In this and in other ways it is part of a more general tendency of individual elements in the novel towards the set-piece; the closures, symmetries, reversals that suggest the shaped autonomy of a fable, a scene in a play, an instructive irony of motive or circumstance. But such periodically recurrent passages of accelerated and summary narrative also contribute to a larger rhythm of tension and relaxation in the movement of the novel as a whole, akin to some of the more extended patterns of reversal. The paragraph which summarises the conclusion of the deal is followed by a ballet of symmetrical reversals, in which the snobbish baronet ends up with an enhanced opinion of the admiral, while the good-hearted admiral develops a genial contempt in return:

Sir Walter, without hesitation, declared the Admiral to be the best-looking sailor he had ever met with, and went so far as to say, that, if his own man might have had the arranging of his hair, he should not be ashamed of being seen with him any where; and the Admiral, with sympathetic cordiality, observed to his wife as they drove back through the Park, 'I thought we should soon come to a deal, my dear, in spite of what they told us at Taunton. The baronet will never set the Thames on fire, but there seems no harm in him:' – reciprocal compliments, which would have been esteemed about equal. (35)

On the surface, this seems like the kind of plague-on-both-houses irony which is one of the virtuoso routines of Augustan satirical rhetoric, as in the comment on the violent inclinations of extremists of opposing factions in Swift's *Sentiments of a Church-of-England Man*: 'And this is *Moderation*, in the *modern* Sense of the Word; to which, speaking impartially, the Bigots of both Parties are *equally* entituled.'[18] The see-sawing reciprocities, and the stinging finality, are also present in Austen in a less ferocious but equally pointed form. In Swift, they are the climax of an argument and the closing words of the first part of a political tract. In Austen, they occur inside a chapter, at no specially strategic point, a momentary crystallisation in a continuing narrative: despite appearances, they are not merely, nor even mainly, an irony of reciprocal blame, since the admiral is not really blamed. They

[18] Jonathan Swift, *Works*, II.13.

look like a Swiftian sarcasm, but they function less as a localised epigrammatic aggression than as part of an intricate system of narrative ironies. The admiral who was under hostile scrutiny passes the test, while the baronet who sat in judgment fails, his pretensions to superiority upstaged by a reversal which puts his presumed inferior on top. This fable of the uppish upped is replayed when the Crofts come to Bath and Elizabeth and Sir Walter decide that they should not be introduced to Lady Dalrymple as 'we ought to be very careful not to embarrass her with acquaintance she might not approve' (157), while the Crofts are totally innocent of any desire for such company: they 'knew quite as many people in Bath as they wished for, and considered their intercourse with the Elliots as a mere matter of form, and not in the least likely to afford them any pleasure' (159). Once again Sir Walter ends up more excluded than excluding: 'He was not at all ashamed of the acquaintance, and did, in fact, think and talk a great deal more about the Admiral, than the Admiral ever thought or talked about him' (159). These recurrent fabular elements not only form a thread of their own within the larger economy of the book. Individually they register an organisational impulse to create local autonomies of significance, rather than surrender an episode to the continuous flow of event or circumstance, even as the narrative is ostensibly committed to reporting that flow.

Ironic reversals and finalities of summation are in some ways a narrative counterpart to the syntactical rhetoric of much Augustan satire, with its stinging definitional containments and its sarcastic paradox-laden antitheses. Narrative is a more spacious and perhaps in Jane Austen a gentler medium, and her fictional world is one that normally excludes the teeming energies of transgression and folly that are the subject-matter of Swift or Pope. The phrase 'regulated hatred'[19] has been applied, in a memorable essay, to her style, and finely conveys its mixture of hard-edged perception and decorous restraint. There are occasional intensities which are not covered by that phrase, and perhaps the most startling of these occurs in *Persuasion*. In 1.vi the memory of a deceased son of the Musgroves who had once served in the navy under Wentworth briefly enters the story. Louisa reports that her mother was 'out of spirits', having been reminded of him by a report that Wentworth was coming back.

[19] D. W. Harding, 'Regulated Hatred: An Aspect of the Work of Jane Austen', *Scrutiny*, 8 (1940), 346–62. Reprinted in Ian Watt, ed., *Jane Austen: A Collection of Critical Essays*, Englewood Cliffs, NJ, 1963, pp. 166–79.

Louisa thinks they should divert her mind from 'such gloomy things'. At this point the narrator weighs in:

The real circumstances of this pathetic piece of family history were, that the Musgroves had had the ill fortune of a very troublesome, hopeless son; and the good fortune to lose him before he reached his twentieth year; that he had been sent to sea, because he was stupid and unmanageable on shore; that he had been very little cared for at any time by his family, though quite as much as he deserved; seldom heard of, and scarcely at all regretted, when the intelligence of his death abroad had worked its way to Uppercross, two years before. (51–2)

This is not spoken by a character whose callousness might be the focus of attention. Unlike some other passages registering malicious attitudes, there is no suggestion of even a shadowy traffic between the authorial voice and any less official consciousness within the story. It comes over as a starkly authorial intervention, especially gratuitous since the young man had not hitherto been any part of the story. The eruptive force is almost surreal, in the context of a surrounding narrative whose ironies are more indirect and low-key, and in a novel whose prevailing atmosphere is usually felt to be kindlier and mellower than the rest of Austen's work. The paragraph has the aspect of a formal 'character', a prose counterpart to some of the portraits in Pope's *Moral Essays*. But one of the remarkable features of this explosion of definitional bravura is that, unlike Pope's portraits, it contains little definition. We learn almost nothing specific about what the young man was like, and the aggressive play of balance and antithesis consists more of *ex cathedra* adjudications than of a precise detailing of the person's characteristics. It is so out of keeping with its context that one senses an unbalancing focus of private malice, a secret settling of scores. It is brought startlingly into relief, unlike its Popeian analogues, which are more naturally accommodated within the generic frame of a satirical epistle engaged in a listing of types, and whose settling of scores is neither secret nor anomalous.

Austen won't let this subject go away, and the deceased Richard continues to exercise his surviving family for the remainder of the chapter. The interplay of outlooks between author and characters is resumed. In a follow-up reflection by the author, harsh summation gives way to a pretended incomprehension: 'that Mrs. Musgrove should have been suddenly struck, this very day, with a recollection of the name of Wentworth, as connected with her son, seemed one of those extraordinary bursts of mind which do sometimes occur' (52–3).

This seems the antithesis of the earlier rhetoric of summary definition. It projects an alternative mastery, that of the unspecific applied to quite precise effects. It resembles the knowing mock-incomprehensions of Fielding (as when he claims that he has 'never met with any one able to account for' the frenetic discriminations between high people or low people, or announces that he will not presume to determine the motive for some obvious folly or nastiness), but with an enhanced and more concise sense of the inexplicability of things. Fielding's incomprehensions imply that he knows the answers, Austen's here that they can't be known, though both employ a similar rhetoric of sharp certainty as to the fact itself of humanity's irrational ways.

Part of the difference is accounted for by the fact that Austen's discourse even here moves with greater fluidity between the author's perspective and those of her characters. A novelistic manner which cultivates interactions with alternative outlooks, and whose exploitation of free indirect style has a greater intimacy and finesse than Fielding's, is more naturally adapted to projecting an incomplete or unresolved comprehension. A sentence like 'Anne sighed and blushed and smiled, in pity and disdain, either at her friend or at herself' (170) would be unlikely to occur in Fielding except, perhaps, in a bouncy parade of omniscience as he conveyed to the reader that both of them know perfectly well what he does not pretend to have grasped. But the remark about 'those extraordinary bursts of mind' is closer to Fielding than this, though in a more subtly manipulative manner. No reader would find them extraordinary. A mother is reminded of the death of her son, and we do not usually marvel at the phenomenon. The shocking insistence on inexplicability forces into relief not the oddity of the mother, but the son's exceptional undeservingness. It is a cunning irony of displacement, as tight as any epigram, without the epigram's accoutrements of verbal wit, registering incongruities of circumstance or character (ironies that eschew verbal wit are more in the style of Johnson, a more freely admired predecessor, than of Fielding). The perverse or contrary character is all in the (alleged) facts, so strange that they do not invite explicit summations, but hardly inexplicable.

Nevertheless, the 'absurdity' of Mrs Musgrove on the point continues to engage Austen as the mother of the son is gradually assimilated into the flow of narrative. Two chapters later, Wentworth is shown being tactful to her. Anne surmises that, as the boy's commanding officer, he had 'probably been at some pains to get rid of him', but he 'shewed the kindest consideration for all that was real and *unabsurd* in the parent's feelings' (67: italics added). *Unabsurd* is a word brilliantly chosen, its slightly laboured inelegance conveying exactly the limits of grudging concession, a word that Richardson might have used, but not Pope or Fielding, more fastidious as they were in their displays of the masteries of style. And Wentworth's determination to maximise the unabsurdity is then surrendered to a merciless fantasia of comic obesity and social gaucherie. Anne and Wentworth

were actually on the same sofa, for Mrs. Musgrove had most readily made room for him, – they were divided only by Mrs Musgrove. It was no insignificant barrier indeed. Mrs. Musgrove was of a comfortable substantial size, infinitely more fitted by nature to express good cheer and good humour, than tenderness and sentiment; and while the agitations of Anne's slender form, and pensive face, may be considered as very completely screened, Captain Wentworth should be allowed some credit for the self-command with which he attended to her large fat sighings over the destiny of a son, whom alive nobody had cared for. (67–8)

The *tableau* is very funny, and the extent to which it is a *tableau*, framed within the sofa as a composition, is striking. The present-tense description of how Anne's sitting position 'may be' visualised, an unusual show of surrendering tight narrative management, almost suggests a stage-direction, and even more perhaps a film scenario. The preceding paragraph had offered intimations of Anne's perspective into the exchanges between Wentworth and the bereaved mother, but by now we are more unequivocally back to an official authorial voice, and this seems confirmed by the paragraph which immediately follows:

Personal size and mental sorrow have certainly no necessary proportions. A large bulky figure has as good a right to be in deep affliction, as the most graceful set of limbs in the world. But, fair or not fair, there are unbecoming conjunctions, which reason will patronize in vain, – which taste cannot tolerate, – which ridicule will seize. (68)

The idiom again approximates briefly not to Fielding or Pope, but to Johnson. The style looks back to his way, pondered and literal-minded, of giving to commonplace observations a peculiar combination of pathos and gravitas. The Johnson who has been described, honorifically, as a satirist *manqué*, whose literal truthfulness and compassionate instincts shrank from the ironic distortions and the cruelty of satirical discourse, and who responded instead with palliating explanations, seems to be at work. The reader is here reminded that the grief of fat people is also grief. But the concession is then withdrawn, in an unJohnsonian way, perhaps even with an arch note of parody of the Johnsonian version of the rhetorical triad: 'which reason will patronize in vain, – which taste cannot tolerate, – which ridicule will seize' – an amusing variation on the mini-anthologizing discussed earlier in connection with Sir Walter's reluctance to move from Kellynch-hall ('had no success at all – could not be put up with – were not to be borne').

The later Christmas scene at the Musgroves', with their noisy children and grandchildren, has something of the effect on Anne and Lady Russell that Fanny Price's return to her Portsmouth family had on her (*MP* 343ff.), except that the degrading squalors of indigence at Portsmouth do not exist at Uppercross. 'It was a fine family-piece', the account concludes, and the sarcastic phrase implies, once again, a framed composition, parodying the happy family *tableaux* which were a stereotype of the novel of sentiment: Mrs Musgrove guarding the Harville children from her own grandchildren, Mr Musgrove trying to talk to Lady Russell above 'the clamour of the children on his knees', 'a roaring Christmas fire' (127). Anne, thinking of Louisa's illness, 'would have deemed such a domestic hurricane a bad restorative of the nerves', but Mrs Musgrove's happy comment on the proceedings is 'that after all she had gone through, nothing was so likely to do her good as a little quiet cheerfulness at home' (128). It is usually difficult, in the portrayal of this kindly lady, to distinguish between affection and contempt. If the portrayal is not merely the product of unprocessed animus, it may mark an incipient sense of the radical incomprehensibility of 'character', unusual in the earlier novels.

Contributing to the Christmas *brouhaha* were the Harvilles' children, brought over 'to improve the noise of Uppercross, and lessen that of Lyme' (127), and it may be that the Harvilles are also mildly derided as types of domestic devotion and felicity, surviving difficult times. This is not a sign that Austen was against families, but that she may have been exercised by ambivalent feelings about another fictional stereotype, that of the virtuous family in stricken circumstances, especially frequent in the novel of sensibility and even found, with varying degrees of irony, in the more 'sentimental' parts of Fielding's novels: the Heartfrees in *Jonathan Wild* and the Booths in

Amelia provide some examples. Harville is, for the most part, a solid fellow and a good naval officer, greatly liked by Wentworth, and 'no reader' (96), unlike his sentimental friend Benwick, who reads Byron and Scott and to whom Anne has to recommend a dose of prose-reading (98–9, 104, 106, 158: in all Austen's novels, people's characters are defined by whether they read, and what). But he has a pointedly 'novelistic' name, recalling Mackenzie's Man of Feeling, Harley, and Burney's Orville, among others, and is in this respect unusual among serious characters in Austen. (The early burlesques contain a Sir George and Lady Harcourt, and a half-page novel, 'The Adventures of Mr. Harley', about a young man 'destined by his father for the Church & by his Mother for the Sea' and who, 'desirous of pleasing both', combined the careers of future Austen heroes by becoming a chaplain 'on board a Man of War', *MW* 33ff., 40). The Harvilles have something of the same faintly insipid passivity as Fielding's Heartfrees, and are exposed to similarly good-natured, but unmistakably uppish, put-downs from their creator: 'Captain Harville, though not equalling Captain Wentworth in manners, was a perfect gentleman, unaffected, warm, and obliging. Mrs. Harville, a degree less polished than her husband, seemed however to have the same good feelings' (95). 'Perfect gentleman' has unsettling echoes of Mr Shepherd on Admiral Croft: 'quite the gentleman' (26–7). Harville's lameness, a vaguely Byronic trait, is the result of a war-wound (92, 95), but such romantically 'interesting' debilities tend to get short shrift in Austen's novels. In this regard, her outlook may not have changed much from the time when the unreformed Marianne could find something erotically 'interesting ... in the flushed cheek, hollow eye and quick pulse of a fever', but has to settle instead for Colonel Brandon and his rheumatism (*S and S* 31–3). In *Persuasion* Austen goes out of her way to make sure that the Crofts, who are the novel's only example of a truly successful and long-standing love, are given unromantic ailments: the Admiral has gout and Mrs Croft a blister 'as large as a three shilling piece' (155, 157, 161).

The example of the Harvilles, and in an opposite sense that of the Crofts, suggest that Austen experienced a certain awkwardness in assimilating the 'sentimental' sympathies which, as many readers agree, are given fuller expression in *Persuasion* than in most of her previous work. The Crofts seem to show a special determination to give these sympathies a middle-aged expression. It is not merely that they are happily married, but that emphasis is given to them as models for young lovers, even as their middle-aged eccentricities and ailments, and their headlong accident-prone way of life, come over as almost ostentatiously unglamorous. Early in the novel they come to represent for Anne an ideal of happy love equal to what she had once felt between herself and Wentworth: 'with the exception, perhaps, of Admiral and Mrs. Croft, who seemed particularly attached and happy, (Anne could allow no other exception even among the married couples) there could have been no two hearts so open, no tastes so similar, no feelings so in unison, no countenances so beloved' (63). That this middle-aged couple are in their married state comparable to a hero and heroine in courtship, is not merely glimpsed by Anne in her nostalgia for her courtship days, now seemingly over. Nor is the observation confined to a serious-minded heroine like herself, whose view of such things might not be dependent on the glow of romance. Even more strikingly, Louisa Musgrove sees the Crofts in the same way, and tells Wentworth: 'If I loved a man, as she loves the Admiral, I would be always with him, nothing should ever separate us, and I would rather be overturned by him, than driven safely by anybody else' (83).

Austen's insistence against all 'romantic' expectation in investing this pair of aging eccentrics with an aura of emotional grace normally confined to young protagonists is evidently self-conscious. The Admiral himself seems almost aware of the generic reversal when he accuses Wentworth, the novel's official romantic lead, of lacking gallantry. It is a passage of exquisite irony because it pits the values of the Crofts against codes of conduct to which, in any final analysis, Jane Austen would give her endorsement. The issue is Wentworth's unwillingness to admit ladies on board ship, except for brief visits, because as Wentworth replies, life on a ship is too rough: 'There can be no want of gallantry ... in rating the claims of women to every personal comfort *high*.' Mrs Croft reacts warmly to this 'idle refinement': she has lived on board ship with her husband, and she hates to hear Wentworth 'talking so, like a fine gentleman, and as if women were all fine ladies, instead of rational creatures' (68–9). At this point, where present-day readers might be most inclined to acquiesce in Mrs Croft's general position, it seems likely that Austen's own assent is being withheld. There is no suggestion, when Anne eventually marries Wentworth, that she will live on his ships as Mrs Croft did. Mrs Croft's declarations about her happiness on board ship have symbolic value for the case of Anne and Wentworth, because they speak of the value of putting love before prudential considerations. As literal models for them to follow they have nothing to offer, however, and their comic dimension as generous eccentrics safely preserves the novel from taking them seriously in any precise operational sense. They are so remote from prevailing custom in the society of Austen's novels that they acquire the privileges and limitations of Quixotic irresponsibility.

That Austen should have denied the Crofts a centre-stage position in the story does not take away from their uniqueness in her fiction, though it could be argued that love in Austen's novels almost always has a middle-aged, or at least an unyouthful, aspect. The heroes are usually substantially older and wiser than the heroines, and some-times display a quasi-paternal authority over them. Some of the younger heroines (Marianne, Emma) marry men in their middle or late thirties. These things are not usually made an issue of, or presented as romantically anomalous. In *Sense and Sensibility*, where the issue arises of marrying an older man against the heroine's original wishes, there is a last minute attempt to salvage some of the proprieties of romantic love: 'Marianne could never love by halves; and her whole heart became, in time, as much devoted to her husband, as it had once been to Willoughby' (*S and S* 334). But whereas Brandon represents for Marianne a safe and rational choice, the Crofts, middle-aged on both sides, represent the success of the exact opposite, and their example speaks poignantly to Anne of all that she has missed by holding back. As Marianne had been unwisely led by 'romance' in her youth and eventually became prudent, so Anne, who 'had been forced into prudence in her youth ... learned romance as she grew older' (33). Age is partly, of course, a rhetorical matter: Mrs Croft is 38, and her younger brother Wentworth is by now 31. But Anne (now 28) and Wentworth remain, several years after their first courtship, cast in the role of *jeunes premiers*, in a situation where their author wishes to assert that status with all the conventional novelistic honours, while insist-ing at the same time, without entire artistic conviction, on the rights of the middle-aged to such things.

Lady Russell is of interest in this context. She plays what would, in a conventional romantic plot, be the role of the interfering elder who tries to manipulate the heroine along mercenary or prudential lines, like an underided Mrs Western. What is interesting is not only that (although shown to be wrong) she is represented in a respectable and even sympathetic light, but that Austen has gone out of her way to indicate that she had a warm loving nature: 'She was a benevolent, charitable, good woman, and capable of strong attachments' (17). In this regard, she resembles another Fielding character, Squire Allworthy, who stands for the civic virtues and admonishes the impetuous Tom Jones for his lack of prudence, but whose gravity has to be shown against the evidence not to be obstructive or stuffy: 'he had possessed much Fire in his Youth, and had married a beautiful Woman for Love' (vi.iv). The disclosure has absolutely no function in the story of *Tom Jones*, other than to maximise sympathy for a character whose identification with prudential values might seem unattractive to readers (and authors) whose main sympathies are with the young lovers. It is interesting that Austen should have made a similar point of stressing Lady Russell's ardent nature, somewhat in opposition to her thematic role, even where the official purposes of the novel require her to be seen to be mainly in the wrong.

That indeed is Jane Austen's main problem. Lady Russell partly upholds Elinor's values at a point in Austen's evolution when her sympathies have moved closer to Marianne. It is not exactly a case of 'reckless middle-age' finding itself 'restrained' by the primly moral young.[20] The middle-aged Austen has not exploded into passion, but mellowed towards it. The most active energies of her earlier imagination were, perhaps paradoxically, critical ones: whatever secret sharing there may have been in the portrayal of Marianne's loving and sensitive side, one is conscious of a strongly willed drive to restrain or ridicule it, as the exuberant unprocessed energy of the early burlesques testifies. We should not forget that exuberant derision of 'sensibility' did not cease with Austen's youth: as we have seen, the unfinished *Sanditon* is slightly later than *Persuasion*. The case is at all stages fraught with ambivalence, but a redistribution of sympathies is evident within the 'serious' novels, which are the works which embody the author's fullest imaginative engagement with her material, and in which the material is human rather than merely bookish. One of the issues for Austen in *Persuasion* was how to project some strong anti-prudential sympathies without, so to speak, being disloyal to Elinor.

Lady Russell is the result. Her influence has to be discredited without forfeiting affection or respect. Hence the assurances of her

---

[20] The words are from W. B. Yeats's epigram, 'On Hearing that the Students of our New University have Joined the Agitation against Immoral Literature', in *Poems*, ed. Finneran, p. 94.

capacity for feeling, and the curiously weighted assertion that 'she was a woman rather of sound than of quick abilities' (16): a combination traditionally prized in English estimates of social worth, often given, in Swift's approving words, to paying 'more Regard to good Morals than to great Abilities', but subject also to imputations of mediocrity and often dedicated to obstructing persons of more remarkable character or talent, as Swift also noted, with withering sarcasm.[21] Jane Austen seems poised between the two valuations not, like Swift, in separate contexts of equal and opposite affirmation, but in a single inclusive and slightly unfocused view. Lady Russell's early response to Wentworth is a revealing example. She 'had little taste for wit; and of any thing approaching to imprudence a horror'. Thus Frederick Wentworth, charming, witty, confident, 'full of life and ardour', seemed to her dangerously 'brilliant' and 'headstrong' (30–1).

Wentworth is sometimes taken by critics at Lady Russell's valuation, as an unsound type whose 'personal philosophy approaches revolutionary optimism or individualism'. Marilyn Butler's vivid and otherwise compelling chapter on *Persuasion* seems to me part of a consistently reductive misjudgment of Wentworth which extends Lady Russell's censures in the very direction where Austen, as well as Anne, believe them to be most misguided. The dangerous 'revolutionary optimism' is apparently to be discerned in Wentworth's praise to Louisa Musgrove of ' "resolution", "decision", "firmness", "spirit", and finally, in truly Godwinian phraseology, "powers of mind" '. These phrases are, in fact, being applied to no more revolutionary a character than Louisa herself, in a fit of gallant speech-making which contrasts Louisa's 'firmness' with some vacillating behaviour by her sister Henrietta earlier in the day. They occur in the same conversation as his mock-pompous oration on the virtues of the nut ('Here is a nut ... To exemplify, – a beautiful glossy nut, which, blessed with original strength, has outlived all the storms of autumn ...', 86), an exercise in rhetorical parody in the genre of Swift's famous 'Meditation upon a Broom-Stick', and delivered, as Austen tells us, 'with playful solemnity', which Butler reads as the serious reflections of a man 'of high moral aspirations ... in the grip of ... a personal bias that perverts his judgement'.[22] The 'personal bias' is not a matter of wilfulness, still less of revolutionary optimism or dogmatism, but bitterness at Anne's failure to exercise 'firmness' when Lady Russell

[21] On this, see *Order from Confusion Sprung*, pp. 35ff.
[22] Butler, *Jane Austen and the War of Ideas*, pp. 275, 278.

'persuaded' her to break off their engagement. This is how Anne interprets the 'serious warmth' she detects in the more 'earnest' parts of his speech (86), and this is surely their natural impact on the reader. But even without this inappropriately solemn reading of the discourse on the nut, and the tenuously grounded politicisation of Wentworth's outlook, Butler's view of Wentworth's imputed deficiencies is over-stated. As Mary Poovey says, it 'needs to be qualified both by Austen's approving treatment of the naval meritocracy in *Persuasion* and by the personal pride she took in her own brothers' advances in the navy'.[23] It must also be qualified by much in the novel itself, by the evidence of Wentworth's own generosity and good sense, by the affection and respect in which he is held by the other characters, and above all by Anne's feelings for him.

Nevertheless, Lady Russell's perspective is not wholly repudiated, despite all the havoc it has caused in the lives of Anne and Wentworth. Anne insists even at the end that she was right to take Lady Russell's advice, though the advice itself was wrong. Even that concession is cautiously phrased: 'I am not saying that she did not err in her advice. It was, perhaps, one of those cases in which advice is good or bad only as the event decides.' Anne adds that she herself would never 'in any circumstance of tolerable similarity, give such advice', but she sticks to her other point (232). Austen completes the rehabilitation at the end, when she grants that Lady Russell 'had been less gifted' than Anne in 'quickness of perception', but adds (as she had found it necessary to add at beginning) that her emotional priorities were the right ones: 'if her second object was to be sensible and well-judging, her first was to see Anne happy'. Austen concludes with a striking quasi-parental variation on her treatment of Marianne's eventual whole-hearted acceptance of Brandon at the end of *Sense and Sensibility*, her warm and loving nature conquering earlier resistance. Lady Russell 'loved Anne better than she loved her own abilities; and ... found little hardship in attaching herself as a mother to the man who was securing the happiness of her other child' (235).

Even Lady Russell's 'prejudices on the side of ancestry' (17), which may to present-day readers seem the least defensible elements in the combination of misjudgments which disrupt Anne Elliot's life, are ones which in an only slightly modified form are broadly endorsed in Austen's fictional world. If *Persuasion* shows ambivalence over this, it differs from the other novels not in the fact of ambivalence, but in the

[23] Mary Poovey, *The Proper Lady and the Woman Writer*, Chicago and London, 1984, p. 268 n. 12.

degree of discomfort, the feeling of conflicting loyalties unresolved, which are more acutely evident in this novel than elsewhere. The elaborate pieces of summary-portraiture of Lady Russell at the beginning and end, even more than the presentation of her in the main course of the action, suggest not so much a complexity of which the author has a comprehensive grasp, as an uncertainty as to which of her characteristics is to be approved or disapproved. This uncertainty extends to some of the other characters, and not only to the extent that part of our view of them is filtered through hers, or responds to behaviour precipitated by her. Although Austen seems to have maintained in principle her faith in traditional notions of 'character' as stable, definable, and subject to clear moral judgment, and although she specifically admired Richardson for 'preserving the consistency of his characters' (5), she may in this last novel be on the edge of a more open and destabilised perception of human personality and behaviour.

Index

Index

Masson, Bernard, 33n.
Maury, Jean Siffrein, abbé, 191n.
Maxwell, Dr William, 248, 252
Maynial, Edouard, 51n.
Mayo, Henry, 236
McGann, Jerome J., 98n., 112n., 113n.
Medwin, Thomas, 102n., 112n.
Memis, Dr John , 256
Miller, Eugene F., 136n.
Miller, Perry, 148nn.
Milton, John, xiii, 4, 8, 63, 99, 106–29
     passim, 173n., 180; Eikonoklastes, 68n.;
     Paradise Lost, 14, 45 and n., 54 and n.,
     75n., 76, 93, 106–29 passim
Mirabeau, Honoré Gabriel Riqueti, comte
     de, 180, 184
Mirror, The, 208
Mitchell, L. G., 133n., 160n., 180–2nn., 192
     and n.
Mitchell, W. J. T. 69–73
Monboddo, James Burnett, Lord, 233
Moniteur, Le, 128, 180n.
Monitor, The, 208
Montagu, Lady Mary Wortley, 143ff., 151,
     213, 220, 249
Montaigne, Michel de, 35–6, 53, 54n., 56,
     177 and n., 191 and n.; 'Des
     cannibales', 191, 192; 'De la coustume',
     36; 'De la cruauté', 35–6; 'Des coches',
     36n., 54n.; 'Des Destriers', 54n.
Moore, Thomas, xii, 258–65; Epistles, Odes
     and other Poems, 263; Irish Melodies, 259;
     Lalla Rookh, 258–9, 263; Odes of
     Anacreon, 258; Poetical Works of Thomas
     Little, 263–4
Moorehead, Alan, 56n.
More, Sir Thomas, 37, 38n., 45 and n., 55,
     58, 59, 64; A Dialogue Concerning Heresies,
     37, 38n.; Utopia, 54 and n., 55n., 56n.,
     64, 193n.
Moreux, Françoise, 139n.
Morisot, Jean-Claude, 38n.
Mossner, E. C., 138n.
Mozart, Wolfgang Amadeus, 196
Murray, Gilbert, 65, 86

Narcissus, 19
Nash, Richard (Beau), 218
Needham, Joseph, 53n., 56n.
Neillands, Robin, 68n.
Nero, 3, 26, 37, 39, 43; Troica, 44 and n.
New Testament, John, 173n.; Luke, 32n.;
     Matthew, 170n.
Nicholson, Andrew, 99
Nidditch, Peter H., 148

Nochlin, Linda, 136n., 164n.

O'Brien, Conor Cruise, 133–4 and nn.,
     170n.
Oakeshott, Michael, 158n.
Observer, The, 208
Old Testament, 1 Chronicles, 32n., Genesis,
     41; Job, 238; Psalms, 32n; 2 Samuel,
     32n.
Oldham, John, xi, 12–27, 95; 'Apology' for
     the 'Satyr Against Vertue', 21, 22;
     'Bion', 19, 20, 25; 'Counterpart' to the
     'Satyr Against Vertue', 21; 'A
     Dithyrambique on Drinking', 17; Art of
     Poetry, 16; 'In Praise of Homer', 17; The
     Eighth Satyr of Monsieur Boileau, Imitated,
     54n.; 'Lamentation for Adonis', 19;
     'Letter from the Country', 24; Remains
     in Verse and Prose, 12; 'Sardanapalus',
     15, 18–19, 23, 25; 'Satyr Against
     Vertue', 17, 18, 26; Satyrs upon the
     Jesuits, 14, 15, 24, 25, 26, 27; Some
     New Pieces, 13, 16; 'To the Memory
     of Mr. Charles Morwent', 17; 'Upon
     the Author of the Play call'd Sodom',
     23, 24
Ollier, Charles, 105n.
Orpheus, 19
Orwell, George, 73; Nineteen Eighty-four,
     47–8, 48n.
Orwell, Sonia, 48n.
Otway, Thomas, 27
Ovid, 8, 9, 12, 16, 20, 21, 40n.; Amores, 9
Owen, W. J. B., 125, 172n.
Ozouf, Mona, 134n., 184n.

Page, Norman, 269–77 passim, 282
Pagliaro, Harold E., 38n., 156n.
Paine, Thomas, Common Sense, 159; Rights of
     Man, 160, 170 and n., 174–5, 178n.,
     181, 193n., 194, 195n.
Paracelsus, 64
Parnell, Thomas, 'Allegory on Man', 78n.;
     Homer's Battle of the Frogs and Mice, 78n.,
     91; 'A Letter to a friend. On poets',
     253
Parr, Samuel, 227, 260
Parrot, The, 208
Pascal, Blaise, 183
Paulhan, Jean, 224
Paulson, Ronald, 162n., 170n., 186n., 192n.,
     193 and nn.
Perrin, Noel, 54n., 56nn.
Perry, Ruth, 213
Petrarch, 49

305